WOMEN'S POLITICAL REPRESENTATION IN IRAN AND TURKEY

For my parents.

WOMEN'S POLITICAL REPRESENTATION IN IRAN AND TURKEY

Demanding a Seat at the Table

Mona Tajali

EDINBURGH
University Press

Edinburgh University Press is one of the leading university presses in the UK. We publish academic books and journals in our selected subject areas across the humanities and social sciences, combining cutting-edge scholarship with high editorial and production values to produce academic works of lasting importance. For more information visit our website: edinburghuniversitypress.com

Edinburgh University Press Ltd
The Tun – Holyrood Road
12(2f) Jackson's Entry
Edinburgh EH8 8PJ

First published in hardback by Edinburgh University Press 2022

Typeset in 11/14pt Adobe Garamond by
Cheshire Typesetting Ltd, Cuddington, Cheshire,
Croydon, CR0 4YY

A CIP record for this book is available from the British Library

ISBN 978 1 4744 9946 0 (hardback)
ISBN 978 1 4744 9947 7 (paperback)
ISBN 978 1 4744 9948 4 (webready PDF)
ISBN 978 1 4744 9949 1 (epub)

CONTENTS

TABLES

FIGURES

ACKNOWLEDGEMENTS

One of the blessings (or perhaps misfortunes) of being raised in a politicised family is that you acquire a sixth political sense for nearly everything in life. As a young girl coming of age in post-revolutionary Iran, the lively conversations about politics that occurred around the family dinner table firmly instilled in me the idea that inquisitiveness, engagement and passion for a given issue were important. I trace my interest in gender and politics to these discussions and my many follow-up questions that the adults in my life endeavoured at the time to answer. Indeed, the theocratic regime under which we lived invested much of its resources towards the creation of Iran's next generation of revolutionary youth, effectively creating a duality that I and many of my school-aged peers were forced to navigate with grace and apparent obedience. On the one hand, we became keenly aware of our gender through both state gender regulations and extensive societal expectations concerning our dress, our behaviour, and even our fields of study, while on the other we were exposed to powerful and outspoken women, in our families and beyond, that challenged these same expectations. The contradictory aspects of our lives were intriguing, to say the least. Such apparent contradictions persisted when I moved to the United States, where gender roles and relations are also based on societal and political expectations, leading me to my own passion of inquiry: namely, the political implications of ideological frameworks that aim to limit women's political roles and influence, and how women respond and push back against systemic marginalisation.

This book, which has been years in the making, is the product of many discussions and exchanges about women's political rights and representation, with relatives, scholars, women's rights activists, female politicians, and cohorts. My first debt of gratitude is to the Iranian and Turkish women activists, politicians, journalists/bloggers and scholars, who gave me their time, and shared with me their knowledge and experiences regarding women's political representation. I am very grateful that in both countries, despite many challenges, these women and men welcomed me in their homes or offices, to share details of their activism, experiences, ideas and opinions. This research would not have been possible without them, and is for them.

I am extremely fortunate to have been guided and supported by exceptional mentors and scholars throughout this journey exploring women's political rights and roles in Muslim contexts. This book draws heavily on my doctoral dissertation research under an exceptional committee at Concordia University in Montreal, Canada, chaired by Homa Hoodfar, now a dear friend and colleague. I will remain forever indebted and grateful for her incredible support and guidance. When I first walked into her office on a warm summer afternoon as an international student in Canada, I could have never imagined how fruitful our relationship would become in the following years, and luckily decades. She masterfully taught me much of what I know about the complexities of researching and writing about women in Muslim contexts, while also encouraging me to pursue my own passions. As I deepened my knowledge about global discussions on women and politics under her guidance, she provided me with the exceptional opportunity to co-author a book with her – *Electoral Politics: Making Quotas Work for Women* (WLUML 2011) –which to date remains one of the most valuable experiences of my academic life. Her belief in my intellectual abilities has been an important motivation. Despite various challenges, including the attacks on her fundamental rights to academic freedom, I am fortunate to be able to call her a colleague, as we continue to collaborate on various projects, as much work remains.

I am also eternally grateful to Kimberley Manning, who graciously served on my advising committee and whose courses and close readings of my writings enhanced my appreciation for feminist political science that looks beyond formal institutions. Also at Concordia, I benefited from Lynda Clarke's guidance and motivation both in my research and teaching. Her valued input greatly shaped my approach to researching Muslim women's agency. Other scholars who contributed to my studies at Concordia include Richard Foltz, David Howes, Yesim Bayer and Bina Freiwald, among many others. I am extremely thankful for all that Concordia offered me to initiate this project, including funds to conduct field research in the Middle East, particularly since as an international student I was ineligible for funding from many Canadian foundations. I hope that having been awarded the best doctoral dissertation prize by the American Political Science Association's (APSA) Women and Politics Research Section in 2015 confirms to Concordia the significance of such support to their graduate students.

Following the completion of my doctoral studies, I landed at Oxford University for a Postdoctoral Fellowship in Middle East Studies at the School of Interdisciplinary Area Studies. This opportunity provided me with exceptional intellectual support and generous funds thanks to the Sasakawa Peace Foundation, to conduct additional field research in the Middle East to extensively revise and update the book. In particular, I am thankful to Phillip Robins, Sachiko Hosoya, Sahar Maranlou, Homa Katouzian, Soraya Teremayne, Mastan Ebtehaj and Derek Penslar. I am also grateful to the cohort of Iranian and Turkish students and scholars who welcomed me to Oxford and included me in their reading groups and thought-provoking discussions. My time at Oxford helped me sharpen and tighten this book's analyses as I sought to highlight the complexities of cases that are often presented in simplistic and essentialist ways.

Since January 2016, I have found a home at Agnes Scott College, in Georgia. From the very beginning, I was welcomed by a group of supportive colleagues in various disciplines, all of whom have been invested in my success. I have particularly appreciated the many times that my more senior colleagues have gently intervened to block in-service requests wending their way towards me, to allow me the time to find myself in my new role and to work on this book. Since my arrival, Cathy Scott has not only been a supportive colleague, but has also graciously read my work and provided me with exceptionally helpful feedback. I promise to continue to supply her imported wine collection as she reads through my many drafts and edits. Gus Cochran, Ellie Morris, Yael Manes, Beth Hackett, Katherine Kennedy, Patricia Schneider, and many others have proved excellent role models since my arrival at the new-for-me environment of a liberal arts college for women. I have been particularly fortunate to find a close group of colleagues who have been my life-line at Agnes Scott College and beyond: Reem Bailony, Rachel

Hall-Clifford, Roshan Iqbal and Scarlett Kingsley. I will be forever indebted for their friendship, advice and for simply being there for me, both for support in overcoming my failures and for celebrating my accomplishments. It is a blessing to share important professional and personal moments with them.

Research of the Middle East is never easy, but access to sufficient financial and logistical support can greatly facilitate fieldwork in the region. This project would not have been possible without numerous internal and external funding sources. Among them, I was fortunate to be supported by an American Association of University Women Publication Grant in 2019–20, which allows scholars to budget for childcare expenses, a fundamental provision that greatly assists scholarship production for those with care duties. Agnes Scott College's Office of Academic Affairs and Faculty Development Funds have been generous, providing me with financial support coupled with sufficient time off from teaching to conduct research in the Middle East. I truly appreciate the guidance and support of Emily Stone in helping me access and apply for funding, both through and from Agnes Scott College, to support the completion of this manuscript. Other sources of funding that made this project possible include the American Political Science Association's Small Research Grants, Women Living Under Muslim Laws Publication Grants and the Carrie Chapman Catt Prize for Research on Women and Politics.

Many people at other universities, organisations and research institutions both in the Middle East and beyond helped me think through various aspects of this project and provided me with valuable support and input. From Turkey, I am very grateful for the guidance and support of Sertac Sehlikoglu, Nurhayat Kizilkan, Fatma Bostan, Ilhan Dögüs, Nil Mutluer, Iffat Polat, Merve Kavakci, Yesim Arat, Filiz Kerestecioglu, Hidayet Tuksal, Binnaz Toprak, Ibrahim Mazlum, Ilhan Keki, Necla Tepekule, Begum Uzun, Fezal Gulfidan and Cigdem Aydin, and many others. My research in Iran benefited from advice and input of various scholars and activists including Fatemeh Sadeghi, Jaleh Shaditalab, Nasrin Afzali, Nima Namdari, Noushin Tarighi, Sanaz Allahbedashti, Touran Valimorad, Tahereh Rahimi, Mariam Behrouzi, and others who for their own security cannot be thanked by name.

I am extremely grateful to the many individuals who read and commented on this manuscript. Earlier drafts of this work have benefited from suggestions and thoughtful input from Homa Hoodfar, Kimberley Manning, Aili Mari Tripp and Heather Macdougall, while parts of it have been carefully read and commented on by Sarah Childs, Lisa Baldez, Marc Lynch and several anonymous reviewers. This book is also greatly indebted to years of scholarly theoretical and social analysis from around the globe related to women's political participation and representation. I was greatly inspired by the works of key scholars such as Ziba Mir-Hosseini, Lihi Ben Shitrit, Mona Lena Krook, Lisa Baldez, Sherine Hafez, Abdullahi An-Na'im, Louise Chappell, Elin Bjarnegård, Georgina Waylen, Alice Kang, Deanna Ferree Womack, Anne Phillips and Pamela Paxton, among many others. I also deeply admire the works of social scientists working particularly on human rights, gender and activism in the Middle East, such as Nazanin Shahrokni, Arzoo Osanloo, Mehrangiz Kar, Asef Bayat, the late Parveen Paidar, Shahla Haeri, Minoo Moallem, Mehdi Moslem, Nayereh Tohidi, Jenny White, and many more.

This book has benefited from the careful read of Marlene Caplan, whose craft with words and interest in gender and social sciences is inspiring. I am thankful for her willingness to take on an additional manuscript on top of all of her other commitments. At Edinburgh University Press, I am grateful for Emma Rees's careful read over my materials and her support of the project, as well as other members of the production team. I appreciate the anonymous reviewers who engaged with this work, and made important suggestions for improvement. All of these efforts, most of which have been non-compensated and carried out by women during a global pandemic, were crucial to the success of this project.

Last but not least, I thank my family and friends, who are spread across the world, for their love and support throughout this very long journey. I am grateful to my brother Reza, whose generosity in stepping in to support the demanding logistics of my multiple travels to the field and numerous conferences gave me peace of mind. I am thankful to my relatives in Iran, from my inquisitive cousins, to caring uncles and aunts, for all of their hospitality and support when I needed it most. My mother-in-law, Gisela Frank, deserves a particular note of appreciation, as this book would not have been possible without her selfless cross-border travels to care for my family as I spent months in the Middle East for research. I am especially thankful to my amazing friend, Mariam Hajialilu, who for the past decades has known how to give me just the right dose of encouragement to finish drafts, degrees, and to simply enjoy life.

My partner in life, Filipp Frank, stood by me through all of the challenges and celebrations of researching and writing a book. I appreciate his patience and many sacrifices to provide me with the time and space to bring this project to fruition. It was not always easy, but I am thankful that I have found a loving partner in him. We are now prepared for me to begin my next book! My children, Benyamin and Leon, have also been extremely patient and understanding as I often left our Lego games unfinished to type away in my office. Thank you for serving as my utmost sources of joy and much needed distraction.

Finally, I appreciate my parents, Farideh and Mohammad, for instilling in me the desire to protest injustice and speak my mind. I also thank them for their innumerable selfless acts to provide a better future for their children. I dedicate this book to them.

1

INTRODUCTION: WOMEN AND POLITICS IN MUSLIM COUNTRIES

'We have many qualified women for political office.' These were the words of Maryam Behrouzi, a fervent adherent of the Islamic Republic, former Iranian parliamentarian and long-time ardent supporter of the conservative faction of the Islamic Republic.[1] 'Women are present in all spheres of Iranian society, ranging from education to health services, they should also be present in political decision-making, so that they can represent women's unique experiences and realities.' Behrouzi went on to detail the efforts of the influential conservative women's organisation, the Zeinab Society, of which she is a key and founding member, towards increasing women's access to political leadership. For example, thanks to lobbying by the Zeinab Society, in 2009 the Islamic Republic appointed its first, and to date only, female minister since the revolution. Marzieh Vahid Dastjerdi, a gynecologist, former parliamentarian and long-time Zeinab Society executive board member, became Iran's Minister of Health under ultra-conservative President Ahmadinejad. In our 2011 interview, Maryam Behrouzi described her as 'one of the best ministers in President Ahmadinejad's cabinet given her level of qualification, dedication, experience, intellect, and thoughtfulness'. When I asked Behrouzi why there are so few women holding political office when there are so many qualified and wishing to do so, she responded with

---

[1] In this research, Iran's conservatives are those who support the theocratic regime and its clerical oligarchy, though they have rebranded themselves as 'Principlists' or fundamentalists (*usulgara-yan*).

I

a sigh: 'Because many men do not want to give up their seat for a woman' (personal interview, 21 July 2011).

In Turkey this sentiment was echoed by Ceren (a pseudonym),[2] an active member of the ruling Justice and Development Party (*Adalet ve Kalkinma Partisi* – AKP)[3] since its founding in 2001. I first met Ceren, a lawyer by training, in June 2015 while she was campaigning for a parliamentary seat in one of Istanbul's multi-member districts. Her low ranking on the closed-candidate party list for the district meant her chances of getting elected were slim. 'I went into politics to address the injustices I saw, including the banning of the Muslim headscarf and the forced closure of Islamic parties. The establishment of AKP revived my trust in politics . . . But as I moved up the party ladder, I realised that some of my male party peers held masculinist tendencies.' Given her years of party activism, including helping found and serving in the Istanbul Provincial AKP Women's Branch, Ceren attributed her low rank on the party candidate list and subsequent failure to win a seat in parliament on gender discrimination from some male party leaders, who resented her 'devotion to women's rights' (personal interview, 7 May 2015). Her continued dedication to the party and the backing of AKP leader Recep Tayyip Erdoğan eventually saw Ceren elected as one of forty-three women mayors out of 1,389 mayoral races in the 2019 local elections across Turkey.[4]

---

[2] Several of my informants are identified only by their rank, position or professional status for security reasons. I use pseudonyms for individuals who I quote frequently, except for those who were public about the views and events they shared with me and consented to forgo anonymity.

[3] Justice and Development Party (*Adalet ve Kalkinma Partisi* – AKP or AK Parti) was founded in 2001 by former members of disbanded Turkish Islamist parties, including the Welfare (*Refah*) and Virtue (*Fazilet*) parties. It won a landslide victory in 2002, and has since steadily increased its percentage of the popular vote in general elections. AKP identifies itself as a 'conservative democratic' rather than 'Islamist' party. Due to AKP's support of a secular system that also espouses public displays of religion, I identify this party as 'pro-religious'. Similarly, I describe the female supporters of AKP as 'pious' rather than 'Islamist' or 'Islamic', per my Turkish interviewees' preference.

[4] In Turkey, women's political representation at local levels is lower than at national levels. According to KADER, the Association for Supporting Women Candidates, as of 2019, women comprise only 3.09 per cent of total mayors, whereas 17.3 per cent of members of the national parliament are women.

Similar to many other parts of the world, women's access to high-level political positions is limited in Iran and Turkey. Although women constitute highly politicised and mobilised demographics in both countries, and significant numbers are politically experienced and aspire to political decision-making roles including but not limited to representing women's interests, gender-based restrictions create considerable challenges. Women not only face the burden of convincing male party elites of their merit to run for office, they must also navigate widespread undemocratic political and social elements present in both countries (which will be elaborated on later) that mitigate against female political representation.

However, recent years have also nonetheless witnessed a rise in elected female politicians in both countries, including on behalf of conservative religious parties, as well as the appointment of women to high-level office. As mentioned earlier, post-revolutionary Iran's first female minister was, surprisingly for most observers, appointed by ultra-conservative President Ahmadinejad, who unlike his more reformist and liberal counterparts, had never campaigned in support of women's access to high-level decision-making positions, and whose party's ideology relegated women primarily to the domestic sphere.[5] Likewise, in Turkey, recent increases in the percentage of female parliamentarians (a more than four-fold increase from 2002 at 4.4 per cent to 17.3 per cent elected in 2018) coincided with the conservative pro-religious AKP's rise to power and, despite its conservative gender ideology, the party has at times supported more female candidates for office than its main opposition, the secular Republican People's Party (*Cumhuriyet Halk Partisi*) or CHP. Though modest, these changes in women's political representation are important, particularly since they have occurred under parties that hold patriarchal ideologies, coupled with constraints imposed by authoritarian and undemocratic political systems in which they operate.

This book explores the puzzle of why women in many Muslim-majority countries have achieved surprising successes despite the significant constraints imposed by conservative gender ideology and authoritarian political parties

[5] As will be detailed later in this book, after his contentious re-election in 2009, Ahmadinejad nominated three women (Marzieh Vahid Dastjerdi, Fatemeh Ajorloo and Soosan Keshavarz) as potential cabinet members. The conservative-dominated parliament approved the appointment of only one, Marzieh Vahid Dastjerdi, who became Iran's minister of health (2009–13). Ahmadinejad's more moderate successor, President Rouhani, did not nominate any women cabinet ministers and was highly criticised by the Iranian women's movement for this.

and systems. To examine the underlying dynamics of these gains the book problematises the false stereotype that women are passive and apolitical subjects in their contexts, and looks at the activities and strategies of women's rights groups around female political representation, as well as political elites' responses to women's rights organising efforts. Through a comparative focus on Iran and Turkey, both countries with long histories of negotiation between women's rights groups and political elites concerning women's political representation, the book explores the conditions that engender greater willingness on the part of male political elites to support women's access to political office. Based on extensive data collection including many in-depth interviews with women from various demographics in both countries, including politicians, aspiring politicians, activists and ordinary women, as well as with male political elites, I suggest that the recent increases in women's political representation in Iran and Turkey, and similar trends in several other Muslim countries, can be best understood in terms of the strategic interactions that take place between women's rights groups and political elites, both of which depend on the support of the electorate. I show that women's groups across the political and ideological spectrum strategically interact with political elites to address women's political under-representation. At the same time, political leaders are increasingly sensitive to the power of women's votes, and in attempting to increase their female support base, increasingly take measures to enable and appoint women to leadership positions. Thus, when opportunities arise within the given structural political context, women's rights actors and political elites use each other to further their respective interests.

To help explain the recent unexpected rises of women to political office in authoritarian and gender conservative settings, such as in Iran and Turkey, the book focuses on the intersections of political and institutional structures, religious and cultural norms and values, and voter behaviour in terms of women's political representation. It examines these questions through a comparative study of women's political participation and representation in Iran and Turkey – countries that share a number of similarities, but also differ in important ways and so offer an interesting comparison. While both Iran and Turkey are Muslim societies with low levels of female political representation,[6] they differ in their founding state ideologies, political

---

[6] Women in both Iran and Turkey are under-represented in political decision-making positions, with parliamentary presence that is below the global average of 24.5 per cent. As

frameworks, institutional transparency and, in particular, the role of religion in defining women's role in the public sphere. By comparing a theocracy (Iran) and a secular state (Turkey), which have both formally instituted paths towards political modernisation while also experiencing a rise in political Islam in recent decades, this research also sheds light on the role of religion in shaping women's access to positions of political authority. Such analysis provides a theoretical framework for understanding the factors and actors that keep women out of politics in the institutionally, ideologically and politically distinct contexts of Iran and Turkey, and examines how women act to address their under-representation in political office.

By placing women's mobilisation and organising for access to positions of political leadership at the centre of its analysis, this book demonstrates that women's demand for a seat at the political decision-making table transcends religious and ideological affinities. Since at least the mid-1990s, women's rights groups across the Muslim world, including in Iran and Turkey, have been demanding women's increased access to political leadership. Studying women's organising efforts shows how women manoeuvre within their respective institutional and ideological structures to address women's political under-representation, and the conditions under which they succeed in convincing ruling elites and the general public to value women's political inclusion.

The role of male party leaders as primary gatekeepers in terms of women's political representation has received the bulk of scholarly consideration around the issue of women's access to political power; the male-dominated political sphere privileges men's political advancement through gender discriminatory structures and behaviours (Bjarnegård 2015; Paxton and Hughes 2013). Hence, the credit for increases in women's political nomination and recruitment often mistakenly goes to male party leaders (Tran 2009), with little acknowledgement of decades of women's rights organising to mobilise the

---

of 2019, women in Iran constitute only 5.9 per cent of parliamentarians (MPs), despite gaining the right to vote in 1963. In Turkey, 17.3 per cent of Turkish MPs are female, and while Turkey's rate is notably higher, it is important to note that in 1934 Turkey was the first Muslim-majority country in the world to grant women the right to vote. Additionally, this notable increase in women's parliamentary presence occurred only over the span of four rounds of elections (from 4.4 per cent in 2002 to 17.3 per cent in 2018), the reasons for which are explained in this book. Women in both countries remain under-represented in other major political bodies such as ministerial positions, local councils or judiciary.

public and pressure elites to address women's political under-representation. It is the purpose of this book to analyze women's rights groups' campaigning efforts for women's political representation in authoritarian and semi-democratic contexts, recognising that even autocratic leaders have an interest in advancing women's political roles when it is too costly for them not to do so.

Recent research has highlighted the need for scholarly analysis of unexpected women-friendly measures taken by autocratic leaders (Tripp 2019; Valdini 2019). Rather than merely dismissing expansion of women's political representation in authoritarian and semi-democratic countries, which are often in token amounts, as window dressing or as a way to appeal to the international community or to women's rights activists, these important studies are examining why and under what circumstances authoritarian and semi-authoritarian states take measures to enhance women's rights, including their access to political office. More specifically, Aili Mari Tripp (2019) argues that authoritarian leaders in the Maghreb (Morocco, Tunisia and Algeria) strategically use women's rights to serve instrumental purposes such as creating a modernising image of their societies. Similarly, Melody Valdini (2019) explores the circumstances under which women's inclusion in government benefits leaders by signalling progressive and democratic qualities of the party or government.

My research does show that the expansion of women's political roles is often motivated by interest-driven considerations of the ruling elites, among them the desire to appear more democratic and modern, or to distinguish themselves from more conservative political forces (Tajali 2011). Women's rights groups across the ideological spectrum are well aware of these motivators and intentionally draw on them in their organising and lobbying efforts, with some success. My findings thus complement recent studies by presenting the women's side of the equation, particularly by showing how women's rights groups play a central role in influencing the 'calculations' made by male elites around the inclusion versus marginalisation of women from power (Valdini 2019). My research shows that women organise – both from within and outside of party structures – to make the political marginalisation of women costly for male party elites, and activists use available opportunity structures to promote the election of female colleagues and allies. Thus, while the promotion of small numbers of women to political office by male leaders and male-dominated parties to serve their own political ends may be a matter of expediency, prepared women's groups drawing from the support of the electorate have at times seized such opportunities to increase women's descriptive representation in ways that have important implications for women's political empowerment.

The issue of women's political representation in Muslim societies such as Iran and Turkey is complex and multifaceted, involving many actors and factors, impacted by diverse obstacles and opportunities arising out of each nation's specific political, legal, institutional and social structures. A close analysis of these obstacles and opportunities helps illuminate the reasons for the gap between women's high level of political participation and their low rates of representation in many Muslim countries, as well as helping explain recent unexpected increases in female political representation on behalf of conservative parties in Iran and Turkey. Here I focus on the interactions between women's groups and political elites: the individuals who influence women's access to political decision-making. Recognising that both groups depend on public support, this research finds that women's rights groups and elites strategically interact with each other to further their respective agendas: women's political access on one side and electoral appeal on the other. I argue that the broader political and cultural contexts of each country distinctly shape the opportunities for local women's groups to engage with political elites and the electorate to advocate for women in politics. Different opportunities mean that though access to political decision-making positions for women has long been a central demand of many women's rights groups in both countries, efforts towards this goal have not always been successful.

My findings suggest that while religious, cultural and institutional obstacles certainly play a role in the low percentage of women in formal politics in Iran and Turkey, the ability of women's rights groups to mobilise the public to support women in politics, and their interactions with political elites, deserve close scrutiny. This book's frame of analysis is particularly relevant given recent political shifts unfolding in the Middle East and North Africa (MENA), many of which are opening up avenues for women's activism. Indeed, the political uprisings across many countries of the MENA region are providing local women's rights groups with important opportunities to demand women's increased presence in political decision-making. Shedding light onto Iranian and Turkish women's strategising and framing in their interactions and negotiations with political elites and the electorate can enrich our understanding of the most effective tactics and processes towards achieving gender parity in elected bodies.

In this introductory chapter, I address some of the assumptions that underlie this lack of attention to women's political roles in parts of the Muslim world, and show why it is necessary to examine the impact of multiple factors, including institutional structures, on women's rise to political office. I also outline why research on women's political representation is important, even in authoritarian contexts in which the general integrity of elections is questionable.

Political Activists who Rarely Become Political Leaders

This book grew out of my reaction to the disconnect between my own observations and experiences around women's political engagement in many Muslim-majority countries, including my own country of birth, Iran, and the near absence of women in political decision-making positions in these same places. As the youngest and only daughter of a politicised family, born soon after the 1979 Iranian revolution, I grew up hearing about and witnessing my female relatives' political engagement. I heard stories of my own mother's participation in the 1979 anti-Pahlavi organising, which included protesting, underground meetings to plot opposition strategy, and hauling used tyres in the back of her car for demonstrators to burn as they tried to fend off the military. After the revolution, as a young girl, I often accompanied my mother to her weekly women-only Quran circle (*doreh*) in Tehran, which grew increasingly critical of the theocratic regime, to the extent that after the arrest and persecution of many members, she stopped attending. Nearly four decades later, she explains her actions were to 'stand with the people as they protest repressive regimes', and rarely considers such activism as 'political' (*siasi*), but rather a necessity, or even a way of life, for many 'ordinary individuals who refused to be silent' (personal communication, 30 July 2018). Decades later, as I embarked on my graduate studies, I sought to highlight similar individuals who refused to remain silent.

I began my research in Iran by studying women's rights groups, particularly secular women's rights activists, many of whom were educated and young urbanites. I became fascinated by their boldness as they protested the gender discriminatory rulings and practices of their societies, universities, and even families. Thanks to my involvement with the feminist transnational solidarity network Women Living Under Muslim Laws (WLUML), and our travels and training courses in Iran, I observed over the years the ways women's dress, demeanour and on-line presence, all of which were seemingly apolitical, become the means to challenge authority and demand change. Women's greater access to political office was one of women's central demands, a topic to which I had the privilege to contribute given my work and collaboration with WLUML on parliamentary gender quotas (Hoodfar and Tajali 2011). Our training moved beyond Tehran and I recognised similar passion and demand among diverse women's groups in various Muslim countries, including Turkey, where I had the opportunity to exchange experiences and knowledge on this topic with KADER (the Association for the Support of Women Candidates), an influential Turkish organisation devoted to enhancing women's access to political office.

Such exchanges and interactions demonstrated to me that women in Turkey and Iran constitute highly politicised and mobilised segments of their societies. In fact, women's political engagement in both countries is illustrated by their notably high voter turnout, engagement in voter-recruitment, and active campaigning and organising efforts, including on behalf of conservative and pro-religious parties. However, women's political activism at grass-roots levels and efforts to enter high-level formal politics rarely translate into seats at the decision-making table. Analysis of this disconnect will underline the multiple factors that contribute to the dearth of female political representation in Turkey and Iran, as well as exposing the strategies activists employ to navigate the institutional structures and ideological constraints they face as they try to correct this political gender imbalance.

Women in Iran played a key role in toppling the monarchy, taking to the streets in the tens of thousands as revolutionaries, and voting in massive numbers in support of the Islamic Republic in 1979 (Nashat 1980; Paidar 1995). During the eight-year Iran–Iraq war (1980–8), women tended the wounded on the front lines and, with the support of the Islamic regime, formed organisations and societies to support the families of dead and disabled soldiers. Revolutionary women also formed women's organisations and parties, among them the influential Zeinab Society (*Jameh Zeinab*), to continue to politicise and mobilise women on behalf of the theocratic regime. During the political openings of the reform era (1997–2005) under the presidency of Mohammad Khatami, diverse groups of women, including secular women, became increasingly politically active to the extent tolerated by the regime. Much of the gender activism during this period involved establishing women's rights non-governmental organisations (NGOs) and grass-roots campaigning. Thanks to such political openings, the number of registered women's NGOs rose from sixty-seven in 1997 to 480 in 2005 (Mir-Hosseini 2006a).

Women in Iran also constitute an important voting bloc, to the extent that electoral campaigns by male politicians cannot afford to ignore them. While Iran, like Turkey, does not track voter turnout according to gender, female voters constitute at least half of the electorate.[7] During presidential elections where presidential candidates underscored women's rights among other reform promises, overall voter turnout increased notably. This was particularly evident for the 1997 and 2009 presidential elections, when voter turnout surpassed 80 per cent, in part thanks to women's organising for the mobilisation of the female electorate. Women in the Islamic Republic take their voting rights very seriously and often see elections as opportunities to try and improve their situations given the overall authoritarian nature of the state (Mir-Hosseini 2002; Tohidi 2009).

The politicisation of Iranian women is also apparent in the increase in the numbers of women who register as candidates for presidential, parliamentary and local elections, though they face major institutional obstacles, including being subject to the Council of Guardian's 'approbatory supervision'.[8] While to date, a female candidate has yet to be approved by the Council to run as president, hundreds of women usually aspire for a parliamentary seat; currently seventeen out of 290 members of parliament are women.

In Turkey, women have also been very active in both informal and formal political spheres, but in contrast to the powerful female Iranian voting bloc, Turkish women have been unable to prove their political might at the polls, largely due to ideological cleavages between secular and pious female demographics that have prevented the emergence of a unified women's movement. A well-documented aspect of Turkish women's political participation over recent decades has been their involvement with political parties though party women's branches, particularly in voter recruitment (Arat 2005; Kavakci

---

[7] There was a 73 per cent voter turnout for the 2013 Iranian presidential elections (39 million votes), and it is safe to assume that means that almost 20 million women voted.

[8] The most significant hindrance to free and fair elections in Iran is the Council of Guardians. According to the Iranian constitution, this body has 'approbatory supervision' over potential candidates for the presidency and parliament. This power hinders women's access to political leadership, due to the Council's conservative backing.

2010; White 2002). Women's organising on behalf of religious parties played a key role in bringing to power Islamist and pro-religious parties, such as *Refah* (Welfare), *Fazilet* (Virtue), and currently, the AKP. Their involvement has grown to the extent that for the past decade the AKP's women's branch *Kadın Kolları* lauds itself as 'the largest political women's organization in the world' with approximately 5 million members as of 2020 (AK Parti 2011; Fazli 2020; Kaplan 2018).[9] Members of the various parties' women's branches are seeking candidacy for decision-making positions after gaining experience, confidence and credibility through grass-roots organising, thus creating opportunities for themselves to climb the political ladder.

In addition to deep involvement in grass-roots party organising, women in Turkey are also active in organisations concerned with women's rights and issues. Although secular and pious women's organisations in Turkey rarely join forces on the issue of female political representation, I observed a shift beginning to occur during the 2011 parliamentary elections when most of the influential women's organisations, regardless of ideological affiliation, began to support the right of headscarved women to have a place in parliament. As discussed in Chapter 5, for the first time in Turkish history various women's organisations across the political and ideological spectrum formed alliances to demand that parties increase access to parliament for *all* women. Such organising fostered competition among parties to appeal to women voters.

An Institutionalist Analysis of Women's Political Under-representation

The literature on women and politics has generally categorised the main obstacles hindering women's access to political decision-making positions as *cultural and social*, which impact the supply of qualified or willing female candidates, or *institutional and structural*, which impact the demand for female politicians by the state's political institutions (Larserud and Taphorn 2007; Paxton and Hughes 2007; Paxton *et al.* 2007; Randall 1982). While such categorisation may appear rather reductionist given the multiplicity of reasons and situations contributing to women's under-representation in the political sphere, they nonetheless help us outline and analyse women's political rights and status in a given context, as well as their strategies to address these obstacles. Significantly, the different types of obstacles are interrelated.

---

[9] Although this number could be in decline in recent years with AKP's intensified gender discriminatory approach.

For instance, many of the institutional and structural obstacles that limit women's rise to political power are based on the assumptions of political elites of prevailing cultural attitudes that women are apolitical or that the public is unwilling (not ready) to elect women.

Institutional or structural barriers include political systems, electoral rules, political party structures, state ideology, and institutional cultures, such as campaign financing priorities, which tend to discriminate against women. Research has documented specific mechanisms within political party or electoral structures that work to limit qualified and experienced female candidates' entry into top decision-making positions (Kittilson 2006; Lovenduski and Norris 1993; Paxton and Hughes 2007; Phillips 1998b).[10] In recent decades, we have witnessed 'an institutional turn in feminist political science' in which the impact of both formal and informal 'rules of the game' on women's political roles and influence are examined (Bjarnegård 2015; Hern 2017; Krook and Mackay 2011; Manning forthcoming; Waylen 2007). With this shift in focus, scholars increasingly view the state to be composed of a series of competing institutions, many of which are gendered or work to reproduce gendered power relations, shedding light on the institutional processes and practices that reinforce and reproduce gender inequality (Krook and Mackay 2011).

Given the prevailing assumption that *Muslim culture* and undemocratic governments underlie women's political under-representation, an institutionalist analysis highlighting the interactions of political actors and institutional rules and structures within a given political culture and history has seldom been applied to study women's political status in Muslim contexts.[11]

---

[10] As will be further explained in Chapter 4, scholars have argued that majoritarian electoral systems, such as the first-past-the-post (FPTP) system hinder women's access to political leadership positions more than plurality systems, such as the list proportional representation (List PR) system, since the chances for a female candidate to be elected are higher when voters vote for a political party and its list (as it is done in List PR systems) rather than for an individual candidate (as it is done in FPTP system) (Matland 2005; Matland and Studlar 1996).

[11] While recent research by scholars such as Kang (2009), Tripp (2013, 2019), Beck (2003), Benstead (2016) and Shalaby (2016), among others, have sought to analyse the impact of institutional obstacles on women's political representation in Muslim contexts, only a few have adopted a comparative approach, and even fewer have analysed women's political roles in non-Arab states. My comparative research on Iran and Turkey, the two non-Arab Muslim states of MENA, contributes to 'gendering comparative politics' (Tripp 2006).

The limited attention to women's political activism, particularly that which supports conservative political parties, has resulted in scholarship that treats the political arena as monolithic, and dissent and contestation on issues such as women's rights within conservative ruling or powerful parties as inconsequential. This homogenising narrative obscures more nuanced understandings of political parties and groups in the Muslim world, in particular the dynamism and diversity among their members and supporters.

In this book I address this oversight by examining specific institutional and structural obstacles facing Iranian and Turkish women attempting to access positions of political authority. I evaluate the impact of each country's electoral system, political party structure, government framework and state gender ideology as they relate to female political representation, and examine how women's rights groups organise for women's greater access to formal politics from within such structures. This institutionalist approach is particularly useful for understanding the behaviour of political actors, including both women's rights advocates and ruling elites in 'hybrid regimes' concerning women's political rights and representation. Hybrid regimes 'combine elements associated with both dictatorship and democracy' (Keshavarzian 2009b: 227), for example holding regular elections for major institutions such as the legislature, though the elections themselves may not be free or fair (Diamond 2002). Despite such undemocratic elements, many scholars of the Middle East, including Arang Keshavarzian (2009b), argue that institutions matter even in authoritarian contexts since they can enable or restrict the behaviour of political actors and organisations. Thus, the specific institutional arrangements of hybrid regimes, including electoral rules and the structure of party systems, can facilitate strategic interactions between ruling elites and social groups, including women's rights groups. The intricacies of institutional competition help explain the puzzling trend of autocratic leaders advancing women's rights and roles in hybrid regimes.

Iran and Turkey are examples of such regimes, combining democratic elements such as participation and competition during major elections with authoritarian practices and institutions, though to different degrees.[12] As the

[12] Various institutions of the Islamic Republic, such as the Council of Guardians and its supervisory role over elections, were established to protect Iran's clerical oligarchy. Similarly, one of the major hurdles to democracy in Turkey has historically been its military as it launched major coups to protect the state's secular establishment. In recent years, monopolisation

chapters in this book demonstrate, women's groups in both countries have exploited their respective republican, authoritarian, and in the Iranian case, 'Islamic' institutions to further their bargaining efforts for women's greater access to political office. Despite their differing state ideologies, political structures and levels of institutional development, women in both Turkey and Iran are active in electoral politics as voters, campaigners, organisers and aspiring candidates. Although statistical documentation on rates for both formal and informal female political participation is limited in both countries,[13] for Turkey, scholars including Yesim Arat (2005) and Jenny White (2002) have shown the significant role of women's grass-roots organising and voter recruitment in the electoral success of religious parties. Likewise for Iran, Parvin Paidar (1995), Azadeh Kian-Thiebaut (2002) and Sanam Vakil (2011), among others, have documented women's political mobilisation and voter turnout as a powerful political force that male elites cannot afford to ignore, even in Iran's authoritarian context. Indeed, one of the unintended consequences of the populist and revolutionary discourses that mobilised masses of women in support of the 1979 Iranian revolution was the enduring politicisation of a female electorate determined to use the state's few republican avenues to challenge the clerical elites' firm hold on power, as exemplified by Iranian women's overwhelming support for reformist candidates in the late 1990s and early 2000s. Acknowledging such contradictory and unintended outcomes illuminates state–society dynamics, and the fact that state institutions, even in closed authoritarian contexts, do not operate in isolation from other social groups and networks (Keshavarzian 2007).

Women's high rates of political activism however has not translated into higher levels of *political representation* or access to formal political decision-making positions. Although scholars have sought to explain the reasons behind women's political under-representation in many Muslim-majority countries, their findings have been incomplete, often based on mono-causal

of power into the hands of AKP leadership and censure of independent media and rights organisations have undermined democratisation in Turkey.

[13] As do a number of feminist political scientists, I include in my definition of political activity women's engagement in *formal* politics, including elections, political candidacy and holding political positions, as well as in *informal* politics including social activism, community engagement, active membership in organisations, and 'street politics' such as campaigning and demonstrating (see Waylen 2007: 5), since both types of political activism influence policy and the distribution of resources.

explanations. As Tripp (2006: 251) notes, such shortcomings in the subfield of gender and comparative politics derive in part from the relative newness of the field, as well as recent methodological trends in political science that 'have lessened the interest in country-based fieldwork that would produce the kind of research that would elicit more in-depth understanding of gender processes'. I agree with Tripp that much of the research on Middle East politics lacks a gender perspective, despite the clout of the female electorate and their presence in major political parties. Certainly the practical difficulties of doing fieldwork, especially cross-national field research, can and do result in incomplete studies that fail to adequately represent both regional differences and global trends (Tripp 2006). My extensive research, with its comparative focus on women's political organising in two Muslim countries, aims to address part of this deficit, and present a more comprehensive picture of women's political rights and representation in Iran and Turkey, by emphasising the intricacies involved in women gaining access to formal political office. Furthermore, much of the research on electoral politics in the Muslim world, fails to adequately include women's demands, experiences and political aspirations.

Religion: One of Many Factors Keeping Women Out of Politics

What is evident from the existing literature on the mechanisms that exclude women from political processes and power, is that women's political under-representation is a global problem, regardless of countries' levels of democracy, political and institutional development, or degree of secularisation (Dahlerup 2006; Paxton *et al.* 2006; Phillips 1995; Tripp 2004, 2019). However, since women in Muslim majority countries are among the most politically under-represented across the globe, some scholars have emphasised religious and cultural factors, namely Islam and 'Muslim culture', as the main barriers to female political participation (Fish 2002; Inglehart and Norris 2003; Norris and Inglehart 2002). This body of literature, widely embraced following the 9/11 terrorist attacks in the US, built on the simplistic East/West, religious/secular dichotomies of modernisation theorists (Huntington 1996) to argue that Muslims hold distinctively patriarchal attitudes which hinder democratisation and gender equality. In one widely cited study, Inglehart and Norris (2003) argued that culture matters greatly, and identified 'an Islamic religious heritage' as 'one of the most powerful barriers to the rising tide of gender equality' that is being witnessed in Western and secularising countries (p. 71).[14] By emphasising culture and/or religion (which are often falsely equated), such essentialist categorisation of the Muslim world as 'non-egalitarian' or 'less-developed' ignores vast political, historical and other distinctions between Muslim countries, assuming that 'Muslim culture' is monolithic and disregarding that 'culture' is ever-changing, flexible, fluid and contested (Bayat 2007; Ciftci *et al.* 2019).

In recent decades, I, along with other scholars, have questioned the claim of religion as the main culprit of women's political under-representation in Muslim contexts (Kang 2015; Sabbagh 2005; Shalaby 2016; Tajali 2016a, 2017; Tripp 2019). As has been pointed out, the 'religious conservatism' explanation is clearly inadequate when we consider the high levels of women's political activity as voters, voter recruiters and grass-roots organisers, including on behalf of religious conservative parties (Arat 2005; Hoodfar and Sadr 2009; Tajali 2016a, 2017; White 2002). It also fails to account for the wide variation among Muslim-majority countries: Muslim-majority Senegal has one of the world's highest percentage of elected female parliamentarians – currently 41.8 per cent thanks to its gender parity quota – while Oman (1.2 per cent) and Yemen (0.3 per cent) are among the lowest (Inter-Parliamentary Union 2021). Women in the Maghreb – Algeria, Tunisia and Morocco – hold on average 28 per cent of legislative seats, compared to an average of 10 per cent for the rest of the Middle East and North African regions (Tripp 2019: 63). Furthermore, a number of Muslim countries such as Pakistan, Indonesia and Bangladesh have democratically elected female heads of states, strongly countering any claim that religion or patriarchal culture are the primary determinants in how women fare in electoral politics.

Claiming Islam as the primary barrier to women entering politics also fails to account for the modest increase in women assuming political office despite the rise to power of conservative and Islamist forces in a number of Muslim-majority countries. Religion is an undeniable factor in the negotiation of everyday life in both Turkey and Iran; what is notable and of research interest is that in Turkey the pro-religious and conservative AKP has been outperforming its main secular opposition the Republican People's Party (*Cumhuriyet Halk Partisi* – CHP) in nominating women for parliamentary seats, while in Iran it was ultra-conservative President Ahmadinejad who

---

[14] Significantly, Inglehart and Norris's (2003) study left out 110 cases from their research, all of which were developing countries, given limitations on datasets (Tripp 2006).

appointed post-revolutionary Iran's first female minister, rather than his more reformist counterparts. Significantly, scholars have identified similar trends in a number of other Muslim countries, including in Yemen and Jordan (Clark and Schwedler 2003) and Tunisia (Marks 2013), where conservative religious parties have been recruiting and nominating women to decision-making positions in higher proportions than their secular and more liberal counterparts.

Since this book also aims to contribute to the debate on religion's roles in women's political representation, I define what I mean by *Islam*. For the purpose of this study, in line with scholars such as Ziba Mir-Hosseini (1999, 2006a) and Fatima Sadiqi (2006), I distinguish Islam as a source of individual faith from the religious organisation in which patriarchal institutions and rulings in the name of Islam dictate a particular division of resources (and power) among various social demographics.[15] This important distinction, applicable to other religions as well, recognises that those in power have often used religion to justify certain practices and behaviours, and that others have challenged such claims with reference to the same religious sources. In this research I point to both the dominant clerical discourses that have shaped law, certain institutions and society, often to the detriment of women's political roles, particularly in theocratic Iran, as well as to how individual believers, especially women's rights activists, understand and practice Islam in ways that may appear at odds with the version of Islam perpetuated by clerical elites and institutions. For Iran, I demonstrate that religious organisation, especially the gender discriminatory laws and institutions of the theocratic republic, greatly limits women's political representation. However, women activists, including those who identify themselves as devout Muslims with allegiance to the state, are actively challenging such gender discrimination in their quest to reach political decision-making positions. Framing their demands for women's access to positions of authority in religious terms based on Islamic principles facilitates their reception in a Muslim society that has placed religion at the core of its value system and social structure.

[15] Fatima Sadiqi (2006) persuasively demonstrates for Morocco that 'liberal feminists were conscious of the use of Islam by patriarchy' in their efforts to enhance women's rights, and that articulating this distinction between Islamic faith and patriarchy enabled them to form important alliances with women affiliated with Islamic associations and parties, and work together with them for the adoption of a very progressive Family Law in 2004.

Because I understand religion to operate in the contexts where I am examining its role as both embedding and responding to the practices of its adherents, it is by definition ever-changing, based on different interpretations and understandings. This conceptualisation legitimises 'women-centred re-readings' of religious texts (primarily the Quran and Hadith),[16] as put forward by some religious women's rights activists (and at times reformist clerics), contesting centuries of male-dominated textual (*mis*)interpretations that denied women their divinely ordained rights and status. I consider the analysis of such contestations among different actors to present us with a better picture of Islam's role in shaping women's access to positions of political and religious authority (Tajali 2011). By viewing Islam as a 'space' within which such debate takes place, this research moves away from perceiving Islam as a dominant voice of authority as represented by often male *fuqaha* or experts in Islamic jurisprudence, to one in which diverse voices can emerge from within the same religious sources, but with new and reform-oriented interpretations. Valuing such diversity of voices, enables us to examine the opportunities for advancing women's rights and status that can arise through religious discourses. In fact, a major opportunity for women's access to political leadership in Iran is anchored in the unresolved debate among even the highest-ranking religious clerics on whether women can serve in positions of authority.

Aside from religion, other factors scholars have analysed as important in contributing to women's political under-representation in Muslim contexts include tribal allegiance (Charrad 2001), oil production (Ross 2008), women's limited role in the labour force (Moghadam 2013), patriarchy (Kausar 1997; Sadiqi 2006) and particular electoral and political systems (Hoodfar and Tajali 2011; Shalaby 2016), all of which can be found in non-Muslim contexts as well. Mounira Charrad (2001), Gihan Abou-Zeid (2006) and Linda Beck (2003) identify tribal, kin-based or patronage networks as stronger factors than religion in gender unequal policies, including women's access to political leadership.[17]

---

[16] The two dominant sources of Islam are its holy book, the Quran, and the Hadith, the sayings and teachings of Prophet Mohammad, both of which are subject to different interpretations and readings across times and cultures. Since this book is more interested in the practice of religion rather than its sources, I will focus on how individuals in contemporary Iran and Turkey understand the (in)compatibility between Islam and women's political leadership.

[17] While this factor may be significant in many Arab countries where gaining political office

Michael Ross (2008) argues that women's extreme political under-representation in oil-rich Muslim countries is due to the very low level of female employment in the formal economy, which limits women's opportunities to mobilise to challenge male domination of the public sphere. However, like other simplistic explanations, this study loses sight of the complexities at play, while concurrently essentialising women by viewing their political involvement as entirely dependent on states and institutions. It fails to account for the role of gender quotas, which have worked to offset the impact of natural resource exploitation on women's access to political office, as well as for women's capacity to organise and to negotiate with state elites. In response to Ross, Kang (2009) and Tripp and Kang (2008) have demonstrated that women's political representation in oil-rich Muslim countries including Iraq, Algeria, Tunisia and Indonesia has increased with the introduction of gender quotas. This mechanism is increasingly implemented in Muslim-majority countries,[18] largely in response to women and civil society organising. For the adoption of 'fast-track' approaches such as quotas, scholars emphasise the importance of national women's movements and international normative influences (Dahlerup 2008; Tripp and Kang 2008).

Women's low labour force participation has also been recognised by Moghadam (2013) as a cause for women's political under-representation in various Muslim countries, including in Iran (pp. 192–3). Such emphasis on modernisation and industrialisation, which has helped explain expansion of women's political roles in Western countries, however, may not necessarily apply in various non-Western contexts. As Tripp (2019: 4) writes,

> the mechanisms that explain women's representation in terms of labor force participation and the expansion of the welfare state, which are linked to the spread of democracy and cultural change in Europe, simply are not as important in countries where women are primarily engaged in agricultural production, in the informal economy, or working in the home.

Instead, she suggests looking to women's movements, in relation to top-down institutional reform, to understand the dynamics of expanding women's

---

is strongly connected with male-organised tribal affiliations, it is less applicable to the case studies of this research.

[18] Particularly in the Maghreb.

political representation especially in Muslim-majority countries with low formal female work-force participation. While Iran has exceptionally low levels of women in the formal labour market (data on women in the informal economy is lacking), and this limits to some degree women's presence in the public sphere generally, my in-depth interviews with women in both countries finds that there are adequate numbers of women interested in, and qualified to seek, political office but they face numerous institutional obstacles. Research which is focused on a single factor such as labour-force participation overlooks that adequate numbers of women do have the experience and skills to participate in political decision-making, but are disadvantaged by majoritarian electoral systems in patriarchal societies where running a woman candidate is considered risky, and by undemocratic candidate selection mechanisms controlled by male leaders.[19]

To date, little research has specifically analysed women's political *aspirations* in Muslim-majority countries, including in Iran and Turkey. And while there are some studies focused on women's rights campaigns and lobbying efforts for female representation, specifically analysing campaigns for gender quotas in the Middle East and North Africa (Abou-Zeid 2006; Araujo and Garcia 2006; Tripp 2004; Tripp *et al.* 2006), few studies have focused on the efforts of conservative party-aligned women to increase women's access to high-level decision-making. Most of the research on women's participation in religious conservative political movements, including in Islamist parties, has focused on women's activism at informal levels rather than on women's aspirations to political decision-making positions (Arat 2005; Iqtidar 2011; Jad 2011; Shehabuddin 2008; White 2002). Only a few recent studies, including my research on Iran and Turkey, address women's political representation on behalf of conservative religious movements (Ben Shitrit 2016a; Jad 2018; Tajali 2015b, 2016a, 2017).

This book is thus the first in-depth study of party women activists across the ideological spectrum that looks specifically at the conditions that shape

---

[19] While it is true that the male-dominated culture of politics in many Muslim majority nations discourages women from aspiring to political leadership posts (Arat 2005; Kar 2005; Kausar 1997), my findings show there are always qualified women who do have political aspirations, and even where only small numbers of women have formal political aspirations in such contexts, this does not equate with political disinterest or apolitical inclinations, which are sometimes used to explain, if not justify, the absence of mechanisms to support women's political participation.

their strategies and the outcomes of their efforts to promote women's political aspirations. Through extensive field research in two Muslim countries, it challenges portrayals of women as passive subjects or mere 'foot-soldiers' in political parties by showing how women in Iran and Turkey, including those aligned with conservative religious parties, are publicly challenging the gender discriminatory actions and attitudes of male elites and the movements in which they are involved. The accounts of women's activism and agency presented throughout this book highlight the ways women organise and manoeuvre within existing institutional structures to gain posts in formal politics.

Why Women's Political Representation?

Over the last decades, feminists, rights activists and the international community have increasingly campaigned to address women's global political under-representation, including in some of the most democratically advanced countries in the West. The presumption behind the demand to increase women's numbers in national legislatures is that a 'politics of presence', which refers to women's *descriptive representation* in electoral politics, will lead to a 'politics of ideas', or women's *substantive representation* in which their interests and demands are represented (Phillips 1995). Phillips (1995) argues that there is a correlation between 'who' our representatives are and 'what' is represented.

While more analytical research has questioned the simplistic link that the 'sheer number' of female legislators produces women-friendly laws or substantive representation (Childs and Krook 2006, 2008; Franceschet and Piscopo 2008; Htun *et al.* 2013), the fact remains that historically women have been systemically marginalised from politics, and this has stifled their voices and demands. However, merely increasing women's numbers in legislative bodies will not result in feminist outcomes, precisely because of the nature and structure of political institutions engineered to undermine egalitarian initiatives and demands. Male party leaders in authoritarian and semi-democratic regimes are particularly prone to marginalise women political aspirants who are sympathetic to feminist concerns, or who are advocates for more democratic institutions. By exposing such obstacles that prevent women's access to political decision-making, this study contributes to our understanding of the overall and systemic frameworks that seek to maintain the political status quo.

Greater access to political decision-making has been a long-standing demand of women's rights groups in Muslim-majority countries, including in Iran and Turkey. Indeed the rise of feminist consciousness in many of these countries correlated with nationalist movements for independence, where equality and democratic rights, including women's suffrage, were among the central demands (Jayawardena 1986; Paidar 1995; Tekeli 1995). Women continue to be a force for democratisation as is evident by their prominence in pro-democratic uprisings that regularly erupt across the region in countries such as Lebanon, Sudan, Iran and Algeria.

Nevertheless, some may question the validity of research on women's political representation in authoritarian contexts, where, as noted earlier, the general integrity of elections is questionable and the public's interests (regardless of gender) are sacrificed for the interests of a select few. Echoing Melody Valdini (2019), I also problematise the assumption that the mere presence of women in a legislature necessarily equates a democratic turn on the part of the state, since as noted, increases in women's descriptive representation may be a matter of political expediency on the part of autocratic leaders.[20] In some instances, electing conservative party women and appointing them to (at least nominally) powerful positions can help maintain limited rights for other marginalised social groups (e.g. LGBT – lesbian, gay, bisexual and trans – communities), and justify continued authoritarian rule. However, my research highlights the need to recognise the complexities and heterogeneity within presumptively homogenous social groups, including women identifying as conservative. Thus, far from composing like-minded groups, the conservative party women discussed in this research are complicated individuals, some of whom publicly protest the dominant gender ideology of their male party leaders, while others are less interested in ideological battles. Studies have echoed the need for more nuanced understandings of the links between religiosity and political tendencies such as voting behaviour (Biagini 2020a; Ciftci *et al.* 2019). Exposing such diversity is important for recognising the dynamism of politi-

---

[20] Valdini convincingly argues that several democracy indices, for example the Democracy Barometer, misguidedly include women's descriptive representation in legislatures as a variable in the measurement of quality of democracy, ignoring the fact that 'in several countries with record-breaking levels of women's representation, women's power remains low and limited and the regime remains thoroughly authoritarian' (2019: 148).

cal groups and institutions, including of conservative religious parties and their members.

My research thus supports the argument that women's greater presence in political office is a step towards democratisation in Iran and Turkey, as it diversifies representation at least descriptively and symbolically, if not immediately substantively (Pitkin 1972). This is especially true in these two countries, where women's groups are central to grass-roots calls for democracy, gender equality and rule of law (Hoodfar and Sadr 2009; Sedghi 2007), and wield pressure on those who achieve political power or position, regardless of gender. Indeed, in both countries women's rights groups have used the democratisation card to support their demands for female representation when democratisation has been on the government agenda; for example, in Turkey the pro-government women's rights organisation KADEM (Women and Democracy Association) has campaigned to increase women's political representation using the slogan 'Kadın Varsa Demokrasi Var' – which translates as 'If there are women there is democracy' (KADEM 2019).[21] Arguably, KADEM, which has served as an important policy tool for the conservatives, is referencing democracy strategically to carve a place for like-minded women, rather than a plurality of women in Turkish formal politics. However, my research of this group also points to their complexities and shifting positionalities, as apparent by their occasional protests and public disapproval of AKP male elites –with some of whom they hold familial ties – as exemplified by their defence of the Istanbul Convention on violence against women despite the party's call for Turkey's withdrawal from this agreement, which eventually took place in early 2021 (Buyuk 2020).

Women in most Muslim countries have been demanding gender quotas to address some of the systemic discrimination that has kept women out of political leadership. Indeed, the achievement of higher levels of female political representation in some Muslim countries, notably Senegal, Algeria, Afghanistan, Iraq and Tunisia, only occurred with the implementation of parliamentary gender quotas.[22] While women's rights groups in both Iran

---

[21] Such tactics are most effective when ruling elites have themselves waved the flag of democratisation to mobilise their support base, as was the case for Turkey's ruling AKP.

[22] The percentage of female parliamentarians in Algeria, for example, rose from 8 per cent in 2007 to 31.6 per cent in the 2012 national elections as a result of adoption of a quota law in January of that year, stipulating at least 30 per cent female representation (Inter-Parliamentary Union 2019; International IDEA and Stockholm University 2018).

and Turkey have been campaigning for parliamentary gender quotas since at least the mid-1990s, neither country has adopted as yet any laws to guarantee women's parliamentary presence. Turkey's leftist pro-Kurdish rights parties have adopted a voluntary 40 per cent 'gender-neutral' quota for candidate lists in local and national elections since the early 2000s.[23] As Chapter 4 discusses, this voluntary quota has prompted other larger parties to increase the rate of women on their candidate lists as a way to maintain their electoral appeal.

At the international level, the 1995 Beijing Platform for Action shifted the discourse on women's under-representation from blaming women for being apolitical to holding states accountable for ending exclusionary practices and integrating women into politics. This important shift engendered significant changes at the national level as indicated by widespread parliamentary quota adoption in many countries (Dahlerup 2008; Krook 2009; Tajali 2013). But what explains the variance whereby some Muslim countries have been responsive to domestic and international pressures (such as Senegal, Algeria and Tunisia), while others continue to resist any measures to address women's historical political marginalisation?

As the following chapters of this book demonstrate, particular obstacles and opportunities influence the extent of advocacy groups' effectiveness in addressing women's political under-representation as they publicly campaign and negotiate with elites. While public calls for democracy and greater transparency in combination with the international community's support have provided local women activists with important opportunities to demand expansion of women's access to political office, undemocratic structures (such as candidate selection processes) and particular institutional characteristics (such as the absence of organised parties) greatly challenge their efforts. Given these complexities, this research focuses on women's descriptive representation, aiming to explore and understand the various obstacles and opportunities that shape women's efforts to be elected to office. Analysis of women's substantive representation – the extent to which female elected officials 'act for' women – is beyond the scope of this research, as it deserves its own analytical inquiry.

---

[23] A 'gender-neutral quota' dictates a maximum for both sexes; in this case, that neither sex should occupy more than 60 per cent or less than 40 per cent of the candidate list in each district. Such framing, by distancing itself from the more common 'women's quota' tends to be better received in patriarchal contexts (Hoodfar and Tajali 2011).

Why Iran and Turkey?

The neighbouring countries of Iran and Turkey offer an interesting comparison of the issue of women's political representation due to a number of differences and commonalities. Despite women's ongoing agitation for increased access to political decision-making in both countries, women continue to be under-represented in these Muslim-majority societies. Comprising only 5.5 per cent of total parliamentarians in Iran, and 17.3 per cent in Turkey as of 2020, women's parliamentary presence is below the global average of 24 per cent (Inter-Parliamentary Union 2021), and is low in other political bodies as well. There are generally only a token number of female ministers in the Turkish government regardless of who is in power (two or three out of a dozen ministerial posts), while in post-revolutionary Iran, as of 2020, only one woman has ever held a ministerial post. Neither country has ever popularly elected a woman to a top-level leadership position.[24]

Both states have similarly experienced top-down projects of political and social modernisation, including the establishment of modern political structures since the early part of the twentieth century (Azimi 2008; Kuru and Stepan 2012). Although both countries declare themselves *republics,* holding regular popular elections, domestic and international observers have deemed that feature as imperfect, though to different extents as I later explain. In the past decades, both states have also experienced the rise of political Islam – though to different degrees – as well as what sociologist Asef Bayat calls a 'post-Islamist turn', a growing trend of increasing emphasis from religious political parties and constituencies on the compatibility between 'religiosity and rights, faith and freedom, Islam and liberty' (Bayat 2007: 11). For at least the past two decades and increasingly since the mid-2010s, both countries have witnessed extensive popular protests against the corrupt and authoritarian aspects of their respective regimes. Women's groups have played central roles in such public protests, and many activists and academics have paid high prices for their involvements.

---

[24] Turkey's Tansu Ciller was not popularly elected, but rather chosen by her party to replace leader and Prime Minister Suleyman Demiral in 1993, when he was elected President following the vacancy created by the death of President Turgut Ozal. She served in that role from 1993 to 1996.

Iran and Turkey, however, depart from one another in several areas; among them, government structure, founding state ideology, level of institutional development, and extent of integration into the international community are the most relevant to this research. Iran has been a theocracy since 1979, maintaining power in the hands of a clerical oligarchy through strong authoritarian structures. In contrast, Turkey has been a secular state since its founding in 1923, with a historically imperfect democracy given its frequent military coups and periods of authoritarian rule. Many observers consider Turkey's recent transition in 2018 from a parliamentary to presidential system under the rule of Recep Tayyip Erdogan as a step towards authoritarianism (Cook 2016; Gardels and Shafak 2018; Taş 2015). While Erdogan and his Islamist predecessors have pushed for increased public and to an extent legal religiosity since the 1990s, my research shows that this has not undermined women's access to the political sphere (the subject of this research), in contrast with theocratic Iran. Indeed, despite some important reforms in women's rights since 1979, women in Iran continue to face major legal discrimination, some of which hinders their full participation in the political sphere. On the other hand, Turkey's early state feminist projects that emphasised women's public presence coupled with its legacy of strict secularism – or 'laicism'[25] – has prevented the adoption of similar gendered restrictions; though in recent decades, Islamist and pro-religious political parties have gained increasing power. Since 2002 with the rise to power of the pro-religious AKP (Justice and Development Party), the role of religion, government and ideology in Turkey are being redefined and re-drawn, with male political leaders – many of whom hold conservative religious tendencies – having overwhelming control over such processes. While it remains to be seen what Turkey's recent political shifts will deliver for women's political roles, this book can nonetheless illuminate religion's impact on women's roles in two Muslim countries relative to other institutional, ideological and social factors (see Table 1.1).

These countries also differ from one another in terms of institutional development and political transparency of party politics, and their electoral

---

[25] As will be explained in Chapter 3, Turkish laicism differs from secularism, in that instead of merely separating religion from politics, a 'laic' state actively subordinates religion and works to control the parameters of all religious practice (Shively 2005). This was one of Kemal's founding principles, intended to unite the people under Turkish nationalism by undermining religious and ethnic differences.

Table 1.1 Key factors and structures that impact women's political rights and roles in Turkey and Iran.

Category	Turkey	Iran
Political framework	Hybrid State founding ideology: Secular Republicanism	Hybrid State founding ideology: Islamic Republicanism
Dominant ruling gender ideology	Complementarian	Complementarian
De jure or *de facto* gender discrimination on women's access to political office	*De jure*: No legal gender discriminatory provisions *De facto*: Various gender discriminatory practices and attitudes hinder women's political recruitment and nomination	*De jure*: Iranian constitution is ambiguous on women's access to the office of presidency; national legislation bans women's judgeship; any legal requirement for religious training for political office also hinders women's access given the lack of clerical consensus on if women can serve as *Marjas* (source of emulation in *Shi'i* Islam), *Mujtahids* (those with the religious authority to conduct independent reasoning or *ijtihad*) or *Faqihs* (Muslim jurists). *De facto*: Various gender discriminatory practices and attitudes hinder women's political recruitment and nomination
Electoral system	Closed list proportional representation system (List -PR)	Two-round system (TRS)
Degree of integration into the international community (with some instances)	Moderate United Nations (founding member); North Atlantic Treaty Organisation (NATO); Organisation for Economic Co-operation and Development (OECD); Organisation of Islamic Cooperation (OIC); Group of Twenty (G20); Inter-Parliamentary Union (IPU) Convention on the Elimination of all forms of Discrimination Against Women (CEDAW): ratified 1985 From 2012 to 2021: Council of Europe Convention on preventing and combating violence against women and domestic abuse (Istanbul Convention)	Low United Nations; Organization of Islamic Cooperation (OIC); Inter-Parliamentary Union (IPU); Group of 15 (G15)
Political party structure	Multi-party system	Weak party structures (factional politics)
% Women in the parliament (2021)	17.3	5.5
Global gender gap index ranking (2021)	133/156	150/156

Sources: Inter-Parliamentary Union, *Monthly ranking of women in national parliaments*, https://data.ipu.org/women-ranking?month=6&year=2021; World Economic Forum, *Global Gender Gap Report 2021*, http://www3.weforum.org/docs/WEF_GGGR_2021.pdf.

systems differ in determining the allocation of seats following elections. Perhaps the starkest difference, and most relevant for the purpose of this research, is that Turkey supports a tradition of organised and extensive political party structures that have been able to mobilise the public, including women, to engage in formal politics. The process of Turkish state formation in 1923, based on republican ideals rather than on a monarchy as was the case for Iran, eventually contributed to the development of institutions, including a multi-party system, which helped foster state–society interaction.[26] Turkey also utilises a list proportional representation (List PR) electoral system, which can help facilitate the election of women to parliament from multiple parties. In Iran, however, organised party structures are largely absent due to factional politics, which have prevented the formation of strong, organised political parties. Although post-revolutionary Iran has been holding regular elections since 1979, the country's continued authoritarianism has precluded the development of genuine or robust party politics as a vehicle for democratic practices (Azimi 1997). Similar to the period prior to the revolution, the banning of opposition groups from organising and contesting elections has continued. Instead of well-structured political parties that organise around specific platforms and actively recruit supporters, Iran has political factions (*firaksiyun*) that coalesce mostly around individual political leaders and lack a clear platform (Amanat 2007; Arjomand 2009; Moslem 2002). Iran also utilises a majoritarian two-round electoral system (TRS) that fosters competition between dominant political groups, a system that is considered fairly antagonistic to women's nomination and election in male-biased socio-political contexts.

Another major difference between the countries is Turkey's greater integration into the international community, largely due to the Republic's historical and until recently ongoing embrace of Westernisation, secularism and democracy, which garnered the support of many powerful Western states. Turkey has been a NATO (North Atlantic Treaty Organization) member since 1952 and a long-running candidate for European Union (EU) membership.[27] On the other hand, Iran's 1979 popular uprising abruptly put

---

[26] Although, prior to 1946, Turkey was essentially a single-party state, the first multi-party elections were held in 1950, beginning the process of organised political protest and activism that persists (Eligur 2010; Howe 2000; Tugal 2009; Wuthrich 2015).

[27] Although Erdogan's pro-religious AKP came to power with a strong commitment to

an end to a Western-backed monarchy and led to the establishment of a theocracy hostile to the West, resulting in its increasing marginalisation from the international community. The degree to which each country is integrated into the international community impacts the extent to which their respective civil society members can rely on international support and resources for demands such as women's increased political representation. Though women's rights groups in both countries are acutely aware of global debates and trends around women's political representation, I found that women's groups in Turkey have better access to international support for their campaigning efforts. Although Iranian women's rights activists have at times sought international platforms and advocacy for their efforts to expand women's formal political participation, Iranian political elites have been less than responsive, and at times hostile, to such efforts.

Iran and Turkey also provide meaningful comparative case studies given their comparable political, social and ideological histories, which both include constitutionalism, Westernisation and Islamisation in the span of a century. These have greatly influenced the contemporary political and social realities of each country. As Nader Sohrabi (2011) argues, major shifts such as revolutions do not occur in a vacuum, rather they are motivated by diffusion of ideas, interests and institutions across borders, which are adapted and reworked according to local exigencies and manifest in specific ways in each context. Historical cross-border exchange of ideas and experiences between the neighbouring countries of Iran and Turkey have influenced conceptualisations of women's rights and status in each country, further validating a comparative analysis. In both countries I often encountered interlocutors eager to compare and contrast women's political accomplishments, political institutions and dominant gender ideologies of each country with me. Some of these conversations resulted in Iranian publications on Turkish women in politics (Koolaee 2015; Tajali 2016b).

---

integrate into the EU (unlike his Islamist predecessors), accession talks have been suspended due to the EU's concerns over Turkey's human rights record, particularly following the government's harsh response to the 2013 Gezi Park protests. Two decades since coming to power, Erdogan still publicly supports eventual EU integration (Batchelor 2018).

The Argument: Opportunity Structures and Strategic Framing

This book argues that although religious, cultural and institutional obstacles play key roles in women's political under-representation in Muslim contexts, the organisational efforts of women's groups and their strategic interactions with political elites are rapidly opening new opportunities in the quest to increase women's rate of political representation. Women's rights activists in Iran and Turkey take advantage of political and discursive opportunity structures to mobilise public support and pressure elites to expand women's access to formal politics.

To analyse the nature and extent of interactions and negotiations between women's rights groups and political elites, I employ two central elements of social movement theory: political opportunity structures and framing processes. The concept of *political opportunity structure* refers to 'consistent – but not necessarily permanent – dimensions of the political environment that provide incentive for collective action by affecting people's expectations for success or failure' (Tarrow 1998: 77). Social movement theorists have argued that certain openings or constraints in the political environment shape whether movement actors achieve their political goals (Meyer 2004; Meyer and Minkoff 2004; Tarrow 1998). Scholars have identified a number of factors that contribute to movement actors' success, ranging from formal political rules and institutions that provide challengers with points of access, to willingness of political elites and positive public opinion (Amenta and Caren 2004; Amenta and Halfmann 2012; Baldez 2002; Chappell 2002; McCammon *et al.* 2007). However, social movement success is complex as it is dependent on the extent to which various circumstances work in conjunction with one another.

The existence of various openings in the political environment is not sufficient, if movement (or contentious) actors do not *perceive* them as opportunities or as worth the effort of mobilising around (Baldez 2002). The way that actors 'articulate their interpretations of the social or political problem at hand, its solution, and the reasons why others should support efforts to ameliorate the condition' is *framing* (McCammon *et al.* 2007: 726). Framing processes entail actors strategically engaging in interpretative actions to perceive, identify, label, legitimise and articulate occurrences in a way that garners optimal support for their cause and maximises pressure on elites (McAdam 1997). Effective framing processes require careful consideration of the broader cultural and political contexts, including the hegemonic discourses (or salient beliefs or values) in society and politics. *Discourse* refers to the use of language in speech and writing to grant meaning to norms and practices of society and the state. Both state and non-state actors reinterpret, reformulate, rethink and rewrite discourses to further their interests, and hence engage in *discursive politics* (Katzenstein 1998).

My analysis of organising and lobbying efforts to expand women's access to political decision-making positions in Iran and Turkey reveals that they are most successful when they take advantage of the available opportunity structures through careful framing. The dependent variable of this study is the recent unexpected increase in women's political representation in both countries. Opportunity structures and effective framing constitute the main independent variables in this study. I argue that the presence of two particular opportunity structures greatly contributes to advancing women's organising and lobbying efforts: meaningful electoral competition, referring to electoral structures that allow distinctive political parties or groups to appeal to the electorate; and discursive opportunity structures, referring to how rights activists frame their arguments in consideration of the broader cultural and political norms and values. McCammon and colleagues define *discursive opportunity structures* as 'ideas in the larger political culture that are believed to be "sensible", "realistic", and "legitimate" and that facilitate the reception of certain movement frames' (2007: 731). Following Rita Stephan (2010) and Lihi Ben Shitrit (2016a), I also find that an analysis which considers both social constraints and women's capacities to act within them to promote change, as a more comprehensive approach towards understanding women's agency, particularly in non-Western contexts where family relations, religion and cultural norms also act as structures shaping women's tactics and outcomes. I demonstrate that women's groups in Iran and Turkey frame their demands for increasing women's access to political decision-making primarily through utilising the local regime discourse or according to international human rights discourse.

The analysis of the relationship between political and institutional structures and women's organising to expand their political rights and roles in Iran and Turkey enables me to highlight two central theoretical points. The first is the reorientation from a long-standing focus on Islam and Muslim culture as the main barrier to women's political representation. As evident from the recent notable increases in the nomination and recruitment of women to political office on behalf of religious political parties, partly as a result of women's active participation in these parties, and the fact that many pious women frame and justify their demands for women's increased political representation in religious terms, this research questions Islam as the main cause of women's political under-representation. Instead, by looking at institutional obstacles, such as undemocratic candidate selection processes and limited party competition, this work emphasises the complex range of factors that hinder women's access to political decision-making, many of which are not limited to Muslim contexts.

The second is the introduction of the concept of *religious discursive opportunities*, which I show enable activists to legitimise and justify women's access to positions of political authority in religiously conservative contexts. My study of religious party women's organising for women's political representation reveals that in fact, religion can serve as a motivating source for contentious activism and for women's political aspirations, as it fosters values and ideals that people hope to see reflected in their society. In this sense, religion is an important discursive opportunity structure for women activists operating in a political and cultural context where religion is a salient feature – as in theocratic Iran – and can facilitate the reception of certain movement frames widely considered legitimate (McCammon *et al.* 2007). This finding contributes to our comprehension of women's agency in Muslim contexts by demonstrating that pious women's demand for gender equal access to positions of authority may not necessarily be based on liberal or feminist thought, but rather on local religious and value-oriented understandings.

Women's Activism and Aspirations within Conservative Religious Political Parties

Women's engagement in conservative religious political movements and parties[28] has received limited scholarly attention. The paradox of women supporting movements that undermine their rights and status has deterred many feminist scholars from critically analysing the types of, and incen-

---

[28] Conservative religious movements, including but not limited to Islamist movements, are widespread across the globe. What they share in common is a conservative gender ideology that relegates women primarily to the domestic sphere (Ben Shitrit 2016a). When these movements succeed electorally, they form political parties. Such parties need women's electoral, political and economic support.

tives and interests motivating women's activism within such movements. Women's mobilisation on behalf of conservative religious and Islamist parties and movements in the Muslim world falls into this gap in the literature. The scholarship that does exist for women's participation in conservative religious parties across the Muslim world has mostly focused on women's roles as grass-roots organisers and voter recruiters, but rarely addresses women's activism or aspirations for high-level political office (Arat 2005; Iqtidar 2011; Shehabuddin 2008; White 2002). Other studies explain women's activism in conservative religious political movements in terms of supporting larger nationalist or religious goals in spite of their subordinate political and social status within such movements (Ben Shitrit 2016a; Biagini 2020a; Jad 2011, 2018; Mahmood 2005). Among these works, Saba Mahmood's *Politics of Piety* (2005), an anthropological inquiry into pious women's involvement in Egypt's mosque movement, radically challenged conceptualisations of Muslim women's agency by moving away from liberal and feminist thought that only located it in acts of resistance or self-empowerment, towards a more nuanced and expansive understanding that recognises agency also in one's subjectivity. According to Mahmood, these women, who desire a subordinate status, are not autonomous subjects and their activities are not products of their independent wills . . . but rather they are 'the products of authoritative discursive traditions whose logic and power far exceeds the consciousness of the subjects they enable' (Mahmood 2005: 32).

My book also explores the subjectivity and agency of pious women in Iran and Turkey who are involved in conservative Islamic political movements;[29] however in contrast to Mahmood's (2005) findings, I found that many pious women in Iran and Turkey, who also derive their subjectivity from religious discourses, utilise these discourses not to subjugate themselves, but rather to demand equal access to positions of authority, including over men. Hence, unlike the women of Egypt's mosque movement, the central objective of many conservative party women in Iran and Turkey is in fact to resist and reform central 'authoritative discursive traditions' which had until then

---

[29] The term 'conservative party women' in this research refers to activist members of conservative and pro-religious parties and/or movements. In both Iran and Turkey, these women tend to be pious, understood as devout, Muslims. However, while in Iran many conservative women activists support a theocracy, in Turkey their counterparts generally support a secular state, where religious expression in the public arena, such as donning a headcovering, is permitted.

mostly denied women equal access to leadership positions. Thus, religious women's rights activists at times framed their demands for increased access to political decision-making through reference to religious discourses by contesting patriarchal *mis*interpretations of religious doctrine and highlighting the endorsement of gender equality in such texts. The women included in this research saw no contradiction between Islam and women holding positions of power.

Yet, I also find that politically active women's level of religiosity was secondary to whether they framed their demand for women's increased political representation in a religious discourse (using holy texts) or according to a 'rights' discourse (based on international human rights documents, such as the Convention on the Elimination of All Forms of Discrimination against Women, or CEDAW),[30] in public campaigns. Indeed, the same groups of women would exhaust one framing approach, before strategically switching to the other to gain the most support and yield the most pressure. Complicating previous dominant narratives presenting conservative party women as mere foot-soldiers in religious political movements, or as loyal supporters of religious and/or nationalist interest, this research highlights women's diversity and agency in shaping and leading the movements in which they are involved. In line with arguments in social movement theory, my study confirms that emotions and values play important roles in changing political discourse (Ferree and Merrill 2000).

My work and more recent scholarly analysis of conservative party women emphasise the heterogeneity among this social group, and the diverse ways they engage with elites in their ever-shifting contexts (Biagini 2020a; Hafez 2011). Erika Biagini (2016, 2020a), studying the Egyptian Muslim Sisterhood's activism of the past decades, similarly argues that important opportunities, such as the 2011 uprisings that ousted Hosni Mubarak, acted as an important instigator of women's political participation, forcing their conservative Muslim Brotherhood counterparts to be more accepting of women's political roles. In her careful study of the Muslim Sisterhood's negotiations with the Brotherhood on women's political roles, Biagini documents instances of women's resistance to gender discriminatory discourses of the party (2020a), though she also highlights the limitations to women's

---

[30] CEDAW is an international treaty adopted in 1979 by the United Nations General Assembly.

outspokenness, as Salafi-leaning male leaders often prioritised the rise of obedient women to influential posts, contributing to tokenistic representation (2020b). Conservative religious parties also vary from one another in their treatment and inclusion of women. For instance, while the Muslim Sisterhood is fully segregated from the central Muslim Brotherhood bodies (Biagini 2020a), this is not the case in either Turkey or Iran, as women's branches or commissions are integrated into the central conservative party structures. Turkey's Justice and Development Party (AKP) is notable in this regard, since the chairwoman of its women's branch is also a member of the party's executive board.

Notes on Method

This is the first book-length comparative study of women's political participation and representation based on fieldwork in two Muslim-majority countries. To this end, between 2009 and 2019 I conducted more than 140 in-depth interviews with past and current female politicians and candidates, with party elites, women's rights activists, scholars, journalists and bloggers from both Iran and Turkey. I encountered my informants mostly through snowball sampling, asking each person that I interviewed to refer me to other activists and party women who might comment on this topic. Given my multiple visits to each country over the span of a decade, I also revisited and interviewed certain key individuals over time to get a better sense of major political shifts' impacts on gender politics. In Turkey, I conducted my interviews in Istanbul and Ankara; in Iran, most of my informants were based in Tehran. In order to protect identities, I assigned pseudonyms to all individuals, except those who chose to be identified – generally women who had already shared their views publicly.

In an effort to gain a deeper understanding of women's actions as well as the public and political elites' reactions and responses to campaigns in demand of increased female political access and power, I arranged most of my field visits to coincide with major elections in both countries. During these periods, I followed female candidates from various parties as well as women running as independents as they campaigned, observing their interactions with the electorate and male elites, and interviewed them about their experiences. I attended and observed many meetings, gatherings and conferences of women's rights activists and party members. I also analysed political party and state documents, reports from women's groups and organisations, and hundreds of media reports to better understand the motivations of different actors, the constraints that they faced and the political climate in which they debated about women's political roles. Additionally, as a researcher and trainer on issues related to women's political representation with the transnational feminist organisation Women Living Under Muslim Laws (WLUML), I incorporated into the research feedback and responses I received from local women's rights activists during workshops. Outside of the field, I continued to closely follow the debates on women and politics in both countries, which also assisted a multi-sited project that I lead on this topic with WLUML. Given my proximity to women's rights networks in Muslim contexts, I quickly learned about major campaigns and negotiations on women's political rights, with access to relevant webinars and virtual closed-group sessions that have been popular with many women's rights advocates who face travel or media restrictions.

In both countries, the women fighting for female access to political decision-making come from across the political, ideological, ethnic and class spectrums, and their diverse experiences are included in this research. Using an intersectional lens, I demonstrate how women's multiple positionalities impact their political standing and access in these two Muslim-majority countries. For instance, I highlight the institutional obstacles that hinder Left-leaning women in Iran, and the structures that until 2013 barred women in Turkey who wore headscarves from political office. While I categorise women and women's groups as 'secular', 'feminist', 'conservative', 'Islamist' or 'reformist', based on how they identified themselves and according to the political party/tendency that they supported, I recognise that (a) these identities are not necessarily mutually exclusive and can be overlapping identities, and (b) political/ideological affinities are complex and shift over time. However, noting such distinctions highlights women's diversity, particularly in terms of political views, social concerns, civic demands, ideologies and religiosity. Thus, among my informants are left-wing women who are feminist, and/or reformist, and/or secular, or every combination thereof, as well as women who are right-wing social conservatives, or those associated with Islamist and conservative religious parties, all of whom support women's increased access to political leadership.

In Iran, at one end of the spectrum, secularists and most reformists favour separation of religion and state and emphasise gender equality (some even identify themselves as feminists); on the other end, conservatives support Iran's theocratic regime, reject feminist ideology and decry Western influence. Despite these differences, I show that since the theocracy's founding both groups of women have managed to join forces regularly in their campaigning efforts. In Turkey, while the political and ideological spectrum is equally broad, ranging from secular to pious to conservative, all of the major women's groups included in this research, regardless of degree of piety or conservatism, supported a secular political framework and emphasised international human rights norms on gender equality in their demands. However, the divide between secular and pious women in Turkey is deeply rooted in the country's historical and political background, and manifests in debates around the extent to which religion and religious symbols (i.e. the Muslim headscarf) should be present in the public sphere, given the Republic's founding principle of laicism as addressed earlier.

In both Iran and Turkey, for women allied with or members of political parties, party allegiance trumped unity on gender issues across party lines.[31] Women's level of devotion to the party platforms, even if it countered their personal gender ideology, increased as they moved up the party hierarchy; this seemed primarily a function of the fact that male party leaders were most likely to promote the women who least challenged the status quo. Instances of internal criticism were more apparent at lower party echelons, where more outspoken women occasionally voiced concerns regarding a candidate nomination process, or discriminatory practices and attitudes among the male political elite. My research tries to expose all the relational complexities at play as women attempted to access political posts.

I initiated my field research by contacting women's organisations and activists across the ideological spectrum advocating for increased numbers of female decision-makers at all levels of government (see Appendix). Thus, in Turkey, I became well acquainted with board members and trainers of a historically secular women's organisation, KADER (Association for the Support of Women Candidates), that specifically works on addressing women's political under-representation. I also interviewed directors and activists from organisations of pious women, some with linkages to the ruling AKP party, such as KADEM (Women and Democracy Association), as well as non-partisan

---

[31] This research contributes to the major question in the politics and gender literature of when gender issues predominate over partisan concerns (Schwindt-Bayer and Taylor-Robinson 2011).

groups that had campaigned for headscarved women's access to the public and political spheres, such as AKDER (Women's Rights Organization against Discrimination) and the now dissolved CCWP (Capital City Women's Platform).[32] In Iran, state hostility towards independent women's organising meant comparable women's organisations were not necessarily obvious; this led me to seek out similar types of women's mobilisation efforts, under the auspices of Iran's two major factions, reformist and conservative.

In addition to non-partisan activists and organisations, I also interviewed women members, candidates and politicians of various political parties and groups. Because party women's branches are common and very active in Turkey's multi-party system, I was able to contact and interview women's branch heads and female political party members of all stripes. To fairly compare the degree of female grass-roots involvement in political parties, I contacted women's branches in districts where the parties were most active and popularly supported, as derived from the most recent election results. Election campaigns provided me important opportunities to connect with and observe female candidates and incumbents as they canvassed for their posts, and to record their own accounts of their efforts, the obstacles they faced and the tactics they employed in their quest to open the field to female politicians. Istanbul's three electoral districts are composed of diverse populations and are among the largest in the country with ninety-eight representatives, meaning all of the major parties have a good chance of seeing some of their candidates elected to parliament.[33] In Istanbul alone, I interviewed women campaigning on behalf of all of the major parties, including the Justice and Development Party (AKP), People's Republican Party (CHP), the pro-Kurdish Peace and Democracy Party (BDP) later the People's Democratic Party (HDP), and Nationalist Movement Party (MHP). I also interviewed a number of independent women candidates, and those running on behalf of the smaller parties that rarely gain parliamentary seats but are nonetheless quite active during election periods, such as the Islamist Felicity

---

[32] Capital City Women's Platform (CCWP), a renowned religious women's rights organisation since the 1990s, dissolved in 2019 as a result of rifts among its key members over their ability to criticise the ruling government, particularly following the 2016 failed coup attempt, which pressured religious groups to 'pick sides' between AKP and Gulen supporters (personal interview with a CCWP founding member, 19 August 2019).

[33] Istanbul's three districts were previously represented by eighty-five seats in the parliament (2002–15); the number increased to ninety-eight seats for the 2018 elections.

Party (*Saadet*) and the currently disbanded leftist Equality and Democracy Party (EDP). During my visits to Ankara, the country's capital, I interviewed several current and former female parliamentarians from the AKP, CHP and pro-Kurdish HDP.

In Iran I spoke with women from the two major political factions: reformist and conservative, including those who identified as independents. I held extensive interviews with key female figures from reformist and conservative parties that most actively worked on increasing women's access to political office, notably the reformist Islamic Iran Participation Front (*Jebheye Mosharekate Iran-e Islami* or *Mosharekat*) and the conservative Zeinab Society (*Jameh Zeinab*). Because the issue of women's political rights and status is increasingly a source of unity across ideological lines among Iranian women's groups, reformist women activists were able to refer me to their conservative counterparts. However, unlike in Turkey, my access during the time of my fieldwork to serving female politicians and parliamentarians was very limited. Given Iran's relative lack of transparency and the fact that I was based and educated in the West, I was advised not to pursue the background checks, government clearances and authorisations required to meet with members of the Iranian parliament and other high-ranking officials. I partly corrected for this by interviewing former female parliamentarians from both factions, and relying on published media interviews and public statements from serving politicians and officials. For this research, reformist women were generally much more willing to speak with me than their conservative counterparts, who needed more convincing. Determined to gather the perspectives of a wide range of Iranian women and thanks to the comparative nature of my research with Turkey,[34] I was ultimately able to win the trust of and interview a number of influential party women from the conservative faction as well.

Another challenge throughout my fieldwork in both countries was including the voices of male politicians, particularly male parliamentarians. Given that the project highlights issues around female political representa-

[34] The comparative nature of my research and my attention to women's organising in Turkey – particularly on religious women's concerns such as lifting of the headscarf ban – greatly enhanced my access to conservative party women in Iran given their interest in major political and social shifts unfolding in neighbouring Turkey. Such interest led various conservative women's organisations and journals to invite me to publish in Persian on my findings in Turkey. Such exchanges and publications further enabled me to gain their trust, while also facilitating an important cross-national exchange on women's political experiences.

tion, my emphasis was on speaking with women in politics; as well, many of the party men I encountered seemed uninterested in the project or immediately referred me to women in their party offices. Access to male politicians and party officials in Iran was even more limited given Iran's gender segregated political atmosphere, in which one-on-one interaction between unacquainted individuals from the opposite sex in spaces like offices or homes is socially unacceptable. Nonetheless, in both countries I was able to interview a few men involved in party politics as well as several male activists, including bloggers and journalists advocating for the political rights and status of women and ethnic minorities. As a political scientist doing participant observation (Gillespie and Michelson 2011), my presence during election campaign activities and meetings also allowed me to observe and document the interactions and reactions of many men during their exchanges with women candidates.

My interviews were informal semi-structured discussions aided by a questionnaire I created to cover the topics of interest. The language of the interviews differed in each country. My fluency in Persian/Farsi allowed me to interview my Iranian informants in their first language. My limited command over Turkish meant most of my interviews in Turkey were in English. This did not prove to be a serious limitation since my informants, primarily politicians, women's rights activists or academics, spoke fluent English, and many had been educated in the West. Only seven of the twenty-six Turkish women parliamentarians and parliamentary candidates I interviewed, as well as several women active in the local women's branches of their parties, did not speak English. These informants were interviewed with the assistance of a translator familiar with my research topic and objectives, a PhD candidate with expertise in Turkish politics and gender relations.

I complemented my qualitative research with an analysis of government and private reports of statistics on women in politics. I collected data on percentages of women who received training and support to run as candidates, women registering for candidacy, women candidates on party lists and the percentage of women elected to political positions. The triangulation of research methods enables a comprehensive analysis of factors contributing to and inhibiting women's political representation in Iran and Turkey.

Organisation of the Book

Following this introductory chapter, Chapter 2 expands on the theoretical framework of the book including a discussion of the two main opportunity structures that have enabled women's groups in Iran and Turkey to increase their level of political representation, which I identify to be: (1) electoral competition structures and (2) discursive opportunity structures. Chapter 3 introduces the Turkish context of this research, presenting Turkey's political history, state ideology and political structure, as well as how significant political and social shifts relate to women's current political status. This historical analysis highlights the role that Turkish women have played and continue to play as political agents, and examines the increasingly significant role of the pious female constituency with the rise of pro-religious parties in the contemporary political landscape. Chapter 4 presents the specific strategies of Turkish women's groups addressing female political under-representation, in particular how they have taken advantage of party competition as a political opportunity structure in the past decades. This chapter delves deeper into Turkish women's campaigning efforts and lobbying of political elites given the country's robust multi-party structure and female-friendly electoral system. Still with reference to Turkey, Chapter 5 discusses framing processes, particularly those of groups comprised of pious and headscarved women, who are increasingly demanding seats at the decision-making table, given their years of political involvement with pro-religious parties such as the AKP. This chapter highlights the convergence of secular and pious women's rights activists due to the strategic framing by pious women's groups of political demands using a secular discourse, and their outspokenness against discrimination and injustice.

Chapters 6, 7 and 8 are devoted to a discussion of Iranian women's political rights and status and the nature of their strategic interactions with political elites and the electorate regarding increasing women's political representation. Chapter 6 introduces Iran's political framework, with particular emphasis on its theocratic structure and factional politics. This chapter explores women's political status throughout Iranian history, and outlines the key obstacles to female political representation. Chapter 7 delves into the impact of Iran's factional politics on women's political representation, in particular how individual women's particular political or ideological affinities shape their access to decision-making positions. Chapter 8 explores women's framing processes and their strategic use of religious discourses to justify their demands for increased representation. This chapter elaborates on the concept of 'religious discursive opportunities' as the means through which religious women legitimise their claims to access positions of authority and find resonance with Iran's ruling elites. It also discusses how occasional strategic convergences between women's groups across ideological and political divides have supported the effort to increase women's descriptive representation.

Chapter 9 summarises the key findings of this research. This chapter highlights the strategies that have been the most effective in increasing women's formal political power given the respective structures and constraints in each context. It reiterates the opportunity structures present in Turkey that led to the notable rise in women's parliamentary presence there, and the absence of those particular opportunity structures in Iran, and shows how Iranian proponents of women's political participation work within the particular opportunity structures available to them. It concludes with a final analysis of the relationship between movements around women's political rights and status and democratisation processes, an analysis that can be helpful in addressing this question within the larger Muslim world.

2

OPPORTUNITY STRUCTURES: STRATEGISING FOR WOMEN'S POLITICAL REPRESENTATION IN TURKEY AND IRAN

In 2013, as newly elected President Hassan Rouhani was finalising his cabinet, Shahrzad (pseudonym), a sociology professor who researches women in Iran, received a call from the president's office, asking her opinion on potential candidates for Vice President for Women's Affairs in the new administration. 'They called me to ask for my thoughts on a few shortlisted candidates they had in mind. I later found out they had also called other members of the women's rights activist and academic communities' (personal interview, 6 June 2015). Among the shortlisted candidates was Shahindokht Molaverdi, an experienced lawyer with expertise in international human rights law and life-long advocate for women's issues ranging from violence against women to women's political representation in both governmental and non-governmental settings (Molaverdi 2003, 2006, 2007, 2008, 2014). 'I expressed support for Molaverdi and highlighted her history working within Iran's political system to promote women's rights.' A few weeks later, in a move welcomed by many Iranian women's rights activists, President Rouhani named Molaverdi to his cabinet as the Vice President for Women's Affairs.[1]

[1] Shahindokht Molaverdi served as Vice President for Women's Affairs from 2013 to 2017. During his second term (2017–21), President Rouhani replaced her with the former Head of the Department of Environment Masoumeh Ebtekar, and named Molaverdi President's Assistant for Citizenship Rights instead, arguably a less influential position from which to address women's rights (personal interview with women's rights activists and scholars, 24 March 2018). Unlike his predecessor President Ahmadinejad, Rouhani did not nominate any women ministers during his presidency.

43

The process that led the president of the Islamic Republic of Iran to consult with members of the Iranian women's rights movement in finalising his cabinet highlights the nature of engagement between political elites and women's groups, as they influence and inform one another to address their respective interests (Banaszak *et al.* 2003; Chappell 2002). This process entailed movement actors utilising the opportunities presented by elections to organise across the ideological spectrum in support of women's demands, including increased female political representation (Ahmadi-Khorasani 2013). This strategic and extensive organising led Rouhani, a moderate cleric, to campaign on the issue of addressing gender inequality to appeal to the female electorate. Rouhani's promises, including his pledge to create a ministry of women's affairs, a novel institution in post-revolutionary Iran, resulted in overwhelming support from women voters, leading to his landslide victory over his five, more conservative rivals. Following his election, women's rights groups lobbied him to include female cabinet ministers, even issuing a public statement 'Selection criteria for ministers in the new government' (Hamandishi Zanan 2013). However, to their great displeasure, on inauguration day Rouhani named only men as his proposed ministers and made no mention of a Ministry of Women's Affairs.

Rouhani's roster of all-male cabinet ministers provoked public protests by women against what to many signalled continued marginalisation of women from all spheres of decision-making. Among those who publicly criticised Rouhani's proposed cabinet was Shahindokht Molaverdi. At a meeting in Tehran on the shape of the future government, Molaverdi stated, 'Everywhere in Rouhani's programs, there was talk of equal participation for women, and we were expecting to see – in the framework of moderation – the presence of women along with men in the cabinet' (as quoted in Esfandiari 2013). According to journalist Golnaz Esfandiari (2013), 'perhaps bowing to pressure', Rouhani began appointing women to his cabinet as vice presidents, a position of less authority than minister, and which does not require parliament's approval. It was in fact surprising to many observers that Rouhani's team even considered the outspoken Molaverdi as a potential cabinet member; her subsequent appointment came after a great deal of behind-the-scenes lobbying (personal interview with Iranian women activists, June 2015). He also increased the influence of Iran's sole women's policy apparatus by promoting the head of the Women and Family Affairs Office from 'advisor to the President' to Vice-President, a cabinet-level appointment whose holder is legally mandated under Article 124 of the Iranian constitution to lead an organisation related to presidential affairs and perform presidential constitutional duties (Kadivar 2012). Ultimately, for his first term, Rouhani named three female vice presidents, for environment, legal affairs, and Molaverdi for women and family affairs. Having worked in the Center for Women's Participation under reformist President Mohammad Khatami (1997–2005), Molaverdi had been successful in tactfully advocating for women's rights in a way that emphasised their compatibility with Islam.[2]

Molaverdi's appointment presented an important opportunity to advance women's rights from within the official administration of the executive branch, and signalled the responsiveness of male-dominated state institutions to sustained pressure from women's lobbying. While women's lobbying activities are not always met with success, nevertheless the skilful targeting of particular state actors can lead to tactical concessions by the state that help promote women's rights or advance the gendering of policy approaches (Chappell 2002; Krook and Childs 2010; Valdini 2019). Indeed, though lacking full executive powers, throughout her term as Vice President for Women's Affairs (2013–17) Molaverdi addressed issues that had until then received very little government attention, including promoting programmes to support female-headed households and female breadwinners, especially in Iran's remote rural areas, and implementing stricter policies to combat violence against women (Tajali 2022). Molaverdi's appointment illustrates how activists effectively took advantage of existing opportunities – Rouhani's relative moderatism and its appeal to the electorate; the desire of a large segment of the electorate to be heard (women) – and created a new opportunity: space for the appointment of an ally in an influential governmental post. Rouhani's responsiveness to women's demands, though limited, was also in hopes of maintaining women's support of his administration through his frequent conflicts with more conservative forces.

This book builds upon feminist scholarship that emphasises the dynamic between state institutions and civil society in advancing women's rights concerns, contributing to our understanding of the nature of interactions between them. Rectifying women's political under-representation

---

[2] During the reform era (1997–2005), Shahindokht Molaverdi, a devout Muslim, worked tirelessly on Iran's bid to join CEDAW, hence helping bridge the gap between religious and secular approaches to women's rights (Molaverdi 2014).

requires state support, and though some scholars have questioned the value of feminist activism targeting the state given its inherent patriarchal character (MacKinnon 1983; Mies 1986), other analyses conceive of the state as dynamic and heterogeneous, and therefore more susceptible to strategic manoeuvring by women's rights actors (Banaszak *et al.* 2003; Chappell 2002; Connell 1990; Zheng 2005).

This move away from the idea of the state as a fixed, monolithic entity enables analysis of the differences in gendered relations within various, sometimes competing state institutions, including parties, parliament and bureaucracies (Chappell 2002), with attention to how these divergences may provide opportunities for women's rights activists. According to Georgina Waylen (2007), to fully understand women's under-representation in the electoral arena, one must also consider the gendered nature of political institutions that recruit politicians. If, as she argues, 'gender is present in the processes, practices, images and ideologies, and distributions of power in the various sectors of social life' (p. 9), then much of what appears 'neutral' in institutional behaviour is, in fact, gendered. The complexities and mutability of state institutions and their gendered norms provide feminists with valuable opportunities to challenge and destabilise them; opportunities that would not be apparent if the state were perceived as a monolithic patriarchal entity. When feminists are stymied in their efforts within one institution, they are able to direct their energies to other avenues. For instance, women may find important allies in leftist political parties that place women's issues on their agenda. However, if such woman-friendly parties lose electoral seats or are removed from power, women may refer to other institutions, such as women's policy agencies or analogous branches (Chappell 2002).[3]

Similar to Chappell (2002) and Waylen (2007), my research finds that this dynamic interaction between civil society actors such as women's rights groups, and state actors and institutions, defines the process through which each constituency influences and informs the other. It is this mutability of structures that allows activists to create more opportunities and provides space for unlikely alliances between patriarchal state institutions and women that result in the expansion of women's political presence, particularly given

---

[3] Since the institution of political parties has historically provided women with important opportunities to increase the number of female political representatives, this work will pay particular attention to them.

the popular demands for greater gender equality and democratisation heard even in authoritarian contexts.

This book identifies two particular opportunity structures that assist women's groups in addressing women's political under-representation in secular Turkey and theocratic Iran: (1) electoral competition structures and (2) discursive opportunity structures. Here, drawing on aspects of social movement theory, I elaborate on how these opportunities create space for the organising efforts of diverse women's groups to lobby for greater access to political decision-making. I also analyse the use of particular opportunity structures as they intersect with activists' ideological/political positionalities, particularly in terms of framing strategies. My research shows that women with ties to conservative religious parties are better positioned than their secular counterparts to use religious framing to articulate their demands, while 'feminist' actors receive more legitimacy and support from the international community in their lobbying efforts.

Political and Discursive Opportunities and Women's Organising

In an effort to deliver lasting change, women's rights activists in Iran and Turkey, as in other contexts, target both cultural and institutional barriers and the underlying attitudes that keep women out of politics. While some women's groups are working on shifting their society's patriarchal culture by emphasising egalitarianism, others are tackling the institutional obstacles that limit women's political presence, pressuring political elites to reform electoral laws or to adopt gender quotas. When opportunities arise, women's rights activists have to be prepared to frame and present their demands and concerns in ways that mobilise maximum support, or to reframe a particular issue to their advantage (Baldez 2002; Merry 2006; Waylen 2007). According to Snow and Benford (1988, 2000), framing processes occur when movement actors, as signifying agents, produce and maintain meaning in order to mobilise potential adherents and constituents, to garner bystander support, and to demobilise antagonists. By analysing women's rights activists' framing processes, I highlight women's agency in co-opting discourses arising out of national and international contexts.

My analysis of the framing processes adopted by women's groups in Turkey and Iran shows that for each context the broader political and cultural realities determine the specific discursive opportunities used in campaigns to increase women's rate of political representation. I found that Turkey's increased integration into the international community until recently, including its candidacy to join the EU, greatly assisted women's groups fighting discriminatory rulings and attitudes in the nomination and recruitment of women for political office. These groups effectively utilised the international human rights discourse, in particular the language of anti-discrimination in CEDAW, to frame their demands for women's equal political representation. This has been effective in lobbying those political elites who value international inclusion – including ranking members of the ruling AKP – to increase women's access to decision-making bodies in order to resonate with the international community's rhetoric of democracy and gender egalitarianism. The reference to secular human rights documents by Turkish women's rights groups is consistent across the ideological spectrum; as I discuss in Chapter 5, many pious women's rights activists used CEDAW to demand headscarved women's access to the parliament. Borrowing from Myra Marx Ferree's (2003) distinction between 'resonant' and 'radical' frames, the choice by pious women's rights activists to articulate their demands using secular international human rights discourse can be considered radical framing since this approach does not accord with their core identity or with the larger community with which they identify, and at first glance seems opposed to the ideology of the AKP's conservative and pro-religious elites. However, this framing was based on the AKP's at the time over-riding goal of international integration,[4] and reflects the agency of activists who choose the discursive frame most likely to effectively achieve their goals. I consider such framing to be strategic since its subscribers, despite their religious tendencies, opted to wage pressure on conservative elites using a secular liberal discourse rather than one derived from their religious traditions. Pious women's reference to international human rights documents also led to an important unity between secular and pious women's rights groups in Turkey on expansion of women's access to politics.

In contrast, Iran's increasing marginalisation from the international community has limited women's groups' abilities to frame their demands according to international human rights discourse, particularly as any reference to international rights documents or organisations is often dismissed by

---

[4] As noted in the previous chapter, although the EU talks are currently at a standstill given Turkey's authoritarian turn, long-term ruling President Erdogan continues to support an eventual EU integration (Batchelor 2018).

the Iranian authorities as bowing to Western domination.[5] Despite decades of effort by Iranian women's rights groups, Iran is still not a signatory to CEDAW; the regime cites cultural inconsistencies as the main reason. Given this context, Iranian women's rights activists frame their demands, including greater political representation, according to the prevailing national discourse, with reference to the religious and revolutionary ideals of the regime. Such framing resonates with the institutionalisation of religious discourse that is the hallmark of the regime and society at large, while emphasising its indigenous basis and compatibility with the values and slogans of the Islamic Republic. Iran's theocratic political context has transformed religion into a discursive opportunity structure for advocates of policy reform, given the state's insistence on legitimising rulings in religious terms. To avoid being labelled 'Western inspired feminists', Iranian women's rights activists often use examples of strong female leaders of early Islam including Fatima and Zeinab (Prophet Mohammad's outspoken daughter and granddaughter), or the Quranic story of the Queen of Sheba. While conservative party women are at the forefront of such framing, I found that many of their reformist counterparts who had initially campaigned for Iran to join CEDAW and hence supported an international human rights approach, switched to a religious framing when the state became increasingly hostile to the international community. Over the years, this trajectory of strategic framing has to a degree coalesced women's groups across the ideological spectrum, from secular to conservative, to tackle gender discrimination with a unified voice.[6]

Through an analysis of the strategic use by women's rights activists of the opportunity structures described above,[7] I demonstrate why activists in

---

[5] Fernandes (2005) has also found that in Cuba, where similar to Iran, the ruling elites are unwilling to relinquish power to feminist groups with international backing, appeal to international norms can actually impede progress.

[6] An important instance of union among ideologically diverse Iranian women's groups was the campaign started in 2008 against President Ahmadinejad's Family Protection Bill, which included provisions supporting polygyny, among other controversial proposals. The powerful opposition from a united front of women's rights groups including secular and conservative women's rights activists prevented the adoption of the bill.

[7] By *acting strategically*, I refer to the fact that women in Iran and Turkey consider the larger political and social context in their framing processes, and that they switch between these approaches when contexts shift. Significantly, there is no clear division between when women act strategically or sincerely, since their faith, beliefs and ideological tendencies can

Turkey have been more successful in increasing women's political representation compared with their Iranian counterparts, despite the similar imposition of conservative gender ideology and authoritarian parties and systems in both. This success is in large part due to Turkey's competitive electoral culture and structure, which has till now fuelled competition for votes in ways that increases parties' vulnerability to pressure from women's groups, and the historical desire and willingness of key recent Turkish political elites to appeal to the international community, including the EU. Conversely, in Iran's more insular authoritarian context, where a clerical oligarchy has hindered the development of healthy electoral competition, Iranian women's rights activists have a harder time convincing political elites and undemocratic institutions to address women's political under-representation. However, women's rights activists in Iran have been able to take advantage of the limited opportunities available under the regime's authoritarian structures, including elections and the occasional rise of relatively moderate leaders in response to shifts in public demands, to press for reform, forming unlikely alliances with elites and male-dominated state institutions in the process.

Electoral Competition as a Political Opportunity Structure

Electoral competition or the 'contagion effect',[8] particularly competition among well-structured political parties, provides a significant political opportunity structure for women's groups to push for female political representation. Previous research by scholars in Western contexts (Baldez 2004; Krook 2009; Matland and Studlar 1996, 1998) has illustrated that electoral competition drives parties to adopt successful electoral strategies developed by their competitors. In recent decades, a focus on social justice issues,[9] in particular gender equality and female political representation, has become

---

still influence their organising, though depending on the political context it may not dominate their public campaigns.

[8] The contagion effect refers to a situation where parties attempt to outperform each other – in this case by competing for broad support from women – creating a dynamic that opens up political space for women.

[9] For the purpose of this work, the term 'social justice' is understood to include the elimination of discrimination and oppression, as well as the more common notion of material justice. This comprehensive definition is particularly applicable to the Muslim context, as the Quran emphasises various elements of social justice, ranging from equality, to charity, to compassion, and more (Hasan 1971).

an increasingly important electoral strategy in many contexts. This is largely due to women's rights movements' successful politicisation of the issue of female political representation, which has forced political parties to enhance women's access to politics as a way to appeal to the electorate.

One popular approach to this has been the adoption by parties of gender quotas, a swift, viable and public way to increase the number of women in political office. Matland and Studlar (1996) and Phillips (1998a), who write on women's access to national parliaments in Western contexts, argue that as smaller and more leftist parties start to promote women's political representation, larger and more conservative parties often do the same to remain electorally competitive. Since gender equality, democracy and social justice have entered the public discourse, parties that actively promote female representation gain electoral advantage. Research from Latin America shows that implementing gender quotas and nominating more women onto party lists is an effective and expedient strategy for appealing to the electorate by appearing egalitarian and democratic, while leaving the actual power to select candidates in the hands of the party leader (Baldez 2004). By nominating women, parties are also able to demonstrate that there is no electoral penalty associated with women candidates, echoing research that highlights fear of public antipathy toward women candidates is groundless (Matland and Studlar 1996). The desire of parties to appear 'woman-friendly', 'democratic' and hence 'modern' by promoting female representation in political decision-making is not unique to the West; it has also been on the rise in Muslim societies and even among conservative religious parties (Ben Shitrit 2016a, 2016b; Tajali 2015b; Towns 2010; Tripp 2019; Tripp *et al.* 2009).

My findings show that competition among political parties with organised and widespread structures that reach local levels is key to effective pressuring of elites by women's rights groups for the expansion of women's access to political office. As I demonstrate in Chapter 4, Turkey's strong party structure and party-list proportional representation electoral system have fostered electoral competition among multiple parties. Such fierce competition creates a valuable political opportunity for women's rights activists, who can capitalise on the differences in gender ideologies and nomination patterns between parties to their advantage, pressuring parties to adopt gender equal policies to gain women's votes. Thus, when in the mid-2000s women's organising led to the adoption and successful implementation of voluntary gender quotas by a leftist pro-Kurdish rights party, activists then pressured larger parties including the ruling AKP to follow suit. Turkish major political parties have since nominated record numbers of women to their party lists, and even adopted similar informal quota measures to ensure women's greater access. Conversely, in the Iranian context where organised party structures are limited and the dominant factions compete in a majoritarian system, women's rights activists have less leverage to demand attention to women's political under-representation.[10] Thus, Iran's factionalism and ephemeral party politics greatly hinder women's lobbying opportunities.

Discursive Opportunity Structures: International Discourse

International norms as articulated in the recommendations, documents and actions of the international community, have been diffusing around our globalised world. Throughout the past decades they have been advocating for women's equal access to political decision-making positions at national levels. Research suggests that links with the international community through international or regional organisations can positively influence a country's domestic policies, including concerning women's political rights (Hughes 2009; Keck and Sikkink 1998; Merry 2006; Paxton *et al.* 2006; Ramirez *et al.* 1997; Towns 2010). These types of progressive policy changes are becoming widespread in two central ways. First, international and transnational actors are increasingly influencing or pressuring countries to abide by global norms, and urging states to become signatories to international documents. Second, non-state actors, particularly members of civil society, use international documents and procedures to demand local reforms to discriminatory policies. The more deeply a country is integrated into the global community, the more women's rights activists can access the support offered by international declarations and networks. Hence, state actors are often pressured to address injustice and gender inequality from both within and outside of their borders.

My research recognises the important role of international influence in promotion of women's rights at national levels, but also finds that externally driven efforts are of limited value in contexts where outside influenc-

[10] A political faction is understood as group of individuals and elites who pursue a specific interest or ideology but outside of organised political party structures (Fabbrini 2010). Iran's factions may form temporary political parties for competing in elections, but often lack a party platform, consistent structure or organised party hierarchy. Generally, Iran's dominant factions include reformists, moderates and conservatives.

ers are considered illegitimate. Previous research on the spread of women's rights norms argues that any external efforts must work in conjunction with internal factors, including the mobilisation of civil society and the receptivity of ruling elites, to be successful (Kang 2015; Liu 2006). Similarly, my research shows that effective campaigns to address women's political under-representation include local women's groups accessing the opportunities the international community provides them, while at the same time mobilising public support. In particular, I explore the role that international human rights documents play in the framing processes of women's rights activism in Iran and Turkey. Since Turkey has signed and ratified CEDAW, women's rights groups can legitimise their demands for reform with reference to its provisions (Marshall 2009).[11] Significantly, pious women activists effectively used the anti-discriminatory discourse of CEDAW to fight the ban on head-scarves in the public sector, which included parliament. This strategic framing contributed to the lifting of the headscarf ban in 2013, which had until then barred headscarved women from public office. As I explain in Chapter 5, an important outcome of the use of secular human rights discourse by pious Turkish women was the development of important alliances with their secular counterparts in the quest for an expanded political presence for women in Turkey. Conversely in Iran, which has not signed CEDAW and is largely marginalised from the international community, activists are not able to draw on international rights discourse to legitimise their demands for increased female political presence to any great effect. Utilisation of such discourse is even more limited with the coming to power of hard-liner conservatives who fiercely attack CEDAW and similar international human rights documents.

Discursive Opportunity Structures: Regime Discourse

Authoritarian political systems work to minimise political competition and maintain power in the hands of a leader or small elite, monopolising state control and the dominant ideological discourse (Tripp 2013).[12] This dominant

---

[11] Turkish women's rights activists have been using international human rights documents in their framing efforts, particularly since 1999 when Turkey became an official candidate for EU membership at the Helsinki Summit, and the country's gender policies and practices became more intensely scrutinised by the international community (Marshall 2009).

[12] Previous research has documented the link between authoritarian structures and limited grass-roots organising, as well as the development of competitive discourses that may challenge state authority (Azimi 2008; Fish 2002; Tripp 2013).

regime discourse, often rooted in a founding ideology, aims to shape societal and political norms from the top down. However, the processes by which dominant state-sanctioned discourses and ideologies are taken up and debated by the population are complex, as diverse sections of the society may interpret or value them differently based on their varying political and ideological positionalities. In this regard, the dominant regime discourse, with its inevitable inherent contradictions, may provide an opportunity structure for activists to challenge and debate the norms prescribed by the regime. Women's rights groups in particular have used official state ideology as a discursive opportunity structure to fight for reform in authoritarian contexts. For instance, as Dongxiao Liu (2006) notes in her analysis of the Chinese women's rights movement, 'The All China Women's Federation tended to fall back on orthodox Marxist–Leninist ideology to reassert the importance of women's equality', when the Chinese state failed to deliver on its promises of gender equality as espoused by the Marxist–Leninist creed which was the alleged basis for the revolution (p. 934). Framing their demands according to the language of official state ideology enabled women's groups to find resonance with the political elites, and pressure them for failing to meet their own oft-stated ideals.

Similarly, I found that Iran's authoritarian theocratic structure has resulted in women's rights groups framing their demands according to official regime discourse, which provides both religious and revolutionary discursive opportunities. Given the regime's hostility towards international human rights discourse and its marginalisation from the international community (Osanloo 2009), out of legal and tactical necessity, many women activists tend to co-opt regime discourse to articulate their demands to resonate with Iran's clerical oligarchy. This approach also enables activists to shame the Iranian elites for failing to respect women's rights and justice as ordained by holy texts and as promised by the 1979 revolution. Such women's rights activists, many of whom are deeply pious, highlight overlooked egalitarian religious rulings, while also arguing that discriminatory religious rulings are due to clerical misinterpretations.[13] They emphasise the compatibility of Islam with women's access to political decision-making, often through reference

---

[13] As Osanloo (2006) argues, under Iran's theocracy, 'religious rights' have replaced the 'universal rights' advocated by international human rights documents, which further explains activists' strategy of framing women's rights claims in religious terms.

to examples of female political leaders in the Quran or early Islamic history. Indeed, application of such 'religious discursive opportunities' has enabled some women's rights activists to argue that Islamic holy texts are superior to international rights documents such as CEDAW in guaranteeing women's rights and gender equality. In addition to religious framing, Iranian activists also turn to the Republic's founding revolutionary discourse to legitimise women's political leadership, particularly Ayatollah Ruhollah Khomeini's support for women's political participation and promises of 'justice' and 'equality' that mobilised many against a despotic monarchy in 1978–9.

While activists' framing of political demands in religious terms can be attributed to the rise of Islamic feminism, or 'a feminist discourse and practice articulated within an Islamic paradigm', it is important to keep in mind that the label 'feminist' is rejected by many women's rights activists who emphasise compatibility between Islam and gender equality (Badran 2002). Despite this, important coalitions have developed among a broad spectrum of Iranian women's groups, ranging from secular feminist to religious conservative, since the founding of the Islamic Republic in 1979, as claims based on religious texts have proved effective in reforming various gender-discriminatory legislations and expanding women's rights (Kar and Hoodfar 1996; Paidar 2001). Women's rights' activism across the ideological spectrum has helped create a strong women's movement, which has in turn fostered the development of a female voting bloc. This politicised female electorate, which often votes according to its collective interests rather than along lines of political affiliation, is a major force in Iran's political landscape, to the extent that one scholar declared Iran's popular elections as 'rare occasions when women determine the fate of men' (as quoted in Kian-Thiebaut 2002: 57).

Similar utilisation of the regime discourse or reference to religious texts in justification of women's political roles is uncommon in Turkey. This is largely because the dominant positions and discourses of the ruling AKP have shifted frequently throughout its two decades in power, with the recent years witnessing an overtly authoritarian and patriarchal turn. Indeed, the party's initial slogan of 'Islamic democracy' which included recognition of basic rights of ethnic Kurdish minorities or greater integration into the international community, have now been replaced by hostile nationalist discourses that have greatly curtailed basic freedoms of large sections of the society. On the specific issue of women's political representation, while the party has maintained a conservative gender ideology that advocates traditional gender

roles based on the public versus private divide, in practice it has been willing to enhance women's access to political office, albeit when it best suits its
interests. For instance, under Erdogan's leadership, the party has appointed
a number of influential women to key positions on women's rights, such
as Fatma Sahin as the Minister of Family and Social Affairs, who sought to
enhance women's rights through greater collaborations with international
human rights bodies (personal interviews with Turkish women's rights activists, September 2019). AKP has also been willing to increase women's access
to the parliament and other bodies, in most cases, at higher rates than the
secular CHP opposition party. Turkish women activists have often attacked
the party's conservative gender stance, while simultaneously advocated for
expansion of women's political roles, often through citing international
expectations, to which the AKP (at least until recently) was susceptible.

Organising for Political Representation across the Ideological Spectrum

As noted earlier, expanding women's descriptive representation in government is a goal of women's rights activists in both Iran and Turkey, regardless
of political, ideological, ethnic or class differences. A major contribution of
this research is to explore how women's multiple positionalities impact their
political standing and access. Of course, socio-political status also constrains
men's access to formal politics, but the chapters that follow clearly illustrate
that the intersection of non-gendered status markers with gender additionally
constrain women's opportunities to access high-level decision-making positions. Thus, for example, there are particular obstacles to achieving political
office faced by Left-leaning women in Iran or (until 2013) visibly pious
women in Turkey that are not encountered by their male counterparts. While
categorising women according to political, ideological and ethnic differences
has the hazard of eliding diversity within groups and might potentially minimise other complex diversities, I contend that such categorisation is helpful
for analytic purposes to demonstrate that these markers affect the nature and
degree of activists' engagement with political elites and the public. Hence, my
introduction of women's activist groups is presented with the understanding
that these categories are nuanced, complex and shift over time. Furthermore,
as Jenny White (2012) warns, many dichotomously structured categories
– such as 'secular' relative to 'Muslim' – are not as clear-cut as they might
appear, and do not map neatly onto assumptions we might hold, as she finds
is the case for contemporary Turkey. Such categories are similarly complex

in Iran; nevertheless, as political actors, activists in both countries identify themselves using various labels that highlight their particular ideological positions as they manoeuvre through the complex political and institutional terrain of their respective contexts.

Women's Ideological Diversity in Turkey

The 1980 military coup was a major turning point for Turkish politics and society, including for women's rights. The emergence of what is generally termed a second wave of feminism followed the coup,[14] critical of the paternalistic Turkish state which, activists claimed, maintained a patriarchal order despite its feminist projects.[15] Assorted women's rights groups, ranging from pious to ethnic Kurds came to the fore (Tekeli 2010) and, although Turkish women's rights activism continued to be dominated by middle-class secular women, the political openings of the post-coup era re-energised and expanded the diversity of the Turkish women's movement. In line with definitions proposed by Alvarez (1990) and Beckwith (2000), my study highlights the heterogeneous, polycentric and expansive nature of women's movements.[16] During my research, the principal Turkish women's groups working for equal access to political decision-making used respective identity markers of

---

[14] Following Jayawardena (1986) I understand feminism as the awareness of women of their subordinate status within a patriarchal society, and the ideas and actions to change this situation. However, I proceed to use the phrase 'women's rights activism' rather than 'feminism' in what follows, since even this basic definition of feminism is controversial for many women in Iran and Turkey; some consider it a foreign concept, threatening to the family or to the fabric of Muslim society.

[15] During the feminist reforms following the founding of the Turkish Republic in 1923, Turkish women gained formal equality with men in divorce and inheritance but did not gain suffrage. Women's rights activists founded a party to fight for the women's vote in the late 1920s, which was subsequently shut down by the Kemalist elite. Women activists responded by establishing the Turkish Women's Union, which successfully fought for women's voting rights, granted in 1930 for municipal elections and in 1934 for the general election (Tekeli 2010).

[16] I define women's movements as the collective of mostly female participants (consisting of women's groups and individuals) who mobilise and make claims on cultural and political systems regarding women's gendered experiences, women's issues, and women's leadership and decision-making (Beckwith 2000). To this basic definition I add that although women's movement activism at times seems fragmented or less focused due to ideological, class, or other divisions, or moments of political crisis, such ruptures do not necessarily result in a loss of solidarity and comradeship in activism.

pious, secular or Kurdish; though notably these categories are not mutually exclusive and there are degrees of overlap. Regardless of self-imposed labels and whether they were affiliated with political parties or were non-partisan, all these groups considered themselves part of the larger Turkish women's rights movement, and shared the goal of higher levels of women's representation in formal politics.

Pious women activists gained political relevance following the 1980 coup with their critical stance against Turkey's strict secularist ideology and its increasing restrictions on women's religious dress in certain public spaces.[17] Many demanded the right for public expressions of piety, in which headscarved women are not discriminated against in their efforts to access state institutions such as universities or the parliament. Significantly, Islamic political movements capitalised on the emergence and growing visibility of pious, headscarved women in the public sphere, since women who forcefully spoke their mind against the secular state while advocating a religious lifestyle improved the image of Islamic movements and served as an important challenge to the conventional view equating Islam with 'women's imprisonment' in the home (Acar 1995: 47). However, in contrast with their Iranian counterparts, many pious women in Turkey do not reject feminism and acknowledge its contributions and significance. Sibel Eraslan, head of the now banned Islamist *Refah* party women's branch, referred to herself as a 'feminist with religious conviction', in the feminist magazine *Pazartesi* (Arat 2004). In 2019, I also met and interviewed a number of pious women's rights activists, among them Berrin Sönmez, who proudly describe themselves as Muslim feminists (*musalman feminist*) and publicly write and speak about the compatibility between Islam and gender equality (personal interviews, August and September 2019). Many pious women in Turkey, while having received their feminist convictions from religion, are rarely required

---

[17] Many of the activists who campaigned on headscarved women's rights in Turkey asked me to refer to them as 'pious' (*dindar*) rather than 'Islamist', given their campaign's emphasis on religious lifestyles and beliefs while opposing political Islam or the establishment of an Islamic state. I was often told, 'we do not want to become like [post-revolutionary] Iran', where religion dominates political, legal and social structures. In order to decrease the emphasis on women's dress or head-covering, these women also preferred the term 'pious' over 'headscarved', which to them also included practicing Muslim women unable to wear the headscarf due to state limitations and women who chose not to wear a head-covering despite their religiosity.

to refer to Islam in their public campaigns. This is because at least until recently they have been mostly making their claims from a secular structure or from parties, including the AKP, that have largely avoided using religious references in their turn towards conservative gender politics (Aksoy 2015). Pious women activists included in this research range from supporters and members of major pro-religious parties such as the AKP, as well as activists of non-partisan women's organisations, such as the Capital City Women's Platform (CCWP), or Women's Rights Organization against Discrimination (AKDER).[18]

At the other end of the spectrum 'secular' and 'secular feminist' activists believe religion should be relegated to the private sphere, and do not use Islam as a point of reference, though many are practicing Muslims. As is the case for pious Turkish women, the secular camp is far from homogenous, including activists tolerant of public expressions of religiosity such as the headscarf; those who see headscarved women as a symbol of Islamisation, synonymous with women's subjugation; and those who publicly denounce their pious counterparts as anti-statist and a threat to the rights gained by women under Kemal's state feminism (Sirman 1989). Secular feminists have been at the forefront of organising for women's equal access to political office, establishing the Association for the Support of Women Candidates (KADER) in 1997 to fight discrimination against women in politics (Tekeli 2010). Though non-partisan, KADER's secular and leftist tendencies have hindered its ability to form durable relations with the powerful AKP women's organisation in the polarised Turkish political atmosphere. During the 2015 and 2018 general elections, however, KADER worked closely with women members of the main leftist opposition People's Republican Party (CHP) and Pro-Kurdish People's Democratic Party (HDP).

Ethnic Kurds have been the most influential women's rights activists in the fight for women's political representation, outperforming what their secular counterparts began decades earlier. Their prominence is tied to both domestic factors, such as the overarching discourses of democratisation and feminism

---

[18] Capital City Women's Platform (CCWP) and Women's Rights Organization against Discrimination (AKDER) were major pious women's rights organisations since the mid-1990s. In the late 2010s, however, these organisations became inactive as a result of increasing cleavages among pious women's rights activists over their proximity with AKP elites (personal interview with former CCWP board members, 17 August and 3 September 2019).

that facilitated mobilisation of Kurdish women in the post-1980 coup era, as well as international factors, including pressure from the European Union on Turkey to expand minority rights as a precondition to EU membership. Pro-Kurdish rights parties were the first major political force in Turkey to adopt voluntary gender quotas, including co-leadership between both genders at every administrative level, proving the power of sustained pressure by women's rights activists for implementing measures towards gender equality in political bodies (Tajali 2015a). Despite these accomplishments, Turkey's Kurdish minority continues to face repression rooted in the homogenising policies of the early Turkish state and contemporary Turkish nationalist sentiment of the ruling AKP (White 2012).

In sum, the women's rights movement in Turkey, which consists of diverse groups across the ideological spectrum, has been successful in placing the demand for women's political representation on the national agenda. Women's efforts have included either working with or against the state, at times with a unified voice across the ideological spectrum, while in other instances individual organisations have strategised using their particular positionalities. For example, the non-partisan, secularly oriented KADER has continued to pressure all party elites through media campaigns, including public exposure ('name and shame') of blatant gender discrimination by party leaders in political recruitment and nomination processes. However, many AKP party women, given their proximity to the government, have opted for a more conciliatory approach, trying to reform the party's patriarchal culture behind closed doors, and only publicising their party leadership's gender discriminatory attitudes and behaviours when all else has failed.

Women's organising across the ideological spectrum has however been undermined by persistent political (party-allegiance) and class cleavages. While collaborations have formed among secular and pious women, with the occasional inclusion of Kurdish women, they have been temporary, as fierce competition between AKP and its allies on the one side and its opponents on the other prevents meaningful convergences for sustained pressure on party elites across the board. Fierce political rivalry between AKP, CHP and HDP reverberates among their female supporters who become embroiled in reactionary party politics (Cavdar 2006). These intense partisan rivalries have seriously constrained the development of a unified women's movement and the formation of a female voting bloc in Turkey.

Women's Ideological Diversity in Iran

In Iran, distinguishing groups of women according to degrees of piety or religious ideology is more challenging than in Turkey given the inherent duality of an 'Islamic Republic' and the consequent nuances and complexities rendering the boundaries of such identity markers more difficult to establish. The regime's legal sanctioning of religious dress for women in public has in effect stripped the *hijab*[19] of its religious significance for many; rather, the degree of observance of *hijab* by various female demographics signals the gradation of political allegiance or opposition to the theocracy.[20] Nonetheless, Iranian women's rights activism comprises various groups holding diverse agendas and perspectives, particularly regarding the role of religion in government and legislation as it pertains to women's status (Afshar 2002; Hoodfar and Sadr 2009; Paidar 2001). For the purpose of this work, I distinguish Iranian women activists according to the political and ideological labels by which they refer to themselves, to each other, and which are used by the media and the public at large, rather than the labels 'Islamic' or 'secular feminist' commonly used by other scholars of Iranian gender studies (Mir-Hosseini 2007; Najmabadi 2000; Paidar 2001; Sedghi 2007).

My findings show that women's groups who have been active on the expansion of women's political representation in Iran can be generally divided into the three categories of 'conservative', 'reformist' and 'secular'. While these groups are not homogenous and women's identities and political tendencies are fluid, these labels are nonetheless descriptive of their political positioning, and to some extent interests and demands. Secularists advocate

---

[19] *Hijab* (also *hejab*) in Islamic tradition refers to modesty in attire and behaviour, though its current common usage refers to a head covering worn by some Muslim women in public or when in the company of non-familial men. Similar to other forms of dress that marks one's identity, *hijab* is highly politicised and subject to much discussion and extensive campaigns as women (and men) advocate to claim their right to dress in response to top-down Islamisation and secularisation forces of their respective contexts.

[20] As will be discussed in later chapters, in both Iran and Turkey women's dress signifies both religious and political tendencies of the wearer. For example, in Iran, where female *hijab* is mandatory in public, women's religious and/or political tendencies can often be determined by the degree of their *hijab*. Conforming women often wear the theocratic regime's ideal form of dress for women, the *chador* (a tent-like wrap which covers women's head to toe, except the face), while others wear the also-sanctioned *manteau* and headscarf, or a long coat accompanied with a head covering.

for a separation between religion and state, questioning the legitimacy of the theocratic structure, which requires all parties and candidates to declare allegiance to the regime in order to stand for elections. This means proponents of secularism can only seek to influence the regime through informal and civic channels since they are precluded from official posts. In contrast, conservatives 'seek to preserve the status quo that places a large degree of formal authority and discretionary power in the hands of the Supreme Leader, unelected councils under his supervision, and state-affiliated religious charities and economic foundations' (Keshavarzian 2005: 69). Somewhere between these extremes stand reformists, trying to gain power through the electoral process, to advocate for expansion and empowerment of the regime's republican institutions, which in turn would support greater citizen participation and pluralism. While internal divisions have always existed in Iranian politics, a major one is between conservatives and reformists, or hardliners and softliners, which has intensified in the midst of Iran's increasing political, economic and social problems (Keshavarzian 2005).[21] Moderates, represented most recently by President Hassan Rouhani (2013–21), often opt for a more pragmatic approach between reformists and conservatives.

Conservative Iranian women identify themselves with Iran's conservative or 'principlist' (*usul-gara*) right-wing political faction, which lauds 'the family' and employs a rhetoric of gender complementarity relegating women's primary responsibilities to the domestic sphere. However, despite their espousal of the construct of social gender complementarity and their strong allegiance to the regime, I encountered many conservative women outspoken about the need for more women in positions of political and religious authority.[22] As I have argued elsewhere, having devoted years of activism to the Islamic movement in Iran, many senior conservative women are at the forefront of the demand for women's greater access to political leadership (Tajali 2017). Using Islamic texts referencing gender equality and justice to argue there

---

[21] While conservatives tend to have greater support in provincial capitals, among the older population and among those directly benefiting from revolutionary organisations such as *bonyads* (charitable foundations) or the Islamic Revolutionary Guard Corps, reformists tend to appeal more to the urban youth, women and educated populations (Keshavarzian 2005).

[22] Conservative women activists have received little attention from Western scholars researching Iranian women's movements and activism, since until recently most scholars considered 'reformist' or 'secular' women as the main representatives and proponents of women's rights in Iran (Mir-Hosseini 2002; Najmabadi 2000; Paidar 2001; Sedghi 2007).

is no contradiction between Islam and female authority, these activists are engaged in redefining the role of women in society. Many are well versed in Islamic teachings and favour reform of discriminatory legislation, which they see as a product of patriarchal culture rather than Islam. They also advocate for women's access to religious knowledge, training and positions of religious authority, and oversee many of Iran's female seminaries (*houzeh*), particularly in the city of Qom (Oladi Ghadikolaei 2009). Conservative women's rights activists advocate for indigenous approaches to reform, especially through religious reinterpretation, and generally reject Western and feminist models for addressing women's rights.

Since the founding of the Islamic Republic, the only women likely to access high-level political decision-making positions have been those with strong ties to the regime. I explain in the Iran part of this book that as conservatives have increasingly controlled the candidate vetting processes in recent decades, reformist women are increasingly less likely than their conservative counterparts to gain political office. Many conservative women are also active in grass-roots women's organisations, though most are man-aged in a hierarchical manner, with the primary aim of promoting women's 'Islamic duties' and politicising and mobilising Iranian women on behalf of the regime to protect the revolution's ideals. As the numbers and influence of these organisations have grown, so has their ability to pressure male politi-cal elites to address their demands (Tajali 2011, 2016a). Arguably, the most influential conservative women's organisation was until recently the Zeinab Society (*Jameh Zeinab*), founded and directed by Maryam Behrouzi with Khomeini's blessing soon after the revolution, who remained active until her death in 2012.[23] As explained in Chapters 6 and 7, Behrouzi's proxim-ity to Iran's ruling elites helped her lobby for women's increased political representation. Towards the end of her life, Behrouzi boldly advocated for gender quotas as a way to guarantee women's political presence, though these requests largely fell on the deaf ears of her male colleagues.

The reformist front emerged from within Iran's larger Islamic politi-cal landscape in the 1990s to fight for greater freedom, transparency and

---

[23] While the Zeinab Society functioned for many years as the central conservative women's organisation on women's political representation, this organisation's influence declined fol-lowing the death of its founder Maryam Behrouzi in 2012. Chapters 6 and 7 outline some of the central ways that this organisation campaigned for women's political leadership.

democracy within the Iranian political system. Reformist (*islah-talab*) women have been particularly vocal and active in the movement for women's greater political presence, and during the political openings of the reform era (1997–2005 under President Khatami) seized the opportunity to place women's demands for increased access to political power on the national agenda. As discussed in Chapter 7, the reformist *Mosharekat* party (Participation Front) was the first to adopt any form of gender quota, a voluntary quota to ensure women's representation at every administrative level of the party. Many renowned female journalists, lawyers and academics – self-identified reformists – have also published extensively on the obstacles keeping women out of politics in Iran, and ways to address them. However, these types of efforts and awareness campaigns have often withered under attacks from hardliners on reformist parties and leaders, including their influential women activists. Indeed, in 2009 the non-elected conservative authorities, out of fear of losing control over the country, responded to the eruption of public protests following the disputed re-election of conservative President Ahmadinejad by shutting down all major reformist parties, including *Mosharekat*, and imprisoning male and female reformist leaders and party officials. The conservative-backed Council of Guardians also often disqualifies prominent reformist women activists from political candidacy, posing a major obstacle to women's substantive discrimination, as further analysed in Chapter 7.

The reformist 'Islamic feminist' approach, which seeks to address gender inequality through reference to Islam's inherent egalitarianism, has been widely examined in Western scholarship (Badran 2002; Mir-Hosseini 2006b; Najmabadi 2000; Paidar 2001). However, many Iranian women, regardless of political or ideological tendencies, reject the label 'feminist' as too loaded in the context of post-revolutionary Iran (De Groot 2010). Many pious women's rights and gender equality activists credit Islam rather than 'feminist' consciousness as their motivator, by arguing that Islam is inherently egalitarian and holds women in high esteem (personal interviews, 2 and 13 July 2011).

Secular women's rights activists more comfortably identify as feminists than those with official ties to the Islamic state and generally align with the international human rights and gender equality perspectives, advocating for Iran's greater integration into the international community and working with international and transnational feminist networks. However, in the context of a theocracy and state oppression of secularist activism, these activists have been forced to adopt tactics similar to those of reformist women. In my interviews with activists from both camps, it became apparent that on various occasions secular and reformist women have joined forces to push for gender-sensitive reforms, using religious framing to win the support of the clerical elites. While secular activists are a major force in the larger Iranian women's rights movement, the extent to which they can actively shape the public discourse on women's rights, or whether they must retreat underground, is determined by the ever-fluctuating levels of hostility directed towards them by the Islamic regime.

Central Contributions to the Literature on Women and Politics

This comparative analysis of the main factors impacting women's political representation in Iran and Turkey makes a number of contributions to the larger literature on women and politics. Despite the dominant feature of Islam in both countries, it highlights the heterogeneity among Muslim countries and their citizens, including their institutional structures as well as the varying interpretations and justifications on women's rights and roles made by authorities through reference to religion largely for political reasons. This book is among the first in the literature to analyse the impact of factional politics on women's access to representative bodies in Iran's electoral processes. Because Iran's factionalism has in effect prevented the formation of political parties, women activists are constrained in their capacity to lobby party elites and to gain formal political experience, since the absence of organised party structures limits local-level formal political involvement. I demonstrate that this also greatly limits state–society interactions, leaving powerful state institutions barely responsive or accountable to civil society outside of major elections. Functioning similar to a dual-party system in a majoritarian context, fierce competition between reformists and conservatives has led neither faction to prioritise women's political representation, while the non-elected gate-keeping institutions of the authoritarian regime outlined earlier also hinder women's access to positions of political authority, in particular the presidency.

In contrast, Turkey's well-structured party system, reaching all the way to the grass roots and with active women's branches at every administrative level, provides women more opportunities to work towards increased female political representation. Highlighting the significant role that political parties can play in recruiting and nominating women confirms previous research that shows this institution as a key mechanism for increasing women's political representation (Kittilson 2006; Wylie 2018). However, an important obstacle preventing Turkish women's access to parliament has been the absence of a democratic mechanism in candidate selection onto Turkey's closed electoral party lists, since candidate selection in practical terms remains the prerogative of male party leaders. Turkish women's rights activists are working to address the discriminatory practices of party leaders, who nominate few women or place women so far down the candidate list as to significantly decrease their chances of getting elected, practices that scholars have identified in other cases as well (Kittilson 2006; Paxton and Hughes 2007; Tripp and Kang 2008).

The findings in this book also contribute to our understanding of women's political rights and status in Muslim-majority countries. I deconstruct essentialised portrayals of Muslim women as apolitical by mapping out their varied demands and their diverse strategies for increasing women's political representation, while demonstrating the extent to which women view themselves as political agents in patriarchal societies. Iranian and Turkish women adopt multiple tactics to address the political gender imbalance, many of which upend the conventional binaries of Islamist or feminist trajectories. Furthermore, while, much of the scholarship on women and politics in Muslim contexts focuses on women's participation in grass-roots politics (Arat 2005; Iqtidar 2011; Shehabuddin 2008; White 2002), I emphasise women's efforts to translate their participation in informal politics into gains in more formal arenas of politics during major elections. I show how women campaign for increased access to positions of political authority, for instance by making strategic alliances with key civil, political or religious groups and figures, or by campaigning for gender quotas. Indeed, gender quotas have been identified as a critical tool to help level the playing field in electoral politics. My research on the limited instances of quota adoptions in Iran and Turkey highlights that these affirmative action measures enhanced women's descriptive and substantive representation as previous studies had shown (Franceschet and Piscopo 2008).

While much of the emphasis in this research is on activism by women's groups in Iran and Turkey to increase women's access to political decision-making, and the consequent elite responses and reactions, the role of the public is also considered, in particular the electorate, whose support of women's demands is essential for effective lobbying of political leaders. Elections provide women's rights advocates with important opportunities to pressure elites at a time when they are most receptive. When elections are not a viable route for addressing women's rights, I contend that activists engage in other means, including grass-roots organising, public awareness raising, or even engaging in religious reinterpretation. Indeed, a key tactic of women's groups in both Iran and Turkey has been to mobilise public support and utilise grass-roots calls for democratisation and gender equality to legitimise their demands for women's greater access to positions of authority when negotiating with state actors. In both countries activists engage in raising public awareness through the media, in particular through women's magazines and journals, some run by 'Islamic feminists', which tactfully but insistently promote the need for more women in the political sphere.[24]

The following chapters outline the most important approaches used by diverse women's rights groups in Turkey and Iran to enhance women's political representation, following a brief historical discussion of the status of women's political rights and roles in each country. Through a comparative analysis, I show how discursive and political opportunities are structured differently in each country, resulting in different impacts on women's access to formal politics. To move away from simplistic explanations that focus on Islam or Muslim culture, this book highlights the complex factors and actors that impact women's political representation, among them level of party system consolidation, electoral competition, political ideology, religion, and more. Despite their authoritarian contexts, it also shows women's ingenuity and resilience as they work within challenging institutional and political circumstances to address women's political under-representation.

---

[24] In Iran, a number of women's magazines, such as *Zan-e Rouz* (*Today's Woman*), *Hoqouq-e Zanan* (*Women's Rights*) and, perhaps the most popular, *Zanan* (*Women*), and more recently *Zanan-e Emrooz* (*Today's Women*), played major roles in entering women's political representation in the national discourse. Scholars in the West have referred to the editors of such influential magazines, such as Shahla Sherkat and Ashraf Geramizadegan, as 'Islamic feminists' given their emphasis on compatibility between Islam and gender equality (Mir-Hosseini 2006b).

TURKEY

3

TURKISH WOMEN AS POLITICAL AGENTS: BETWEEN SECULARISM AND ISLAMIC REVIVALISM

Even prior to Ataturk, Ottoman feminists fought for women's presence in the public sphere, including the right to education, employment and to even be a representative. More than a century later, Turkish feminists are still fighting for these rights, but often from two opposing camps of secular and pious (*dindar kadınlar*). It is a shame that today the issue of women's rights is so politicised that Turkish women can't campaign for them in a unified voice.

–Personal interview with Hidayet Tuksal, a pious
women's rights activist, 17 June 2011

The struggle for women's rights, including political rights, has a long history in Turkey. Indeed, the rise of Turkish women's rights activism dates back to the declining years of the Ottoman Empire in the late nineteenth century, when demands for women's greater presence in the public sphere and enhanced family rights were publicly articulated. Women's organising eventually intersected with the modernisation goals of the Turkish elites, and in 1934 when Turkish women were granted full suffrage, Turkey became the first Muslim country to enshrine the rights of women to both vote and run for office. Despite this progressive history, Turkey is among the lowest ranked countries in terms of gender equality as measured by the World Economic Forum's annual Global Gender Gap Report. The report, which measures relative gaps between women and men in four key areas (politics, education, economics and health), ranked Turkey 133 out of 156 countries in 2021.[1] In formal politics, women make up only 17.3 per cent of total Turkish parliamentarians, and only 3.23 per cent of mayors from metropolitan, city, district and sub-district levels following the March 2019 local elections.

While a number of factors have contributed to women's lower societal status, the historical ideological tensions between secularism and Islamism, and by extension between secular and pious women, which came to the fore during the founding of the Turkish Republic in the early 1920s, inhibited concerted, effective women's rights organising. In their promotion of republican principles, Mustafa Kemal and his supporters set in motion binaries between religion (presented as tradition and backwardness) and secularism (presented as modernity and progress), with lasting effects on Turkish society and politics, including on women's rights activism. In this chapter I show that these historical divisions among Turkish women, in combination with Kemal's state feminism projects and his concurrent shut-down of independent women's organisations, weakened Turkish women's rights activism. It was not until the post-1980 military coup era that Turkish women's groups finally had an opportunity to effectively organise to address codified gender discrimination with a unified voice. The rise of religious parties in the 1990s and early 2000s intensified the binaries between religious and secular lifestyles, at the centre of which was the 'woman question', including women's bodies as markers of each dominant ideological tendency. This is made apparent by the fact that for decades, headscarved women's access to state facilities, including universities and the parliament, was a major source of controversy in Turkish society and politics.

However, despite their secular–religious divide, I argue that Turkish women across the ideological spectrum have throughout modern Turkish history worked to take advantage of opportunity structures to expand their political rights and status. For instance, Turkish women gained suffrage in 1934 because they were prepared to seize circumstantial opportunity structures in the form of broad support coming from the international community and Kemal's eagerness to seem modern by enfranchising women. More recently, the near quadrupling of women's parliamentary presence in

---

[1] Iran, the other case examined in this book, ranks 150 out of 156 (World Economic Forum, *The Global Gender Gap Report 2021*, http://www3.weforum.org/docs/WEF_GGGR_2021 .pdf (accessed 19 October 2020)).

less than two decades (from 4.4 per cent in 2002 to 17.3 per cent in 2018) is largely thanks to opportunities (that arose for reasons elaborated on later in this book) for strategic interactions between Turkish women's groups and party elites. While parties such as the ruling and pro-religious Justice and Development Party (*Adalet ve Kalkinma Partisi*; henceforth AKP) and its predecessors rely on women's grass-roots organising efforts for voter-recruitment purposes, women have simultaneously used their leverage to lobby party elites to expand women's access to political decision-making positions, which in turn has increased the party's support base and electoral appeal. My analysis of women's groups' strategic engagements with political and party elites throughout Turkish history highlights the diverse opportunities and obstacles that impact women's access to political decision-making. Significantly, this chapter shows that opportunities to expand women's political representation may arise during periods of both secularisation and Islamic revivalism.

Secular and Pious Women's Rights Activists: Fierce Opposition or Gradual Fusion?

Hidayet Tuksal is a theologian, scholar, and one of the key members of the pious women's movement in Turkey. Referred to as a 'feminist theologian' by the media and her peers, she has written extensively on women's rights from within an Islamic framework, as well as the need for feminist reinterpretation of religious texts to reformulate misogynous *mis*interpretations in Islam. As a headscarved woman, she was also an outspoken critic of the secular state's now-overturned restrictions on headscarved women's access to official buildings (often referred to as the 'headscarf ban'), as well as the patriarchal attitudes and practices that limit women's opportunities to participate in the public sphere, including in political decision-making.

My meeting with her was illuminating as it introduced me to a leading voice of the pious women's movement in Turkey,[2] but also emotional, as I was able to witness the pain and hardship visibly pious women faced until recently in Turkey. At the time of our first meeting, not only was Hidayet banned from public buildings such as her local library because of

---

[2] As briefly explained in the first chapter, the pious women's movement in Turkey consists of observant Muslim women (some of whom are headscarved) who demand expansion of women's rights. I consider the pious women's movement part of the larger Turkish women's movement.

her headscarf, she was also 'othered' by some of her secular peers. 'I am a product of this country and its strictly secular education, legal, and political systems . . . but when I choose to wear the headscarf, I am looked at as a foreigner . . . as someone who does not belong here' (personal interview, 17 June 2011). I could see the pain in Hidayet's face as she spoke about the need to continuously defend her feminist identity to Turkish feminists from more secular backgrounds. She is often told that unless she criticises the 'Islamic understanding of the female body' she cannot call herself a feminist. In response, Hidayet advocates women's freedom of expression, while she reminds her secular feminist peers that Turkish feminism should try to address *all* of Turkish women's rights. Considering herself a member of the Turkish feminist movement, Hidayet has publicly criticised both the limitations of the secular system as well as AKP leadership for not doing much for headscarved women.

Hidayet introduced me to a woman I will call Oya, a self-identified member of the Turkish feminist movement, active for decades within leftist secular parties, who had been imprisoned during the 1980 coup because of her activism. At the time of our meeting in 2011, Oya held a high-level position in the opposition Republican People's Party (*Cumhuriyet Halk Partisi*; henceforth CHP). Although she had at times been an outspoken critic of CHP and its leadership for being 'patriarchal and elitist, characteristics that do not fit a social democratic party like CHP', she joined the party after Kemal Kılıçdaroğlu was elected leader in 2010, to 'help him steer the party in the right direction' (personal interview, 17 June 2011). Oya shared with me her experiences of helping to establish the first autonomous women's shelter in Turkey in the early 1990s, as well as her work with multiple feminist organisations and journals. When during our conversation I asked about her relations with pious women's rights activists, some of whom are headscarved like Hidayet, Oya told me that while she respects activists like Hidayet, and collaborated with her to prepare a CEDAW shadow report,[3] for her a central problem is that many pious women's rights activists prioritise addressing

---

[3] Since Turkey's ratification of the Convention on the Elimination of Discrimination against Women (CEDAW), Turkish women's rights activists can present reports on instances of gender discrimination to CEDAW Committee sessions, which in turn pressures the state to implement CEDAW. The preparation of these so-called shadow reports is an opportunity to bring diverse women's rights activists together.

discrimination against headscarved women, 'as if women in Turkey have no other problems'.

> I see this as a major reason for why we cannot come together to address the main problems of Turkish women, like high levels of women's illiteracy or providing social services for disabled women. When you only focus on the headscarf, this makes it hard for many of us to come together. (Personal interview, 17 June 2011)

When I suggested that perhaps pious women's rights activists need acknowledgement from their secular counterparts that the decades-long headscarf ban is a significant problem for many Turkish women, Oya responded, 'OK, we acknowledge, but when we ask them to also acknowledge the significance of homosexual rights, many of them remain silent' (personal interview, 17 June 2011). Indeed, the debate on the rights of sexual minorities is a highly sensitive issue, and at times used by secular feminists to reproach the whole religious women's movement as intolerant, discriminating or undemocratic. However, as Hürcan Aksoy (2015) finds in her important research on activists of autonomous pious women's organisations such as the Capital City Women's Platform (CCWP) or Women's Rights Organization against Discrimination (AKDER), members of such entities are not homogenous in their stance on homosexuality, with prominent pious activists such as Hidayet Tuksal of CCWP publicly condemning discrimination against LGBT individuals.[4]

While the headscarf ban is now lifted, the ideological rifts between pious and secular women's rights activists persist in Turkey, undermining the potential for uniting in the fight against patriarchy and gender discrimination. Like Oya, many secular women's rights activists disagreed with the headscarf ban, but generally did not prioritise it in their organising efforts, probably because they did not share the experience of discrimination endured by headscarved women like Hidayet on a daily basis. As well, many secular women's rights activists see a contradiction between feminism and adherence to codes designed to hide women's bodies from the male gaze, which they claim uphold gender inequality, while pious women's activism increased

---

[4] Similar to Aksoy (2015), I also identified diversity among pious women's rights movement in Turkey, and found their outspokenness against the discriminatory actions and attitudes of AKP leaders to contribute to democratic consolidation in Turkey.

in support of headscarved women in the 1990s, in response to secularist discriminatory policies that restricted their access to higher education and employment.

The ban on religious markers in state institutions, including parliament, presented a major obstacle to pious women who aspired to public office but were also committed to the public expression of their piety through the wearing of the Muslim headscarf. Significantly, no concomitant situation faced pious men, who in Turkey do not necessarily have any visible markers of religiosity. The secular establishment's distaste for the headscarf even led the pro-religious AKP to avoid nominating any headscarved parliamentary candidates for more than a decade after coming to power, fearing the party's closure on the basis of undermining the Republic's secular ideals. In fact, the secular establishment had succeeded in shutting down AKP's predecessor Islamic parties of *Refah* and *Fazilet* and, in 1999, secular elites prevented Merve Kavakci, the only headscarved woman democratically elected to parliament, from serving in her post. This was despite the fact that there was no formal 'ban' on headscarves in parliament; the only formally stipulated dress code in place required that women wear 'skirt suits', hence outlawing trousers for women.

The de facto restrictions on headscarved women's access to state institutions such as parliament were eventually removed in October 2013, when AKP leaders unveiled a package of democratic reforms, which included lifting the controversial headscarf ban for most civil servants, along with other measures such as improving rights for minority Kurds. Immediately following the announcement of these reforms, four AKP women Members of Parliament (MPs) entered the parliament wearing headscarves, signalling an important expansion of women's political representation in Turkey. The 2015 parliamentary elections marked the first time that the ruling AKP nominated headscarved candidates onto their candidate lists. According to Ayşe Böhürler, an AKP founder who also wears the headscarf, 'It took more than 80 years for the right to political representation to also extend to headscarved women, since women's suffrage in 1934 only recognised this right for non-headscarved women' (personal interview, 19 May 2015).

Böhürler's comment captures the sense of disenfranchisement that many pious women felt for much of their adult lives, as a result of the secular state's harsh and gendered policies since the 1980s restricting public expressions of piety. Educated and aspiring headscarved women particularly felt discriminated against when their full participation in certain professions was hindered due to the ban, such as headscarved lawyers' inability to enter courthouses. This discrimination led many pious women, who comprise a large segment of Turkish society, to spurn the early Republican era's state feminist policies, and favour instead moderate religious parties that promised to elevate the status and opportunities of visibly pious women.

Briefly outlining the roots of ideologically diverse women's rights groups, this chapter contends that while Turkish women's rights activism remains divided on many issues, in recent years secular and pious women's rights activists have been able to form important fronts on the issue of female political representation, in particular headscarved women's access to the parliament. However, this gradual alliance has been challenging to achieve and impacted by various political and social shifts. To better comprehend the factors that have led to the historical divide between secular and pious women in Turkey, as well as the sensitivity surrounding women's bodies and dress as markers of national identity, it is necessary to analyse where Turkey's founding principles intersect with the 'woman question'. Such historical analysis will clarify the nature of interactions between women's groups and political elites throughout Turkish history, beginning with the Ottoman era. This chapter also briefly outlines the ways that women have bargained for their political rights during moments of both intense secularisation *and* Islamic revivalism in Turkey. Rather than passive subjects, women in Turkey have strategically addressed their marginal status in formal politics over the course of their country's democratisation process. While it is important to recognise that Turkey's increasing authoritarianism since 2013 under the leadership of Recep Tayyip Erdogan has undermined the women's rights movement along with other civil rights efforts, women as active agents of Turkish society have not ceased to agitate for greater political roles, and are in fact an important force for democratisation.

From Ottoman Feminism to State Feminism of the Turkish Republic

The roots of the modern Turkish state lie in its Ottoman history. The Ottoman Empire, which is considered among the largest Muslim dynasties in the Middle East, ruled from 1299 until 1922, when Mustafa Kemal 'Ataturk' founded the Republic of Turkey in 1923. At the height of its power in the sixteenth and seventeenth centuries, this Islamic empire spanned over three continents. The complex web of its institutional framework enabled

Ottoman rule over diverse territories, encompassing multi-ethnic and multi-religious populations (Cleveland 2004).

The Empire's most significant tensions lay in managing the dynamic between its Islamic base on one hand, and pressures from foreign and Western influences and powers on the other. To maintain the Empire's independence and still compete with the rest of the world in terms of influence, the Ottoman elites shifted often between Western and Islamic tendencies, at times adopting measures to reform and modernise governmental institutions such as the military and the education system according to Western models, at others emphasising the Empire's Islamic foundation as a way to differentiate themselves from Europe. However, most often these two tendencies co-existed in Ottoman society, resulting in complex and at times contradictory policies and relations both internally and with external forces (Cleveland 2004: 101).[5]

At the centre of dualist trajectories of Westernisation and Islamisation was the 'woman question'. While 'progressive' elites argued that women's emancipation was a prerequisite to civilisation and modernisation, understood as economic and social progress similar to the West, Islamic forces argued that social life should be organised according to Quranic rulings, deviation from which could lead to corruption and moral depravation (Kandiyoti 1989; Sirman 1989). This polarity politicised women's rights concerns, such that any critique of practices such as gender segregation and polygamy was declared by those in the Islamic camp an attack on Islam in favour of Westernisation, and their defence a means to counter foreign influence on Ottoman 'tradition'. Conversely, secular or self-proclaimed progressive elites saw support for such practices as regressive.

Women were not silent in these debates, voicing their perspectives and demands in newspapers and journals of the time. Their most significant demand centred on girls and women's right to education, presented as a prerequisite to the transformation of women's roles in society and thus to societal development. As early as 1868, a feminist writing in the political journal *Yerakki* (*Progress*) (which devoted all of one page to women's issues) condemned the idleness of wealthy urban women and advocated women's

[5] According to Yavuz and Esposito (2003), the Empire's source of power was the 'complex web of relationships between a military and a bureaucratic system, on the one hand, and Islamic institutions, on the other' (p. xix).

education 'to help transform them into useful human beings' (Sirman 1989: 3).[6] The latter half of the nineteenth century, until the foundation of the Republic in 1923, witnessed the rise of a viable women's movement, which mobilised to achieve women's basic rights, ranging from education and employment to important family rights (Tekeli 2010).[7] This period saw the founding of a number of women's associations, and the existence of over forty women's magazines, addressing diverse issues (Ilkkaracan 1997). However, given the extensive rate of women's illiteracy during the Ottoman era, women's publications mostly circulated among upper-class and educated women.

As illustrated by this chapter's opening quote, contemporary Turkish women are proud of the historical record of Ottoman women's movements, which confirm a significant level of women's activism prior to the Republic's state feminism projects, and provide models for current women's rights activism at the intersection of ideological divisions between Islam and Western-styled modernity in Turkey. Ottoman era rights activists strategically adopted a discourse aiming to reconcile Islam and modernity, in an attempt to depoliticise women's rights for both reformists and traditionalists. They framed their position in terms of justice and development/progress, while trying to respect the sensitivities of the public regarding the social and political forces of both tradition and Western dominance at play.

The transitional period from the Ottoman Empire to the establishment of the Turkish Republic witnessed the creation of additional women's organisations and increased circulation of women's journals. It was at this time that women's demands for equal political rights began to be heard publicly. To ensure that women's rights were part of the reformist agenda, activists, many of them members of the elite, educated female nationalist bourgeoisie that played a key role in Turkey's independence movement and the founding of the Republic, pressured for women's citizenship rights. As part of their activism in the Turkish independence movement and the battle against European forces for the former Ottoman Empire, elite women's rights activists donned

---

[6] Such demands were voiced in Turkey some thirty years before Egyptian Qasim Amin's celebrated book, *The Liberation of Women* (1899), in which he also posited female education as necessary for societal progress.

[7] Women's demands concerning reform of family rights included women's right to divorce, prohibition of polygamy and arranged marriages, and women's access to property and inheritance.

the *çarşaf* (the Islamic head covering)[8] in public demonstrations, to illustrate their solidarity with women of other classes as well as their opposition to Europeanism. Their strategic use of Islamic dress as a marker of nationalism and political ideology during this transitional period has occurred in mass demonstrations in other nations as well, including during the 1979 Iranian revolution when many secular women covered their hair to publicly protest Western (mostly American) influence in Iran, and to show solidarity with the masses of pious Iranian women (Hoodfar 1999).

With the fall of the Ottoman Empire at the end of World War I, Mustafa Kemal (1881–1938), an Ottoman army commander, led the Turkish War of Independence (1919–23) against imperialist forces. This war provided a major opportunity for women to enter the public sphere, given men's deployment to the war fronts. As women acquired jobs in civil service and mainstream professions, they agitated for further rights and protections. Women were admitted to universities in 1914, and public service and factory jobs were opened to women in 1915 (Tekeli 2010). The Committee of Union and Progress, a liberal reformist movement that emerged in the late 1880s and evolved into Turkey's ruling political party from 1913–18 during the transitional period between Ottoman rule and the founding of the Republic, responded to the changing circumstances by adopting a new family law in 1917 that expanded women's rights. This law not only placed family courts (the last remaining judicial branch under religious jurisdiction) under the authority of the Ministry of Justice, but also recognised women's right to divorce and restricted the grounds for polygamy. By 1919, suffrage became the key issue of women's rights campaigning along with the demand for women's access to the political field, to try and ensure that women (and their basic rights) were not ignored by male decision-makers. Looking at the tactics and substance of their campaigns, it is clear that women's rights activists of the late Ottoman period had significant connections with the international women's movement, whose steps and strategies they carefully monitored and adapted (Tekeli 2010).

In 1920 the Turkish National Movement established the Turkish Grand National Assembly, with Mustafa Kemal as its president (Cleveland 2004).

---

[8] *Çarşaf* is the traditional Islamic head covering used in Turkey and other countries in the region. It fully covers the hair, neck and shoulders, and some versions are tent-like and cover the entire body. *Çarşaf* has also been the prevailing dress code for pious women in Iran, where it is called *chador* (literally 'tent').

In order to appear modern, Kemal emulated European governing structures, opting to be 'elected' as the new republic's president (albeit through a single-party system of his own design and by a band of his supporters), rather than establishing a monarchy, which army commander Reza Pahlavi pursued in neighbouring Iran in 1925.[9] Despite its actual limitations, and the novelty of choosing a republican model over a monarchy, this move by Kemal significantly set the tone for democratic development in Turkey and the region as early as the 1920s, although Turkey only held its first democratic and multi-party elections in 1950. By establishing a parliament and elections, the formation of the modern Turkish state followed a drastically different model than other countries in the region, including Iran. These institutional developments greatly assisted democratisation as they enabled public participation, including women's activism.

The reforms that occurred following the end of the Ottoman period were geared towards establishing a modern republic, modelled after Western powers. Deeming Turkey's Ottoman past and Muslim heritage as sources of Turkish traditionalism and backwardness, Kemal's reforms aimed at secularisation and Westernisation, which he equated with modernisation and progress. His central ideology, which became known as Kemalism, was that modernity and democracy require secularism. According to Yavuz and Esposito, 'in order to bring modernity, Islam had to be either kept under strict state control or confined to personal conscience' (2003: xiii). By 1926 secular law applied to all aspects of society, including family law. According to Cleveland, Kemal did not seek to abolish Islam as a personal belief system, but rather to remove it as an institutionalised regulating agent in the affairs of the state and society (2004: 181–2). In this sense, Kemalist ideology was to replace religious ideology in Turkish society and politics.

Turkish secularism: the founding principle of a nation-state
The ruling elites instrumental in the Turkish Republic's founding claimed 'secular' as their identity (*laik* in Turkish), and defined secularism as progressive (having faith in science), modern (i.e. European) and nationalist (Turkish) (Yavuz and Esposito 2003: xxiii). This identity framework became

---

[9] Although Kemal sought to establish popular sovereignty in the new constitution, and emphasised the rule of law, as president he also had overwhelming power to persuade the national assembly to pass new laws that he demanded (Cleveland 2004: 192).

increasingly hegemonic with the ongoing implementation of state policies according to this secularist ideology, which in practice marginalised anyone who did not fit the state's definition of a '*laik* Turk'. A large body of scholarship has analysed the impact of the Kemalist secularist ideologies on various institutions and structures, including the military, the judiciary, and of course, the Directorate of Religious Affairs (the *Diyanet*) that aimed to administer and regulate the public's religious needs in the secular society (Atasoy 2005; Gulalp 2005; Gurbey 2009; Tugal 2009; Yavuz and Esposito 2003).[10] Much of such literature has highlighted the complex and ever shifting approach of the secular state to religious control in a Muslim-majority country. For the purpose of this research, I am interested in the gendered aspects of Turkey's top-down secularisation since its foundation, especially as it relates to women's political participation and representation.[11]

The Turkish founding elites' secularising ideas influenced the early party politics, as the Kemalist state prohibited the establishment of any political party or organisation that departed from Kemalist ideology, resulting in de facto single party rule, which lasted from the Republic's foundation in 1923 until 1950, when Turkey held its first multi-party elections (Arat 1989). Mustafa Kemal founded the Republican People's Party (*Cumhuriyet Halk Partisi*, henceforth CHP) in 1923, as the only functioning political party, which embodied the centre-left ideology that became known as Kemalism. In 1935, Kemal codified the six principles of Kemalism to guide the party, the state and the nation: nationalism, secularism, republicanism, populism, reformism and statism (referring to a state-controlled economy) (Cleveland 2004: 180). Today, CHP functions as the main opposition party to the ruling pro-religious AKP, and many of its leaders boast of their Kemalist legacy. As a former military commander, Kemal also underlined the role of the Turkish Armed Forces in guarding the secular state.[12] He and his follow-

---

[10] The *Diyanet* is a state institution responsible for dictating acceptable measures and practices of religiosity, and blocking the expression of alternative versions of Islam that might emerge from within civil society (Yavuz and Esposito 2003: xxiii).

[11] While as of this writing we are currently witnessing yet another important shift in Turkish politics at the hands of a conservative religious party – that poses increasing threats to Turkey's secular ideals – my research is more concerned with women's experiences and the ways they seek to increase women's political rights between the competing discourses of secularism and conservative Islam.

[12] Throughout Turkish history, this responsibility has resulted in numerous coups, as the mili-

ers presented themselves as the guardians of the Turkish people, pursuing policies in the best interests of society. This paternalistic approach particularly implicated Turkish women, who were expected to participate by nurturing future generations of modern, civilised citizens of the Republic.

Turkish women's rights during the early Republican era: women as national symbols

In addition to the creation of strong state institutions, another significant development of the early republican days was the realisation of women's suffrage. The Kemalist state granted male adult suffrage upon the Republic's establishment in the 1920s, and extended suffrage to women roughly a decade later. In 1930 women gained the right to participate in municipal elections, and in 1934 universal suffrage was extended to adult women for national elections, making Turkey the first country in the region to recognise women's political rights. Many scholars credit this significant development to Kemal's top-down modernisation projects and his equation of women's full participation in the public and political spheres with Westernisation (Arat 1999, 2005; Ilkkaracan 1997). For instance, Hala Maksoud (1991) states 'Turkey might be the only country in the world where women's liberation in politics is not the result of women's activism . . . women were granted their universal suffrage without a suffragette movement' (p. 678). However, others credit women's efforts in the late Ottoman era for their achievement of political rights, noting that campaigns by activists for women's political rights preceded by many decades any response to their demands. Tekeli (2010) argues, 'the women's revolution accomplished by the young Turkish Republic was in fact the result of 50 years of activism by Ottoman women' (p. 120).[13]

In fact, women's suffrage in Turkey resulted from women's extensive organising efforts as well as the opportunities that Turkey's modernisation and nation-building objectives provided. Indeed, campaigns for women's suffrage at the beginning of the twentieth century continued after the Republic's foundation, as a handful of women established the Turkish Women's Union,

---

tary sought to 'protect' the Republic from parties or governments that threatened Turkey's secular establishment.

[13] Turkish women were enfranchised at a time when neither France nor Switzerland, the two countries Kemalists used as models for the Turkish Republic, had female enfranchisement. This highlights the internal civil society pressure that mobilised Turkish women's enfranchisement.

bridging women's movements from the Ottoman to the Republican era, and actively campaigned for female suffrage between 1926 and 1934. The Union sought to establish itself as a 'woman's party', and put forth candidates for the 1927 national elections and for the 1931 municipal elections. According to Gol (2009: 4), the Union's decision to nominate women in the 1927 elections, prior to full female suffrage, was a tactical move to place the issue on the national agenda and create public discussion. However, the move generated a great deal of criticism given the patriarchal nature of Turkish society, and Kemal himself demonstrated little support for this autonomous women's group.

Nonetheless, Turkey's nation-building project created significant opportunities for women's demands for political inclusion to be heard, since, after decades of rights activism, the birth of the Republic modelled after Western-style modernity provided space for consideration of women's enfranchisement. Women's suffrage as a norm was spreading rapidly across Europe and North America, and Turkey did not want to be left behind (Towns 2010); both Turkish women's groups and Kemalist elites engaged with transnational feminist networks on the issue of women's political rights. For instance, the Turkish Women's Union committed to host the Twelfth Congress of the International Alliance of Women for Suffrage and Equal Citizenship scheduled for 1935 in Istanbul,[14] in part to again place the demand for Turkish women's suffrage on the national agenda and to garner transnational support. However, in a rather surprising move, Kemal extended the right to vote to women just months before the congress, as part of his effort to shape the image of the young republic as modern and liberal. During the congress, he delivered a speech in which he remarked, 'I am convinced that the exercise of social and political rights by women is necessary for mankind's happiness and pride. You can rest assured that Turkish women together with world's women will work towards world peace and security' (Kemal 1935). Soon after the conference, however, he 'invited' the Turkish Women's Union to close, leaving Turkey without any organised association for women (Cinar 2008: 901; Tekeli 2010: 120). The state's reasoning was that the Turkish Women's Union and other independent women's organisations were redundant since women had achieved equal legal status with men (Tekeli 2010). However many argue that

---

[14] A pioneer transnational women's network working on the issue of female suffrage was the International Women Suffrage Alliance (IWSA), which was founded in Berlin in 1904 by delegates from eight nations ('International Alliance of Women Records', n.d.). Such networks greatly strengthened the Turkish women's movement.

the closure of the Women's Union, like that of the People's Party of Women in 1923, was motivated by the state's desire to maintain single-party dominance and its intolerance of any civil society organisations that might dilute or undermine its control (Gol 2009; Kandiyoti 1989; Sirman 1989; Tekeli 2010). According to Tekeli (2010: 120), the Turkish Women's Union's closure 'marked the end of the women's movement for 40 years to come'.

Consequently, the Kemalist state's extension of the vote to women lacked sincerity and was primarily designed to enhance Turkey's international standing. Male elites have typically used women and women's issues as pawns in their political struggles, and the Kemalist project on women had little to do with women's own concerns, but was rather conceived as part of the larger project of nationalism (Gulalp 2005; Kandiyoti 1989). By cracking down on independent women's rights organisations following women's enfranchisement, the male elites hindered the rise of a feminist movement geared towards addressing the needs of a diverse female population and empowering women to shape their own rights and realities.[15]

Women's bodies as signifiers of national identity

That women are used as 'symbolic pawns' in political shifts and struggles is particularly apparent by the manipulation of women and their bodies to signify a national identity or political affiliation (Baron 2005; Joseph 2000; Rao 1999; Shively 2005). Ironically, Kemalism, like the religious ideologies it aimed to overturn in the name of modernity and democracy, sought to determine Turkish women's proper societal place, including aspects of dress, behaviour and lifestyle. The ideal Turkish woman was to symbolise progress through her education and employment, while at the same time serving the Republic as a model wife and mother. Given the state's emphasis on women's presence in the public sphere, women's bodies, as well as men's, became an important site for the national imagining, in which attire associated with the 'backward' Ottoman or Islamic past was either banned or discouraged.[16]

---

[15] Scholars such as Arat (2000) and Kandiyoti (1987) argue that while Turkish women were emancipated in the early republican years in terms of formal gender equality, they were not liberated as these reforms did not trickle down to all segments of the society, and the public realm continued to be a patriarchal space where women were treated as second-class citizens.

[16] While soon after the Republic's foundation the state banned the fez (traditional Ottoman hat for men), it only discouraged women's religious head covering, while promoting the wearing of Western style hats (Gulalp 2005).

Mustafa Kemal himself saw 'veiling as a malady, a "barbarous posture" or an "object of ridicule" that needed to be corrected' (Cinar 2008: 901). His anti-veil stance and emphasis on secularising women's dress became a critical and sensitive issue for Kemalist elites for decades to come.

Women's responses to top-down state feminism projects varied according to their societal position and ideological tendencies. While many upper-class women viewed Kemal and his 'state feminism' policies as their saviour from tradition and backwardness, many others, including feminist intellectuals, saw the policies as top-down, authoritarian measures implemented to serve the nationalist agenda. The state's closure of autonomous women's organisations further demonstrated to many that women were being used as pawns in the secularist project (Gunduz 2004; Ilkkaracan 1997; Tekeli 2010).

Similar to most other countries in the region, Turkey's state feminism project primarily benefited upper-class women, since literate, urban women were more likely to be aware of changes to laws and government policy. But the majority of poor and rural women remained largely unaware of new rights or policies enhancing women's status, due to lack of state resources for sensitisation and, especially, because the women's organisations which would otherwise be advising and helping women access new rights had for the most part been closed down by the government, weakening the development of the Turkish women's movement and sharpening ideological divisions among women. On one end of the spectrum were women supporters of the Kemalist agenda, who viewed Islam and the veil as the main threats to women's rights, progress and modernity; on the other end were those critical of the Kemalist regime's authoritarian approach to modernising and secularising, especially the restrictions on public expressions of religiosity. These divisions would have lasting effects in Turkish society, as each group of women viewed the other as 'other' – with opposing values, objectives and priorities.

Turkey's first women parliamentarians
In line with Kemal's modernisation efforts, Turkey became the first Muslim country to elect women to the parliament. Just months after women's enfranchisement in 1935, eighteen women entered the parliament, composing 4.5 per cent of the total parliament (see Figure 3.1). Although at the time this constituted among the highest rates of female lawmakers in the

Mebrure GÖNENÇ	Hatı ÇIRPAN	Türkan ÖRS BAŞTUĞ	Sabiha Gökçül ERBAY	Şekibe İNSEL	Hatice ÖZGENER
Huriye Öniz BAHA	Fatma MEMİK	Nakiye ELGÜN	Fakihe ÖYMEN	Benal Nevzat İŞTAR ARIMAN	Ferruh GÜPGÜP
Bahire Bediz MOROVA AYDILEK	Mihri PEKTAŞ	Meliha ULAŞ	Esma NAYMAN	Sabiha GÖRKEY	Seniha HIZAL

Figure 3.1 First female parliamentarians of the Turkish parliament (1935). (Credit: 'First female MPs of the Turkish parliament' by Kemalist Yurtsever is licensed under public domain.)

world, the undemocratic nature of Turkey's elections and CHP's single party rule cast a shadow over the early parliaments of the Republican era (Arat 1989; Tekeli 1981). Indeed, like their male counterparts, all eighteen female parliamentarians were handpicked by the political leaders of CHP, and all were expected to uphold the party line. However, by facilitating women's access to formal politics, the state's symbolic move to 'elect' female MPs to help Turkey appear modern in the eyes of the world also had wider and lasting implications in terms of conceptualising women's political roles. The involvement of women in high-level political decision-making in Turkish government as early as 1935 was extremely progressive, considering that most other governments, including a number of Western states such as France and Switzerland, had yet to recognise the significance of women's political representation.

Regardless of the CHP party nepotism involved, the election of these first female MPs helped cement the legitimacy and legacy of women in political leadership in the history of the founding of the Republic and its institutions. Their recruitment opened the door for other female politicians in an otherwise patriarchal and paternalistic society. In fact, although the high level of women's representation during the early days of the Republic was short-lived – as illustrated in Table 3.1, future generations of Turkish women have often used the 1935 percentage to pressure male political elites by highlighting the willingness of the early leaders of the Republic to nominate women, something many Turkish feminists point out was subsequently absent for many decades in Turkish politics (personal interview with women's rights activist Fezal Gulfidan, 3 June 2011). Female parliamentary representation only came close to 1935 levels again in 2002, with ascendancy of the pro-religious AKP, and has been continuously increasing ever since.

Table 3.1 Percentage of women parliamentarians in Turkey.

Parliament	Percentage of Women
1930: *Women gain the right to vote;* **1934:** *Women gain the right to stand for elections.*	
1935–39	4.5% (18/395)
1939–43	3.7% (15/400)
1943–46	3.7% (16/435)
1946–50 *(first multiparty national elections)*	1.9% (9/455)
1950–54 *(first time CHP was not the ruling party in parliament)*	0.6% (3/487)
1954–57	0.7% (4/535)
1957–60	1.1% (7/610)
1961–65 *(dual chamber legislature is created)*	0.7% (3/450)
1965–69	1.7% (8/450)
1969–73	1.1% (5/450)
1973–77	1.3% (6/450)
1977–79	0.9% (4/450)
1983–86 *(first elections after 1980 coup and new constitution; legislature becomes once again unicameral)*	2.9% (12/410)
1987–91	1.3% (6/449)
1991–95	1.8% (8/449)
1995–99	2.4% (13/550)
1999–2002	4.2% (23/550)
2002–2007 *(AKP enters parliament)*	4.4% (24/550)
2007–2011	9.1% (50/550)
2011–2015	14.4% (79/550)
2015–2018	14.7% (82/550)
2018–Present	17.3% (104/600)

Sources: Sirin Tekeli (1981), 'Women in Turkish Politics', in Abadan-Unat Nermin, Deniz Kandiyoti and Mubeccel Belik Kiray (eds), *Women in Turkish Society*, Leiden: Brill, p. 300; Inter-Parliamentary Union (IPU), www.ipu.org.

From State Feminism to Multiple Feminisms: Turkish Women's Political Status Before and After the 1980 Coup

Despite Mustafa Kemal Ataturk's important feminist reforms, women's true equality was not achieved at the stroke of his pen; the struggle for women's liberation in Turkey has been long, arduous and ongoing (Arat 2000; Kandiyoti 1987). While many of women's political and citizenship rights were recognised during the early years of the Republic, these reforms did not really penetrate society beyond a small, urban elite. According to Tekeli, from the 1930s until the 1960s, many Turkish women activists identified with Kemalism rather than feminism 'both because they got some important rights and were given new opportunities, and because they were forced to do so by repression' (1995: 12). Most women's organisations formed during this period equated protection of women's rights with loyalty to Kemalism and the secular establishment, believing these to be the only guarantors of their acquired rights in the face of Islamic tradition. Fierce loyalty to Kemalism also caused many elite women to ignore the patriarchal reality of Turkish society, including the suffering of common Turkish women, and the perpetuation of a number of discriminatory rulings, such as features of the 1926 Civil Code which still recognised husbands as the head of the family (Tekeli 1995: 12).[17]

The limited extent of women's political empowerment during the first decades of the Republican era is also evidenced by the significant and sustained drop in female parliamentary presence following the transition to multi-party competition after World War II (see Table 3.1). The lowest level of women's political representation in Turkish history – a mere 0.6 per cent – occurred following the 1950 parliamentary elections, which was the first time that CHP was not the ruling party, and the Democratic Party (DP) won the majority of the parliamentary seats.[18] In the 1950 multi-party election, the symbolic importance of female representation lost ground to increased party

[17] Although the 1926 Turkish Civil Code included several radical reforms for its time – such as banning polygamy and recognising women's equal rights in divorce, child custody, and inheritance – it still included a number of patriarchal provisions which limited women's rights (Sirman 1989).

[18] While the 1946 elections were Turkey's first ever multi-party elections, many scholars, such as Yesim Arat (1989), consider the 1950 elections as the beginning of true multi-party competition, since this election effectively put an end to CHP's decades-long single-party rule, as the Democratic Party gained a majority of the votes in a mass voter turnout.

competition. According to Arat (1989), although the women parliamentarians who served between 1950 and 1980 were more independent-minded relative to their predecessors during the single-party rule era, they were still unable to deliver significant changes for Turkish women, given their low numbers as well as the expectation that they toe their respective party lines in order to maintain their positions.

Nonetheless, the 1950s shift towards democratisation opened space for the growth of civil society, including women's rights movements. During the 1960s and 1970s, Turkish women began to be drawn into various brands of leftist ideology, which among their many demands sought freedom from repression and class domination. It was at this time that various youth groups and intellectuals began to mobilise against the state, referencing concepts of economic development, imperialism, inequality and class exploitation. As the emergence of a feminist consciousness expanded, and more and more Turkish women questioned their oppression and exploitation and the official state discourse of 'gender equality', women's rights activism increasingly integrated with socialist and leftist groups. However, women's rights issues were framed according to struggles against the class system rather than against patriarchy, since Marxism in Turkey was fundamentally anti-feminist. This weakened Turkish women's rights activism through the 1960s and 1970s, since the demands of key activists and organisations in the development of global liberal feminist discourses in Turkey were subordinated to leftist ideology and the 'larger' goal of eliminating class exploitation (Sirman 1989; Tekeli 1995).

The 1980 military coup, a response to the ongoing political and economic contest between leftist and right-wing Turkish groups embroiled in the proxy wars between the Communist bloc and the United States, is considered a major turning point in Turkish history, including for the development of Turkish feminism.[19] During the coup all political activity was banned and left-wing movements were crushed. However, the military junta did not

---

[19] Despite political integration of previously marginalised groups and their bottom-up modernisation efforts, Turkey's increasing political and economic instability led to a radical politicisation of diverse groups throughout the 1970s. By 1975 Turkey had plunged into political turmoil and urban violence, and deep divisions between Left versus Right, Turk versus Kurd, and Alevi versus Sunni dominated the political landscape (Cleveland 2004: 282–5). The government's inability to calm the situation, as well as the severe socioeconomic problems of the late 1970s, resulted in a military coup to restore secularism and stop the state's fragmentation among diverse political fronts.

consider Turkish women's organising or feminist ideology to be threats to the state, and this provided important opportunity structures for the emergence of an autonomous women's movement in Turkey (Ilkkaracan 1997). Feminist consciousness in Turkey was also bolstered by major women's rights developments at the international level, such as the United Nations Decade for Women (1976–85) and various international women's conferences: in Mexico City (1975), Copenhagen (1980) and Nairobi (1985). These gatherings, and the discussions and documents they produced, provided Turkish feminists with legitimacy for their own claims and demands (Tekeli 1995; Towns 2010).

Since Turkey's post-1980 feminist movement developed largely in opposition to 'state feminism', it was able to accommodate voices within the Turkish women's rights movement that were previously marginalised (personal interview with Turkish women activists, June 2011). The three groups that came to the fore of the women's rights movement in this period were secular feminists (including those with socialist tendencies), Islamic feminists and Kurdish feminists. While they often were allied and cooperated on particular issues and campaigns, such as a successful campaign against domestic violence, on other issues ideological differences precluded collaboration. Nonetheless, Tekeli (1995) considers the Turkish feminist movement to be among the first democratic and public oppositions to military rule during one of the darkest moments in Turkey's modern history.

Turkish feminist activism after the 1980 coup included a very significant shift in discourse thanks to its disengagement from leftist parties: instead of targeting class exploitation, Turkish feminists began to target patriarchy and male dominance, which they realised was present in Kemalism, Islamism, and even leftist ideology. The movement was successful in politicising the 'woman question' in the public sphere, but this time through pluralism, in which the views, interests and needs of diverse groups of women were highlighted and addressed. Although the main actors came from different backgrounds and diverse societal positions, they all agreed on an autonomous women's movement that actively supported the proliferation of women's groups representing a wide variety of ideological positions, exemplifying a democratic movement in Turkey.

Through its extensive awareness raising and publicising of activities, Turkey's feminist movement successfully placed various women's issues on the national agenda by the end of the 1980s. The decade's most effective collaborative campaign (called the Campaign Against the Battering of Women) targeted violence against women. The prevalence of domestic violence across Turkish society, combined with the patriarchal indifference of the state to the issue, made it a rallying point for women from all backgrounds, classes, education levels and ideologies.[20] Aside from affording women campaigning experience, among the most important achievements of the Campaign Against the Battering of Women were important legal reforms and the establishment of the Purple Roof Foundation, which continues to provide counselling and shelters for battered women. These achievements were followed by the repeal of Article 159 of the Turkish Civil Code in 1990, which had required a husband's permission for a wife to be employed, after a number of women's groups brought the case against the Constitutional Court (Ilkkaracan 1997; Tekeli 1995).

The re-emergence of feminism in Turkey and the consequent awareness and mobilising around women's issues in the post-1980 coup era forced political elites to address and respond to women's demands. The strength and the autonomy of women's groups meant the first wave of politicians who came to power after the coup had to reckon with the growing power of the female electorate, and gender discourses gradually entered the political sphere as politicians increasingly sought to emphasise women's issues in their campaigns. For instance, Turgut Ozal, the leader of the centre-right conservative Motherland Party (*Anavatan Partisi* – ANAP) that came to power in the first post-1980 coup elections, sought to integrate headscarved women into public life as he viewed this increasingly powerful section of society as a potential support base (Kavakci 2010: 53). Similarly True Path Party's (*Dogru Yol Partisi* – DYP) Suleyman Demirel, in an attempt to rejuvenate his party to be competitive with ANAP in the 1990s, recruited a woman, Tansu Ciller, to his party's higher echelons, which eventually led to her becoming the first Turkish female prime minister. Demirel believed that having a young, female, Western-educated economist in the ranks would save his party from its 'old man's club' image and garner women's support. Demirel, who often

[20] While women's organisations actively raised public awareness around this issue starting in the early 1980s, it was a judicial ruling in a 1987 divorce case citing the Turkish proverb 'One should not let a woman's back without a stick or her womb without a baby', that triggered mass women's protests against domestic violence. Women's persistence in highlighting this issue resulted in a march in the same year, which was the first 'legal' street demonstration since the 1980 coup (Ilkkaracan 1997).

consulted Ciller on economic issues, made the crucial move of promising her a bright future in the party. In 1991 Ciller was elected one of eight female MPs that term, due to her high placement on the True Path Party's candidate list. Ciller later rose to the party's leadership, and eventually became Prime Minister when the sitting President Ozal died and Prime Minister Demirel resigned to take his place (Arat 1998: 8).

Although Ciller's prime ministership (1993–6) was not associated with passage of women friendly laws, and she herself was inattentive to women's rights and feminist groups' demands, she, like other politicians, brought women into the centre of her electoral discourse through strategic rhetoric and activities designed to benefit her campaign and position using the fact of her sex when expedient. For instance, while campaigning she justified the crack-down on Kurdish rebels with reference to herself as Turkey's 'mother and protector' (Arat 1998: 16). However, once in office, she downplayed her gender and generally painted herself as everyone's representative, code for her conservative stance on gender (Arat 1998: 9). According to Arat (1998), secular feminists, who harboured great hopes with a female prime minister, were hugely disappointed in Ciller when she formed a coalition with the Islamist *Refah* party, the same party against whom she had campaigned. However, simply by virtue of being appointed to the nation's highest political decision-making position, Ciller broke many gender taboos that had constrained women's political ambitions and roles. While during her tenure and since, feminists have critiqued Ciller's silence on women's rights, they acknowledge the significance of having had a female political leader in Turkey's patriarchal context.

The Impact of Islamic Revivalism on Women's Political Participation

The post-1980 coup era witnessed the rise of various social and political movements, including Islamic revivalism. The upswing in religious organising in secular Turkey resulted from a number of political openings and social factors. First, mass urbanisation and politicisation of diverse groups throughout the 1980s intensified the interactions between civil society and state actors, and the post-coup, military-supported Turkish state could no longer ignore the religious and ideological orientations of much of society. Second, during the 1980 coup, Turkish generals purposefully used Islamic movements to counter the rise of leftist and communist groups, which they considered greater threats to Kemalism than Islam (Yavuz and Esposito 2003). The military's apparently surprising shift towards Islam can be understood in the context of the Cold War and the presence of communist movements in Turkey. Significant international and regional events of the late 1970s and 1980s illustrated the power of religious organising to defeat communism and leftist ideology, which are inherently anti-religious. During the same period, Turkey witnessed both the aftermath of the 1979 Iranian revolution and how Islamic factions undermined all opposition parties including communists; and the Soviet invasion of Afghanistan, which eventually saw the United States relying on religious fighters, namely the Mujahedin – then referred to as 'freedom fighters' – to engage in a proxy war against the Soviets. These events led Turkish leaders to reason that the population's engagement with religion would serve as a counterweight to leftist ideologies, and Islam experienced a kind of political rehabilitation as mainstream secular leaders used religion in the ideological battle against secular leftist ideology. The military introduced compulsory religion classes in primary and middle schools, and opened religious schools to train preachers and prayer leaders. By the early 1990s, approximately 300,000 students were enrolled in these, many of whom came from the historically disenfranchised and religious constituencies of central Anatolia. However, the secularist strategy for a safe Islamic outlet backfired as the void left by the repression of the political Left was filled by Islamic-oriented groups who offered alternative solutions to the marginalised populations (Cleveland 2004: 524). These new Islamic groups eventually rose to political power in the 1990s. According to Eligur (2010: 76), 'following the elimination of the left, the urban poor, who had been voting for left-wing political parties in the pre-1980 coup period, started to vote for the political Islamist parties'.

Ironically, the post-1980 coup era's relative tolerance of Islamic networks and religious organising, as well as the disruption of existing power arrangements, were important opportunity structures for the consolidation of Islamic movements that eventually hardened into political parties. The strategic tolerance of Islamic organising by the military regime also legitimised the now transnational religious movement Fethullah Gulen, which started in Turkey as a provider of religious education and training. Significantly, the interactions between the state and Islamic movements were 'not a bipolar clash of identities and ideologies, but rather occasional co-optation, confrontation or symbiotic interaction' (Yavuz 2009: 41). According to Berna Turam, the Turkish Republic 'has displayed ongoing swings of the pendulum between repression and toleration of Islam', and Islamic social forces were often tolerated by the military and Kemalist elites until they were thought to pose a threat to the secular state (2007: 6). This is evident when we consider that despite the military regime's increased tolerance of Islam, it nonetheless banned Islamist parties, such as Necmettin Erbakan's National Salvation Party (1972–81), and sought to restrict public visibility of religious symbols, including women's headscarves and men's beards, as they signified an Islamist turn from Kemalism.

The emergence of pro-religious political parties following the 1980 coup played a major role in expanding the political participation of pious women, who were largely marginalised and ignored by the secular establishment. The most significant development in this regard was the establishment of the Islamist *Refah* party (Welfare Party) in 1983 under the leadership of Necmettin Erbakan, whose mandate was to move away from Westernisation and modernisation in the quest for 'cultural and moral development' (Arat 2005: 32–3). *Refah* drew the support of pious women by lauding maternal roles and duties as a pillar of the moral order, thus acknowledging and politicising pious women's contributions to society for the first time in Turkish political history. Despite emphasising women's domestic role, this discourse eventually opened the space for pious women to enter public and political life, albeit under the guidance and protection of male party leaders (Arat 2005; White 2002).

Refah's major tactic for enhancing pious women's access to the political sphere was through the establishment of women's branches at various levels of the party structure. According to Arat (2005), the party was eager to appeal to marginalised groups and those living in peripheral rural and urban settings, and very soon after its founding set out to capture the support of women. 'The earliest and most vocal advocate of the idea of organizing women within the party organization . . . was [Recep] Tayyip Erdogan, at the time the head of the *Refah* Party Istanbul organization' (Arat 2005: 40). Despite much opposition from within *Refah*, Erdogan argued that recruiting women to the party could help recruit men as well; this was a significant shift from the belief that women vote for the same leaders as their husbands and fathers. Beginning in 1989, Erdogan personally trained the women who would form the first women's branches of *Refah*, mainly housewives who were relatives and friends of male party leaders (Arat 2005: 40).

Women's organising and activism in *Refah* was extensive and its female membership far exceeded that of any other Turkish political party. '*Refah*

Party women registered close to one million women members in about six years', and male members widely acknowledged that many women were instrumental in persuading their husbands to register as well (Arat 2005: 8). The success of the *Refah* party's women's branches manifested itself in the 1995 election when *Refah* won the highest percentage of the vote with 21.4 per cent.[21] In Istanbul alone, in the run-up to the 1995 parliamentary elections, 18,000 *Refah* women activists met face-to-face with 200,000 women voters to garner their support (Arat 1999; White 2002: 235). This intensive voter recruitment, under *Refah*'s Istanbul women's branch head Sibel Eraslan, set the bar for future grass-roots party organising in Turkey. The work of *Refah* women, and their crucial role in the party's success through the 1990s, engendered a saying common among party activists across the political spectrum: 'Work like a *Refah* woman!' (personal interview with Merve Kavakci, 1 December 2011).

The involvement of pious women in party politics in the 1990s resulted in strategic interactions between women and party elites. While *Refah* officials such as Erdogan, who in 1994 became Istanbul's mayor, had facilitated women's involvement in party organising in hopes of increasing the party's support base, women also took advantage of the opportunity structures this created to enter the political and public spheres and to eventually champion their own interests. Through *Refah*, previously marginalised pious women accessed significant openings for participation in formal politics that aligned with their religious and ideological beliefs, particularly regarding freedom of religious expression in public. Despite *Refah* women's opposition to the secular establishment's restrictive attitudes towards religious expression, they nonetheless upheld the democratic ideals of mass participation and organising. In this sense, *Refah* women crossed the boundaries between the traditional and the modern, private and political, and secular and religious.

Refah party women's success in entering formal politics and their contribution to Turkey's democratisation as they worked to elect an opposition party was met with some criticism by Kemalist and secular feminists, who castigated *Refah* for using women as mere 'foot-soldiers' in the party's quest for power, without providing for female parliamentary representation or status

---

[21] The 1995 victory was a drastic increase from the 1987 elections, in which *Refah* received only 7.2 per cent of the votes, forcing it to form an alliance with a nationalist party for the 1991 elections in hopes to pass the 10 per cent threshold (Arat 2005: 32).

within the party hierarchy (personal interview with pious woman parliamentary candidate, 30 May 2011). Indeed, of the thirteen female parliamentarians elected in 1995 (2.4 per cent female representation), none were from *Refah*, while seven were from Tansu Ciller's True Path Party. In 1999, responding to criticism from secularists and to pressure from pious women activists and the international community concerning women's political rights, *Refah*'s successor party *Fazilet* (Virtue Party), nominated seventeen female candidates to its lists, including a headscarved candidate, Merve Kavakci (Kavakci 2010). Although the percentage of female parliamentarians rose to 4.2 per cent in the 1999 elections, only three of the twenty-three female parliamentarians elected were from *Fazilet*, suggesting constraints remained within the party hierarchy in terms of true support for female political representation. As pious party women became increasingly savvy to the manipulation of their constituency by party leaders, they increasingly pressured for internal reforms to enhance women's access to political leadership positions. Erdogan, who left the party as he grew disenchanted with Erbakan's anti-Western rhetoric, helped found the AKP in 2001 and played a major role in finally bringing women's parliamentary presence back up to 1935 levels by placing female candidates higher on the party's electoral lists. With his party's landslide 2002 victory the percentage of female parliamentarians rose to 4.4 per cent, with the two biggest parties – the AKP and the secularist CHP – each sending eleven women to the parliament (see Table 3.2). While the AKP's strategic placement of female nominees has been considered by many women's rights activists to have been a tactic designed to enhance the party's woman-friendly image and distance itself from predecessor Islamist parties, it was also due in large part to AKP female members' lobbying of party elites to enhance women's access to decision-making positions (personal interviews with women's rights activists, May and June 2011). Today, both AKP and CHP have informally accepted that women should comprise at least 20 to 33 per cent of their parliamentary candidate lists, and in most elections, they generally nominate a similar percentage of women to each other. The pro-Kurdish parties since 2007 have more formally adopted voluntary gender quotas, striving to ensure that women comprise at least 35 to 40 per cent of the total MPs the party sends to parliament (see Tables 3.3–3.7).

Despite the increase in women's parliamentary presence in recent years, including the near doubling of the percentage of female parliamentarians from 9.1 per cent in 2007 to 17.3 per cent in 2018, women continue to be

Table 3.2 Turkey's 2002 parliamentary elections (total women elected: 24/550 or 4.4%).

Party	Women candidates on party lists	Total seats gained from each party	Women elected from each party	Party women in proportion to total women MPs
AKP	5%	66%	3.03%	45.8%
	27/550	363/550	11/363	11/24
CHP	7.3%	32.4%	6.18%	45.8%
	40/550	178/550	11/178	11/24
Independent	N/A [a]	1.6%	22.22%	8.3%
(mostly pro-Kurdish)		363/550	2/9	2/24

[a] Unlike nationwide party lists, independent candidates tend to only run in certain districts, where voters vote for those individual candidates on the ballot.

Sources: Data compiled by the author from the Grand Turkish National Assembly, http://www.tbmm.gov.tr/TBMM_Album/Cilt3/index.html; and reports on women's electoral performance of the Association for the Support of Women Candidates (KADER).

Table 3.3 Turkey's 2007 parliamentary elections (total women elected: 50/550 or 9.1%).

Party	Women candidates on party lists	Total seats gained from each party	Women elected from each party	Party women in proportion to total women MPs
AKP	12%	62%	8.8%	60%
	67/550	341/550	30/341	30/50
CHP	10%	20.4%	8.3%	20%
	57/550	112/550	10/112	10/50
MHP	6.7%	13%	2.8%	4%
	37/550	71/550	2/71	2/50
Independent *(mostly pro-Kurdish)*	55 independent women ran for office [a]	4.7% 26/550	40% [b] 8/20 From the pro-Kurdish Democratic Society Party *(DTP)*	16% 8/50

[a] Independent candidates mostly run in presumably winnable districts, where voters vote for those individual candidates on the ballot. [b] Twenty from the total twenty-six independents elected to the parliament joined the pro-Kurdish Democratic Society Party (DTP). Among the twenty DTP parliamentarians there were eight women elected (40%), while the remaining six independent parliamentarians were all men.

Sources: Data compiled by the author from the Grand Turkish National Assembly, http://www.tbmm.gov.tr/TBMM_Album/Cilt3/index.html; and reports on women's electoral performance of KADER.

Table 3.4 Turkey's 2011 parliamentary elections (total women elected: 79/550 or 14.4%).

Party	Women who applied for candidacy in proportion to total	Women candidates on party lists	Total seats gained from each party	Women elected from each party	Party women in proportion to total women MPs
AKP	15.3%	14%	68.2%	14.06%	58.2%
	855/5,599 [a]	78/550	327/550	46/327	46/79
CHP	22%	20 %	24.5%	14.07%	24%
	783/3,500	109/550	135/550	19/135	19/79
MHP	N/A	12%	9.6%	5.7%	3.7%
	from 2,500	68/550	53/550	3/53	3/79
Independent mostly from the leftist and pro-Kurdish Labour, Democracy and Freedom block	N/A	37% 13 women nominated by the 35-member Labour, Democracy and Freedom Block	5.3% 29 [b] /550 joined the pro-Kurdish Peace and Democracy Party (BDP)	38% 11/29	14% 11/79 from BDP

[a] About fifty women who applied for candidacy with AKP in 2011 were headscarved (personal interview with women candidates). [b] Among the thirty-five total independent candidates who entered the parliament in 2011, twenty-nine (twenty men and nine women) joined the pro-Kurdish Peace and Democracy Party (BDP) after the election.
Sources: Data compiled by the author from the Grand Turkish National Assembly, http://www.tbmm.gov.tr/TBMM_Album/Cilt3/index.html; reports on women's electoral performance of KADER; and the 2011 parliamentary elections party candidate lists, available from http://www.ysk.gov.tr/ysk/docs/2011MilletvekiliSecimi/KesinAdayListesi2011.pdf.

Table 3.5 Turkey's June 2015 parliamentary elections (total women elected: 98/550 or 17.8%).

Party	Women candidates on party lists	Total seats gained from each party	Women elected from each party	Party women in proportion to total women MPs
AKP	18.4%	47%	16.3%	42.8%
	101/550	258/550	42/258	42/98
CHP	20%	24%	15%	20.4%
	109/550	132/550	20/132	20/98
MHP	12.2%	14.5%	5%	4.08%
	67/550	80/550	4/80	4/98
HDP	45.3%	14.5%	40%	32.6%
	249/550	80/550	32/80	32/98

Sources: Data compiled by the author from the Grand Turkish National Assembly, http://www.tbmm.gov.tr/TBMM_Album/Cilt3/index.html; Inter-Parliamentary Union, http://archive.ipu.org/wmn-e/classif-arc.htm; and reports on women's electoral performance of KADER.

Table 3.6 Turkey's November 2015 parliamentary elections (total women elected: 81/550 or 14.7%).

Party	Women candidates on party lists	Total seats gained from each party	Women elected from each party	Party women in proportion to total women MPs
AKP	13%	57.6%	10.8%	42%
	71/550	317/550	34/317	34/81
CHP	23%	24.3%	15.7%	26%
	127/550	134/550	21/134	21/81
MHP	14%	7.2%	7.5%	3.7%
	78/550	40/550	3/40	3/81
HDP	43%	10.7%	39%	28.4%
	234/550	59/550	23/59	23/81

Sources: Data compiled by the author from the Grand Turkish National Assembly, http://www.tbmm.gov.tr/TBMM_Album/Cilt3/index.html; and reports on women's electoral performance of KADER.

Table 3.7 Turkey's 2018 parliamentary elections (total women elected: 104/600 or 17.3%).

Party	Women candidates on party lists	Total seats gained from each party	Women elected from each party	Party women in proportion to total women MPs
AKP	21%	49.2%	18%	51%
	126/600	295/600	53/295	53/104
CHP	22.8%	24.3%	12%	17.3%
	137/600	146/600	18/146	18/104
MHP	11.5%	8.1%	10%	4.8%
	69/600	49/600	5/49	5/104
IYI	22.3%	7.16%	7%	2.8%
	134/660	43/600	3/43	3/104
HDP	38.3%	11.16%	37.3%	24%
	230/600	67/600	25/67	25/104

Sources: Data compiled by the author from the Grand Turkish National Assembly, http://www.tbmm.gov.tr/TBMM_Album/Cilt3/index.html; and reports on women's electoral performance of KADER.

AKP Trend for Women's Nomination and
Election for Parliament 2002–2018

• • • • Women Candidates on AKP Lists
▬▬▬ Women Elected from AKP

CHP Trend for Women's Nomination and
Election for Parliament 2002–2018

• • • • Women Candidates on CHP Lists
▬▬▬ Women Elected from CHP

MHP Trend for Women's Nomination and
Election for Parliament 2007–2018

• • • • Women Candidates on MHP Lists
▬▬▬ Women Elected from MHP

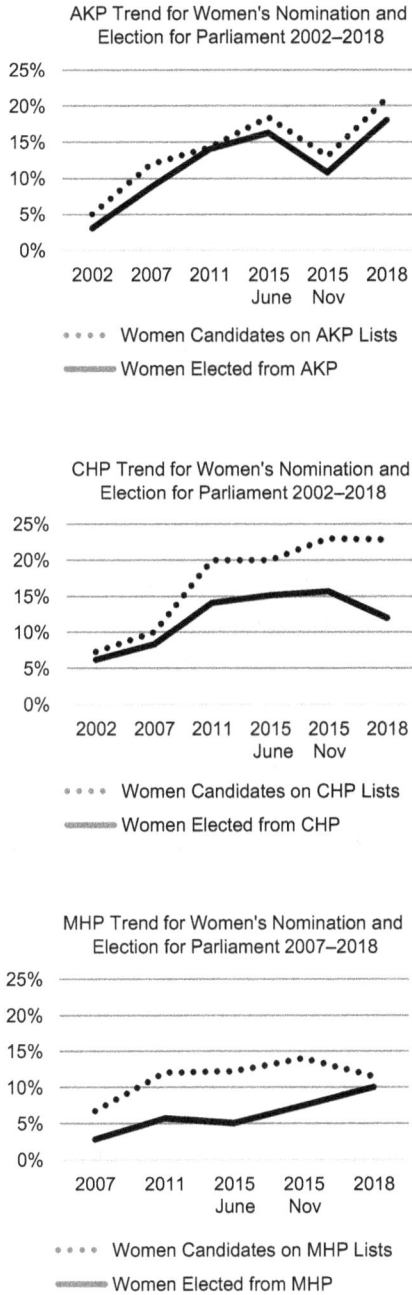

Figure 3.2 Trends of women's nomination and election for AKP, CHP and MHP in recent elections.

marginalised from formal politics. Women's numbers are even more dismal at the local level. Following the 2019 local elections, the Association for the Support of Women Candidates (KADER) reported that women composed only 3.23 per cent (45 out of 1,389) of mayoral positions at the metropolitan, city, district and sub-district levels.[22] At the national level, the major parties of AKP and CHP continue to nominate a limited number of women to elect-able positions, though as the charts in Figure 3.2 show, AKP has a notably narrower gap between the percentage of its women parliamentary nominees than CHP and MHP, while it also tends to send the most women to the parliament in proportion to its total MPs, second only to the pro-Kurdish HDP that has adopted a gender quota.

Although Turkish male elites often blame women for female politi-cal under-representation, arguing that women are apolitical, unqualified or inexperienced, much evidence points to the contrary. Aside from the well-documented high levels of female political participation in grass-roots party organising (Arat 2005; White 2002), official statistics point to a gap between the percentage of women aspiring for formal political positions, such as the parliament, and those who reach them. For instance, during the 2007 parliamentary elections, some 4,912 women (19 per cent of the total number of applicants) applied to political parties for candidacy, and 1,261 (18 per cent of the total number of candidates) were nominated on party lists (OSCE/ODIHR 2007).[23] However, women constituted only 9.1 per cent of total parliamentarians, indicating that the percentage of women trying to enter politics in Turkey is significantly higher than their actual level of representation, a trend that is also witnessed in Iran. The gap between the high rates of women's candidacy and their lower levels of acquiring political seats has persisted in Turkey.

---

[22] As further explained in Chapter 4, the successes at the national level have not been repli-cated at the local level since local women's groups, utilising the support of the international community, have prioritised women's parliamentary presence; though many, including KADER, are currently working to address this gap at the local level as well.

[23] Similarly for the 2011 parliamentary elections, some 3,500 women applied to be candi-dates for seven political parties, from the total of fourteen parties that competed ('Women's platform seeks equal political representation in Turkey', *Hurriyet Daily News* (2011), http:// www.hurriyetdailynews.com/default.aspx?pageid=438&n=8220women-who-are-right-plat form8221-seeks-for-equal-representation-in-politics-2011-03-17 (accessed 10 July 2013)).

Turkish women constitute a highly politicised and active segment of their society. Given the discriminatory attitudes and practices of party leaders, women across the ideological spectrum continue to pressure for access to political leadership positions. As elaborated on in the following chapter, women's groups look to the pro-Kurdish parties as models for other parties to emulate. Adopting a feminist ideology, Turkey's pro-Kurdish parties, such as previously the Peace and Democracy Party (*Baris ve Demokrasi Partisi* – BDP) and currently the People's Democratic Party (*Halkların Demokratik Partisi* – HDP), are co-led by one man and one woman at each administrative level, and implement voluntary gender quotas to guarantee a minimum of 30–40 per cent representation by gender. With BDP's success in ensuring that at least 40 per cent of their representatives were women in the 2007 national elections, Turkish women's rights activists have been lobbying for the adoption of gender-neutral quotas of 50 per cent, to increase women's political representation. However, as of 2021, no other major Turkish party has formally adopted gender quotas to be applied to their parliamentary candidate lists, though most parties have – at least in theory – internal party quotas to ensure women's presence throughout the party structure, as discussed in the following chapter.

Conclusion

Women's rights groups are key actors in increasing women's political representation, both in terms of numbers (descriptive representation) and in addressing women's interests (substantive representative). The absence of a unified women's movement, as in Turkey, can contribute to women's lower societal and political status, including access to political decision-making positions. The decades-long ideological split between secular and pious women's groups, which has its roots in the early Republican era's secularisation projects and prohibition of independent women's organisations, has negatively impacted Turkish women's activism. Women's bodies/dress has been a particular source of contention between secular and pious women's groups throughout Turkish history. Although feminist consciousness has played a role since the Ottoman era, feminist organising in Turkey began to make real impacts on politics and women's rights following the 1980 military coup. The activities of such women's groups in recent decades have begun to tackle Turkish women's under-representation in formal politics.

Today, Turkish women's rights activism is a key democratic force in Turkey's politics. Turkey's transformation from state feminism to multiple feminisms has at times brought together previously opposing groups of women, namely pious, secular and Kurdish, to combat male dominance in politics. Women such as Hidayet Tuksal, the feminist theologian I cited earlier in this chapter, highlight the complex identities of pious women who adhere to a secular political framework, while seeking to build alliances with other women's groups and engage in strategic interactions with ruling elites. Such complexities of the current Turkish women's movement can force the ruling elites to be more responsive to women's demands for democracy, gender equality and justice, including freedom of expression. Significantly, women's rights groups across the ideological spectrum have been among the boldest proponents of democracy and human rights, actively resisting Turkey's increasing authoritarianism. The Gezi Park protests in 2013 clearly demonstrated women's courageous stance against autocracy. Such fierceness has intensified in recent years, with increasing outspoken women demanding peace, justice, equality and democracy, including among women who were previously supporters of the ruling AKP.

4

STRATEGIC INTERACTIONS:
MULTI-PARTY POLITICS AND THE
LOBBY FOR FEMALE REPRESENTATION

'Although politics in Turkey is a man's world, women are learning how to play by the rules, *and* at the same time, manipulate the system to their advantage.' These are the words of a well-known female journalist who lost her campaign for a parliamentary seat in 2007 (personal interview, 27 July 2010). Throughout our interview, her emphasis on the need to 'play the political game' to attain decision-making positions spurred me to further analyse women's engagement with party politics, in particular the ways women strategically 'play' the political and electoral rules and systems to their advantage. This led me to explore what significant opportunities and obstacles have influenced women's political representation in Turkey, and in particular to uncover the factors supporting the notable rise in the percentage of female parliamentarians over the past several elections from 4.4 per cent in 2002 to 17.3 per cent in 2018.

In this chapter I demonstrate that this increase in female parliamentary representation is largely due to women's strategic manipulation of the opportunity structure of party competition. Specifically, three important factors engendered the successful exploitation of the multi-party electoral structure by diverse women's rights groups to expand women's access to parliament. First, in contrast with Iran, the institutionalisation of political parties has a long history in Turkey. Since the transition from single-party rule to multi-party elections in 1946, most Turkish political parties have prioritised creating organised and widespread party structures including at the grass-roots level, with women's branches at all levels. In recent decades women have been increasingly involved in party organising and voter recruitment through participation in women's branches, which in turn provides women with a direct channel to male party elites. Second, Turkey utilises the List Proportional Representation (List PR) electoral system, which research shows is more supportive of female candidacy and representation compared with majoritarian systems (Matland and Studlar 1996, 1998; Meier 2004).[1] Finally, the successful implementation of gender quotas by one party encouraged women's groups to pressure other parties to follow suit. These three factors have fostered competition for women's votes among the major parties in Turkey, to the benefit of women's rights activists.

After years of fighting for female political representation, many independent and party-affiliated women's groups are well equipped to exploit such opportunities, pressuring party elites to increase women's access to political office or risk losing women's votes and political viability. As I will show, one event in particular raised the stakes in this regard. A small pro-Kurdish rights political party successfully implemented voluntary gender quotas on its candidate lists for the 2007 parliamentary elections (and for subsequent national elections); women's rights activists and party women subsequently lobbied other major parties, including conservative ones, to do the same, using the power of women's votes to press their point. Their extensive organising and lobbying met with a certain willingness on the part of political elites to nominate and recruit more women, to broaden their parties' electoral appeal. This responsiveness illustrates the dialectical relationship that can emerge between women's groups and male elites to advance women's political rights, as they influence and inform one another to address their own interests (Chappell 2002; Waylen 2007).

The notable increase in women in Turkish national politics over the past two decades can be attributed to other factors as well, including a global movement to increase women's presence in political decision-making. This

---

[1] Turkey utilises a closed-list proportional representation system under which parties create a ranked list of candidates for each constituency and citizens vote for a party, not a specific candidate. Each party is awarded seats in proportion to its share of the votes received. Thus, the higher on the list the candidate, the more likely s/he is to win a seat. List PR systems can be favourable to women candidates if the party wishes to promote gender-balance and/ or female representation by nominating women, and by placing them high on its list. In this system parties tend to nominate women to their lists in order to broaden their appeal (Virgint 2016).

international momentum coupled with Turkey's shifting dynamic wherein women are increasingly politicised has made it costly for party leaders to ignore demands for women's political representation. However, despite their effective capitalising on party competition at the national level, Turkish women continue to face obstacles to being elected. For instance, while the current electoral system includes woman-friendly features such as ballot selection of party candidate lists rather than individual candidates as performed under majoritarian systems, the process of candidate selection and ranking remains in the hands of male party leaders. Hence, while more parties have women on their lists, women rarely appear at the very top of lists, with many parties placing female candidates in unwinnable positions low on the list (personal interview with the Association for the Support of Women Candidates (KADER) board members, 2011, 2015 and 2019). These aspects of the Turkish electoral system challenge the assumption that a List PR electoral system inevitably promotes women's political representation, suggesting that further analysis of factors contributing to the system's actual impacts would be helpful. Additionally, the recent increases in women's political representation at the national level have not been replicated at the local level, where women's access to district, municipal, village and other local councils continues to be well below 5 per cent. In part this is because political parties and local women's rights groups have prioritised female representation at the national level, which is in turn a function of the international community's emphasis on and support for women's access to national politics (personal interview with KADER board member, 17 May 2015). Furthermore, the successful gender quota implemented by the pro-Kurdish rights party, which influenced similar measures by other major parties, was only applied at the national level, since at the local level, pro-Kurdish parties are only viable competitors in Kurdish-dominated districts.

Impact of Electoral Competition

Electoral competition between multiple political parties, that is elections involving three or more parties, as briefly introduced in Chapter 2, is considered a major political opportunity structure enabling women's rights activists to pressure party leaders to address women's political under-representation and further democratise politics (Adams 2012; Baldez 2004; Kenny and Mackay 2014; Krook 2009; Matland and Studlar 1996, 1998; Meier 2004). As parties strategise to increase support during election campaigns they tend to adopt successful electoral strategies that appear to be winning support for their competitors.[2] With the increasing global and domestic rhetoric on democracy and gender equality, and the ongoing successful politicisation of women by women's rights movements concerning female access to political decision-making positions, platforms promoting women's access to parliamentary seats are increasingly seen as an important electoral strategy in both the West and the Muslim world (Baldez 2004; Krook 2009; Phillips 1991; 1998a). Women's groups strategically cultivate and broadcast grass-roots calls for democratisation and gender balance in politics to legitimise their lobby for more representative legislative bodies.

Gender quotas are a quick and publicly prominent way for political parties to promote and increase female representation and gain attention and support in the process, and are thus widely used (Krook 2009). As a result, much of the scholarship on party competition and women's representation focuses on trends in party quota adoption. For instance, Matland and Studlar (1996) and Phillips (1998a), who write on women's access to national parliaments in Western contexts, argue that as smaller but competitive parties start to actively promote women through quotas, larger parties will begin to emulate them.

Gender quotas have been on the rise as countries transition to democracy, exemplified by the wave of quota adoption in Latin America, where the nomination of more women onto party lists has served as a democratising strategy that also broadens electoral appeal. In the Latin American context smaller and leftist parties have also proven there is no electoral penalty associated with running female candidates. Rather, by visibly championing gender balance in politics this strategy fosters the appearance of party support for true representative democracy, though in reality candidate nomination remains in the hands of the (generally male) party leadership (Baldez 2004: 234). While the increasing use of gender quotas has been documented in Western democracies since the early 1970s (Dahlerup and Freidenvall 2005; Krook 2006, 2009), recent research indicates that the desire to appear 'woman-friendly', 'democratic' and hence 'modern' by promoting female

---

[2] For instance, when Norwegian and German leftist and smaller parties increased the percentage of women on their party lists through the adoption of quotas, conservative parties followed suit for fear of otherwise losing votes to these smaller parties (Matland and Studlar 1996; Phillips 1998a).

representation or nominating women to leadership positions is on the rise in Muslim societies as well (Abou-Zeid 2006; Ben Shitrit 2016b; Kang 2009; Tajali 2013), particularly as the international community and electorates are becoming increasingly attentive to human rights, democracy, gender equality and social development issues (Towns 2010; Tripp *et al.* 2009). Indeed, research by Lihi Ben Shitrit (2016b) documents that even ultraconservative religious parties in the Middle East, including Hamas in Palestine and the Egyptian Muslim Brothers, were forced by gender quotas to support female candidacy in ways that have helped to legitimise the principle of women in politics and support female representation.

Turkey is no exception to global trends towards democratisation and gender equality, where calls for democracy and transparency remain a public priority. These calls strengthened after the 1980 coup, following which diverse ideological groups, including the Islamist movement, formed political parties to compete in elections (Wuthrich 2015). The 1980s and 1990s also witnessed the strengthening of Turkish women's rights movements, successfully campaigning for various important reforms, including addressing violence against women and patriarchal aspects of the Turkish penal code. Since 1999, when Turkey became an official candidate for EU membership, its democratisation efforts, institutional development, and respect for minority and women's rights have come under global scrutiny. Notably, one of the conditions set by the EU for Turkey's accession was legislation of gender equality in various arenas, including in formal politics. The Turkish public's demands for pluralism coupled with international support for democracy has resulted in an increase in party competition in Turkish elections, with anywhere between twelve and eighteen parties competing in general elections, though generally only three or four win parliamentary seats due to rules requiring a minimum 10 per cent of the national vote to enter parliament, as explained below.

My ethnographic and empirical research on the past two decades of Turkish general elections shows that party competition has indeed provided women's rights groups in Turkey with an important opportunity to notably expand women's access to parliament given the three key factors listed above. Women's descriptive representation in the national parliament rose again in 2018 to 17.3 per cent from 14.7 per cent the previous term, largely because of the willingness of political elites to nominate women (see Table 3.1 in previous chapter). In this election, the leftist pro-Kurdish HDP (People's

Democratic Party) and conservative AKP (Justice and Development Party) sent twenty-five and fifty-three women to parliament respectively, three-quarters of all female MPs elected (seventy-eight out of a total 104). HDP's high levels of women's nomination and elections are thanks to its voluntary gender quota, while AKP has remained outspoken in its opposition to formal gender quotas; despite this, 21 per cent of AKP's parliamentary candidates were women, and almost half of these won seats.[3] High-ranking AKP women shared with me that their party has an informal quota for the parliament, in which women compose around 20 to 30 per cent of those elected (personal interview, 2 September 2019).

Political Party Structures: The Power of Women's Branches

As discussed in the previous chapter, in a novel move in 1923, Mustafa Kemal and his co-founders sought to establish a parliamentary Turkish Republic, at a time when many of its surrounding neighbours, including Iran, maintained their monarchical rule. Although for its first few decades Turkey had single-party rule (Kemal's secularist People's Republican Party or CHP), its founding principle of republicanism nonetheless supported the prospect of future multi-party electoral competition. Turkey held its first multi-party election in 1946, and the following election in 1950 saw the breakaway Democratic Party (DP) upend the CHP's longstanding single-party rule. In the ensuing decades there has been a proliferation of political parties.

Ironically, democratisation of Turkish politics with its move away from single-party rule led to a decline in women's parliamentary presence (from 3.7 per cent in the 1943 elections to 1.9 per cent and 0.6 per cent in the 1946 and 1950 elections, respectively). This was largely because fierce competition between CHP and DP resulted in these parties prioritising gaining popular support over the decades-long CHP strategy to ensure women's parliamentary access as a marker of its modern stance.[4] However, the birth of multi-party politics engendered competition for votes, including women's

---

[3] As Table 3.7 of the previous chapter illustrates, in 2018, in contrast to the strong performance of HDP followed by AKP, secular CHP elected only 12 per cent women (18 of its 137 female candidates), in part because the party did not rank enough women sufficiently high on the party lists to enable their election.

[4] As further elaborated on, when competition is fierce between two parties, women's political recruitment may not receive sufficient attention by either party. This can however change when three or more parties compete, and one takes the lead in including women.

votes, spurring the formation of women's branches within political parties. The CHP was the first to establish a women's branch, in 1955, following its loss to DP. Cavdar argues, 'While [women's] visibility and participation as representatives and politicians declined with the introduction of the multi-party system, women became more influential than before as actual voters' (2006: 98–9). The early women's branches operated mostly during elections, to mobilise the female electorate and provide venues for women to discuss the branch party's goals and objectives. CHP women's branches during this era focused particularly on raising women's awareness of Kemal's legacy on women's rights. Though limited in scope and reach, this was the beginning of grass-roots voter mobilisation. In fact, most women's branches were dormant if not defunct between election campaigns, meaning direct links between the female electorate and party headquarters ceased following elections.

In the aftermath of the 1980 military coup, Turkish political parties, spearheaded by parties rising out of Turkey's Islamist movement, became increasingly effective at grass-roots political organising (Eligur 2010). The Islamist movement recognised the importance of mass support at the local level, particularly from the large disenfranchised segments of society, namely religious and rural populations. The *Refah* (Welfare) Party (1983–98), founded under the leadership of Necmettin Erbakan, aimed to mobilise mass support for reforming Turkey's secular-democratic structure into a type of Islamic democracy. *Refah* party activists embraced all segments of society regardless of class, gender, ethnicity or faith, attempting to build a network around a 'politicized collective identity' (Eligur 2010: 10–11). A key distinctive feature of *Refah*, which set it apart from many conventional parties in Turkey, was its creation and maintenance of strong, direct links between members and supporters at the local level and the party leadership in Ankara, while continuing to function hierarchically with top-down decision-making. Spreading the party's message was accomplished through *Refah*'s comprehensive party network that reached all the way down to local neighbourhoods.

Through the establishment of women's branches (called Ladies' Commissions)[5] across the country, *Refah* was able to cultivate and mobilise a female base and politicise previously marginalised segments of Turkish society. Moving beyond the CHP's intentions for women's branches as gathering

---

[5] See Arat (2005: 41–3) for more on the history of *Refah* and the choice to call the Women's branches Ladies' Commissions.

places for women, *Refah* party leaders, including Recep Tayyip Erdogan,[6] prioritised the establishment of women's branches for the purpose of voter recruitment and grass-roots election organising. In the run-up to the 1995 general election, the efforts of *Refah*'s Ladies' Commissions mobilised close to a million women to vote for the party (Arat 2005: 8), increasing *Refah*'s seats in parliament to 158 from sixty-two in the previous election and helping it to victory with 21.4 per cent of the vote out of a field of thirteen competing parties.

Refah's Ladies' Commissions arranged neighbourhood gatherings, home visits, tea parties, and other voter-recruitment events. While these efforts initially focused on politicising and mobilising women to support the party, the leadership also recognised women's great influence on male household members' voting choices, and thus intentionally worked to spread its political message out from the Ladies' Commissions into households and local districts. Pious women who supported *Refah*'s religious and populist message welcomed the opportunity to become political actors for a party in line with their religious and ideological convictions. The party's conservative/faith-based platform helped legitimise women's political engagement and presence in the public sphere as grass-roots organisers; in fact, some women heralded their political involvement a form of religious activity. Ethnographic research on *Refah* party women's activism in the conservative and lower-middle class neighbourhood of Umraniye found that Ladies' Commissions politically empowered many pious women, and female organisers increasingly began to make demands that were in some respects 'universalist, modernist, and even feminist ideas about women's roles', including demanding that headscarved women have access to university (White 2002: 239–40).

When I began my research in Turkey in the late 2000s, many women activists of *Refah* had transitioned to the AKP or the Islamist *Saadet* (Felicty) party. Many of these women (alongside their relatives) credited the grass-roots focused approach of *Refah* for their eventual politicisation and inclusion in politics. As discussed below, during the 2015 parliamentary elections, I also interviewed a number of AKP women candidates who were

---

[6] Erdogan, who found his way to politics through the youth branches of the Islamist National Salvation Party (*Millî Selâmet Partisi* – MSP) in the 1970s, become the head of *Refah*'s Istanbul branch, and was eventually elected Mayor of Istanbul in 1994, recognising the value of grass-roots mobilisation.

the daughters and relatives of former *Refah* women activists, highlighting the extent that activism even at lower party echelons as it was in *Refah* in the 1990s, can pave the way for women to enter politics, including in leadership roles.

The successful organising and voter mobilisation of *Refah* women's branches in the mid-1990s spurred other Turkish parties to emulate them. Most of Turkey's major parties now have similarly structured networks at each level of Turkish administrative hierarchy; parties thus have national, provincial (*il*), district (*ilce*) and neighbourhood (*mahalle*) women's branches.[7] While women's branches or commissions are often headquartered in a party's central office in Ankara, they are replicated at each administrative level.[8]

AKP Kadın Kolları

Since its founding in 2001, *Refah*'s successor party the ruling AKP has been particularly successful in applying the lessons of effective grass-roots mobilisation and voter recruitment through its auxiliary women's branches that is integrated within party organisation at all administrative levels. Similar to *Refah*, AKP provincial, district and neighbourhood offices across the country, even in many remote areas, generally include a women's branch (*Kadın Kolları*). At the headquarter level in Ankara, the Chairwoman of AKP Women's Branch (*Genel Merkez Kadın Kolları*), elected like all deputy chairpersons during the party congress from a list of candidates prepared by the party leadership, also sits on the party's twenty-one-member Central Executive Committee (*Merkez Yürütme Kurulu*) to represent women's interests on the AKP main executive organ (Evans and Efe 2012). According to official party documents, AKP's women's branch has two primary responsibilities: (1) to organise at the neighbourhood, district, provincial and headquarter levels to assist in institutionalising, increasing, enhancing, auditing and guiding women's issues

---

[7] There are eighty-one provinces (*iller*) in Turkey, which are divided into 957 districts (*ilceler*). The districts are further divided into neighbourhoods according to population density.

[8] The exception being some leftist pro-Kurdish minority rights parties. For example, HDP (People's Democratic Party) has a Women's Congress not women's branches, which as discussed below, arguably may end up marginalising women's issues from the main party discourse. According to party guidelines, the Women's Congress has independent authority and its primary mission is to mainstream women's concerns into the workings of the party (Tajali 2015a).

onto the larger party agenda; and (2) to increase women's social, political and economic participation and awareness through national and international projects and activities (AK Parti 2011). AKP's women's branch often lauds itself as 'the largest political women's organization in the world'; as of April 2020, its Chairwoman, Lütfiye Selva Çam, claimed that AKP had over 4.7 million female members, while the membership for the entire party was just over 10 million, meaning that almost half of AKP members are female (AK Parti 2011; Fazli 2020).

Many of my informants credited the repeated electoral success of AKP since its initial rise to power in 2002 to its organisational network's mobilisation and politicisation of supporters, and to the commitment of AKP workers and volunteers. According to a Turkish women's rights scholar, unlike other parties, AKP organisers are active year-round and between election cycles, rather than just around elections (personal interview, 14 July 2010). Indeed, my field visits to Turkey during general elections revealed the organisational power of the party's Women's Branch at every administrative level to connect candidates, particularly female candidates, with constituents. Face-to-face meetings with various constituents ranging from business owners to educators to housewives are crucial during the allotted one-month campaign period, and women's branches are well positioned to organise high-impact meetings with important local groups in a timely manner. As I followed female parliamentary candidates on their campaigns, I realised that every hour of the day (usually beginning at 7:30 in the morning and ending at 11:00 at night) was organised with input from the women's branches in the district that they were visiting. A typical day began with an early morning meeting in the local branch office to confirm the day's schedule. Usually by 8 a.m., often accompanied by high-ranking local branch women, the candidate set off for a series of 'meet and greets' with constituents, rolling through the streets in a campaign van bearing their image and the party logo, music blaring as loudspeakers announced the candidate's presence (see Figure 4.1). Women candidates are able to access spaces that are either private, such as homes, or gendered female, such as nursing homes, daycares, or women's factories, spaces social norms render off-limits to their male counterparts. Conversely, there are few contexts socially barred to female candidates, who thus ably campaigned in male-dominated spaces such as coffee shops, businesses and vocational schools alongside their male peers. Hence, despite AKP's conservative stance, with the support of women's branch members

Figure 4.1 AKP women campaigning in Istanbul during the June 2015 election. Left: AKP parliamentary candidate Ravza Kavakci campaigning in Istanbul's Beykoz district in May 2015. Right: A typical AKP campaign van, this one promoting parliamentary candidate Seyma Dogucu in Istanbul. (Images by author.)

female candidates were well positioned for effective public campaigning, at times even more intensely than their male counterparts.

Witnessing the level of women's political interest and influence, AKP's *Kadın Kolları* has also developed training courses for women at all administrative levels to increase their political roles. '*Kadın Kolları* acts as schools of politics for women', according to a high-ranking official of the AKP Women's Branch Headquarters in Ankara. In her explanation, this official discussed that party organisation at different administrative levels – ranging from the neighbourhood to the province – hold regular training for women members of their respective *Kadın Kolları* on how best to address their economic, social or political problems, while also educating them on key political structures and processes. 'These training courses are an important way to not only discuss women's issues and concerns at the local level, but also empower them to aspire for political posts that can potentially address them.' These training modules are budgeted for by the central party branches at each administrative level, and are a way of contributing to 'women's empowerment in Turkish society', which was a central objective of the party according to this *Kadın Kolları* official (personal interview, 2 September 2019). A close study of such training courses and seminars as advertised on *Kadın Kolları*'s website reveals that they cover various general themes as opposed to providing focused training on running for political office similar to the ones offered by the non-governmental Association for the Support of Women Candidates (KADER). Hence, while the participants on such training courses are educated on various ways of addressing their political and economic concerns, it is unclear whether they are trained in successful campaigning strategies for political office, or how to build coalitions on women's rights, topics that KADER covers in their training courses.[9]

The training support for local women is complemented with an elaborate computerised feedback system that allows members and officials at women's branches across the country to anonymously submit the concerns or issues of their constituents to the *Genel Merkez Kadın Kolları* in Ankara. 'This system was created so that we can track women's needs and issues at every corner of the country, and then strategize on ways to address them' (personal interview, 2 September 2019). Roughly 30 per cent of the total annual party budget is allocated to its *Kadın Kolları*, much of which is spent on funding such projects. Most of the activists of *Kadın Kolları*, whether at the local or the headquarter levels, work voluntarily.

The impact of women's branches on party competition

The multi-level organisational structure of Turkish parties, particularly grass-roots mobilisation mechanisms, has significantly shaped party competition in Turkish politics; increasing reliance on grass-roots organising means the demands of constituents are more likely to be heard and addressed by parties vying for electoral support. Since women constitute half the electorate, Turkish political parties across the ideological spectrum are working to appeal to and mobilise women, increasingly through encouraging their participation within the party. This has engendered increasingly widespread politicisation among Turkish women, who have come to expect responsiveness to their demands from politicians, including the demand for increased female access to positions of authority.

Party women's branches were initially created to foster voter support during elections, and parties such as *Refah* rarely imagined women's roles within the party progressing beyond the function of grass-roots 'foot-soldiers' to help win elections; however, increasingly there is a push both within and outside of party structures to expand women's political participation, includ-

---

[9] *Kadın Kolları* regularly advertises its training courses and seminars, such as one held in March 2019, titled, 'Financial Literacy Mobilization', held in all eighty-one provinces. For more information, visit http://kadinkollari.akparti.org.tr/haberler/finansal-okuryazarlik-sef erberligi-semineri-81-ilimizde-gerceklesti.

ing nomination and recruitment to high-level office. Internally, this push is being driven by the many women, often from parties' women's branches, who have devoted much of their adult lives to grass-roots party organising and who are increasingly demanding greater representation in higher party echelons and political office. After decades of activism and consequent hard-earned political experience, many party women feel the time has come for their share in decision-making to shape and influence the direction of their parties, their communities and their nation (personal interview with an AKP member, 15 June 2011).

A number of non-affiliated women's rights activists and groups view party women's branches as key channels for directing more women into political leadership positions, driving the push to increase women's political representation in Turkey. Among them, the Association for the Support of Women Candidates (KADER) has devoted the past decades to campaign extensively, lobby, and publicly pressure major parties to address women's political under-representation, while it also trains women to run and serve in political office. KADER links with party women's branches to reach and recruit already politicised women for the periodic training sessions it runs to encourage and prepare women for political leadership. The campaigning efforts of KADER over the past decades and other women's rights groups have helped politicise the Turkish electorate on the importance of women's political presence, fostering public interest in scrutinising parties' rates of female nomination. Not surprisingly, this has spurred competition between parties to out-nominate and out-recruit their rivals in terms of female candidates. I was told by one pious parliamentary candidate that the conservative pro-religious parties that succeeded *Refah* had no choice but to support increased female parliamentary representation after a great deal of castigation from secular parties and feminists, who accused them of exploiting women's grass-roots efforts during election campaigns while denying them real political power (personal Interview, 30 May 2011).

Additionally, party women's branches have provided women's rights groups with direct channels to influence and pressure party leaders to address women's political under-representation. For instance, KADER's training courses bring together women from all political parties for workshops, including on the importance of female representation at every level. This message reaches party leadership when female party-member participants in KADER workshops discover the shortcomings of their respective parties around the political recruitment of women, and bring pressure to bear on leaders. In turn, parties are spurred to outdo each other to gain support from the female electorate.

However, Turkish party women's branches have also been subject to criticism by feminist scholars, who accuse them of acting to segregate rather than integrate women and 'women's issues' into party politics (Arat 2005; Cavdar 2006). Cavdar argues that separate women's organisations within parties can lead to the 'creation of "ghettos" of women, which generally enjoy a degree of autonomy within their own organizations but have little to no impact on the central party organization, where all the significant decisions are made' (2006: 96). KADER and other feminist organisations also note that women's branches can negatively impact women's political representation in Turkey. According to KADER board member and trainer Fezal Gulfidan, women's branches can become a way for parties to 'seem as if they are interested in women's issues and their representation', when in reality their primary interest is in capturing women's votes. Gulfidan also told me that members of the women's branches, which are often separated from the main party structure, are rarely provided with opportunities to rise to higher party echelons and leadership positions (personal interview, 20 July 2010). Given these shortcomings, KADER's training of party women branch members is critical, alongside calling for the adoption of legal quotas to guarantee a minimum percentage of female representation.[10] Other Turkish feminists insist that the elimination of party women's branches, or their replacement by other mechanisms, will help support women's integration into the central party structure (personal interview, 17 May 2015).

While many of the criticisms directed at party women's branches are valid, my research demonstrates they are an increasingly important means of expanding women's political presence. Despite their degree of segregation from central party structure, as substantive departments at every administrative level from the central to the local, women's branches have been fundamental to mobilising and politicising masses of women across the country, a key step in the process of stimulating women's interest in and engagement with institutional party politics while familiarising potential female

---

[10] KADER proposes adoption of constitutional gender quotas, with sanctions for parties that do not conform, to guarantee female parliamentary presence in sufficient numbers (personal interview with Fezal Gulfidan, 20 July 2010).

candidates with the needs of their communities. Indeed, throughout my field research in Turkey, I encountered scores of party women aspiring to run for political office and reap the fruits of their efforts after years of devoted activism within women's branches. This was particularly true of AKP women activists, whose political organising accounted for a great deal of the party's continued electoral success. As I later explain in Chapter 7, the absence of similar party structures in Iran has greatly hindered women's rise to political office, who are missing a vital channel to become politically experienced.

Female party activists of the earlier generation have clearly inspired and paved the way for new generations of aspiring female politicians, as evidenced by the daughters, nieces and granddaughters of former *Refah* women's branch members who are increasingly considered for political positions. One such candidate was Fatma Betul Sayan Kaya, whom I met in May 2015 while she was campaigning for a parliamentary seat in Istanbul's third district on behalf of AKP. As I followed this young, American-educated medical doctor on her campaign for one day, I found her enthusiasm and dynamic campaigning remarkable, especially since her election was far from guaranteed given her sixteenth position on the closed party list in a thirty-one-member district, where only the top fifteen listed AKP candidates had won seats in the previous election. Over the course of the day, Dr Sayan Kaya lauded the work done by women of her party before her to 'bring our party to where it is today'. Her own mother had been a long-time women's branch activist during the *Refah* period, and later helped found AKP's women's branch:

> Even most of the men in our party (*Refah*) did not believe that Erdogan would become [Istanbul's] mayor [in the 1994 local elections], but the women believed in him and worked very hard for his victory, all as volunteers. Both of my parents were heavily involved in party politics. Their devotion to the party meant that by age eleven, I had taken over the household chores, looking after my younger sister and cooking. (Personal interview, 8 May 2015)

Her family's devotion to the party, and particularly her mother's involvement, inspired Sayan Kaya to follow in their footsteps, 'to help my people'. She held several high-ranking positions in AKP's Istanbul branch starting in 2009, including Deputy Chairperson for Publicity and Media. When I asked if she was satisfied with her sixteenth place ranking on the party list given her years of activism, she responded, 'Of course not! There are thirteen men in front of me!' Sayan Kaya was not counting the two women candidates that AKP had ranked higher on the list in that district, one in the second and the other in the sixth position. 'If I don't succeed, and only two women enter the parliament from this district, that is too little . . . I expect more from my party.' She added, 'I like them (my male co-candidates), but women are self-sacrificing (*fedakar*) and continuously give, but are rarely acknowledged' (personal interview, 8 May 2015). Sayan Kaya's dismay over her rank on the closed party list was exacerbated by the pro-Kurdish HDP implementation of a much-desired party rule requiring at least every third candidate from the top of the list down to be a woman.

Sayan Kaya did not win a seat in the June 2015 general elections, the first election that AKP failed to secure a majority of the 550 seats since rising to power. However, AKP's failure to form a coalition government following the June elections resulted in a snap general election in November 2015. This time AKP ranked Dr Sayan Kaya in fifth position, in a different Istanbul district, directly behind another experienced AKP woman, Ayşe Nur Bahçekapılı, a two-term parliamentary incumbent.[11] Not surprisingly, this time Sayan Kaya won a seat and Prime Minister Binali Yıldırım named her Minister for Family and Social Policies in 2016, a role she served until July 2018, when the new presidential system took effect.[12] Today, Sayan Kaya is one of AKP's most influential female politicians; in the 2018 parliamentary elections she was ranked second on the list for her Istanbul district (Milliyet Haber 2018). Her rapid rise in the span of only three years speaks to her own and her family's legacy of hard work and devotion to the party, and her conviction that women must gain their share of political power. These also surely played a part in her party's willingness to quickly address Sayan Kaya's dissatisfaction over her low rank on the list in the June 2015 election.

Many women's branch members are increasingly critical of the recruitment of female parliamentary candidates from outside party structures, under

---

[11] In the November 2015 snap general election, AKP regained its parliamentary majority. However, the percentage of total female parliamentarians dropped by roughly three points to 14.7 per cent from 17.8 per cent in the June elections.

[12] Most AKP cabinets have had at least one female minister, usually Minister of Family and Social Policy. In 2018, under the new presidential system, President Erdogan named two women ministers: Zehra Zumurut Selcuk to head the Ministry of Labour, Social Services and Family, and Ruhsar Pekcan as Minister of Trade.

which parties nominate wealthy corporate figures and business owners (or their spouses) who can finance their own campaigns, or celebrities and other public figures of influence who attract votes, rather than unknown party members who have worked for decades at lower party echelons. Their public reproach has shamed many party leaders into nominating more women from within their party structures (Tajali 2017).[13] According to former KADER director Gunul Karahanoglu, the 2015 elections witnessed more party-affiliated female parliamentary candidates ever, including from women's branches; a trend that seems to have been repeated for the 2018 parliamentary elections (Unal 2017). The pro-religious AKP was at the forefront in this regard, in part also due to the lifting of the headscarf ban, which had until 2013 prevented pious female party supporters from competing for political office (personal interview with Gunul Karahanoglu, 7 May 2015). The rise in nominations of party women highlights how grass-roots political engagement in the women's branches can translate into political gains for women in formal political positions.

Though women's rights activists continue to debate the extent to which women's branches help expand female political representation, there is no question they have been a key mechanism for mobilising Turkish women as campaigners and voters, and have enabled pious women's engagement in the political sphere. KADER is hopeful that its training programmes and lobbying efforts will empower party women to demand more access to influential political positions, advance their status in party hierarchy, and increase their influence in Turkish politics. KADER's training sessions for party women focus on raising awareness of their potential power and influence on policy-making, and work to empower them to champion the social, economic and legal inequities faced by Turkish women. Additionally, KADER seeks to educate trainees on existing internal party gender quotas, which are rarely implemented, so that they can call out leaders on non-compliant and discriminatory practices concerning candidate recruitment. This organisation also advocates changing the process for selecting women's branch leaders

---

[13] All parties recruit candidates from outside of the party, particularly in extremely competitive districts. Given women's historical marginalisation from politics, recruiting female candidates from outside party structures especially impacts party women's rise to political office. Thanks in large part to women's protests, this practice is decreasing, and more female candidates are being recruited from within party structures.

from appointment by party leaders, which is the prevailing practice, to election by party members.

Turkey's List Proportional Representation Electoral System and its Shortcomings

The Grand National Assembly of Turkey (*Türkiye Büyük Millet Meclisi*), usually referred to as the *Meclis* (parliament), is Turkey's sole legislative body. With the transition from a parliamentary to a presidential system in 2018, the number of parliamentary seats (*Milletvekili*) increased to 600 from 550, with members elected for a five-year term according to the D'Hondt method, a party-list proportional representation system (List PR). According to this system, voters vote for parties rather than individual candidates, and parliamentary seats are distributed in proportion to the total votes each party receives. Parties present their closed lists for all of the eighty-seven multi-member electoral districts.[14] The number of seats for each district ranges from two to thirty-five (the exception being Bayburt, the only single-member district); in larger districts it is often the case that multiple parties win seats, proportional to the percentage of the vote they receive in that district. So, for example, in the November 2015 election Istanbul's first district, which had thirty-one seats at the time, elected sixteen members from the pro-religious AKP, eleven from secular CHP and two each from the nationalist MHP (Nationalist Movement Party) and the pro-minority HDP (People's Democratic Party).

As noted earlier, many scholars consider proportional representation systems to be more conducive to the election of women compared with majoritarian systems, where voters choose individual candidates rather than a slate of candidates on behalf of a party (Matland 2005; Matland and Studlar 1996). Various elements of the PR system: district and party magnitudes, the formula used in allocation of seats, and the ballot structure, are more responsive to increasing women's access to political participation (Larserud and Taphorn 2007; Paxton and Hughes 2007; Rule and Zimmerman 1994). Because List PR systems present multiple candidates for multiple seats in a given district, they eliminate the pressure to run *the* most 'acceptable' candidate; parties are thus less likely to consider women 'risky' candidates. Larger district magnitudes encourage parties to nominate women in order to broaden their appeal to the female electorate, without risking alienating the

---

[14] In 2018, Turkey's electoral districts increased from eighty-five to eighty-seven.

male electorate. Research in Western democracies has repeatedly shown that the perceived risk of public antipathy towards women candidates is almost completely groundless when multiple parties compete in multi-member districts (Matland and Studlar 1996: 712). In List PR systems gender quotas are more easily implemented, but for a closed-list PR system to be truly favourable to women's election, leaders must promote gender-balance by nominating women and placing them high on their lists.

My analysis shows that in contrast to Iran's majoritarian system, Turkey's proportional representation system is an important opportunity structure for those working to elect more women to parliament. Although historically, since its implementation in 1961, the percentage of female parliamentarians in Turkey has been atypical of a PR system, with women comprising only 1–2 per cent of MPs until the 1990s (see Table 3.1 of the previous chapter), there have been notable increases in recent decades largely thanks to women's rights groups working to bring female political representation on to the public agenda. As an increasingly important democratising force in the post-1980 coup era, Turkish women's rights groups have sought to address the shortcomings and optimise the strengths of the List PR system and address some of the electoral barriers to electing more women MPs.

A significant barrier has been the non-prioritisation of women's political representation by leaders of Turkey's dominant parties. Despite Turkey's move away from single party rule in 1946, for decades Turkish politics was dominated by two parties: the secular CHP and successive main opposition parties, including the Democrat Party, Justice Party (AP), and so on. Fierce two-party competition thwarted the nomination of women, who were considered risk candidates by both parties. Following the 1980 military coup, the adoption of a 10 per cent threshold for parties to enter parliament further hindered the potential for smaller and more leftist parties to enter Turkish politics.[15] Even when major parties were eventually forced by women's groups in the 1980s and 1990s to address the issue of women's access to political office, female candidates were generally ranked too low on party lists to be electable, allowing party leaders to merely pay lip service to female

[15] Turkey requires parties to garner at least 10 per cent of the national vote in order to claim seats in parliament. Upon reaching this national threshold, seats are allocated in proportion to the votes that parties receive at the district level, which can help politicise the electorate at the district level.

nomination. In the closed-list PR system used in Turkey, candidates enter parliament according to their ranking on the party list as decided by party leadership, in proportion to the votes received in a given district by the party (see Figure 4.2). The further down the district party list, the less likely the candidate is to gain a seat. Unlike open lists, voters cannot select their own ranking and express their preference for female candidates; they must vote for the slate, not individuals on the list (Collins 2010).

Recognising the disingenuous move of many parties, including the secular CHP, to mostly nominate women in lower ranks in the party candidate lists, women's groups such as KADER demanded a minimum 30 per cent quota for women on each list, with ranking order rules to ensure that female candidates also appear towards the top (personal interview with Fezal Gulfidan, 20 July 2010). Specifically, in the early 2000s, KADER launched a major campaign to demand that every third candidate from the top of the list down be a woman.[16] Such simple but specific recommendations for addressing female under-representation in Turkish politics are viable in part due to the List PR system. Despite its flaws, Turkey's List PR electoral system has made it possible for women's groups to pressure parties to put forward more gender-balanced candidate lists and to publicly castigate those that do not. As I further demonstrate below, this has been one of several important factors that have engendered improvements in female candidacy and electability as parties compete for support from an increasingly politicised female electorate.

Taking Advantage of Party Competition: Campaigning for Gender Quotas

In addition to an organised and widespread party structure and a women-friendly List PR electoral system, another significant opportunity to exploit inter-party competition in the push for increased female representation presented itself to women's rights groups when a small, leftist party voluntarily adopted gender quotas for the 2007 parliamentary elections. The party's successful implementation of this voluntary quota encouraged women's groups to pressure larger parties to follow suit. KADER, which had worked since the late 1990's to put female representation on the national agenda and began

---

[16] In the June 2015 elections, the pro-Kurdish HDP (in their first attempt to compete in Turkish politics as a party) implemented this rank order rule to ensure that at least one woman is listed in one of the top three slots.

Figure 4.2 Sample ballot for Istanbul's first district for the 2011 election. The ballot, sized at 22 x 96 cm, consists of fourteen party closed lists, each nominating thirty candidates listed below the party symbol and name. This ballot also includes the names of twelve independent candidates running without party affiliation, who may enter parliament if they receive at least 4 per cent of the district votes. Voters mark their choice in the circle provided below the party symbol or the independent candidate's name.

advocating for gender quotas in the early 2000s, was at the forefront of the initiative.

The small but important Democratic People's Party (DEHAP) that took the lead in implementing gender quotas arose from the pro-Kurdish rights movement.[17] In 2004, pressure from its women's branch, along with KADER's campaigning efforts, led the party to adopt a voluntary 40 per cent gender-neutral quota, whereby each gender must comprise a minimum of 40 per cent of any party organ or candidate list.[18] Additionally, the DEHAP introduced a co-leadership system whereby leadership at every level of the party hierarchy is shared by male and female co-chairs (Bilgili 2011). This structural reform, which has persisted in all pro-Kurdish parties, was modelled on the German Green Party to systematise shared decision-making between male and female politicians and administrators, help mobilise female supporters, and created a situation where rural women felt comfortable approaching party leaders with their issues given the presence of a female co-chair at every administrative level (personal interview with a BDP female co-chair, 20 July 2010). The DEHAP experimented with this quota measure for the 2004 local elections, and its successor, the Democratic Society Party (DTP), publicised its use during the 2007 parliamentary elections, which attracted much national attention.

For the 2007 elections, the pro-Kurdish rights DTP ensured that women comprised at least 40 per cent of its candidates most likely to win seats. Given the high threshold of 10 per cent of the national vote needed to enter parliament under a party banner, smaller parties such as DTP fielded their candidates as independents (in which case a winning candidate required a

---

[17] DEHAP was one of the Kurdish pro-rights predecessors to the current People's Democratic Party (HDP). Pro-Kurdish rights political parties, which were first allowed to operate in 1990, have faced numerous closures by the Turkish state for alleged connections to the PKK (Kurdistan Workers' Party) guerilla movement. However, each closure has led to the creation of a new version of the party under a different name. For instance, the pro-Kurdish Democratic Society Party (DTP) was shut down in 2009, but the Peace and Democracy Party (BDP) was established soon after. In 2014, BDP was dissolved and then, in a move to become more inclusive of all minority rights (including Armenians, Alevis, and more), some former BDP leaders founded the People's Democratic Party (HDP). HDP's inclusivity enabled it to reach the 10 per cent threshold and enter parliament as a party for the first time in 2015.

[18] Framing quotas in gender-neutral terms in a male-dominated society allowed the party to deflect somewhat critics who argued that quotas 'undemocratically' advantage women.

minimum of 4 per cent of the vote in their district to gain a seat); once having won seats, DTP MPs acted as a party in parliament. By implementing the quota, women made up a record 40 per cent, or eight of the DTP's twenty MPs; for the dominant AKP and CHP parties, women comprised only around 8 per cent of MPs (see Table 3.3 of the previous chapter). The success of DTP's quota encouraged KADER to revise its quota campaign from lobbying for a 30 per cent female quota to a 50 per cent gender-neutral quota, alternately ranking male and female candidates on party lists in what is termed zipper style. 'Once the pro-Kurdish party showed us it was doable, we realised we needed to demand a 50 per cent quota. They were really ahead of us, even though we're a feminist organisation', one KADER board member told me (personal interview, 16 July 2010). To fan competition for women's votes between parties, KADER worked to raise awareness around the success of DTP in drastically increasing women's political representation, and highlighted the shortcomings of major parties regarding gender inequality in politics. Inspired by DTP and its successor, the Peace and Democracy Party (BDP), KADER launched a '275 Women in Parliament' campaign shortly prior to the June 2011 elections, calling for half the 550 seats in parliament to be filled by women. Although KADER realised that equal representation was not going to happen immediately, it pursued this radical demand as a way to legitimise women's presence in male-dominated Turkish politics; the campaign also created expectations from the Turkish electorate that party leaders respond to the demand for gender equality in politics.[19] According to Fezal Gulfidan, 'We [KADER] consider it a great success that now, prior to national elections, the media and the public discuss how many women have been put forth by each party' (personal interview, 20 July 2010).

In this context, fostered by feminist organising and supported by international calls for greater levels of women's political representation, many Turkish party leaders began to pay more attention to demands for gender balance, as election results showed that the initiatives and rhetoric around inclusion and female representation by leftist pro-Kurdish parties were resonating

---

[19] In the end, while KADER's 2011 gender-balance election campaign fell far short, as expected, it helped increase the percentage of female parliamentarians from 9.1 per cent to 14.4 per cent. The three largest parties coming into parliament increased their rate of female nominations, and two of the three – CHP and MHP – doubled the percentage of female MPs compared with the 2007 elections as Figures 4.3 and 4.4 show.

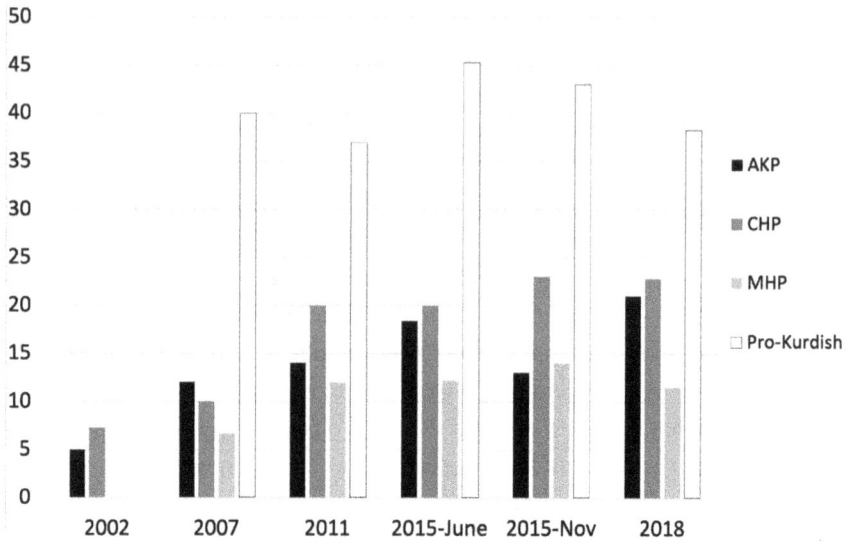

Figure 4.3 Percentage of women candidates by party in 2002–18 parliamentary elections.

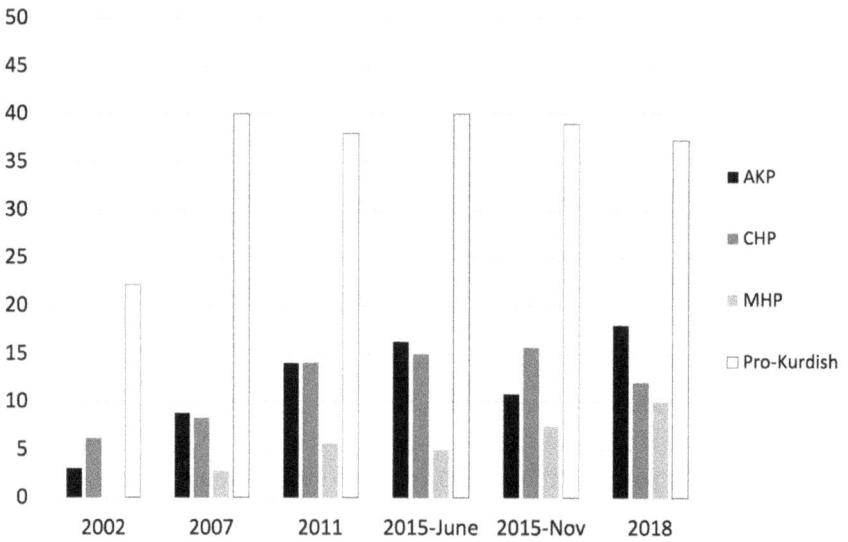

Figure 4.4 Percentage of women elected by party in 2002–18 parliamentary elections.

with large segments of Turkish voters. The public scrutiny and analysis of parties' gender ratios forced even the most resistant party leaders, including those of the main contenders AKP and CHP, to begin increasing women's access to parliament (see Figures 4.3 and 4.4). The leadership of secular CHP, which declares itself a feminist party based on its Kemalist legacy, instituted measures ahead of the 2011 parliamentary elections to increase female candidacy and democratise the candidate selection process, previously entirely in the hands of party leaders.[20] The percentage of CHP female candidates on party lists subsequently doubled to 20 per cent from 10 per cent in the 2007 elections. Despite this notable increase, many observers questioned the party's intentions, given that only 14.07 per cent of CHP candidates elected to parliament were women; the large gap between the percentage of female candidates and percentage of female MPs highlights that many of the female CHP candidates were ranked far too low on their district lists to be electable. The ruling AKP had a more modest increase in female candidates on its party lists, to 14 per cent from 12 per cent in the previous election, but the percentage of AKP female candidates elected (over 14 per cent) closely matched the percentage running. Significantly, in the 2007, 2011 and June 2015 general elections, the two main opposition parties, CHP and AKP, consistently contrived to send almost matching percentages of women to parliament as Figure 4.4 shows, presumably to appear equally 'progressive' or 'woman-friendly' to the electorate. Both parties also oppose formal gender quotas, though CHP has made some efforts towards internal quotas for party structures, with limited success (personal interviews with KADER members, 2011 and 2015).

June 2015 Parliamentary Election and its Aftermath

The June 2015 Turkish parliamentary elections delivered a number of important firsts, some of which drastically shifted the course of national politics. The election not only witnessed the first pro-Kurdish rights party, in this

---

[20] In an effort to democratise the candidate selection process, for the June 2015 elections, CHP introduced primary elections held during its general assembly. From a list of all the potential candidates who registered, party members elected candidates for the closed party lists. With 550 parliamentary seats up for grabs, the party president was allowed to hand-pick only twenty-eight candidates, fourteen of whom would be running in the all-important Istanbul districts, over which party leaders generally like to exercise firm control; the rest were selected by party vote (personal interview with a CHP female incumbent MP, 20 May 2015). The ranking of the final candidates was still in the hands of party leadership.

incarnation the pro-minority People's Democratic Party (HDP), to compete in the election as a party and cross the 10 per cent national threshold by gaining 13.1 per cent of the national vote; it also put an end to thirteen years of AKP majority rule.[21] The June election also witnessed a record number of women elected to parliament, with 17.8 per cent female MPs, an increase of more than 3 per cent from the previous term.

I argue that party competition played a key role in the notable increase in women's parliamentary presence during the June 2015 elections, thanks particularly to the feminist ideology and quota measures of HDP. Indeed, as someone who has extensively investigated dynamics of gender in Turkish elections since the late 2000s through field research, I found the public sentiment ahead of the June 2015 elections to be particularly vibrant, with a wide range of the Turkish population apparently invested in its results, including the gender ratio of parliament. In fact, this was the first general election following the 2013 Gezi Park protests, during which AKP demonstrated its autocratic tendencies when it staged a violent crackdown on peaceful protestors.[22] It was also the first election after the 2013 lifting of the headscarf ban, which removed a major obstacle to women's political representation.[23] In this context, all parties entered into a fierce competition. Among them, AKP was resolute to maintain its majority rule, while HDP was equally determined to win at least 10 per cent of the vote and finally enter parliament as a political party. Recognising that achieving both of these results concurrently was unlikely, both parties redoubled efforts to increase support, particularly from the female electorate, capitalising on the previous work of feminist and women's rights activists.

HDP effectively presented itself as a feminist and pro-minority (as opposed to pro-Kurdish) party, to appeal to other minority groups such

---

[21] HDP's 13.1 per cent of the national vote equated to eighty of a total 550 seats, more than double the number of seats they held in the previous election, when their candidates competed as independents.

[22] The 2013 protests began as a peaceful sit-in to save Gezi Park in Istanbul's Taksim Square from being converted into a commercial centre, challenging AKP's neo-liberalism. However, the violent eviction of the primarily young, environmentalist protestors sparked nationwide protest from many segments of Turkish society, who saw the government's use of force as disproportionate. The supporting protests grew to encompass issues including freedom of expression, of assembly of the press, and more (White 2014).

[23] It can be argued that AKP lifted the headscarf ban in 2013 as a way to regain its legitimacy following its tarnished image from the Gezi Park protests.

Figure 4.5 KADER campaign poster for the 2015 general election. (Credit: Association for the Support of Women Candidates – KADER.)

as Alevis[24] and Armenians, constituents feeling increasingly marginalised by AKP's hegemonic approach. As part of its feminist agenda, HDP publicly declared it would strive for gender parity, with women comprising at least 50 per cent of its candidates, and with zipper-style party lists alternating male and female candidates.[25] Even more radically, HDP adopted a 10 per cent voluntary quota for LGBT candidates, the first party to do so in the Middle East (Tajali 2015a). HDP's progressive, feminist politics was a breath of fresh air for Turkish feminist groups, including KADER. Not surprisingly, KADER viewed HDP's gender platform as an important opportunity to pressure the leadership of the three major parties expected to dominate parliament: AKP, CHP and the nationalist MHP. In a highly publicised campaign poster titled, 'What are we saying and what are you hearing?', KADER compared the reactions of the four major party leaders to the widespread call for more women in political office (see Figure 4.5). KADER's wordplay highlighted HDP's gender-balanced approach, while poking fun at AKP, CHP

[24] Alevis are a heterodox Shia sect that make up more than 10 per cent of the Turkish population (White 2014). In recent elections they tend to support the secularist CHP.

[25] Despite these ambitions, HDP did not succeed in producing gender-equal candidate lists; women made up 45.3 per cent of its candidates for the June 2015 elections. It also failed to implement a zipper-style rank order, but instead ensured that at least one woman's name appeared among the first three candidates on party lists across the country. Since men topped most party lists, and in many districts HDP received only enough votes to send one candidate to parliament, women ended up composing 40 per cent of total HDP MPs entering parliament in June 2015 (see Table 3.5 from Chapter 3).

and MHP leaders' apparently intentional misunderstanding or deafness. For instance, the AKP leader at the time, Ahmet Davutoglu, is portrayed hearing a woman say 'Oh my uncle!' (*Aaa dayım!*), instead of her actual declaration 'I am candidate' (*Adayım*). Of the four parties portrayed on the poster, only HDP's Figen Yüksekdağ and Selahattin Demirtaş acknowledge each other as equals, calling each other '*eş başkan*' (co-leader).

While gender-conservative AKP was not an advocate of gender quotas, leaders knew that support from the female electorate was key in this critical election, particularly from the women who had contributed so much to the party's success in the previous decade. Along with Fatma Betul Sayan Kaya, whose candidacy was discussed earlier, AKP recruited many women from within party structures. It also played up its formal lifting of the headscarf ban in 2013, a move that significantly expanded educational and employment opportunities for a large segment of Turkish women. AKP election billboards all over the country, in every major city and town, boasted of this accomplishment, including a billboard sporting an image of a headscarved woman with the words 'I can now go to University with my headscarf', above the party's campaign slogan 'They Talk; AK Party Does', referring to major reforms delivered by AKP over the course of its rule (see Figure 4.6). For the first time, AKP nominated headscarved women, who, according to a high-ranking Ankara women's branch member, made up 44 per cent of AKP female candidates (personal interview, 11 May 2015). To increase support from the pious female electorate, the party ran several high-profile headscarved female candidates, some of them activists in the decades-long struggle protesting discrimination against headscarved women. These included Ravza Kavakci (in a 'safe' ranking on the party list for Istanbul's first district), the younger sister of Merve Kavakci, an elected Islamist *Fazilet* (Virtue) party MP in 1999 who was prevented from taking the parliamentary oath because of her headscarf.[26] AKP also nominated high-profile, headscarved human rights lawyer and activist Fatma Benli, also in an electable position, on the party list for Istanbul's second district. Running these women candidates in important Istanbul districts at rankings that guaranteed them a seat in parlia-

[26] Merve Kavakci, who for years had lived in the United States following the hostile treatment she experienced after her election, including losing her Turkish citizenship, returned to Turkey prior to the 2015 elections and served as an advisor to the AKP (personal interview with Ravza Kavakci, 15 May 2015).

Figure 4.6 AKP campaign billboard for the 2015 election on finally addressing the headscarf ban. (Image by author.)

ment, served as an important strategy to appeal to the party's female base, many of whom, like Fatma Benli, had devoted much of their adult lives to addressing discrimination against visibly pious women in Turkey's secular context.[27]

HDP's comfortable entry into parliament after gaining 13.1 per cent of the national votes in June 2015 spelled major defeat for AKP, which lost its parliamentary majority, preventing it from delivering on its agenda, including a constitutional reform changing the parliamentary system to a presidential one. In fact, the post-election parliament was unable to form a

---

[27] Fatma Benli has been a high-profile headscarved women's rights activist and lawyer who was personally effected by the secular establishment's headscarf ban (Tavernise 2008). I met her in 2011 as she was working with both domestic women's rights groups (such as AKDER or the Women's Rights against Discrimination Association), as well as the international community (such as the CEDAW Committee's periodic review of Turkey) to address the discriminatory headscarf ban in Turkey (personal interview with Fatma Benli, 30 May 2011).

coalition government and consequently President Erdogan called for a snap election to be held 1 November. The November 2015 election took place in an extremely divisive political climate, particularly between AKP and HDP.[28] AKP blamed its June defeat on HDP, and accused the party's leadership of ties with the Kurdish guerilla group, the Kurdistan Workers Party (PKK). My interviews with those close to party officials highlighted that the hostility and fierce competition between AKP and HDP as they faced off in the snap election engendered a major 'shifting of priorities' for the AKP regarding women's political representation (e.g. Kenny and Mackay 2014; Kittilson 2006: 32). Concern with appealing to the female constituency was no longer considered an important electoral strategy, and AKP reduced its proportion of female candidates from 18.4 per cent to 13 per cent, justified as necessary to 'fix' the candidate lists from June that had resulted in the party's losses (personal interview with KADER board member, 25 October 2015).[29] It appears that in the face of fierce competition for votes against one specific party, AKP leaders considered women to be 'risk candidates'. This observation confirms the significance of meaningful *multi*-party competition, as opposed to dual-party competition, as a key condition for the contagion effect, in terms of enhancing women's political representation.

This finding further complicates our understanding of party competition, which had previously assumed that when a smaller party adopts measures that promote women's candidacy, such as quotas, other larger parties feel pressure to follow suit in an effort to remain competitive (Matland and Studlar 1996). More recent research increasingly highlights the complexities of the contagion effect, in that larger parties 'follow suit' only when the costs of doing so are lower than the potential electoral gains (Kenny and Mackay 2014; Kittilson 2006). AKP's main strategies following the June 2015 elections were designed to defeat HDP, and promoting women's parliamentary presence to appeal to the female electorate was no longer seen as a key means of achieving this. Instead, AKP focused on rhetorically linking HDP with instability and terror in the minds of the Turkish people. Using national-

---

[28] Security threats and bombings, among them bombings in Suruc in July 2015 and Ankara in October 2015 targeting pro-Kurdish and leftist activists that killed close to one hundred activists, exacerbated the divisive political environment, reminiscent of the decades-long clashes between Turkish and Kurdish forces of the 1980s and 1990s.

[29] HDP's percentage of female parliamentary candidates also dropped from the June election to the November election, but insignificantly, from 45.3 per cent to 43 per cent.

ism as a frame, the AKP convinced many constituencies to look beyond HDP's policies of inclusivity, including regarding gender, and made them appear secondary to concerns over national security and border control. On 1 November 2015, AKP regained its majority in parliament; the party's percentage of female MPs dropped to just over 10 per cent from almost 16 per cent the previous June. HDP barely passed the 10 per cent threshold, receiving just 10.76 per cent of the national vote, which translated into fifty-nine of the 550 parliamentary seats, down from eighty seats, though its percentage of female MPs remained almost the same as in June.[30] AKP's victory and the decrease in the number of seats held by HDP led to a notable decrease in female MPs, from 17.8 per cent to 14.9 per cent, causing some commentators to declare Turkish women the biggest losers in the 1 November election, since much of the national discourse around affirmative action measures in support of women's political representation appeared to have been almost reversed in a matter of five months (Tremblay 2015).

The polarised political atmosphere, which intensified with the 2015 elections, spun into ongoing political crises, exacerbated by mounting economic pressures and increasing public distrust of AKP's path forward. In July 2016, a segment of the Turkish military attempted a coup, hoping to topple the government and unseat President Erdogan. Accusing Turkish preacher Fetullah Gulen, self-exiled in the US since 1999 and leader of the religious *Hizmet* (Service) Movement, of instigating the coup, the AKP government declared a state of emergency and began an extensive crackdown on *Hizmet* followers (labelled terrorists by AKP), as well as other opposition groups. Press and academic freedoms were particularly targeted, with many journalists, academics and civil servants removed from their positions as AKP sought to further concentrate its institutional powers. In a final push towards its goal of replacing Turkey's parliamentary system with a presidential one, the AKP held a constitutional referendum in April 2017 on this important matter.

---

[30] Interestingly, CHP and MHP (the other sitting parties in the election), which were not facing off in as fierce a competition as existed between AKP and HDP, increased their percentages of female candidates between the two 2015 elections; both elected their highest percentage of women MPs ever in November.

Women's Political Representation with the Transition to a Presidential System

In the April 2017 constitutional referendum, 51.4 per cent of Turkish voters narrowly approved replacing Turkey's parliamentary system with a presidential one. Arguably the biggest shift in Turkish politics since transitioning from single-party rule to a multi-party system in 1946, Turkey's new presidential system eliminated the position of Prime Minister, strengthening the office of the President, which now acts as both head of state and of government. While detailing the major constitutional amendments that this referendum entailed are beyond the scope of this book, it will suffice to say that most were consistent with previous constitutional referendums of the AKP era, which sought to consolidate more power, such as control over the judiciary and the military, into the party's hands. Some observers argued that many of the reforms were designed with the assumption that AKP would continue its majority rule in the foreseeable future under Erdogan's leadership (Ekim and Kirisci 2017). Similar to the US presidential system, checks and balances between the three branches can be undermined when the president's party controls a critical number of parliamentary seats (which leads to parliament rubberstamping executive decisions). Amid increasing political and economic turmoil in a highly polarised society, the ruling AKP held elections which formalised this transition in June 2018, a year earlier than originally proposed, without lifting the state of emergency.

The number of parliamentary seats under the new system increased to 600 from 550, and the 2018 election witnessed an increase in female MPs from 14.7 per cent in the previous term to 17.3 per cent (equating to 104 women in total), slightly below the 17.8 per cent achieved in June 2015. This was largely thanks to AKP's notable 8 per cent increase in female candidates on party lists, from 13 per cent in the November 2015 elections to 21 per cent in 2018. Having achieved its ultimate goal of strengthening the office of the presidency with the 2017 referendum, it appears that AKP once again turned to wooing the female electorate. Once again AKP looked within the party to recruit many of its female candidates, in a calculated move to reward the women activists who had long supported the party. More importantly, AKP placed a good portion of its female candidates in electable rankings, and following the elections women comprised 18 per cent (fifty-three women) of AKP MPs, only 3 per cent less than their rate of candidacy on party lists.

In contrast, secularist CHP's candidate lists drew much criticism as many women candidates were placed low on the party lists; some publicly withdrew their candidacy in protest (Sevinc 2018). Consequently, although women made up 22.8 per cent of CHP candidates, following the elections women comprised only 12 per cent of CHP parliamentarians.

The second reason for the increase in women's descriptive representation in 2018 was HDP's continued use of gender quotas as part of its feminist ideology. Despite the imprisonment of many HDP leaders following accusations of connections with Kurdish terrorist groups in the aftermath of the 2015 elections, in 2018 HDP's platform of inclusivity, peace and equality resonated with at least 11 per cent of the electorate, bringing the party back into parliament. HDP once again outperformed all other parties with 38.3 per cent female candidates; following the election 37 per cent (twenty-five women) of its sitting MPs were women.[31] Despite this exceptional performance, more than half of all women MPs elected in 2018 were from the AKP.

In the first election under the new presidential system, with six presidential candidates, Recep Tayyip Erdogan won the presidency with more than 52 per cent of the vote. However, Erdogan's AKP failed to gain the majority in parliament, winning 295 out of 600 seats (though the AKP and MHP People's Alliance managed to win 344 seats).[32] As of this writing, it remains to be seen whether the new configuration of the Turkish parliament will lead it to act as a rubberstamp for Erdogan's policies, or if the legislative branch will fight to maintain its constitutionally enshrined checks over the executive (AK Parti 2018).

---

[31] The newly established *Iyi* (Good) Party, led by long-term female politician and 2018 presidential candidate Meral Akşener, was the worst performer: women made up 22.3 per cent of its forty-three candidates, but only three women (7 per cent) won seats (Sevinc 2018).

[32] Prior to the 2018 elections, the AKP-dominated parliament permitted electoral party alliances, to allow smaller parties to form coalitions with larger parties in order achieve the 10 per cent threshold, though each constituent party still receives seats in proportion to the number of votes it garners. AKP entered into an alliance with the conservative right nationalist MHP (National Movement Party), called the People's Alliance, to ensure this much smaller party's entrance to parliament as a potential ally in parliamentary debates/votes. On the other hand, opposition CHP formed the Nation Alliance with the newly established nationalist *Iyi* (Good) Party and the Islamist *Saadet* (Felicity). HDP did not enter any alliances (Shaheen 2018).

Conclusion

The literature on women and politics has recognised party competition as a key opportunity structure that can be exploited by well-prepared groups that have positioned themselves to fight to expand women's access to political leadership positions. In the effort to address women's political under-representation, it is important to recognise the factors conducive to creating party competition. As I have demonstrated here, party competition in Turkey has been facilitated by the existence of organised party structures that reach the grass-roots levels via party women's branches, creating mobilised and politicised female constituents, as well as by a proportional representation electoral system that fosters multi-party competition in multi-member districts. Although some women's rights activists and scholars criticise women's branches as acting to segregate 'women's issues' from the main party structure, my research of the main parties suggests that women's branch members increasingly refuse to be sidelined, and are demanding access to higher-level political positions. By consistently pressuring political parties and effectively campaigning, women have compelled a number of parties to recruit more of their female candidates from within party women's branches, particularly given the years of women's devotion and activism for the party at its lower echelons.

The adoption and successful implementation of voluntary gender quotas by a small leftist party also encouraged women's rights groups to press larger parties to follow suit. This was undertaken in conjunction with extensive public campaigns on the significance of women's access to political leadership. Thus, Turkey's competitive electoral situation, along with effective campaigns by women's rights groups, compelled most of the major political parties to act to increase the percentage of women in parliament and hold on to or increase support from female members and voters. While the larger parties did not adopt gender quotas, they did increase the percentage of female candidates in winnable positions on party lists. As a result of these important recent shifts, a conservative pro-religious party, the AKP, has been in competition with the liberal pro-minority HDP, in terms of women's nomination and election to parliament.

However, the recent push for women's increased access to political office requires attention to certain nuances, such as the distinction between women's descriptive, substantive and symbolic representation (Pitkin 1972).

While this book predominately addresses women's descriptive representation and the recent push to increase the number of women in political decision-making positions, the close study of factors that have led to this rise also shed light on the complexities of women's substantive and symbolic representation. Despite the women-friendly features of Turkey's proportional representation system, which has helped expand women's parliamentary presence as discussed above, various women's rights activists with whom I discussed Turkey's electoral system argued that substantial modifications are required to further democratise Turkish politics and enhance all aspects of women's representation. Their main criticisms included the undemocratic manner by which party leaders nominate candidates onto party lists, and the high (10 per cent) threshold that closes the door to smaller and more liberal parties, some of which keenly support getting more women elected and into office. Male party leaders, as the main gatekeepers to political office, remain overwhelmingly in control of candidate selection, with little input from members. A former board member of KADER pointed to the absence of alliances between female parliamentarians from different parties to pursue women's interests on this undemocratic process, whereby many female MPs feel they owe their positions to party leaders; thus, party loyalty and full support of the party platform trumps any other agenda. KADER has proposed the introduction of primary elections for candidate selection, so that the process is not entirely in the hands of the party leadership (personal interview, 3 June 2011). The high 10 per cent threshold has been another source of controversy in Turkish elections. While its advocates argue that it creates more stable governments by preventing fractured parliaments and multi-small-party coalition governments (Turan 2007), opponents, among them many feminist and women's rights groups that I spoke to, argue that it can lead to unrepresentative parliaments in that it silences smaller parties that tend to be more liberal, and hence more sympathetic to women's issues. The debate on decreasing the 10 per cent electoral threshold is occasionally discussed by the lawmakers, though to date no serious action has been taken on it.

Aware of the system's current pitfalls that constrain their efforts to increase the number of women elected to political offices, Turkish women's rights activists are campaigning for important reforms to Turkey's electoral system, including more democratic processes for candidate selection that bypass control by party elites, and the adoption of legal gender quotas with rank-order rules that guarantee women's access to political decision-making positions. My discussions with various women's groups in Turkey reconfirmed their devotion to address unjust electoral processes in Turkey, particularly given the country's recent authoritarian turn. Despite the extensive crackdowns on civil society, many autonomous women's groups continue to be outspoken.

5

FRAMING FOR POLITICAL INCLUSION: THE DEMAND FOR HEADSCARVED WOMEN'S CANDIDACY

The run-up to Turkey's 2011 parliamentary elections included public debate around the issue of headscarved women's access to parliament. A number of activists I spoke with during this period referred to Fatma Bostan, one of the founding members of the pro-religious AKP, who had gone public urging her party to nominate headscarved candidates. The educated, headscarf-clad Bostan was often mentioned in the media, either as 'brave and outspoken', or as a 'provocateur'. Several months prior to the election, Bostan, who at the time served on AKP's Central Executive Committee, declared her intention to run for parliament, citing her years of political experience and devotion to the party. She also threatened that if party leader Recep Tayyip Erdogan was not ready to nominate her, she would run as an independent to 'pursue her right to political representation', and in effect resign from the party she had helped found in 2001 (personal interview, 15 June 2011).

In the years preceding the 2011 parliamentary election, Turkey appeared on a path towards democratisation, which observers attributed to the diminishing role of the military in state politics, increasing levels of civil society activism, and pressure from the international community including the EU (Atasoy 2005; Kuru and Stepan 2012; Yavuz 2009). But despite promising signs of a more representative democracy, in the wake of the 2011 election, the huge demographic of headscarved women, whom sociologist Dilek Cindoglu (2011) estimated comprises 70 per cent of the Turkish female population, remained highly uncertain that its interests would be represented in the new parliament. Up to that point, this constituency had been excluded from positions of political authority; indeed the civil and political rights of headscarved women had long been subject to serious debate in Turkey, particularly since the 1990s when their presence became more pronounced in urban settings (Gole 1996). The Turkish secular establishment's unease with the electoral victory of political Islam in the mid-1990s and increased visibility of the headscarf in the public sphere eventually led to the banning of this religious symbol, especially in public institutions, such as universities and parliament. The 2011 parliamentary elections, which marked almost a decade since AKP's rise to power, took place amid women's growing frustration with the headscarf ban, and their increasingly vocal calls for qualified women to be nominated regardless of headgear. This demand was particularly directed towards the ruling AKP, a pro-religious party with many headscarved women in its ranks and membership. Many of the headscarved women I interviewed who aspired to political office said they faced discrimination on two fronts: firstly, with respect to male colleagues, and secondly, relative to their bare-headed female peers who are often recruited from outside of party structures, bypassing headscarved party women to run for office (personal interviews with headscarved party women, 2010 and 2011).

As I show in this chapter, activism and campaigns for headscarved women's political rights during this period included an important milestone for the Turkish women's movement and Turkey's democratisation process. For the first time, moderate women from both the secular and pious camps formed strategic coalitions, strengthening the lobby for women's expanded political representation beyond particular ideological and political affiliations. The unifying of women's voices from across the spectrum increased their leverage over the leaders of major parties, who historically had played off the ideological divides between women's rights activists and groups. As a genuine grass-roots call for equal representation, the movement for headscarved women's political rights also sought to further democratise the Turkish parliament by enabling the representation of a marginalised group. Despite vigorous campaigning by Islamic women's groups for their nomination, and the application of around a dozen headscarf-wearing women to be candidates, for the 2011 parliamentary elections none of the major parties, including the AKP, nominated headscarved candidates.[1] However, two years

---

[1] Headscarved women's rights activists demanded institutional change concerning freedom of expression, and hence opposed a select few headscarved women's compromise to remove

later, women's strategic activism contributed to the formal recognition of headscarved women's right to access the parliament when in 2013 the AKP finally lifted restrictions on their access to most public institutions. In the subsequent 2015 parliamentary election, most parties ran headscarved candidates. Expectedly, the AKP took the lead, with headscarved women making up 44 per cent of the party's female candidates, most of them recruited from within the party (personal interview with secretary of AKP Women's Branch Headquarters, 11 May 2015). In the same election the pro-Kurdish HDP, with its platform of inclusivity, ensured that women comprised at least 45 per cent of its total candidates, but headscarved women made up only 10 per cent of its total female candidates (personal interview with HDP headscarved parliamentarian Huda Kaya, 5 May 2015).

Women's organising was effective in that context as activists and organisations were poised to take advantage of the international human rights discourse opportunity structure, predicated on Turkey's growing interest in attracting the support of the international community, particularly the EU, which it hoped to join. This situation greatly enhanced the framing possibilities for demands for political equality from headscarved women and their allies: while pious women are generally linked with conservative pro-religious parties, the framing of their call for the right to run for office using the secular discourse of international human rights spoke to secular institutions and feminist groups. At the same time, as headscarved women they had a legitimacy that could not be dismissed by conservative and pro-religious elites, who were now feeling pressure to overturn gender-biased policy in order to win international approval. In what follows, I demonstrate that a major outcome of pious women's strategic framing was that it brought together women's groups that rarely saw eye-to-eye on women's political representation or public sphere roles. However, it is also the case that despite this important convergence Turkish women's groups remain unable to mobilise and politicise a female bloc to vote based on women's collective interests rather than on party/ideological affiliation. This is largely due to the deep-rooted historical cleavages between Turkey's different ideological factions, which today manifests in the competing party politics between the AKP (recently in combination with the conservative MHP) and its main secular opposition parties, the CHP and

their headscarves once elected, as was settled with one of the seventy-eight AKP female nominees in 2011 (The Associated Press 2011).

HDP. Party leaders of the opposition AKP and CHP have been particularly successful in pivoting women against one another, further undermining the possibilities for a unified women's coalition across party lines.

Strategic Framing Processes in Turkey

As explained in Chapter 1, framing approaches that tap into the broader cultural and political contexts in which they are practiced are most effective in mobilising support and finding resonance with the public and political elites (McCammon *et al.* 2007). According to Gamson and Meyer (1996), opportunities which arise from existing political and cultural realities allow actors to strategically frame their objectives and assign meaning in ways that identify, label and describe events towards furthering their aims. Thus, while opportunities shape movement strategy, movement actions also produce new opportunities. This dynamic interaction between movement actors and opportunities reveals the degree to which actors are agents who make strategic choices within the constraints of existing cultural and institutional structures.

Discursive opportunity structures arising out of a given political and social context shape actor strategy by enabling certain framing processes that garner the most support and yield the most pressure, while effective framing processes can themselves engender other opportunities for actors to construct interpretive schemas whose signification mobilises others and generates change. Actors' engagement in meaning construction and cultural reproduction – in the 'politics of signification' (Benford and Snow 2000: 613) – can lead to important political and cultural openings, including for future social movement activism. Indeed, powerful signifying work can even lead to the creation of 'master frames', which later movements may draw on. For instance, the anti-discriminatory discourse of the civil rights movement enabled the later women's and disability movements to draw upon similar language (Zald 1996).

In this chapter, I present the interaction between structure and agency to explain the evolution of headscarved women's access to political representation in Turkey (Chappell 2002; Waylen 2007). I argue that Turkey's ratification of key international human rights documents, such as the Convention on the Elimination of All Forms of Discrimination against Women (CEDAW), as well as the country's eagerness to appeal to the international community in its bid for EU integration, provided Turkish women with important opportunities, among them the usage of the international human rights discourse.

Turkish women across the ideological spectrum, including pious women, have been able to frame their demands for increased access to political office with reference to international human rights, particularly CEDAW's anti-discriminatory language. I show that although Turkey initially ratified CEDAW in a strategic move to appeal to the international community and without much involvement from women's rights groups, this document has become an important tool in legitimising Turkish women's efforts to expand their political representation. Their framing process, while unsuccessful in getting major parties to nominate headscarved candidates for the 2011 election, succeeded in strengthening and unifying the Turkish women's movement, ultimately leading to the removal of the headscarf ban in 2013.

To make sense of the decision of women's rights groups in Turkey to transform the international human rights document into a discursive opportunity structure for framing headscarved women's access to parliament, it is necessary to first contextualise the nature of the headscarf ban in Turkey.

'The Headscarf has No Place in the Turkish Parliament!'

On 2 May 1999, Merve Kavakci, a headscarved woman elected to parliament from *Fazilet* (Virtue Party), was prevented from taking her oath by members of the opposition Democratic Left Party (*Demokratik Sol Parti*; henceforth, DSP), who jeered her out of parliament. Writing about that day, Kavakci recalls the infamous speech of then Prime Minister Ecevit in the midst of the applause, in which he orchestrates the chanting of 'Get out!' and points to her and yells, 'Put this woman in her place!' Meanwhile, on national television, President Demirel labels her an 'agent provocateur' for wanting to take her oath wearing a headscarf (Kavakci 2010: 76–7). The spectre of a headscarved representative represented a 'deep fundamentalist threat' in the words of President Demirel, and was equated with anti-Turkish and even treasonous sentiments (Shively 2005: 35). The intensely hostile reaction caused *Fazilet* to withdraw its support from Kavakci, and prevented her from attempting to take the oath a second time.

That day marked an important encounter in Turkey between pro-religionists and secularists, played out on the terrain of a woman's body and choice of clothing, both understood to signify a particular political ideology (Tajali 2014). For the DSP, Kavakci's headscarf represented a clear attack on state secularism, nationalism, public unity, progress and modernity. Kavakci was prevented from serving her parliamentary role because of her headscarf;

her male and bare-headed female *Fazilet* party colleagues in parliament carried on, because, as Kavakci notes, 'The most "backward" Islamist man was still better than a headscarved woman in the eyes of the regime, and hence was entitled to be in the parliament' (2010: 78). Nonetheless, months after the 'Kavakci affair', the State Prosecutor opened a case against the *Fazilet* party, despite the party leadership's public censure and criticism of Kavakci for her actions (Meliha and Tur 2005; Shively 2005). The Constitutional Court ultimately shut down the party in June 2001 on grounds of anti-secularist activities, and banned five of its members from politics for five years. Among these were Kavakci herself, and Nazli Ilicak, a non-headscarved female MP also elected on the *Fazilet* party ticket who had defended Kavakci's right to wear the headscarf (Kavakci 2010: 79).

The 'headscarf ban'[2] and closures of parties deemed threatening to the secular establishment have a long history in Turkish politics. While discouragement of the headscarf in the service of secularism initially manifested through government constraints on headscarved women's access to certain state services and institutions, the rise of Islamist parties and a gradual increase in the visibility of headscarved women in public, particularly among female university students in the 1970s and 1980s, eventually led to legal measures to ban headscarved women from many public institutions. In 1981, amid great controversy, the Ministry of National Education announced that female students and staff at public post-secondary schools could no longer wear headscarves (Cindoglu and Zencirci 2008: 33). The Council of Higher Education and several other state bodies took similar measures, as secularist factions grew anxious that Turkey's secularist ideals were under threat, claiming the veil or headscarf was being used as a political symbol of opposition to Kemalism, adopted by women and supported by men as a way to undermine Turkish secularism. Secularist resentment increased as growing numbers of modern, young, professional women assumed the headscarf, despite their years of schooling in the secular state education system, which was intended to indoctrinate the youth with Kemalist ideals (Shively 2005).

With Islamist *Refah* party's unexpected victory in the 1995 general elections, Turkey's secularist forces received a clear warning of the extent of popular support for a more religiously inspired lifestyle and polity. In

[2] 'The Headscarf ban' is the term commonly used for state limitations (legal or assumed) on women's access to state facilities, such as universities, libraries and court houses.

response, the military, considering itself the protector of Turkish secularism and Kemalist ideals, launched a 'soft-coup' in 1997, during which it closed *Refah* and enacted stricter implementation of the headscarf ban in universities and in the public sphere (Çitak and Tür 2008: 458).[3] This more formal ban targeting headscarved university students, staff and faculty had a chilling effect on headscarved women's presence in other public sectors including schools, libraries and hospitals.

The military and Constitutional Court's shadow over religious parties persisted well after the AKP's landslide rise to power in 2002. The AKP's 2008 attempt to lift the ban on headscarves for university students was rejected by the Constitutional Court, and the AKP narrowly escaped being shut down (Cindoglu and Zencirci 2008; Kavakci 2010). This led to an extensive campaign by the AKP government for legal, institutional and structural reforms intended to wrest more power from the secular establishment and its control over the military and the Constitutional Court – the two bodies notorious for closing parties deemed in conflict with secularism – before addressing the headscarf ban. Using the rhetoric of democratisation, justice and making Turkey compatible for EU membership, the campaign was followed by a constitutional referendum in 2010, resulting in public support for the AKP's consolidation of most institutional power in its own hands. In October 2013, Prime Minister Erdogan announced reforms, among them the official removal of the headscarf ban. Immediately after this announcement, a number of female MPs elected to office in 2011 began wearing headscarves in parliament, sending a clear message to the Turkish public that personal religiosity should pose no impediment to public life. In the 2015 parliamentary elections, the AKP successfully nominated headscarved Ravza Kavakci, Merve Kavakci's younger sister, to represent one of Istanbul's districts. As of 2021, both Kavakci sisters hold important political posts on behalf of the AKP.

Significantly, even when regulations banning headscarved women's access to public universities and schools were in place, there was never an explicit ban on headscarves in parliament; the assumption however was that rulings concerning headscarved women's access to state facilities implied a 'ban' on headscarves in parliament. The only dress code for women in

---

[3] Public spaces included schools and universities, courts of law, government offices and other official institutions. The ban applied to students, workers and public servants.

parliament required female MPs to wear skirts – thus banning them from wearing trousers (personal interview with Fatma Bostan, 15 June 2011).[4] In fact, when Turkish courts stripped Merve Kavakci from her elected parliamentary position (and later her Turkish citizenship), they did so on the grounds that she had become a US citizen 'without the permission of the Turkish authorities', and not because of her headscarf (personal interview with Merve Kavakci, 1 December 2011). Despite the absence of a definitive ban on headscarves in parliament, following the Kavakci affair all the major political parties, including pro-religious ones, abstained from nominating headscarved candidates, unless potential candidates agreed – 'out of respect for the secular establishment' – to remove their headscarves if elected (personal interview with a headscarved parliamentary candidate, 15 June 2011). Given the large demographic of headscarved women in Turkey, this discrimination by party leaders eventually led to important campaigns and protests by women's groups demanding equal political rights for headscarved women.

CEDAW: Headscarved Women's Beacon of Hope

Previous research has pointed to the significant linkage between international influence and enhancement of women's rights and status in Turkey (Anil *et al.* 2002; Berktay 2004; Bilgili 2011; Marshall 2009; Tajali 2014). According to Marshall (2009), Turkey's official candidacy for membership in the EU since 1999 in particular opened up important opportunities for activism around minority and women's rights, as the country's policies and practices came under close scrutiny by the international community.[5] Although serious discussions on Turkey's integration into the EU have effectively come to a halt since 2015 for a number of reasons, including the country's increasingly authoritarian turn in recent years (Macdonald 2018), my research also finds that the EU membership process did significantly help women's rights efforts. In the early 2000s, Turkey witnessed significant improvements for women's rights and status as women's groups were poised to exploit the new opportunities EU candidacy presented and to seize on political elites'

---

[4] The ban on women MPs from wearing trousers was also removed with a swift parliamentary vote in November 2013 following the announcement that headscarved women could now serve in the parliament (White 2013).

[5] EU's *Acquis Communitaire*, the set of legislative conditions which candidate states must meet prior to accession, include legal establishment of gender equality.

eagerness to meet the EU's conditions for membership. These improvements included important reforms to the Turkish Civil and Penal Codes, strengthening Turkey's commitments to international documents such as CEDAW, and extensive 'NGOisation' of the Turkish women's rights movement thanks to the international community's support (Keysan 2012).

Many rights groups welcomed Turkey's efforts to comply with EU conditions for integration, which they viewed as a means to further democratisation. Erdogan himself acknowledged this, stating 'We regard Turkey's EU membership as the biggest democratization project after the proclamation of the Republic' (quoted in Yavuz 2009: 202). This type of rhetoric from political elites opened a significant discursive opportunity structure for civil society actors; though many of the state's democratisation actions were strategically directed towards gaining EU membership, in the long-term they opened up avenues for rights activism and civil protest. Among such strategic moves was Turkey's acceptance of CEDAW.

The Convention on the Elimination of All Forms of Discrimination against Women (CEDAW) entered into force in 1981 and has been ratified by most of the world's countries. Often described as an international bill of rights for women, CEDAW consists of thirty articles aimed at ending sex-based discrimination. Concerning women's political representation, articles 7 and 8 of the Convention outline the ratifying states' responsibilities in eliminating discrimination against women in the political and public spheres, at both national and international levels. States that ratify the Convention are required to abide by these articles and enshrine gender equality into their domestic legislation, while repealing all discriminatory provisions from their laws. However, a number of countries that have ratified CEDAW, among them some Islamic states, have done so with reservations, stating that particular articles are incongruent with their tradition, religion or culture. However, these justifications have faced strong criticism from women's right activists across the world, including from Muslim countries, who oppose states' curtailment of women's rights in the name of religion or culture. Indeed, a number of religious women's rights activists in Iran and Turkey who I interviewed emphasised the compatibility between CEDAW and Islamic precepts, which they interpreted to be inherently egalitarian. Given Turkey's secular context, the official discourse of the AKP has rarely referenced religion, but rather emphasised democracy and civil liberties in its plans.

Despite the significance of such international rights documents, states may sign them to appear modern and egalitarian in the face of pressures from the international community, while lacking the commitment to implement the required reforms (Baldez 2014; Simmons 2009). However, regardless of the motivations for signing, once ratified these documents can provide civil society activists with important discursive opportunities. This was the case with Turkey's ratification (with reservations)[6] of CEDAW in 1985, just a few years after it came into effect. Although undertaken as strategy to gain EU support for Turkish EU membership (Kardam 2004; Marshall 2009),[7] signing CEDAW nonetheless opened the way for Turkish women's rights groups to hold the state accountable for its promises on gender equality. Women's activism coupled with Turkey's aspirations to EU membership led Turkey to withdraw its reservations on CEDAW in 1999;[8] Turkey further increased its commitments to CEDAW when it ratified the Optional Protocol in 2003.[9]

Turkey's ratification of CEDAW and its Optional Protocol have created important opportunity structures, both political and discursive, for Turkish women's rights activists to address gender discriminatory rulings and practices. Although Turkish feminists did not play a key role in CEDAW's initial ratification by the state, 'over the years CEDAW became the rock from which Turkish feminists demanded that the state change gender policies' (Marshall 2009: 360).[10] In recent decades, Turkish women's NGOs have been prepar-

---

[6] The majority of Turkey's reservations concerned Turkish family law, which at the time failed to guarantee women's equal rights in marriage, divorce, child custody and property ownership.

[7] Although Turkey was officially recognised as an EU candidate in 1999, it had a long history of applications and rejections prior to that. CEDAW's ratification in 1985 was a strategic move by Turkey to impress the EU (Marshall 2009).

[8] The feminist group Women's Circle (*Kadın Cevresi*), which formed following the 1980 coup in Turkey, played a key role in CEDAW's ratification and eventual removal of the reservations (Bend 1988).

[9] The Optional Protocol to CEDAW (adopted October 1999; effective December 2000) established complaint and inquiry mechanisms to enable women to seek redress for violations of the Convention.

[10] Important reforms included addressing discriminatory provisions in Turkey's civil and penal codes, as well as establishing the first women's policy apparatus, the Directorate General on the Status and Problems of Women, as required by CEDAW (Marshall 2009). Also in 2004, the Turkish constitution included a mandate that in case of conflicts between ratified international agreements on fundamental rights and freedoms and domestic laws, the international agreements shall prevail.

ing shadow reports on instances of gender discrimination as a way to pressure the state to better implement CEDAW.

CEDAW's emphasis on non-discrimination aligns with Turkish women's rights groups' demands for unreserved female access to political leadership positions, as well as with demands from groups fighting for headscarved women's right to political representation. After Turkey signed the Optional Protocol, women's groups used the opportunity to present accounts of discrimination to the CEDAW Committee: in 2010 a coalition of seventy-one Turkish non-governmental organisations presented the Committee with a shadow report on the impact of the headscarf ban on women's rights in Turkey, as well as documenting the state's failure to implement the Convention by continuing to discriminate in this way (Benli 2010b). The result was the first formal international condemnation of Turkey's discrimination against headscarved women: a strongly worded statement from the CEDAW Committee urging Turkey to end the headscarf ban and requiring that Turkey comply with CEDAW by implementing measures to increase access to public and political life for all women. This important milestone for headscarved women's activism marked a clear departure from the earlier position of international and regional bodies that issues around headscarves were a state prerogative (CEDAW Committee 2010).[11] According to human rights lawyer and headscarved women's rights activist Fatma Benli – who in 2015 became an AKP parliamentarian as mentioned in the previous chapter – 'we realised that despite remaining patient and exhausting all of the internal sources of pressuring our politicians, we were not getting anywhere. So we decided to take matters to the international community, while continuing our lobbying efforts [inside the country]' (personal interview, 30 May 2011).[12]

[11] Prior to the Committee's comment, regional and international bodies had ruled against headscarved women's rights in Turkey. For example, in 2005 in Leyla Sahin vs. Turkey, the European Court of Human Rights ruled in favour of Turkey's right to protect its secular ideology above the right of the individual, stating that Turkey's ban on headscarves for university students following the 1997 coup, which prevented Sahin from continuing her medical studies, was justified as she should have 'anticipated such restrictions to her education' (Benli 2010a: 15). According to Fatma Benli, experiences with these types of rulings had discouraged activists from bringing cases of discrimination against headscarved women to international and regional bodies (personal interview, 30 May 2011).

[12] This is an example of what Keck and Sikkink (1998) refer to as a 'boomerang pattern of influence'. The boomerang model describes the effect whereby local lobbying efforts can be boosted by support from the international community, which can in turn reinforce pres-

The CEDAW Committee statement inspired and empowered Turkish activists to confront anti-headscarf regulations and policy, lobbying ahead of the 2011 parliamentary election to try and overturn these obstacles to women's political aspirations, including to becoming MPs.

Strategic Framing: Headscarves and the 2011 Parliamentary Election

The months preceding the 2011 parliamentary election saw the use of CEDAW-informed rhetoric by Turkish women's groups sympathetic to the cause to frame their demand for headscarved women's access to parliament. They highlighted the fact that although 'two-thirds of Turkish women are headscarved, not one of them has a seat in the parliament', attributing this to party leaders' male bias (Birch 2011). Women's groups, particularly pious ones, transformed CEDAW and its Committee's 2010 statement condemning the headscarf ban into a discursive opportunity structure. Their framing of discrimination against headscarved women with reference to the Convention and Turkey's contravention of it was targeted to garner support from Turkey's secular population, while concurrently pressuring conservative party elites, particularly the AKP, who wanted the votes of the headscarved constituency and the approval of the EU.

Campaigning and lobbying efforts for the nomination of headscarved candidates were directed primarily at the governing AKP since many of its female members, including founding member Fatma Bostan, were adamant the time had come for the party to be the example in representing its huge demographic of headscarved members and supporters in politics. Many headscarved women had joined the AKP primarily because its leaders had promised to fight policies hindering their access to state-run institutions, including parliament. More than a decade after the controversial and demeaning 'Kavakci Affair', the AKP had now consolidated its power over the judiciary and military, the state bodies most notorious for closing down parties for alleged contravention of Turkey's constitutional secularism. However, when women's rights activists did not see any sincere effort on the part of the AKP to address headscarved women's marginalisation from political leadership during the 2011 election campaign, they took matters into their own hands.

As noted at the beginning of this chapter, among them was Fatma Bostan.

sure from local/national women's rights groups on political elites (Keck and Sikkink 1998; Marshall 2009).

Even with her vast experience and long involvement with the party, her headscarf made her ineligible as a candidate. While Bostan's husband served as an AKP parliamentarian from 2002 to 2007 despite his shorter history of party involvement, party leaders refused to even consider Bostan as a potential parliamentary candidate. As a devout woman with political aspirations Bostan determined to challenge this discrimination on the grounds that it violated her individual right to political representation and freedom of expression as emphasised by various international human rights documents including CEDAW. The juxtaposition of her religiosity and political ambitions, and her use of the international human rights framework to make her case, made Bostan's stand particularly intriguing.

Bostan's public announcement of her candidacy application to the AKP included a statement saying she was prepared to run as an independent if the party she helped found continued its discrimination and remained unwilling to nominate her (Zibak 2011). This public threat, along with her repeated references to 'rights' and 'anti-discrimination' infuriated AKP leaders. In our interview, Bostan emphasised that her intent was to publicly problematise the AKP's refusal to nominate headscarved women for the 2011 election.

> During last year's *Istisare Toplantisi* (an annual closed party consultation meeting) in October 2010, I raised the issue that two-thirds of Turkish women are not represented in the parliament. At that meeting I also pointed out that in July the CEDAW Committee had asked Turkey to do something about its headscarf ban and address the problem of women's low political representation. So as a signatory to CEDAW, it is time that we (the AKP) respond to this demand and show headscarved candidates in the next elections. (Personal interview, 15 June 2011)

Prime Minister Erdogan's response to her statement at the closed-door meeting (which she chose not to disclose to me) motivated her public declaration. About fifty other headscarved women, including ten close colleagues – one also a co-founder of the Party, applied to run as AKP candidates. 'Although all of these women were qualified, I was 99 per cent sure that AKP was not going to nominate any headscarved candidates.' She continued, 'My main objective in registering for candidacy was mostly to put pressure on the party rather than to get elected. Hence, I only registered with the AKP, so that when they chose NOT to put me on the candidate list, I could talk about it' (personal interview, 15 June 2011).

In addition to pressure and criticism from within the party, the AKP also faced censure from a group of non-partisan women called Women Meet Halfway, many of whom were headscarved. Prior to the 2011 election, this group launched a campaign with the slogan 'If no headscarf wearing candidate, then no vote', threatening to boycott any major party that failed to run a headscarved woman candidate; a move directed again mainly at the AKP, the party likely to have the most headscarved candidacy applicants. According to one campaign organiser, an AKDER (Women's Right's against Discrimination Association) board member,[13] the campaign's objective was to highlight the discriminatory and unjust denial of headscarved women's right to political representation based on dress (personal interview, 23 June 2011). Like Bostan, the campaign organisers framed their demands in terms of rights and justice.

This secular framing by religiously motivated women's rights activists aimed to garner support from secular Turks while also pressuring pro-religious political elites looking for approval from the international community by appearing egalitarian. The choice of this frame was primarily shaped by opportunities presented by international discourses coming out of CEDAW and the EU integration process, as well as Turkey's secular framework. Instead of articulating and justifying their demands in Islamic terms that might have resonated with the AKP government, they used CEDAW and other international documents committed to by Turkey (personal interview with two pious women's rights activists, 17 June 2011). Significantly, this choice was despite the fact that many pious women's rights activists receive their feminist convictions from Islam. For instance, a former director of the now dissolved religious women's organisation, Capital City Women's Platform (CCWP), and one of Bostan's peers, emphasised the compatibility between Islam and international human rights norms. Declaring the Quran as an inherently egalitarian document, she clarified that this document dictates a minimum standard for rights and duties of all individuals, that 'Muslims should expand upon as contexts evolve over time'. To her, CEDAW and other international

---

[13] Women's Rights Organization against Discrimination (*Ayrımcılığa Karşı Kadın Hakları Derneği* or AK-DER) was created in 1999 after the 1997 soft coup that formally deprived many women of their rights to education and work (AK-DER 2019). AK-DER was at the forefront of much activism around headscarved women's rights, and remains active despite the lifting of the ban in 2013.

documents reiterate the Quran's egalitarian message, including on the issue of female political authority. 'The Quranic story of Queen of Sheba (*Bilquis*) justifies women's leadership roles in Islam, and we do not accept any ruling that departs from this' (personal interview, 2 September 2019). Witnessing no contradictions between their faith and international rights documents, many members of CCWP publicly campaign in secular terms to better reach feminists and pressure elites. Using Ferree's (2003) distinction between 'resonant' and 'radical' frames, I find that pious women's framing in secular terms, which may be at odds with their core identity claims, is an example of radical framing, as it opposed the dominant and institutionally anchored conservative gender discourse of the AKP government while it also sought more rapid institutional change. Such framing shows 'adaptation to opportunity' on the part of pious women activists and illustrates how 'differences in discursive opportunity affect the strategic use of frames in the feminist repertoire' (Ferree 2003: 304).

This strategic move to maximise support in Turkey's secular context was aptly deconstructed by one of my headscarved interviewees, a renowned feminist theologian who was adamant in her support for a secular system, but one in which freedom of religious expression is respected. Although engaged in feminist reinterpretations of religious texts, this informant did not consider Quranic reinterpretation a feasible approach to addressing headscarved women's access to the parliament.

> It is a big mistake when secular feminists think that we support a religious system, like those in Iran or Saudi Arabia. We moderates want a secular system! If they group us together with the fundamentalists who want to bring Shari'a, they are shooting themselves in the foot. Women are under pressure from a secular system in Turkey, not a religious one. Perhaps if we had our rights denied based on religion, we would also pursue a religious discourse. However, it is the secular system that denies our rights, but ironically a pro-religious government that also ignores our cries. (Personal interview, 17 June 2011)

To the surprise of many pious women activists, the fiercest opponents to the lobby for headscarved women's access to parliament were various AKP leaders along with their most ardent supporters. A prominent Islamic intellectual, Ali Bulac, publicly attacked the 'If no headscarf, then no vote' campaign as a move to 'destroy the Islamist movement from within'. 'They have stripped the headscarf of its religious significance, reducing it to a simple issue of human rights inspired by feminism' (as quoted in Birch 2011). He further claimed that this demand by headscarved women was a trap set to destroy or at least weaken the AKP by splitting the vote. These attacks did not go unanswered; while religiously conservative men took umbrage at headscarved women's refusal to remain patient and continue to devote themselves to the party, campaigner Hilal Kaplan had a sharp response to Bulac in her column in the conservative daily *Yeni Safak* (*New Dawn*):

> Apparently the reverence some conservative men feel for their covered womenfolk is dependent on their deference to their husbands and betters . . . But if that is what they understand by [the Islamic concept of men's duty to protect women] then, inevitably, they are going to end up being told 'thanks, but no thanks'. (In Birch 2011)

Columnist Nihal Bengisu Karaca responded to the repeated query from AKP government supporters 'where did this demand emerge from?' noting, 'There was always such a demand!' and reminded her readers that systematic exclusion from decision-making of an entire (and very large) demographic (headscarved women) leads to their marginalisation. Referring to AKP leaders, she states, 'When these men manage to acquire certain positions, they forget the women' (in Zibak 2011). The reaction of Islamic elites to the campaign clearly showed the dominance in the pro-religious camp of the idea that women's rightful place was in the domestic sphere as subjects of male control.

For Fatma Bostan, whose position was attacked by many of her AKP colleagues, her surprise was the many allies she found in the secularist camps. 'When I come together with secular women [activists], they like and respect me. Generally, they had viewed headscarved women as obedient and stereotypically weak, but when they saw us raising our voices, we gained their respect' (personal interview, 15 June 2011). The convergence between pious and secular women's groups, engendered by the unwillingness of male party leaders to take action to address women's problems, resonates with research that suggests 'new ways to frame women's issues facilitates coalition building among groups with previously distinct, even conflicting agendas', as Baldez and Kirk found in their analysis of both Chilean and American women's movements (2005: 135).

In the end, although no headscarved women were nominated for the 2011 parliamentary elections by the ruling AKP, the diverse Turkish women's movement triumphed in another way, by bringing together disparate, histori-cally oppositional, secular and pious women's groups. For the first time in Turkish history, secular women's rights activists became aware of pious and headscarved women's agency as they contested patriarchal and discriminatory practices of male leaders. The campaigns and framing process of pious activ-ists shifted the decades-long image of the headscarf in Turkey as a symbol of political Islam, oppression or backwardness, allowing an understanding of headscarved women as independent actors prepared to articulate and fight for their rights. These recent developments have caused many secular feminists to recognise the commonalities they share with headscarved women regard-ing misogynous and discriminatory party politics that undermine women's political rights and influence.

A strategic convergence on headscarved women's right to political representation
An important sign of the convergence between moderate religious and secular women on the issue of headscarved women's access to parliament was the campaign by KADER (Association for the Support of Women Candidates) for the 2011 parliamentary elections. Closely associated with the secular feminist movement since its founding in 1997, in 2011 KADER for the first time addressed the headscarf ban as an obstacle to women's political represen-tation. The organisation's '50/50 campaign' poster, calling for at least 50 per cent female parliamentary representation, was the first KADER material ever to feature an image of a headscarved woman. This deeply significant symbolic shift in the organisation's campaign material and rhetoric was equally impact-ful for Bostan and her pious allies, signifying resonance of their demands with the country's larger women's rights movement.

> While KADER did not support Merve Kavakci in 1999, this time they sup-ported us, and even used the same arguments we did, pointing out that the majority of Turkish women are headscarved. They even raised this issue at their meetings with women from across various parties, and in a way pres-sured parties to nominate headscarved candidates. This was a very positive step for us. (Personal interview with Fatma Bostan, 15 June 2011)

This shift was very evident in KADER's campaign posters; while the posters ahead of the 2007 general elections (known as the 'mustache cam-paign' posters) only featured non-headscarved women, for the 2011 elections KADER posters featured women representative of diverse constituencies,

KADER 2007 campaign poster

KADER 2011 campaign poster

Figure 5.1 KADER campaign posters for 2007 and 2011 parliamentary elections. Top: KADER 2007 campaign poster; bottom: KADER 2011 campaign poster (translation: '275 Women Parliamentarians'). (Credit: Association for the Support of Women Candidates – KADER.)

including well-known handicapped, headscarved, and ethnic minority women's rights activists (see Figure 5.1). The slogan of the 2011 KADER campaign, '275 Women Parliamentarians', called for gender parity in the 550-seat parliament.

The willingness of a traditionally secular women's organisation such as KADER to campaign for headscarved women's political representation resulted from a number of factors, including the very vocal demands, framed in terms of human rights discourse, from pious women's rights activists who publicly protested the discriminatory and patriarchal attitudes of male party leaders. Strategically emphasising the shared battle with their secular counterparts over denial of access to political decision-making based on gender, they highlighted their support for a secular, inclusive and democratic Turkey. This framing engendered positive reaction and support from secular feminists; one KADER board member noted that as an organisation whose mandate claims 'equal distance to all political ideologies and parties', KADER could not continue to ignore headscarved women: 'In KADER we could no longer turn a deaf ear to the demands for political representation of headscarved women, who had been active for years in parties, particularly in AKP, but could not be elected. As a women's group we had to defend *all* women' (personal interview, 3 June 2011).

To join forces across women's organisations for the larger objective of increasing *all* women's access to parliament many pious women's rights activists, including Bostan, strategically chose to emphasise gender discrimination rather than the headscarf as the main barrier to headscarved women's parliamentary presence. According to Bostan, 'Considering that the majority of Turkish women are underrepresented, it is not very productive to continuously single out the headscarf as an obstacle . . . all Turkish women are discriminated against when it comes to politics, so we aim to emphasise anti-discrimination' (personal interview, 15 June 2011). When her efforts and outspokenness during the 2011 elections turned her into a representative of headscarved women, Bostan chose to build alliances and win secular feminist support by strategically using a feminist and anti-discriminatory discourse. During a gathering organised by secularist newspaper *Hurriyet* in collaboration with KADER (Figure 5.2), Bostan, the only headscarved speaker, made sure her speech emphasised the discrimination faced by *all* women aspiring to parliament. She told me she actually removed a sentence from her original text referring to the 'stone wall' faced by headscarved women in addition to the 'glass ceiling' most women in politics encounter (personal interview, 15 June 2011). Bostan's appearance at the event was all the more significant considering she represented women until then considered 'oppressed' or 'fundamentalist' by many of those gathered. Her strategic use of human rights discourse through reference to CEDAW's anti-discriminatory language not only linked her efforts with other feminist and women's organisations, but

Figure 5.2 Image from the Rightful Women's Platform. Fatma Bostan from the women's organisation Capital City Women's Platform (CCWP), seated middle of the back row, the only headscarved NGO representative out of sixteen at the event of the *Hakli Kadın Platformu* (Rightful Women's Platform) in 2011 bearing the slogan: 'We want equal representation of women in the parliament right now!' (Credit: Doğan Holding, https://www.doganholding.com.tr/en/sustainability/corporate-social-responsibility/.)

also depoliticised the very politically sensitive headscarf issue by framing women's lack of access to parliament as gender discrimination rather than religious discrimination.

It is arguable that the nascent unity between secular and pious women's rights advocates in Turkey in 2011 helped strengthen Turkey's women's movement, allowing space for moderate voices, while de-emphasising radical ones. Women's rights activists across the ideological spectrum became increasingly cognisant of the need to fight discrimination on various levels, including around dress regulations. To this end activists engaged in efforts to draw attention away from both extreme and divisive secularist rhetoric demonising headscarved women, and from Islamic fundamentalist rhetoric denouncing feminism as incompatible with Islam. One KADER board member sympathetic to headscarved women's rights told me, 'The headscarf issue is a women's issue, not a political issue. It is women who should gather together and try to resolve it' (personal interview, 16 July 2010). An important milestone in the emerging unity among diverse women's groups in Turkey was a signature campaign that a number of Turkish women's rights activists launched in 2008, featuring the slogan '*Birbirimize Sahip Çıkıyoruz!*'

(We support each other!). While this coalition did not specifically campaign on headscarved women's right to run for parliament, it sought to normalise their access to public spaces and institutions, including universities. The campaign brought together a coalition of feminists, gay rights activists and headscarved women's rights activists (Aksoy 2015; Avramopoulou 2013). 'A public sphere where we cannot all walk arm in arm is not our public sphere', read the headline of their petition, contesting state authority over women's bodies and signalling recognition by secular feminists of the struggles of headscarved women for freedom of expression, education and employment. Theologian and pious women's rights activist Hidayet Tuksal welcomed what she regarded as an act of solidarity in that, while many of the secular feminist organisations involved opposed veiling practices, they signed nevertheless, lending support to religious women's fight for their rights, and against discrimination and oppression (Avramopoulou 2013: 241).

Building a Unified Women's Movement, But Not Quite Yet!

The alliance of secular and pious women's groups around female representation in the 2011 parliamentary elections created an effective front to address headscarved women's political under-representation. Although this unification greatly strengthened the larger Turkish women's movement in decrying headscarved women's lack of rights to party elites, and ultimately helped end the headscarf ban in 2013, my observations suggest that deep-rooted ideological and political differences between diverse women's rights groups have prevented subsequent convergences on other women's rights concerns. To this day, Turkish politics remains highly divided along ideological, ethnic, religious and class lines, hindering the formation of coalitions between women's groups. With Turkey's increasing divergence from the path of democratisation in recent years under Erdogan, these schisms have not diminished and they continue to impede the emergence of a unified women's movement and any effective female voting bloc. Previous scholars have argued that a decline in national organised feminism impedes the emergence of a powerful female electoral bloc, which weakens the lobbying influence and pressure women's groups can wield over political elites (Baldez 2002; Krook 2009; Young 2006). In the case of Turkey, the fractured nature of the women's movement has not allowed for a feminist politicisation of the Turkish female electorate to vote in accordance with its own collective interests, rather than along party lines or political affiliations. This is despite the long history and high level of women's activism in Turkey, in particular KADER's succession of campaigns to politicise female voters and get more women elected.

The divisiveness of Turkish politics stems in part from decades of exclusionary policies aimed at homogenising a heterogeneous society. Such policies often directly or indirectly affected women's rights and societal status, as the Turkish Republic's secularist nationalisation efforts disregarded the experiences of religious, rural and ethnic minority demographics and the interests of women within them. This deeply undermined the development of a unified women's movement, and although women's groups across the ideological spectrum have converged on some issues – including domestic violence, the Turkish civil code and, more recently, headscarved women's access to parliament – they disagree on many others, the most contentious of which are gay rights, and to a lesser extent gender quotas and abortion.[14]

In recent years, the schisms between women's groups are often fuelled by the fierce political rivalry between the ruling pro-religious AKP and its main opposition, currently the secularist CHP and pro-Kurdish HDP, both of which garner enough electoral support to maintain their presence in the Turkish parliament. This means alliances on issues shared by all Turkish women do not form, such as the demand for gender quotas. Given Erdogan's clear opposition to gender quotas for instance, many AKP women have not pursued this demand and instead stick with the party line, diminishing the possibility of joining forces with other women's groups in support of such affirmative action measures. Indeed, AKP's highly gender-conservative ideology has minimised much collaboration and discussion among women's rights activists across the political spectrum.[15]

The issue of parliamentary gender quotas is one that would be well served by an alliance between women's groups. The historically secular-oriented

---

[14] It is notable, however, that many pious activists, including theologian Hidayat Tuksal, fiercely objected when in mid-2012 Prime Minister Erdogan announced a plan to ban abortion, equating it with murder. Women such as Tuksal argued that abortion was a women's issue and should be discussed by diverse women's groups, not decided by male politicians (Sehlikoglu 2013). The stance of these pious women's rights activists on such a contentious topic exhibits their feminist consciousness and their agency, while highlighting their opposition to conservative male leaders.

[15] A notable example of AKP's conservative gender ideology is its efforts to restrict women's reproductive rights within the framework of the valuation of motherhood as the primary role of women (Sehlikoglu 2013).

KADER has been at the forefront of gender quota debates in Turkey and has succeeded in bringing the discussion onto the public agenda; however, their efforts to bring a gender quota into effect receive little support from more pious political and social organisations or activists, many of which are linked with the AKP. According to KADER board member Fezal Gulfidan, the lack of support for gender quotas from many pious women's rights activists is largely due to the fact that Erdogan has publicly criticised them as 'humiliating for women', claiming that merit should be the only criterion determining women's access to political decision-making positions (personal interview, 20 July 2010). Erdogan's vocal public opposition has prevented many AKP women from publicly pushing for gender quotas, and from supporting outside campaigns for their adoption. This is despite the fact that in several conversations I had with a number of high-ranking AKP women, they expressed the need for affirmative action measures to address women's political under-representation. However, when I asked about plans for moving towards adoption of a quota, I was told that the 'timing was not right' given the leadership's opposition. Allegiance to the AKP and Erdogan was further highlighted during one of my visits to the AKP women's branch headquarters in Ankara (*Genel Merkez Kadın Kolları*), after a number of key women leaders had discussed gender quotas with me as 'the next natural and expected step for Turkish women'. But when I asked if the women's branch had raised the issue, I was told, 'It is not right for us to raise this issue, it is a party concern. What we do emphasise is women's *right* to be elected' (personal interview, 16 June 2011). In the run-up to the 2011 elections, many AKP women with whom I spoke said they were prioritising abolishing the headscarf ban and hoping its removal would substantially increase women's access to the parliament. They also expressed hope that Erdogan himself would continue to take the lead in increasing women's access to political leadership and praised him for the informal measures taken by the party to ensure women comprise at least 20 per cent of parliamentary candidate lists as was the case for the 2018 elections (personal interview with a central AKP women's branch official, 2 September 2019). It did not help KADER's cause that its focus on gender quotas for over a decade disregarded the fact that a large section of Turkish women was barred because of their headgear from access to formal political decision-making positions.

A number of other issues of concern for women (and society) which could be well served by a united front of women activists have been sacrificed to Turkey's party politics and deep-rooted ideological rifts. KADER considers the ideological divides that impede the mobilisation of a united female voting bloc one of its key challenges in addressing women's political under-representation. Another KADER board member told me,

> Women in Turkey are not a strong voting bloc, and many of them lack a feminist consciousness. Women are too divided and cannot agree on certain issues . . . but as a women's organisation, we are trying to bring all women together at least regarding women's presence in politics. (Personal interview, 16 July 2010)

Because Turkish women do not vote as an interest group, female politicians have little impetus to join forces across the political spectrum on gender specific demands. Female MPs generally owe their positions to the party, and this impedes both their responsiveness to the electorate and their willingness to take positions not aligned with party policy.

The divide between ideologically distinct women's groups has intensified in recent years with growing political polarisation amidst Turkey's increasing authoritarianism. With the recent transition from a parliamentary to a presidential system under Erdogan, women's rights groups, which until recently functioned as a central democratising force in Turkey, have also been swept up into the heated oppositional dynamic at play between the various ideological and political backers. While 2011 saw a number of important coalitions between historically secular and pious women's rights groups, alliances like these were largely absent during the 2015 and 2018 parliamentary elections. In one stark example of the extent of this division, in contrast with 2011, the marquee event held by *Hurriyet* newspaper and KADER ahead of the June 2015 elections, urging women politicians to be a 'single voice' for women, had representatives from only three parties (CHP, HDP and MHP) in attendance, and none from AKP. These divisions remained during the 2018 election, marking the first vote under the presidential system, which many saw as consolidating even more power in the hands of the AKP. While party women worked hard to win votes for their respective parties, there was little collaboration between women's groups of different political persuasions. KADER continued its campaigns for a gender-balanced parliament, which it largely framed in terms of democracy and justice, urging the adoption of a quota measure, with a zipper ranking system alternating male and female candidates all the way down party lists to ensure women's greater access to parliament.[16] Despite all these efforts, none of Turkey's major parties, including the pro-Kurdish HDP, which does have a gender quota, has yet implemented a zipper-style party list system.

Conclusion

This chapter highlights the interactions between structure and agency present in the strategic use of discursive opportunity structure by pious women's rights activists, who saw an opening in Turkey's acceptance of international human rights documents. Despite targeting the ruling conservative, pro-religious party in their campaign for headscarved women's access to parliament, they effectively framed this demand in secular terms, using CEDAW to support their claim of discrimination. Their agency was evident as they garnered support from secular society while also challenging, and ultimately winning over, the pro-religious elites. A significant outcome of their strategic framing process was the resulting gradual convergence between secular and pious women's groups over the demand for headscarved women's access to parliament.

Despite this historic 2011 collaboration between various pious and secular women's rights groups, Turkish politics, particularly concerning women's rights and roles, continues to be divisive. Party rivalry between the conservative AKP and its main opposition parties, secularist CHP, and more recently pro-Kurdish HDP, continues to supersede most efforts to mobilise a female voting bloc or create a unified voice around gender discrimination. This has greatly limited women's rights activists' opportunities to pressure political elites. This contrasts with the Iranian situation, where, as briefly mentioned in Chapter 8, women's rights activists across the political spectrum have had an easier time joining forces to tackle female political under-representation, largely due to a more unified women's movement, which emerged in response to the Islamic Republic's discriminatory rulings on women. The Iranian women's movement has successfully politicised Iranian women, emphasising that female access to positions of authority is compatible with Islamic

---

[16] KADER's campaign slogan in recent years, 'No Women, No Democracy! No Women, No Justice! No Women, No Freedom!' continues the call to elect more women. As an organisation mandated to be independent of any political party, KADER has refrained from taking a position on Turkey's transition to a presidential system. It continues to encourage standing for office and using the ballot box as the primary means of political expression (KADER 2017).

doctrine. Women's groups' successful mobilisation of a female voting bloc has forced political elites to respond to women's demands. Hence, while Turkish women have successfully utilised party competition and the international human rights discourse as a means to increase women's political representation, in Iran, strategic convergences among diverse women's groups have helped to politicise a female voting bloc, resulting in important milestones for women in politics, including the appointment of Iran's first female minister since the 1979 revolution, as discussed in the following chapters.

IRAN

6

WOMEN AND POLITICS IN IRAN: FROM REVOLUTIONARY TO REFORMIST

I ranian women captured the world's attention during the 1979 revolution when they took to the streets en masse alongside men to topple a monarchy. Their highly visible activism rendered the image of protesting black-veiled women a symbol of the Iranian revolution. Thirty years later, the world again witnessed Iranian women at the forefront of another public uprising, when thousands of women in bright green headscarves swelled street demonstrations contesting President Ahmadinejad's re-election in 2009, in what later became known as the 'Green Movement'.[1]

While the images of politically active women in both uprisings astonished the world, in reality, women's participation in political movements and public protest has a long history in Iran. At least since the early twentieth century, Iranian women struggled alongside men for political, social and economic reform. Their participation in the 1906 constitutional revolution as well as the 1979 revolution, which ended virtually 2,500 years of monarchical

---

[1] Iran's Green Movement refers to the pro-reformist, widespread, peaceful protests against the re-election of President Mahmood Ahmadinejad in 2009. Suspecting widespread rigging of the elections, masses of Iranians poured into the streets, initially demanding, 'Where is my vote?', and then calling for democracy and diminished clerical dominance in Iranian politics, including of the office of the Supreme Leader (*Velayat-e Faqih*). The protests ended under an extreme crackdown from the regime. Various Iranian scholars consider this movement as pivotal in that it witnessed the largest street protests in the history of the Islamic republic, signalling the regime's loss of legitimacy among significant constituencies, as well as the power of the electorate even under stringent conditions (Ehsani *et al.* 2009).

rule, has received much scholarly attention. Over the four decades since the profound transition from secular monarchy to theocratic republic, Iranian women's political ambitions have ranged from revolutionary to reformist, including those who seek gradual reform towards democracy. Today, in Iran's authoritarian context, women constitute a highly politicised, if loosely organised and diverse constituency of voters, campaigners and community organisers, whom political elites can no longer afford to ignore. Women are major participants of the commonly occurring mass protests in Iran, publicising their demands on economics, politics, and more.

Despite their long history of political participation, Iranian women's access to formal decision-making positions continues to be limited in the face of myriad cultural and institutional obstacles, which have hindered their rise to positions of political authority. Since achieving full suffrage in 1963, the percentage of women in parliament has remained below 10 per cent. Following the 2016 parliamentary elections, women constituted only 5.9 per cent of all parliamentarians, and that was a notable increase from 3.1 per cent during the previous term. Therefore, although Iranian women have emerged as leaders and organisers of key civil and political movements, they continue to face major obstacles to accessing political decision-making positions.

This chapter looks at the systematic discrimination affecting Iranian women's access to formal political power and leadership. I argue that while women have been important players in their country's major political and social shifts at least since the turn of the twentieth century, their access to positions of political decision-making has been systematically curtailed during both the monarchy and Islamic regime. Throughout Iranian history, expansion of women's political rights, particularly the right to elect and be elected, has been among the most contentious of issues for political and religious elites, largely due to their desire to maintain male authority. Many Iranian religious (and secular) political leaders have claimed that men are divinely ordained as guardians of women (Amin 2002; Mir-Hosseini *et al.* 2015) and have opposed granting women the ability to decide the fate of men, either as public office holders or voters on this basis. Thus, historically, Iran's male elites have only expanded women's political rights when it served their own interests, often simultaneously creating restrictions limiting women's utilisation of these rights. Currently these include legal and institutional barriers restricting women's access to many positions of public office, including the

Council of Guardians which vets all those hoping to run for political office at the national level.

In analysing the obstacles limiting women's access to political power in contemporary Iran, this chapter also further clarifies the role of Islam. Significantly, while the conservative Iranian religious elites have used Islam to justify women's political marginalisation, Islamic discourse has also been harnessed to support women's political participation and representation. The frequent shifts in religious discourse on women's political roles has demonstrated to Iranian women that Islam, like other religions, is open to interpretation and that even its most stringent rulings can be altered, particularly when they serve a political interest. Similarly, the lack of clerical consensus on this issue has given women activists important opportunities to pressure for legal and institutional reforms. In the face of institutional obstacles and discriminatory practices which undermine the full exercise of their political rights, women have mobilised public support for women's access to political power, and use every opportunity to strategically interact with ruling elites to realise this objective.

Masters of the 'Art': Iranian Women and Political Protest

Reflecting on the 2009 protests and women's roles in them, Nasim (a pseudonym), a young activist, blogger and journalist looked gravely at me and asked, 'Why do you think it was Neda (Aghasoltan) who became the symbol of the Green Movement?' (see Figure 6.1). Seeing my puzzled expression, she continued, 'It was because women were at the forefront, and in a way, leaders of the demonstrations. After all, we (Iranian women) have more experience than men in how to lead demonstrations and escape from the police.' She elaborated with numerous instances of Iranian women's rights activists and feminists peacefully demonstrating and holding rallies for women's rights, often resulting in violent clashes with the authorities.

> Our many sit-ins, protests, and demonstrations gave us much experience. We know for instance that when the police are beating you, you should not look at your attacker in the eye, as he/she will hit you more, or that if you hold your head up, you will be hit stronger . . . we have learned the tricks on how to escape and avoid harassment from the officials. So when the 2009 demonstrations happened, men protestors realised that not only were we their partners, but that we were better prepared and equipped to protest . . .

Figure 6.1 Protestor holding a poster of Neda Aghasoltan during the 2009 Green Movement uprisings. The poster reads, 'Martyr of Freedom Neda Aghasoltan', who was shot dead during the 2009 protests. (Credit: Undisclosed citizen journalist image.)

> When they saw women and girls bravely standing up to the police, and on many occasions leading the march [see Figure 6.2], we gained their respect. (Personal interview, 6 July 2011)

Nasim represents a sizeable demographic of educated, highly politicised and often urbanite Iranian women who came of age during the reform era (1997–mid-2000s), signalled by the unexpected 1997 landslide victory of President Mohammad Khatami. With the reformists' emphasis on civil society, Nasim and many of her peers felt empowered to shape their political and social realities, organising or joining NGOs, participating in reformist political parties, working and writing for journals and newspapers. During this time student, women's and workers' movements became particularly active in their demands for civil and political rights, including freedom of press and expression, and in turn advocated for reform of the theocratic system. However, the ultra-conservatives' takeover of the legislative and executive branches in 2004 and 2005 respectively, put an abrupt end to much of the civil society

Figure 6.2 Iranian women contesting President Ahmadinejad's re-election during the 2009 Green Movement uprisings. (Credit: Undisclosed citizen journalist image.)

building and grass-roots organising encouraged by the reformists.[2] Extensive crackdowns on civil society activists, particularly those associated with the student and women's rights movements, forced Nasim and many of her peers to master the art of political protest under oppression. With increasing harassment by the state and suppression of civil society movements, solidarity intensified among activists (and among many ordinary citizens) as they campaigned for the release of their peers from prison and held meetings in private homes after the closure of their NGOs and other organisations (interviews with student and women's rights activists in summers of 2009 and 2015). Women have continued to participate in major street protests in recent years, and with state crackdown, particularly in the 2019 and 2020 protests, have been among the arrested or killed participants. Their high level of political activity has helped dismantle stereotypical images of Muslim women as apolitical or

---

[2] The 2004 parliamentary elections replaced the reformist-majority parliament with a conservative-majority one. The following year ultra-conservative Mahmood Ahmadinejad defeated more reformist and pragmatic candidates for the presidency.

passive subjects, as the world has witnessed women's ongoing courage in voicing their objections to Iranian politics despite very real threats from the state.

Iranian women's significant involvement in grass-roots and 'street' politics has however not warranted their participation in political decision-making. Deeming such women's political activities trivial, many opponents of women's political representation in Iran – similar to other countries – argue that women's access to political office should be based on merit. Merit is rarely defined and comes up only during election periods, when Iranian officials across the ideological spectrum regularly oppose affirmative action measures, such as quotas aimed at increasing women's political representation, arguing that access to political power should be 'solely based on merit, rather than gender' (Janaati and Zaifi 2005; Kamali 2017; Omidy 2001).

There is extensive literature addressing the assumptions that keep women out of politics, including a bias among recruiters towards the (male-dominant) status quo (Annesley *et al.* 2015; Bjarnegård 2015; Murray 2014, 2015; Nugent and Krook 2016b). In fact researchers have found that women who enter political office with the help of quotas are in fact often better qualified and more experienced than many of their male colleagues (Nugent and Krook 2016a; Weeks and Baldez 2015). Clearly, the quality of representation and of democratic processes is negatively affected 'by having too large a group drawn from too narrow a talent pool' (Murray 2014: 520). My research supports these findings, showing that women's lived experiences, in addition to their deep political engagement and participation in grass-roots politics, are important qualifications for political office. However, similar to women in Turkey (as well as most other countries), Iranian women have been systematically discriminated against by male elites when it comes to political nomination and recruitment.

Indeed, my interest in women's organising and activism in Iran came from observing women's commitment to voicing their concerns despite the authoritarian context. Women's rights activism has been a potent force in Iran's democratisation and human rights efforts, to the extent that Iranian authorities declared the Iranian women's movement (*jonbesh-e zanan*) a threat to national security, in order to justify crackdowns on activists and to harass and arrest members (Gheytanchi 2008).[3] To properly understand women's

---

[3] For example, the extensive grass-roots organising for the 2006 'One Million Signature Campaign' which sought to reform discriminatory gender laws, included door-to-door sig-

collective efforts to realise their political agency and to access political power in contemporary Iran requires an analysis of the history of women's political rights and roles in modern Iran. The following section briefly outlines the major events in the timeline of women's political activism, with a focus on the negotiations between women and political elites regarding their political rights and roles both before and after the 1979 revolution.

Male Authority and the 'Woman Question' in Modern Iran

Similar to Turkey, the 'woman question' in Iran has often been a flashpoint at the intersection of traditionalism (*sonat-garayi*) and modernisation (*modernite*). Traditionalism for Iran has meant the reinforcement of Islamic socio-cultural practices and values, while concepts of progress and modernisation, as advocated by the monarchy, have implied Westernisation and divergence from core Islamic principles (Sanasarian 1982). Throughout the twentieth century, Iran and its women experienced intense socio-political shifts, from modernisation and strong secularist policies under the Pahlavi monarchy to Islamisation following the 1979 revolution.

Given the controversy and sensitivity surrounding women's 'proper' societal status and women's bodies in Iran over the last century, women's rights have often been the battleground for competing ideological factions, whether secular versus religious, modernist versus traditional, and more recently, reformist versus conservative.[4] While limiting women's rights has at times served to build alliances among elites from opposing groups, at other times advancing women's rights has helped to distinguish a given political elite from more conservative sectors or to highlight a party's particular political or ideological position. Political sociologist Parvin Paidar argues that during the constitutional revolution (1906–11) 'women's issues were the most sensitive of all for both anti-constitutionalists and pro-constitutionalists' (1995: 67).

---

nature collection, a website and workshops across the country on the legal challenges facing women and girls. The campaign's potential to mobilise masses of people greatly alarmed the regime and led to arrests and imprisonment of members on charges including 'threatening national security'.

[4] Currently, the dominant competing ideological factions on women's rights in Iran include *reformists* who advocate re-reading and reinterpretation of traditional religious rulings and practices according to modern times (Mir-Hosseini 1999, 2002), and *conservatives* who uphold the traditional religious readings on gender, in particular the division of gender roles, which relegate women primarily to the private sphere.

Despite the outspokenness of some regarding the advancement of women's rights at the turn of the twentieth century, for the most part the controversial topic was abandoned in favour of a focus on debates around establishing a constitution and a parliament to decrease the power of the monarchy (Paidar 1995; Sanasarian 1982).[5] Under the Pahlavi rule (1925–79) women's rights issues remained a point of contestation even during periods of relative liberalisation: at certain junctures elected liberal governments conceded to the conservative clergy and curtailed women's political rights; at other times, as a political move to oppose the clergy, the monarchy enacted liberal reforms advancing women's rights (Paidar 1995). In 1962, Prime Minister Asadollah Alam's liberal government conceded to the clergy and cancelled an electoral law sanctioning women's political participation; one year later Mohammad Reza Shah Pahlavi enacted the White Revolution reforms, including women's suffrage, to demonstrate his opposition to the clergy (Paidar 1995). Similarly, the founders of the Islamic Republic have also shifted their position on women's rights, particularly women's political rights, when it has served their interests. The founders of the Iranian theocracy, including Khomeini, reversed their initial opposition to female suffrage, encouraging women to vote in support of the Islamic regime in 1979, but restricted other aspects of women's political agency, for example banning women from serving as judges and impeding their access to the presidency, as further discussed below.

These arbitrary actions of rulers with regard to women's rights illustrate their prevailing paternalistic and authoritarian inclinations as well as the volatility of women's issues. Historian Camron Amin (2002) explains the political elites' resistance to advancing women's rights through his concept of 'male guardianship', in which he argues that Iranian male elites, regardless of their ideological or political inclinations, have always had a deep-rooted belief in the need to act as women's guardians, which they justify in various ways. For instance, religious conservatives reference the Quran verse 34–5 from the fourth chapter *An-Nisa* (The Women), which they interpret as having established men as guardians (*qawwamun*) over women (Amin 2002), while secular or nationalist elites have explained their position as either guarding

---

[5] The one area of women's rights which greatly improved following the Iranian constitutional revolution, was women's education, on which many intellectuals and rights activists campaigned (Paidar 1995).

women from backwardness when granting them certain rights, or protecting them from Western decadence and assaults on their chastity and dignity when denying them others (Paidar 1995). These diverse justifications for male guardianship impacted activists' organising efforts as they struggled to advocate for gender equality using discourses that resonated with each ideological group. While prior to the 1979 Islamic revolution, women's rights activists often used the discourses of modernity and equal citizenship rights to align with the rhetoric of the Pahlavis, following the revolution and the establishment of the theocratic regime, they began to formulate their demands in religious terms, with reference to the Quran.

My research also demonstrates that throughout Iranian history political rights for women, particularly those that allow women to exercise decision-making that affects men, such as the rights to vote and to hold political office and shape policy, have been especially controversial (Tajali 2011). This is evident when we consider that although women's suffrage obviously aligned with ideals of modernisation and Westernisation championed by the Pahlavi regime, the regime did not address women's lack of suffrage until it served their political agenda/image. Thus, for example, in 1936 the state forced women to unveil as part of its modernising feminism project launched during the reign of Reza Pahlavi (1925–41), but the right to vote, a primary demand of the women's movement from its inception, was not extended to women until 1963 (Paidar 1995).

Reza Shah Pahlavi outlawed the veil following a visit to Turkey, where Mustafa Kemal's modernisation efforts had encouraged women's unveiling, but did not go so far as to ban the veil. In the Shah's quest to modernise however, the Iranian monarch prioritised the regulation of women's bodies over their rights as citizens, in contrast to Turkey where women gained suffrage in 1934 and were left to choose whether to veil or not. The irony of this was not lost on Iranian women, who continued to campaign for their political rights, harnessing the Pahlavi regime rhetoric that women's political rights were essential to national development and progress (Afary 1996; Paidar 1995; Sanasarian 1982). In the end, the prerequisite for Iranian women 's political rights, granted in 1963, was state control of the women's movement, which Mohammad Reza Pahlavi (1941–79) accomplished in 1961 by dissolving independent women's organisations, as discussed below (Paidar 1995: 106–7).

The elites' insistence on the religious and cultural imperative to maintain male authority over women has been a constant barrier to all collective efforts to enhance women's political rights and representation. Following the 1979 revolution, the guardianship of women simply shifted from the monarchy to religious clerics, who appropriated women's bodies as symbols of national identity through forced veiling and attempts to increasingly relegate women to the private sphere. Despite significant controversy and resistance, the Islamic regime enforced a female dress code to further its own political image, not unlike the previous Pahlavi rulers. Although forced unveiling and veiling decrees did unwittingly empower some women by increasing their access to the public sphere, these measures unequivocally demonstrate male authority over women's bodies and choices (Hoodfar 1992; Paidar 2001). In addition to enacting policies that served to diminish women's public sphere access and roles, both regimes' harsh treatment of non-state-affiliated women's rights activists has hindered efforts to engage with political elites on enhancement of women's rights. Nevertheless, Iranian women's rights activists have never ceased to challenge the systemic subjugation of women in Iranian politics and society.

Contesting Male Authority

Similar to most Middle Eastern countries, Iranian women's politicisation correlated with the rise of nationalism (Badran 1995; Hoodfar 1999; Jayawardena 1986; Paidar 1995).[6] Iran's constitutional revolution (1906–11) provided Iranian women with one of the first opportunities to come out of seclusion and join the larger struggles for democracy and independence. With the support of the intelligentsia and the more conservative sectors including clerics and merchants (*baazaris*), Iranian women participated in political actions both peaceful and more aggressive, including boycotting foreign goods and threatening parliamentary deputies with pistols as they called on them to stand up to Russian self-interest (Afary 1996; Jayawardena 1986; Sanasarian 1982).

Pro-constitutionalist women took advantage of the burgeoning political space created by the constitutional movement to campaign for the inclusion of women's rights in the new constitution. When the country's first election law in 1906 denied all women and illiterate men the right to vote, several

---

[6] Although Iran was never formally colonised, it was de facto under the control of Russia (north) and Britain (south) throughout the nineteenth and much of the twentieth centuries.

women writers protested in articles published in nationalist papers (Paidar 1995). In 1911, when the Iranian parliament again denied women the vote and adopted universal *male* suffrage, exasperated women activists continued to pressure the intellectual and clerical elites on women's suffrage and other key women's rights issues (Afary 2005).[7]

With the coming to power of Reza Shah Pahlavi in 1925, Iranians witnessed a wave of social and political developments (Azimi 2008; Paidar 1995). As with Kemal in Turkey, Reza Shah's modernisation scheme included both a state feminism project, referred to as Woman's Awakening (*nehzat-e banovan*), which lasted from 1936–41 and encouraged female education and women's public sphere participation, and secularisation, exemplified by forced unveiling. Ironically, unlike Turkey, Reza Shah's state feminism did not include women's suffrage.

The policies of his successor, son Mohammad Reza Shah Pahlavi (1941–79), also simultaneously emancipated and restricted women, in particular independent women's rights organisations. Although the latter Pahlavi king's limited modernisation and progress efforts benefitted primarily urban, middle- and upper-class women, they nonetheless enable this limited demographic to develop a feminist consciousness and arrive at a set of gender equality demands not tied to their roles as wives and mothers, among them, women's right to vote. Iran's feminists organised for women's suffrage with the creation of the independent Women's Party (*Hizb-i Zanan*) in 1943. In order to find resonance with Iran's ruling elites, this party tactfully emphasised female suffrage as a pre-condition for Iran's 'progress' and 'modernity'. The Party justified women's rights to vote according to international rights discourses, while highlighting the elites' failed promises to deliver true modernity and progress for Iran's citizens, particularly its women (Amin 2002, 2008). However, despite Women's Party's and other independent women organisations' tactful lobbying, Mohammad Reza Pahlavi, similar to Turkey's Mustafa Kemal, banned all independent women's groups, including the Women's Party, as he viewed them as a threat to his absolute control over state affairs (Amin 2002, 2008; Khorasani and Ardalan 2003; Paidar 1995); and instead founded the High Council of Women's Organisations of Iran in 1961 as an umbrella organisation to

---

[7] Early twentieth century women's rights groups also campaigned for female education and to make polygamy and divorce more difficult for men (Paidar 1995).

oversee women's efforts under the presidency of his twin, Princess Ashraf (Paidar 1995).

In 1963, almost thirty years after women gained the vote in Turkey, the Shah proposed women's enfranchisement as part of the so-called White Revolution reforms. Clerics, including leading Pahlavi opponent Ayatollah Khomeini, declared the reforms un-Islamic and called for public outcry against them (Kar 2000; Paidar 1995; Sanasarian 1982). In response, masses of women campaigned supporting the reforms, and teachers, nurses and receptionists held a one-day strike that effectively paralysed the country, proving women's readiness to challenge the elites (Paidar 1995: 145), while Khomeini's call to protest resulted in his exile to Iraq (Hoodfar 1999).

A few months after women's suffrage, the 1963 parliamentary election witnessed the election of seven women (out of 200 seats). The Shah also appointed two women to the sixty-member Senate (Paidar 1995), one of whom (Iran's first female lawyer Mehrangiz Manuchehrian) drafted the proposal for the 1967 Family Protection Law, improving women's legal status concerning marriage, divorce, custody and polygamy.[8] Manuchehrian's appointment to the Senate by the Shah was in response to women's organising, as well as his own realisation of select women's capabilities to enter formal politics. However, Manuchehrian resigned in 1972 when a bill passed requiring women to obtain permission from a husband or male next-of-kin to get a passport or travel. She declared that her Senate seat simply provided good optics for the regime, which claimed progressiveness by pointing to its two female Senators, when 'in effect we cannot do anything for (women's) rights' (Khorasani and Ardalan 2003: 334).

In the ensuing decades it has become evident that to rectify women's marginalisation male authority and dominance in Iranian politics and society must be challenged. To date, after more than five decades of complete enfranchisement, women's political representation remains marginal, peaking at 6.7 per cent in the last Shah's final term from 1975–9, and falling to 1.5 per cent immediately following the Islamic revolution (see Table 6.1). Given the Islamic Republic's claim to a Quranic basis for the exclusion of women from the political sphere, religious women's rights activists are particularly well equipped to debunk this myopic rendering of religious texts, and indeed

---

[8] Although the passage of this important law is often credited to the Shah, it was Manuchehrian who drafted it long before 1967 and lobbied the monarchy for its adoption (Paidar 1995).

Table 6.1 Percentage of women parliamentarians in Iran.

Parliament	Percentage of Women	No. from Tehran	No. from other provinces
1963: *Women gain electoral rights*			
1963–1967	3.5% (7/200)	3	4
1967–1971	4.6% (10/219)	3	7
1971–1976	6.3% (17/268)	3	14
1975–1979	6.7% (18/268)	3	15
1979: *Establishment of the Islamic Republic of Iran*			
1980–1984 (1st)	1.5% (4/270)	4	0
1984–1988 (2nd)	1.5% (4/270)	4	0
1988–1992 (3rd)	1.5% (4/270)	4	0
1992–1996 (4th)	3.3% (9/270)	5	4
1996–2000 (5th)	4.9% (13/268)	7	6
2000–2004 (6th)	4.1% (12/290)	6	6
2004–2008 (7th)	4.5% (13/290)	6	7
2008–2012 (8th)	2.8% (8/290)	5	3
2012–2016 (9th)	3.1% (9/290)	4	5
2016–2020 (10th)	5.9% (17/290)	8	9
2020–2024 (11th)	5.9% (17/290)	5	12

Sources: Hoodfar 1999: 39; Inter-Parliamentary Union 2021; Iranian Interior Ministry.

it is their efforts in their re-reading of the religious texts that have led to the gradual expansion of women's political rights and status in Iran today.

The 1979 Revolution: Revolutionary Women Rise to Topple a Monarchy

While it was primarily women from the educated elite who were active in the 1906 constitutional revolution, during the 1979 revolution masses of ordinary women played key roles in toppling the Pahlavi regime. Though known as the 'Islamic Revolution', it is important to note that many of the millions of Iranians who rose in opposition to the Shah were motivated not by Islam, but by shared frustration and anger at the shortcomings of the monarchy. As Arang Keshavarzian argues, 'the overthrow of more than two millennia of monarchy was speedy and relatively bloodless precisely because the revolution was ideologically inclusive – encompassing self-professed leftists, feminists, nationalists and constitutionalists from almost all social classes' (2009a: 12). Women's active participation in this revolution was a clear indication of their commitment to shaping Iran's political future, after enduring decades of the Pahlavi regime's autocracy and intolerance of independent women's rights groups, particularly those that identified with the secular left.

Masses of women were politicised in the prelude to the revolution by leading intellectuals publicly urging women to look to Islam as the antidote to the excesses and oppression of the corrupt and morally bankrupt Pahlavi regime and its secularisation policies, with which many ordinary Iranian women failed to identify. But it was Islamic ideals and morals that were heralded, not a return to pre-modern 'tradition' as has been widely portrayed. In fact, it is argued that the revolution 'consumed the products of development, integrated itself within modern structures and institutions, and reconstructed a modern political ideology' (Paidar 1995: 172). Muslim reformist Ali Shariati (1933–77) played a key role in fostering a revolutionary image of Iranian women as both political *and* pious (Terman 2010), encouraging them to follow in the footsteps of outspoken Shi'i heroines Fatima and Zeinab (Shariati 1981) and urging them to turn away from both the monarchy's Westernised and sexualised female subjectivity and the passive, secluded woman touted by more traditional clerics. Prior to the revolution, tapes of Shariati's lectures circulated widely, mobilising thousands of dissatisfied Iranian youth into action (Shaditalab 2006). Renowned clerical figures such as Ayatollahs Taleghani (1911–79) and Motahhari (1919–79) also advocated for modernisation of Shi'ism, and wrote extensively on Muslim women's roles in the shifting Iranian social context.[9]

This revolutionary gender discourse politicised many women across the ideological spectrum to oppose the Shah and take actions that risked imprisonment or execution by the state's secret police. Iranian women's activism during the 1979 revolution astonished both national and international observers and indelibly shifted the imagery of women's public roles. Secular

---

[9] Works that shaped modern Shi'i discourse on gender include: Mahmud Taleghani (1979), 'On Hejab', in Azam Tabari and Nahid Yeganeh (eds) (1982), *In the Shadow of Islam*, London: Zed Books; Morteza Motahhari (1978), *Nezam-e Hoghoghe Zan dar Islam (The System of Women's Rights in Islam)*, Tehran: Sadra Publications; Ali Shariati (1980), *Fatima is Fatima*, trans. Laleh Bakhtiar, Tehran: Hamdami and Shariati Foundation.

women's rights activists who were excluded from the state-run women's organisations, publicly expressed their opposition to the Shah by adopting conservative dress in public, including the modern *hijab* (Keddie 2007). As detailed in Chapter 8, contemporary Iranian women activists highlight their indisputable role in the success of the 1979 revolution when pressuring political elites to address their current demands.

Women's mass participation in the anti-monarchy movements forced many conservative clerics, including Ayatollah Khomeini, to reconsider their stance on women's political rights and roles. While in 1963 Khomeini had publicly denounced women's suffrage as anti-Islamic, in 1979 he urged women to vote for an Islamic Republic, and publicly framed its virtues in the most gender-equal terms he could muster (Amin 2008). In a speech specifically addressing women, Khomeini emphasised that women's rights are embedded in Islam, including political participation, education and employment, and noted that no man's permission is required for women to vote or demonstrate, as these are divine duties mandated by Shari'a. He promised that the Islamic regime would grant women divinely ordained rights that far exceeded the rights enjoyed by Western women (Kar 2000; Saidzadeh 1998).

This complete turn-about can be explained in a number of ways. First, women's large-scale participation in the revolution, and the newly iconic image of veiled revolutionary women rendered the regime's founders unable to ignore women as political agents (Hoodfar and Sadr 2009; Keddie 2007; Shaditalab 2006; Vakil 2011). In particular, women from more religious and conservative sectors of society used the revolution's legitimisation of women's public participation as Islamic as an opportunity to enter the public sphere and pursue their interests. The revolutionary fervour encouraged one of my informants, Zahra, then a high-school student and now an active member of a conservative party, to join her school's Islamic girl's group and participate in all the major demonstrations. When her father, worried about violence, tried to restrict her participation in the street protests she stood her ground.

> I was only about fifteen or sixteen . . . and to prove to my father my devotion I packed my suitcase and put it next to my bedroom door. I threatened that if he did not support my right to protest, I would run away. My father, who was a religious man, knew that I meant it, so he eased off and instead prayed for my safety every time I went out. (Personal interview, 11 June 2015)

The new regime's emphasis on women's education in fact supported the goals of women's groups previously stonewalled by the monarchy.[10]

Second, the regime's founders knew the success of the new Islamic Republic required women's support. In particular, Khomeini depended on the female vote to secure the new regime and legitimise his rule, thus his call for women to support Iran's new political system at the ballot box. Clearly Khomeini's reversal of position in support of women's political participation had more to do with political expediency than with divine scripture (Hoodfar and Sadr 2009; Kar 2000; Paidar 1995). In fact Khomeini and the Islamic Republic's founders reversed many of the rights secured by women under the monarchy, particularly women's family rights, by declaring them un-Islamic, while upholding their right to vote (Afshar 1982; Hoodfar 1999; Paidar 1995). Nevertheless, this important reversal in Khomeini's position on women's political duties showed Iranian women that so-called Islamic rulings are not written in stone, and that given contextual opportunities and women's preparedness, even the highest-ranking religious figures can depart from their initial stands on women's rights. This realisation encouraged many Iranian women's rights activists to engage with political elites in hopes for reform of gender discriminatory legislation in theocratic Iran.

Lastly, this shift also highlights the fact that Khomeini and his close allies were keenly aware of a global audience, at a time when gender rights were under scrutiny by the international community (Amin 2008). Ironically, despite the Islamic regime's apparent disregard for international standards on women's rights, various scholars have convincingly argued that the regime's leaders have often found themselves engaging with 'the notion of international standards of women's progress' as something to be met or justify exemption from (Amin 2008; Osanloo 2006, 2009). Turning back the clock on women's suffrage was potentially too costly for even ultra-conservatives such as Khomeini. However, in drafting the new constitution it became clear that while the Islamic regime expected women's full participation as supportive voters and demonstrators, it did not expect their presence at the decision-making table.

---

[10] For example, allocating half of medical and nursing school placements to women. The Islamic Republic's policies of gender segregation and expanded women's education notably increased women's employment opportunities (Hoodfar and Sadr 2009).

Women's Political Representation in Post-revolutionary Iran

Despite their high level of political *participation* during the revolution, women's political *representation* fell drastically in its aftermath. To preserve its image and in an attempt to win the support of the revolutionary women who had helped topple the monarchy, the new regime recruited a few token women to key political positions. For instance, Monireh Gorji was the only woman of seventy-three appointed members of the first Assembly of Experts, which was tasked with drafting post-revolutionary Iran's constitution (Paidar 1995; Tajali 2011; Vakil 2011). As the sole female member, she however failed to enshrine various constitutional rights for Iranian women, despite her clear articulation of the regime's own rhetoric claiming women to be the foundation of the family and of Islamic society (Hoodfar and Sadr 2009). Only four women – just 1.5 per cent of sitting members, entered the parliament, and this continued for the first three parliaments. Only one new woman was elected to replace one of the original four; the others were simply re-elected each round (Koolaee 2012; Vakil 2011). Unsurprisingly, the fundamentalist fervour of the new regime discouraged the candidacy of many women. Furthermore, the Islamic Republic's first female parliamentarians had close familial or professional ties to high-ranking clerics. For instance, Maryam Behrouzi who served in the first four rounds of the post-revolutionary parliament was educated in religious seminaries and backed by the conservatives. The number of women members of parliament has remained low: the highest percentage of women elected was 5.9 per cent in 2016 – the tenth parliamentary session since the revolution (see Table 6.1).

Women's political under-representation in post-revolutionary Iran has greatly hindered the capacity to address women's concerns through formal political decision-making processes. The conservative clerics who have monopolised power reversed many of the hard-won rights secured by women during the monarchy, rights the few women politicians have lacked the support and leverage to defend. A major setback was the reversal of the 1967 Family Protection Law, which had increased women's grounds for divorce, limited male divorce and polygamy rights, and determined child custody based on the child's best interests (Keddie 2007; Nashat 1980; Paidar 1995). These legal changes faced little contestation from the public since most women did not have the knowledge or the means to engage with the court and legal systems. Additionally, many women had more immediate concerns – namely poverty, illiteracy, and an insufficient social infrastructure, all of which the Islamic Republic had promised to address.[11] While a number of key revolutionary women, such as Zahra Rahnavard and Maryam Behrouzi, sought to raise public awareness about the repercussions of these reversals, their efforts proved fruitless under the hard-line clerics' tight grip on post-revolutionary politics (personal interview with a journalist and women's rights activist, 2 July 2011).

Iran's Islamisation process also entailed mandatory veiling and gender segregation (Shahrokni 2020). Many women from religious and conservative backgrounds welcomed these reforms as an important corrective to the monarchy's forced unveiling and pro-Westernisation policies (Hoodfar 1992, 1999; Mir-Hosseini 2007); however, some scholars argue that forced veiling cannot be understood as a tool for religious women's empowerment, given that it severely limits women's rights (Moghissi 1999).

Beyond these competing perspectives regarding the impact of Islamisation for Iranian women's empowerment, my research suggests that the revolutionary gender and social justice discourses have galvanised women's rights activism in part because of the state's failure to deliver on its initial promises of 'Islamic justice' for women, leaving women across the political and ideological spectrums highly motivated to pressure Iran's ruling elites on women's rights and status. While the revolutionary gender discourse mobilised women in support of the Islamic regime and encouraged their entry into the public sphere, post-revolutionary legal reforms in effect prioritised their domesticity, restricted their freedom of movement and rendered them second-class citizens. The regime's contradictory policies, and the gaps between its promised 'Islamic justice' and what it delivered, incited women to rally for their divinely ordained 'Islamic rights' (Osanloo 2009). Although women's demands were initially articulated primarily by educated and middle-class women (of both secular and religious backgrounds), Iranians of both sexes from a wide spectrum of society soon took up the cause of gender equality (personal interviews with two women's rights activists, 2 June 2009 and 12 July 2011).

---

[11] Maxine Molyneux's (1985) distinction between women's 'practical interests', such as poverty and illiteracy, and 'strategic interests', which address women's subordinate status in society through affirmative action measures, helps explain women's ongoing low societal, economic and legal status in Iran. The Pahlavi regime mostly sought to address women's strategic interests, while the Islamic regime attended to women's practical interests; neither addressed these interests simultaneously.

Obstacles to Women's Political Representation in the Islamic Republic of Iran

The Islamic Republic of Iran is a unique fusion of republicanism and religious authoritarianism, with power divided between elected and non-elected (mostly religious) branches. Its republican aspect includes popular elections for a government and parliament, which however wields limited influence; the Islamic feature ensures that ultimate power is in the hands of a clerical oligarchy. In this political structure, Iran's theocracy has limited women's access to formal political decision-making in both official and unofficial ways: legislation has prioritised women's domestic duties over their public and political roles and deploys discriminatory language in constitutional articles outlining criteria for a multitude of positions; and the ruling elites have subtly instituted processes, including candidate vetting, in order to maintain power in the hands of a select few 'qualified' individuals, determined by criteria including allegiance to the theocracy, religious training and previous activities. By default, the specifics of each of these criteria generally eliminate most women, and hence are of significance for the purpose of this research.

As illustrated in Figure 6.3 below, the distribution of political power between non-elected and elected institutions leaves the clerical Shi'i authorities with either direct control or extreme influence over all aspects of the state. The most powerful figure in the Islamic Republic is the Supreme Leader, who is appointed by the popularly elected Assembly of Experts, a body of clerics with extensive religious training.[12] Thus far, the Islamic Republic has had two Supreme Leaders (*rahbars*), Ruhollah Khomeini (1979–89), and since 1989, Ali Khamenei.

While Khomeini generally avoided addressing women's lack of access to decision-making, his successor Khamenei is increasingly forced to grapple with this issue, largely thanks to pressure from the growing constituency of feminist women (and men). Khamenei's speeches and statements on his official website elucidate his conservative stance on women's public roles. In

---

[12] The Assembly of Experts is a constitutionally enshrined eighty-eight-member body of *mujtahids* (those with the religious authority to conduct independent reasoning or *ijtihad*). Though members are popularly elected for eight-year terms, to qualify to run, candidates must be masters of Islamic jurisprudence and be approved by the non-elected Guardians' Council (*Shoura-ye negahban*). To date, the Council has not approved female *mujtahidahs* to run for this office. The Assembly is charged with electing or removing the Supreme Leader and supervising his actions.

a 2014 Iranian women's day speech on women's employment, Khamenei spends more than half of his forty-minute talk lambasting 'feminism and Western thought' for failing and objectifying women, stating 'If we wish to move forward on women's rights in Iran we have to free our minds from Western discourse on gender equality.' He argues that gender equality is unjust because it ignores the natural differences between men and women. 'Why should we delegate "manly" works to women? This does not make sense and it is not fair . . . I feel sorry that at times it is women themselves . . . who persist on this issue and ask "how are we different from men?"' He goes on to justify the exclusion of women from certain fields and positions, declaring 'Discrimination is not always bad . . . it is to protect women and grant them security.' Emphasising women's domestic roles as the priority, he ends his speech saying 'we do not oppose women's employment or even leadership, so long as it does not conflict with their primary roles' (Khamenei 2014).

According to women's rights activist Mehrangiz Kar, having Iran's highest-ranking figure reiterate the regime's official gender discourse in this way makes opposing it very difficult for other male elites and policymakers (Sanij 2017). Long-term parliamentarian Maryam Behrouzi also noted in an interview with me that the 'cultural attitude' of many male elites – which undervalues women's capabilities and contributions and sees men and women as unequal – is a major obstacle to women's political representation (21 July 2011). However, women activists and some of the bolder male elite are increasingly challenging the regime's gender discourse, and recent reasoning from some Muslim scholars and clerics supporting women's access to positions of political and religious authority highlight the lack of clerical consensus on women's roles in Islamic societies, as later discussed in the conclusion of this chapter (Tajali 2011). Despite this rising debate among leading Iranian religious thinkers,[13] the theocracy's founders have ingeniously integrated institutional obstacles that ensure political and religious authority is not only male dominated, but is also concentrated in the hands of a select 'acceptable' few, as further discussed below.

The lack of scholarly attention specifically to institutional obstacles to *women's* political representation in Iran is largely due to the fact that the coun-

---

[13] For a sample of debate among Islamic scholars on female political authority, see Azam Taleghani's 1997 *Payam-e Hajar (Hajar's Message)* magazine (issue 227) on the topic of women's presidency in Iran.

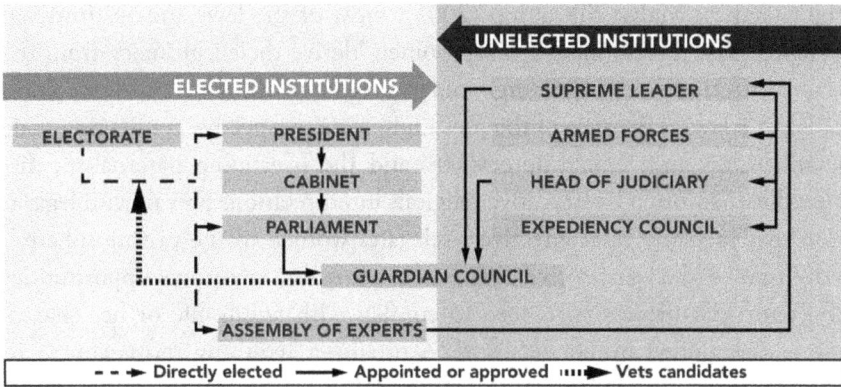

Figure 6.3 Iran's institutional structure: flow of power among unelected and elected institutions.

try's power structure and political system preclude the participation of most individuals, regardless of gender. Based on interviews I conducted in 2011 and 2015 with reformist party members, I believe that this absence of critical analysis of the obstacles keeping women out of politics has fostered an erroneous sense that democratisation, especially reform of the theocratic structure, will inevitably entail women's equal access to formal politics. Hence, even the staunchest advocates of reform lack sufficient understanding of these barriers, or ways to address them. Here, I outline a number of such legal and institutional obstacles, including the role of the Council of Guardians, that lead to women's political under-representation in Iranian formal politics, despite their high levels of political participation as voters, campaigners and organisers.

Legal obstacles

Post-revolutionary legal codes and the Iranian constitution include a number of contentious articles regarding women's rights and societal roles, all of which influence women's access to the public and political spheres. The constitution does not refer to gender *equality*, but rather states that rights are granted 'in conformity with Islamic criteria'.[14] According to Iranian women's

---

[14] For instance, the phrase 'in conformity with Islamic criteria' appears in Articles 20 and 21 of the Constitution with reference to rights and legal protection of all citizens 'both men and women', and 'rights of women in all areas', respectively (The Iranian Constitution, available from http://www.iranonline.com/iran/iran-info/government/constitution-3.html).

rights activist Mahsa Shekarloo (2005), most of the laws and institutional practices that discriminate against women 'derive their legitimacy from the clause effectively subordinating women's rights to the state's interpretation of Islamic law'.[15] Because of the prevailing male perspective concerning male guardianship and female domesticity and the overriding paternalism discussed earlier, often conservative religious interpretations prevail with legislation that in many cases effectively relegates women to the private sphere.[16] For instance, the Iranian civil code limits women's professional opportunities if a particular profession is seen to conflict with family life or her character as determined by her husband. A provision requiring most women to obtain written permission from a male guardian to obtain a passport or travel outside the country is another example.[17] Various women's rights activists have decried these laws as intended to subjugate women and maintain male authority by curtailing women's opportunities in the public sphere. Nobel Peace Prize laureate and longtime women's rights defender Shirin Ebadi said in a 2010 speech:

> How can we have a female minister or deputy to represent Iran's affairs (at the international level), when she must first acquire her husband's permission before she makes any international travel? God forbid she gets in a fight with her husband the night before she is supposed to travel abroad, and her

[15] Shekarloo (2005) further argues that it is due to the requirement of 'in conformity with Islamic criteria' that a major focus of women's rights activists has been to offer interpretations of Islamic jurisprudence that encourage gender equality.

[16] For the purpose of this research, I will elaborate on legal obstacles that specifically curtail women's political rights and roles, though acknowledging that other discriminatory rulings in areas such as family, education and employment can also negatively impact women's political presence. I emphasise that much of the discriminatory post-revolutionary Iran's gender policies are justified according to conservative interpretations within Ja'afari jurisprudence. Iran's Council of Guardians and to a lesser extent the Expediency Council, largely backed by conservatives, are tasked with ensuring that laws passed by the Iranian parliament are in congruence with Islamic law.

[17] While all married women, and females under the age of eighteen, require a male guardian's permission to apply for a passport, single women and all men (whether married or single) over eighteen do not. The conservative government of President Ahmadinejad introduced a bill in 2012 requiring single women under forty applying for a passport to get permission from a male guardian as well, but it faced huge opposition from women's rights groups, including the parliament's own Women's Commission, and parliament ultimately rejected the bill (Radio Farda 2013).

husband refuses to give her a written permission. Then we are stuck with an empty seat at the assembly! (Speech at Concordia University, Montreal, Canada, 3 March 2010)

There are other legal obstacles specifically curtailing women's access to certain political decision-making positions. For example, Article 115 of the Constitution stipulates '*rijal*' as one of the criteria for becoming president. When the Islamic Republic's constitution was being drafted, some members of the Assembly of Experts proposed 'maleness' as a requirement of the office of the presidency. This caused widespread debate as many Iranians, including more liberal members of the Assembly, objected. As a compromise, the Assembly of Experts accepted the criterion of '*rijal*' instead, which technically means men, but in its Arabic usage also refers to women who have been granted honorary male status (Tajali 2011; Taleghani 1997b). The requirement of *rijal* is nevertheless a major obstacle to women trying to access the office of the presidency, since the Council of Guardians, which determines who qualifies to run for president, has thus far refused to accept any of the women who have attempted to register their candidacy, including some who have demonstrated deep commitment to the regime through their political activities, have religious training, and have served in political decision-making positions including parliament. Many Iranian women activists have declared that qualifying a female candidate for this office will be the only satisfactory act that the Council does not discriminate against women.

The legal requirement of religious training for political leadership positions also hinders women's access to key positions since women have limited options for acquiring such training; also, since there is no clerical consensus on whether women can serve as *marjas* (source of emulation in Shi'i Islam), *mujtahids* (those with the religious authority to conduct independent reasoning or *ijtihad*) or *faqihs* (Muslim jurists), women are essentially barred from posts that require these designations.[18] Thus, while the law does not specifically mention gender as a requirement for membership in the Assembly of Experts or the twelve-member Council of Guardians, the requirement to be

---

[18] While only a select few women have reached the title *Mujtahidas* (feminine of *Mujtahid* – a person recognised in the Shi'a tradition as an original authority in Islamic law), there is no clerical consensus on whether they can engage in religious interpretation similar to their male counterparts, since some conservative clergy argue that they can only provide rulings on women's issues.

a *mujtahid* means very few women will have the background required for these positions (Kar 2000), as explained below. Similarly, women are barred from the office of the Supreme Leader (*Vali-e faqih*), the ultimate political and religious authority in Iran, due to the legal requirement of being a *marja*. Although religious women's organisations, such as the Zeinab Society (*Jameh Zeinab*)[19] have been lobbying to increase women's access to religious training in hopes that women can eventually serve in political institutions such as the Assembly of Experts, no significant reforms have yet materialised.

The only position for which the law clearly requires 'maleness' is judgeship. Despite an outcry and organised protests by female lawyers soon after the revolution, Iran's conservatives banned women from serving as judges, a position open to women and held by some prior to the revolution (Paidar 1995). Although many Islamic nationalist and reformist organisations supported female judgeship, Khomeini simply declared that 'women's judgment is against *Shari'a* law' (Kar 2000: 100). In 1995, after sixteen years of sustained lobbying, a reform was adopted allowing women to serve as advisory assistants to male judges in family court (Kar 2000; Osanloo 2009).

Although legal obstacles are a key factor in women's marginalisation from political decision-making, laws are not fixed and several concerning gender have been reformed and upheld by conservative backed institutions in post-revolutionary Iran, subsequent to sustained lobbying by rights activists and progressive religious thinkers. Thus, rights activists across the ideological and political spectrums are focused on the potential for reform of discriminatory clauses constraining women's access to political decision-making positions.

Iranian factional politics
Where Iranian law does not specify gender or religious requirements for political leadership positions – such as membership in parliament, on local councils, or for ministerial positions – a series of institutional obstacles remains. Some of these are unique to Iran's theocratic structure, others are not. Similar to France, Iran utilises the majoritarian two-round electoral system (TRS),

---

[19] Founded in 1986, the Zeinab Society was until recently Iran's largest formally structured women's organisation. It has branches across the country and oversees eight women's seminaries in Qom. The Society lobbies extensively to advance women's rights from within an Islamic framework, particularly women's access to political and religious decision-making positions (personal interview with the Society's secretary, 11 July 2011).

which research has identified as 'less friendly' to women's political representation in comparison to proportional representation systems, such as the one used in Turkey (Matland and Studlar 1996; Reynolds 1999; Rule 1994; Rule and Zimmerman 1994). Under the two-round system voters vote for individual candidates rather than a party list, which in turn decreases party incentives to be inclusive of diverse sections of society. Rather parties are inclined to nominate 'safer' well-connected, middle- and upper-class male candidates over 'riskier' female candidates in order to maximise the perceived odds of winning seats (Hoodfar and Tajali 2011). In Iran, TRS has fostered competition between the two dominant reformist and conservative factions, both of which prioritise winning seats in Iran's male-dominated political context over creating gender balanced institutions.

Ideological competition is among the most salient features of the current Iranian political landscape, as ideological blocs or 'factions' aim to advance their own particular interpretation of issues and policies. Iran's factions are constellations of groups, political parties, organisations, clergy and non-clergy that support the ideals of an Islamic state as originally presented by the Republic's founders, but 'disagree on the nature of the theocracy's political system and its policies in different spheres' (Moslem 2002: 2).[20] Factional power struggles are pronounced during popular elections as each faction strives for control over a particular institution or branch of government – namely the executive or the legislative. However, political power among state institutions is distributed unequally and in a hierarchical manner, with the reformist faction being particularly disadvantaged since currently ultimate power rests in the hands of the conservative Supreme Leader. This power imbalance, whereby certain bodies can override the decisions of others, is a significant feature of the Iranian political framework and a major hindrance to its democratisation. Yet, Iran's factional politics is fluid in that factional control over various state institutions may shift as a result of elections. Hence,

---

[20] For the purpose of this research, I simplify Iran's ideological political camps between the conservatives (also referred to as Principlists or 'usulgarayan') and reformists (or 'islahtalaban'). It is important to note that these categories are heterogeneous in that there is much variety among groups and elites who align with each camp. For a brief introduction to the diverse range of groups within each category and the shifts they have undergone in recent years, see Mohammad Sahimi (2009), 'The Political Groups', in Frontlines' Tehranbureau, https://www.pbs.org/wgbh/pages/frontline/tehranbureau/2009/05/the-political-groups.html (accessed 6 June 2019).

in the past two decades, Iran's executive and legislative branches have experienced swings of control by both reformist and conservative factions.

Unlike Turkey's clearly distinctive political parties, I show that Iran's fluid factional politics presents a major obstacle to women's political representation, as it prevents the development of organised parties with clear platforms to mobilise voters. Thus, while Turkish women's groups can sustain pressure on established political parties and political elites with clear platforms, Iranian women's groups have limited capacity to effectively and extensively lobby political elites and state institutions for structural change (for example electoral gender quotas), or simply to have more women candidates nominated,[21] since parties and more recently, coalitions, primarily form just around elections.

Given the structural hierarchy of the Islamic Republic, the support of the Supreme Leader and his close allies for conservatives over reformists has been detrimental to women's political representation. As will be discussed next, this support includes the intentional marginalisation of influential reformist figures, particularly reformist women, through the Council of Guardians' mass disqualifications of reformists since the 2004 parliamentary elections. In 2009, the state banned two popular reformist parties[22] most supportive of women's political participation, greatly hindering mobilisation for women's political rights. The crackdown on reformists has led to even greater reluctance from reformist elites to support women's political empowerment, fearing additional clampdowns. However, despite the Council's overwhelming support for conservative candidates in recent years, it has been unable to undermine popular support for the reform movement and its objective of gradual democratisation. Since state institutional legitimacy depends heavily upon public support, the Council is forced to accept the nominations of some reformist candidates; and reformist women, who have in many ways planted the seed for women's political engagement at all levels in post-revolutionary Iran, continue to agitate for women's increased political representation.

---

[21] Women's groups in Iran have tended to press for female candidates to be included on party lists, rather than encouraging women's candidacy as independents, since many women lack sufficient resources to finance an election campaign without party advertising support.

[22] The Islamic Iran Participation Front (*Jebheye Mosharekat-e Iran-e Islami;* henceforth *Mosharekat*), the only party at the time that had adopted internal quotas to ensure women's presence within the party structures as discussed in Chapter 7, and Mojahedin of the Islamic Revolution Organization (*Sazman-e Mojahedin-e Enghelab Islami*).

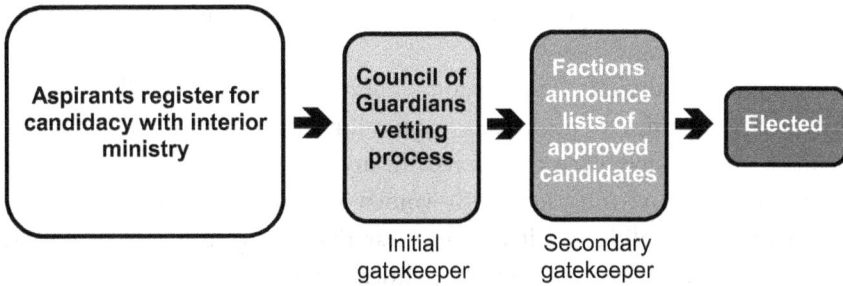

Figure 6.4 The Council of Guardians' process of 'approbatory supervision' for major elections.

The Council of Guardians: The main gatekeeper to women's political representation

A significant and uniquely Iranian institutional obstacle to women's political representation, and democracy and fair elections in general, is the Council of Guardians. This twelve-member unelected body designed by the Iranian constitution following the 1979 revolution, is essentially entrusted with guarding the theocracy.[23] Its two main responsibilities are to ensure that the laws passed by parliament are compatible with Shari'a law and the Constitution, and to supervise elections by vetting all candidates for the Presidency, Assembly of Experts and parliament, referred to as 'approbatory supervision' (Arjomand 2009). Over the years, this supervisory role has come to mean that the Council decides who is 'appropriate' to run for public office based on their commitment to Islam and the Islamic regime, and loyalty to the Constitution and to the rule of the Supreme Leader (*Vali-e faqih*). For parliamentary elections, parties, or more recently coalition fronts, may only select their lists of candidates from a pool of individuals approved by the Council (see Figure 6.4). Eclipsing its constitutionally defined responsibilities, the Council of Guardians has increasingly been disqualifying any candidate it deems a threat to the regime's stability. With few exceptions, the Council in recent elections

---

[23] The Council of Guardians is composed of six clerics selected by the Supreme Leader, and six lawyers elected by parliament from a list provided by the Head of the Judiciary, who is himself appointed by the Supreme Leader. Given the Supreme Leader's de facto control over the Council's composition, members tend to be closely tied to the Conservative faction. The conservatism of the Council is also apparent by their members' frequent remarks disapproving women holding positions of authority (Al Jazeera 2013)

has sought to maintain power in the hands of the conservatives by disqualifying most reformists.[24]

Since the Council's 'approbatory supervision' applies to all registered candidates regardless of gender, its implications for women's political representation have rarely been considered. In my research on Iran's major elections, and extensive interviews with women activists, party women, women candidates and politicians, it became clear that in fact this institution has particular repercussions for women's political representation. I found that the Council's candidate vetting process is a major barrier for women's descriptive, substantive and symbolic representation, which further reiterates the interconnectedness among the different dimensions of representation as previously argued by Pitkin (1972) and Schwindt-Bayer and Mishler (2005).

In terms of women's political aspirations, I observed that the Council's mere vetting process discourages many women from registering their candidacy in the first place, negatively impacting women's descriptive representation. Women in fact comprise less than 10 per cent of all those who register to run for parliament or the presidency (see Tables 6.2 and 6.3). It seems clear that the Council's vetting process adds another layer of intimidation for women to an already unwelcoming and male-dominated political environment. I met many well-connected and politically experienced women who would not entertain the idea of running for office because of the risk of arbitrary disqualification and the consequent inevitable harm to a women's reputation given Iran's patriarchal context. Among women who did dare to register for candidacy, some faced resistance from their husbands or families because of the stigma of a possible rejection.

The Council's vetting process also has negative implications for women's substantive representation in terms of electing legislators who will advocate

---

[24] The Council of Guardians disqualifies many registered candidates it considers secular, too liberal, too controversial, or not completely in line with the regime's structure and the rule of the Supreme Leader (which since the mid-2000s increasingly includes many reformists), even if they have religious credentials and a long history of service and involvement with the Islamic regime. For instance, considering him a threat to the conservatives' power in 2013 the Council disqualified Ayatollah Hashemi Rafsanjani, one of the founders of the Islamic Republic, for the presidency under the pretext of his old age (Milani 2013). For the 2017 presidential elections, the Council also disqualified former ultra-conservative President Ahmadinejad (2005–13) for the sake of political stability given his defiant and divisive nature (Keshavarzian and Sohrabi 2017).

Table 6.2 Women's participation in Iran's parliamentary elections 2000–20.

Year	% ♀ of total registered candidates	% ♀ of total qualified candidates by the Council of Guardians	% ♀ of total elected [a]
2000	7.3% [b]	NA/6,459 [b]	4.1 %
	504/6,860		12/290
2004	11.8% [c]	9.3% [c]	4.5%
	847/7,179	436/4,679	13/290
2008	7.6% [d]	~7-8% [e]	2.9%
	580/7,597	~360/4,597	8/290
2012	7.9% [f]	7% [f]	3.1%
	428/5,395	243/3,460	9/290
2016	10.2% [f]	9.4% [f]	5.9%
	1,234/12,123	586/6,229	17/290
2020	12% [g]	10.9% [g]	5.9%
	~1,900/16,033	782/7,157	17/290

Sources: [a] Inter-Parliamentary Union 2021; [b] Dokouhaki and Tarighi 2000; [c] Ebrahimi 2004; [d] Torfeh 2008; [e] personal interview with party women in 2011 and 2015; [f] Iran Newspaper 2015; [g] Iranian Interior Ministry.

Table 6.3 Women's participation in Iran's presidential elections.

Year	No. ♀ registered	Year	No. ♀ registered
1997	8/238 (3.3%)	**2013**	30/680 (4.4%)
2001	47/814 (5.8%)	**2017**	137/1,636 (8.3%)
2005	89/1014 (8.8%)	**2021**	40/592 (6.7%)
2009	42/476 (8.8%)		

Note: Women have been registering to become presidential candidates since 1997. As of 2021, the Council of Guardians has never qualified a woman to run as a presidential candidate.
Sources: Holland 2013; Iranian Interior Ministry; IRNA 2017.

on behalf of women. The Council's filtering of candidates, which generally favours conservatives, has largely prevented the candidacy of anyone with links to feminist and reformist movements.[25] According to Iranian women's

---

[25] Since the mid-2000s, the Council increasingly performs mass disqualifications and has at times in certain districts rejected close to 60 per cent of those who registered for candidacy,

rights activists across the ideological spectrum, a significant underlying reason for the Council's disqualification of female reformists is their advocacy for women's rights on top of their overall reformist positions. Given the mobilisation and popularisation of the Iranian women's movement during the reform era, the Council of Guardians shows little tolerance for the expansion and strengthening of a liberal gender discourse as presented by outspoken reformist female parliamentarians and their colleagues (personal interview with a women's rights activist and scholar, 4 July 2011). Thus, from the seventh to the ninth parliaments (2004–16) the Council enabled right-wing conservative women to gain seats in parliament and act as mouthpieces for their male peers. These women MPs often sought to limit women's rights rather than advance them. For instance, they pushed for legislation that limited women's employment opportunities by restricting their working hours, and remained silent on a bill making polygamy and man's unilateral divorce easier (Tabnak 2010). Today, very few women aspiring to parliament who demonstrate commitment to women's rights pass the Council of Guardians' ideological filters. The fact that the Council generally does not provide reasons for rejecting candidates leaves female parliamentary hopefuls without any viable avenues to contest the Council's decision.

Having lost faith in conservative female MPs, Iranian women's rights activists chose instead to lobby moderate male parliamentarians on crucial bills. To contest a polygamy bill for instance, activists engaged with the wives of some male parliamentarians, phoning them and asking, 'How would you feel if I married your husband?' (Amnesty International 2011). Under pressure from their wives, these male MPs used every means to avoid discussion on the bill, which has delayed its adoption until now. Constraining advocates of women's rights from entering parliament has negative symbolic implications as well, which profoundly impact women's political and social justice aspirations, since parliament continues to be widely seen as an institution unresponsive to women's demands. Considering that the Council severely curtails female representation by eliminating potential candidates with feminist views, and maintains the parliament as a symbolically male domain,

the majority of them reformists (Ajiri 2016). Given that reformists are generally more sympathetic than conservatives to women's political representation, and that some reform parties support women in politics, these disqualifications have greatly limited women's access to formal politics.

Iranian women's rights activists have in recent years been trying to analyse the Council's mechanisms for sidelining women and strategise ways to surmount its extensive disqualification of women who register for candidacy.

With the high 53 per cent disqualification rate for registered women candidates in the 2016 parliamentary elections,[26] activist Azadeh Davachi (2016) examines whether this was due to candidates' links to reformist or moderate groups or simply hostility to equal representation of women in formal politics. In fact, Davachi highlights the interconnectedness of these two possibilities, but argues that the broad disqualification of female candidates is motivated primarily by the Council's objective of systematically excluding potentially oppositional political groups from interference in the regime's legislative process. The similarly high rate of disqualification of reformist and moderate male candidates supports this conclusion. However, the disqualification of many independent aspiring female candidates suggests the Council's opposition to women parliamentarians goes beyond political or factional considerations. Seeking to maintain power in the hands of a select few, the Council seems to fear that women's presence in formal politics undermines the male dominance that is central to the regime, and that women's rise to power alongside reformists would likely lead to lasting structural changes in political and legislative processes. The regime is highly attuned to the potential for activist women to mobilise Iranian women in general and disrupt Iranian political and social structures, as witnessed during the early reform era and the sixth parliament (2000–4), which I will discuss in the next chapter.

The Council's marginalisation of predominately reformist women does not mean however that women with close ties to conservative faction elites freely compete in elections without any institutional impediments. While the Council rarely disqualifies women members of conservative parties or groups, since that could tarnish the regime's image, conservative party leaders themselves systematically discriminate against women. And, while the Council's rejections are public knowledge, other institutional barriers mostly

---

[26] As discussed later, mobilisation campaigns by activists prior to the 2016 parliamentary elections led to a tripling of the number of women registering as candidates from 428 in 2012 to 1,234. The Council disqualified 53 per cent of these and 48 per cent of all registered men. In some major cities this was extremely pronounced: in Shiraz, the Council disqualified forty-eight out of fifty women who registered to run (Davachi 2016).

function behind closed doors during internal party discussions among male political elites, as I was told by high-ranking party women from the conservative faction who regularly witness or are subject to discriminatory behaviour. Although conservatives justify the restriction of women to the domestic sphere through traditionalist interpretations of religious texts, many women who are affiliated with conservative political groups or parties, particularly those who became politicised during the revolution in support of the ideals promoted by the regime's founders, see no contradiction between women holding positions of political authority and Islam, as further elaborated in Chapter 8.

Political parties as secondary gatekeepers to women's political representation
A number of female members and affiliates of conservative parties and groups spoke in interviews with me about barriers keeping Iranian women out of politics, the most high-ranking of whom was Maryam Behrouzi, who passed away in 2012. A long-term activist for the Islamic movement, prior to the 1979 revolution Behrouzi was among the only female students of Ayatollah Khomeini and became a prominent female preacher, which resulted in her imprisonment by the Pahlavi regime. Immediately following the revolution, she was one of the four women who served in the first four sessions of the Islamic Republic's parliament. In 1986, she founded and until her death directed the largest conservative women's organisation and political party in Iran, the Zeinab Society (*Jameh Zeinab*), with the intention to nurture generations of revolutionary women and increase women's presence in positions of political and religious authority. In a personal interview, Behrouzi spoke candidly about male party leaders' resistance to including numerous female candidates on election party lists.[27] 'In our meetings, I would ask to include at least ten women onto their Tehran candidate lists, from a total of 30 parliamentary seats; but even to add one woman's name (in addition to the two or three token women whom the party had chosen), I would face much struggle.' When I inquired about the type of resistance she encountered, she chuckled and responded,

---

[27] Maryam Behrouzi's Zeinab Society (until her untimely death in 2012) was a major political party among Iran's conservative forces, and even considered as the women's wing of the oldest and most established conservative party in Iran, the Islamic Coalition Party (*hezb-e motalefeh-e Islami*) (personal interview with Iranian women activists and journalists, 2011). Hence, conservative party elites often sought her input in the compilation of candidate lists for elections.

They would tell me, '*Khanoom* (lady) ten women for a thirty-member district list is too much, five or *khoms* is enough'; hence adding only four or five maximum women on Tehran's candidate list, all of whom would get elected to parliament. (Personal interview with Maryam Behrouzi, 21 July 2011)

In this context, the use of the term '*khoms*', which is the Islamic obligation to contribute one-fifth of a certain type of income to charity, illustrates the perspective of male elites that nominating a limited number of women to party lists is a charitable act of generosity from them to women's groups such as the Zeinab Society.

Behrouzi's goal of nominating at least ten women to Tehran's thirty-member district is yet to be realised by either conservative *or* reformist parties. Turning a deaf ear to women's demands, party leaders refuse to adopt gender quotas. However, reformists often campaign on the promise of increasing women's political representation and tend to nominate more women onto parliamentary lists than their conservative counterparts. For the 2016 parliamentary elections, while the main conservative party Tehran district list of thirty included six women (20 per cent), the highest percentage ever for any conservative faction in the history of the Islamic Republic,[28] the main reformist faction list included eight women (26.6 per cent; see Figure 6.5).[29]

Across the ideological spectrum many parties act as secondary gatekeepers, blocking women's political representation through both recruitment and nomination processes unless female candidates serve a particular political agenda at a given point in time, as will be discussed in Chapter 8. In Iran, candidates need the support of parties or strategic political fronts formed on behalf of factions to succeed. Thus, women have not only to clear the Council of Guardian's vetting process, they must also pass through the various filters

[28] The main conservative list only included five women in the 2020 elections for Tehran, all of whom entered the parliament. Reformists refrained from participating collectively in that election given the mass disqualification of their candidates.

[29] In 2016, the eight women nominated by the *Omid* (Hope) List for Tehran with the backing of the Reformists included: Parvaneh Salahshouri, Tayebeh Siavoshi, Fatemeh Zolghadr, Soheila Jelodarzadeh, Farideh Oladghobad, Fatemeh Hosseini, Fatemeh Saidi and Parvaneh Mafi. All of them won seats in parliament. None of the six women nominated by the main Conservative faction – Marzieh Vahid-Dastjerdi, Fatemeh Rahbar, Fatemeh Alia, Laleh Eftekhary, Zohreh Tabibzadeh Noury and Zohreh Elahian, five of whom were incumbents, won seats.

The Principlist Grand Coalition   The List of Hope

Figure 6.5 The 2016 parliamentary election candidate lists for Tehran's thirty-member district. Left: main conservative-backed list: *The Principlist Grand Coalition*. Right: main reformist-backed list: *The List of Hope*.

put in place by political parties. At times the internal party scrutiny of potential women candidates is so harsh that even qualified women who have passed the Council's vetting process are unwilling to subject themselves to it. One high-ranking member of the Zeinab Society shared the following experience of Ezat-ul-sadat Mirkhani, a female *mujtahida*, whom the Society suggested for the main conservative party list for the 2004 parliamentary elections:

> When men (*aghayoon*) want to include women on their candidate lists, they make them pass various filters, mostly in the form of holding meetings and interviews with them (to evaluate their thoughts and beliefs). Mirkhani, who quickly realised the purpose of these meetings, became very offended, and protested, saying, 'You think I am one of your playing chips, and can be used as a tool for your purposes? I have independent thought and will not merely follow orders from the top.' Despite the backing of the Zeinab

Society, Mirkhani quit and the male party leaders were happy to see her leave.

Mirkhani's demeaning experience of candidacy for parliament convinced her not to pursue election to the Assembly of Experts, for which she was also qualified as a *mujtahida* (personal interview, 11 July 2011). Increasingly, many women find political parties' screening processes discouraging and demeaning, recognising that male elites are only seeking token women who will serve their political interests without disrupting institutional structures.

In sum, it has become apparent that the Islamic Republic mostly opens the gates of political power to women who abide by predetermined guidelines set by male political and religious elites. Women's political tendencies (whether reformist or conservative/principlist) and level of allegiance to the regime and its ruling elites play a major role in determining their access to political decision-making positions. Furthermore, my findings indicate that women in leadership roles are more intensely scrutinised than their male counterparts given the potential changes that women's rise to power can bring to Iran's authoritarian structures.

Conclusion: Islam's Role in Structural Obstacles to Women's Political Representation?

A close analysis of the legal and institutional obstacles that keep Iranian women out of politics highlights the extent of systematic discrimination against women constructed by Iran's ruling elites to retain male authority over women. Significantly, Iran's elites justify much of such restrictions through reference to conservative interpretations of Islam, which they present as divine and therefore incontestable decrees. However, as demonstrated in this chapter, such 'Islamic' decrees have been reformed in the past, as with Khomeini's original opposition to women's suffrage, which reversed during the revolution when it served his political interest to be inclusive of women. In fact, at the time of the revolution, Khomeini declared that it was women's Islamic duty to help topple the monarchy and establish an Islamic republic. Iranian women's rights activists across the ideological spectrum are fully aware of such political usage of Islam. For the past decades they too have engaged in re-reading and reinterpretation of religious texts, providing woman-centred analyses challenging the common patriarchal (mis)interpretations that subjugate women socially and politically. As larger female demographics have pushed for more inclusive readings of religious texts, some renowned clerical figures have begun to advocate for reform of religious doctrines that deny women access to positions of political and religious authority.

Among them was Ayatollah Yousef Saanei, a renowned Shi'i *marja*, the highest level of religious authority in Shi'i Islam. Until his death in 2020, Saanei blamed patriarchal rulings for denying women the ability to reach their full political and social potential on erroneous traditions (*sonathay-e qalat*), where historical cultural practices were mistakenly interpreted by clerics as universal religious mandates. On female leadership, Saanei publicly declared that 'women are capable of being the *Vali al-Faqih* (guardian jurist) and that they could lead the prayers while the men pray behind them', seeing no contradiction between female authority and Islamic precepts (Lutfi and Saanei 2007). To this end, Saanei wrote a scholarly treatise from the *Houzeh al Illmiya* (religious seminary) in Qom on women's jurisprudence, which further stated that women can hold the office of president, and called on all Sunni *and* Shi'a colleagues to act accordingly. Saanei's progressive stance highlights the lack of clerical consensus at the highest levels on women's eligibility for authoritative religious and political office. This lack of consensus provides women's rights activists with important opportunity structures within Iran's political structure to engage with Iran's ruling elites on women's leadership and to pressure for reform in alignment with contemporary realities and understandings.

Despite such significant developments, the politically motivated crackdown on reformist tendencies within Iranian society, including writings and speeches of many high-ranking reformist clerics, has once again demonstrated to Iranian women the determination of male elites to maintain authority over women, expanding women's rights only to the extent that it serves their own political agenda. However, male elites continue to engage over women's public role, ranging from access to sports stadiums to fields of education to political office, largely thanks to women's ongoing organising and campaigning efforts for change.

Thus, Iranian women continue to demand expanded roles in politics, and view political decision-making as a viable route to enhance women's rights and status. Despite discriminatory treatment by a patriarchal society and the non-representative institutional structures of the theocratic regime, Iranian women continue to mobilise for greater access to political leadership at all levels. The following chapter discusses specific ways that women's groups organise and exploit their limited opportunities to engage with political elites and the public concerning women's role and influence in formal Iranian politics.

7

ORGANISING AGAINST ALL ODDS: IRANIAN FACTIONALISM AND WOMEN'S POLITICAL REPRESENTATION

After several attempts, I finally reached Tahereh Rahimi, a women's rights activist with deep conservative party affiliations. Despite being hospitalised for cancer treatment, she graciously insisted that we meet in between her treatments at the hospital. In part thanks to her smart phone, Rahimi continued to remain politically active and engaged by tuning into meetings virtually and remaining in touch with her colleagues, even from the hospital.

On 8 June 2015, I arrived on time for our scheduled meeting and hurried to the Oncology Center. Not knowing what to expect, I entered a long, white hallway and rang Rahimi's phone to alert her that I had arrived. Towards the end of the hall a woman appeared, wearing a black and pink flowery headscarf, wrapped in a pale grey cottony *chador*. As she walked towards me with a warm smile, I realised it was Rahimi, and smiled back. Introducing myself, I told her how grateful I was that she was meeting with me under such circumstances. She guided me to the hospital's garden, and as we settled on a bench under the shade of a large tree in the heat of the Tehran summer, with customary Persian hospitality she offered me watermelon.

It turned out that Rahimi had been deeply engaged for decades with the issue of women's roles in Iranian conservative political groups. Her activism included serving on the Zeinab Society's executive board for several terms, founding and directing another Islamic women's organisation,[1] and working

---

[1] Tahereh Rahimi founded and, until her untimely death in 2018, directed the Fatemiyoun Society (*Jami'yat-e Fatemiyoun*), an Islamic women's organisation that was closely linked

with the Islamic Women's Coalition (*E'telaf Islami-e Zanan*), which was a temporary coalition among high-ranking reformist and conservative party women that extensively lobbied the state during Ahmadinajed's presidency (2005–13). She had also completed a Master's degree on women's rights, for which she had researched and written on women's political participation in post-revolutionary Iran. 'The Islamic revolution's victory facilitated a leap (*jahesh*) in women's political and social participation, including women's education, but not in women's leadership roles', she told me. 'Women still face many obstacles . . . among them the male dominated political sphere . . . which results in unfair competition when women aspire for political posts.' Reflecting on her own political experiences, Rahimi noted, 'Since my early thirties I have run for various political posts ranging from local councils to several rounds of parliamentary elections. However, I have never succeeded mostly because of behind the scene wheels and deals (*zad-o band-hay posht-e sahneh*) among men.' She described her first attempt to run for parliament:

> After much organising for the conservative faction in Khorramabad (the capital of Lorestan Province), I was selected (by the party leadership) to become a parliamentary candidate in 2004. The (district party) leader assured me that I would be a candidate for this two-member district, while the party decided between two men as the other nominee. He told me, 'I consider you more qualified than many of the men who are active, and I will fully endorse and even financially support your campaign'.

Rahimi welcomed this opportunity, seeing her political aspirations as 'for God and to pursue God's aims for the society'. However, the (male) party leaders could not agree on the male candidate, and in the end, in backroom negotiations they chose to support both male candidates over her just days prior to the election. 'This was a great injustice to me!' she said, anger in her voice all these years later. 'The same leader who said he completely supported my candidacy given my qualifications, turned around and said in a public setting, "It is true that Imam (Khomeini) said women should enter the political sphere, but that does not mean that women get to directly enter the parliament! Women should rather raise kids . . . who are suitable for political activity".'

with the ultra-conservative United Front of the Followers of the Imam's and Leader's Line, a coalition of Iranian Principlist political groups.

Committed to her candidacy but now without party backing, Rahimi ran as an independent, financing her own campaign with help from her family.

> After the first round I received a few thousand votes. Coincidentally, the male party candidate who had replaced me needed the same number of votes to enter parliament. So clearly (party leaders) felt that my candidacy had cost him the votes he needed to win. Therefore, (for the second round of elections) the party leadership came to me again and offered to reimburse me for all of my campaign expenses plus another 20 per cent, if I dropped out of the race and gave one public speech supporting that male candidate.

Rahimi's response was unequivocal: 'Why should I remove myself from the race in support of a male candidate, when you yourself said that I was more qualified than many of them?' She stayed in the race, and in her campaign speeches highlighted her superior qualifications compared with most of the male candidates.

> I am not saying this to boast, but I think it is important to inform the public of women's qualifications. I would go to the bazaar or to a central square (*meydan*) to campaign, listing my qualifications at the top of my lungs: my political experience, my clean record from corruption, my wanting only to represent the people's interests in parliament. In a matter of minutes, in our patriarchal provincial city, I would have the whole bazaar gathered around me.

Although Rahimi did not win a seat in the 2004 parliamentary elections, she grew more aware of her strengths, including her ability to passionately campaign and gather a crowd despite her gender and youth.

In standing up to the intimidation from her male peers and protesting their discriminatory actions, Rahimi was expressing the internalisation of the revolutionary gender discourse promoted by Khomeini and Maryam Behrouzi[2] and shared by tens of thousands of Iranian women, that women are equal political agents in the Islamic state. In her campaign speeches, she often referred to women's vital roles in the success of the revolution and during the Iran-Iraq war, and reminded audiences that in the time of the Prophet Mohammad 'women were always present and had central roles'. Rather than

---

[2] Behrouzi, the influential revolutionary and founder of the Zeinab Society, mentored scores of women. Tahereh Rahimi was one of her students (personal interview, 8 June 2015).

seeing a contradiction between her Islamic faith and female authority, it was her *hezbollahi* background, as a supporter of Khomeini and his ideals, which empowered her to strive for political leadership.

Despite her devotion to the regime, undemocratic candidate selection processes again prevented Rahimi from running for parliament in the 2008 elections.

> We worked for more than a year, under the leadership of Maryam Behrouzi, to organise and gather all conservative party women under the umbrella of United Front of Principlist Women (*jebjhe motahed zanan usulgara*). To identify suitable female candidates for the parliament, members of the Front ranked the would-be contenders and came up with twelve high-ranking Islamic party women, including Behrouzi and me. We took this list to the male elites of the conservative faction and asked them to integrate these women onto their parliamentary candidate list for Tehran. We asked them to include at least ten women among the thirty total candidates, but they refused. We then asked for eight women, but they still rejected . . . In a compromise, we finally demanded that *we* should at least choose the five or six women that the leaders typically include in their list. But even that, they rejected, and included token obedient (*taabe'e*) women who did not have our support.

In protest the United Front of Principlist Women threatened to run its own women-only list. 'The male leaders did not think that we would do it. But once we announced the list, they waged so much pressure that our two highest ranking women, Maryam Behrouzi and Marzieh Vahid-Dastjerdi, were forced to leave the list.' In the end, the ten remaining women, among them Rahimi, ran without backing or financial support of the party leaders. 'I managed the women in their campaigns. But since we knew that we were not going to win without the party's support, we decided to spend just enough (from our own finances) to show ourselves and raise public awareness (of the absence of women on the main conservative party list).' While all of the five women on the main conservative party list for Tehran eventually entered parliament, none secured enough votes in the first round, which according to Rahimi demonstrated 'lack of sufficient support among the public for these women'.

Rahimi's experiences in her two unsuccessful attempts to run for parliament highlight some of the barriers faced by Iranian women aspiring to political office. Ranging from undemocratic candidate selection processes to gender discrimination by male elites and women's limited financial resources, Iran's electoral and political systems greatly limit women's access to political leadership. This is true even for conservative women, who are more favoured to reach political office given the conservative domination over Iran's political institutions.

While the previous chapter outlined the major legal and institutional obstacles to women's access to political power, this chapter focuses on the impact of Iranian factional politics on women's political representation, including the ways that Iran's weak and unorganised party structures hinder activists' ability to undertake targeted collective action to expand women's political roles. I show that despite decades of women's activism and devotion to conservative and reformist political groups, most women, particularly outspoken ones, are systematically excluded from positions of authority. Such intentional exclusion is rooted in political structures that are undemocratic, including the absence of free and fair elections.

I find that Iran's factional politics have prevented the institutionalisation of diverse and well-structured political parties to compete in elections. In addition to impeding meaningful party competition, Iran's historically weak party structures have also prevented women from being able to apply sustained pressure – whether from within or outside of parties – on male elites to be inclusive of women in several important ways. First, the absence of organised party structures, including distinct platforms and dedicated women's branches mobilising women from the grass roots, greatly limits women's capacity to effectively pressure party elites for inclusion. While in Turkey established parties with clear platforms and party structures allow activists to directly lobby political elites and provide resources to recruit, train and support aspiring female politicians through women's branches, parties in Iran mostly form at the time of elections. This makes effective lobbying and pressure tactics exploiting party competition very difficult. Second, the political dominance of the conservative faction and the power of the ultra-conservative non-elected branch of government, and its frequent crackdowns on reformist and more liberal political entities, undermine the fairness of Iran's elections. Finally, factional divisions skewing heavily towards the conservative are also unfavourable to alliances between party women across factions, as evidenced by the aborted gender quota campaign launched by a coalition of influential party women from across the ideological spectrum, as explained later.

Despite the institutional limitations, this chapter shows that Iranian women continue to organise against all odds. Lacking direct channels for pressuring party leaders, Iranian women activists have instead aimed their lobby for women's political representation directly at the public, with some success. A notable example was the 2016 parliamentary election campaign by Iranian women's rights activists launched with the slogan 'Change the male-dominated face of parliament'. Building on previous campaigns for gender quotas and women's political leadership, this campaign was an attempt to counter the Council of Guardians' discriminatory candidate vetting process and raise awareness among voters to prevent electing misogynous members of parliament. The campaign was successful in raising public awareness on women's political representation and led to the candidacy and elections of a record number of women in post-revolutionary Iran, many of whom were sympathetic to women's issues, though it failed in reaching its goal of electing at least fifty women MPs (only seventeen women entered the parliament) as a result of Iran's women-unfriendly electoral system and factional politics, among other factors.

Implications of Iran's Weak Party Structures for Women's Political Representation

Iran's theocratic political framework, which demands the public's acceptance of the clerical oligarchy, has prevented the emergence of political parties (Arjomand 2009; Azimi 1997, 2008; Baktiari 1996; Kamrava 2010; Moslem 2002). Although Article 26 of the Iranian Constitution allows the formation of political parties, since its founding the regime's key clerical figures have publicly opposed this, evidently fearing that the potential for parties to organise and mobilise might weaken the clerical oligarchy. Ayatollah Mahdavi-Kani, long-time secretary of one of the most powerful clerical groups in Iran – the Society of Militant Clergy (*Jameh-ye ruhaniyyat-e mobarez*) – publicly declared his opposition to party formation stating 'the cleric is the father of the people' and 'the Mandate of the Jurist (the office of the Supreme Leader or *Vali-e faqih*)[3] is not a matter for elections; it is a

---

[3] The office of the Supreme Leader (*Velayat-e Faqih*), the highest office of the Islamic Republic, is the product of Khomeini's radical theory that during the occultation of the

matter of recognition' (Arjomand 2009: 65, 67). Other conservative authorities have declared that parties sow dissention and destroy the sacred unity of the community. Following the 1979 revolution, Khomeini and his supporters successfully suppressed and marginalised all rivals and internal opponents entrenching Khomeini's supreme leadership in large part thanks to the onset of the eight-year Iran–Iraq war.[4] His supporters' slogan was 'Party, only party of God, leader, only Khomeini' (Alamdari 2005). The institutionalisation of such rhetoric has over the years thwarted the formation of strong political parties with distinctive platforms and widespread structures that reach the grass roots, such as well-staffed district offices or women's or youth branches.

The absence of organised party structures has given rise to factions – 'ideological blocs with each group sharing and advancing its own interpretation of issues and policies' (Moslem 2002: 2). Factional membership is fairly fluid with key figures occasionally changing affiliations and political elites spread across the ideological spectrum, with hard-liner conservatives on one end and soft-line reformists on the other. The conservatives (the Islamic Right), who have rebranded themselves 'Principlists', generally support the absolutist powers of the Supreme Leader and related non-elected institutions; while Islamic leftists, or reformists, seek greater powers for republican institutions and a reinterpretation of Islamic texts compatible with contemporary life. In the middle are pragmatists (also known as moderates or centrists) who gained increasing political prominence with the coming to power of President Hassan Rouhani in 2013. With the deliberate marginalisation of reformists from formal political power since 2009, moderates increasingly constitute the main opposition to the Principlists, particularly to neo-Principlists, composed of the Islamic Revolutionary Guard Corps and the most adamant supporters of the Supreme Leader (Safshekan and Sabet 2010). Moderates such as former President Rouhani are less vocal on reform of the theocratic structure and empowering Iranian civil society than are reformists; instead they focus on improving Iran's international and regional standing and on ending nuclear-related sanctions on Iran (Keshavarzian and Sohrabi 2017).

Twelfth Imam Shi'ite jurists have the mandate to establish and rule an 'Islamic government' (Arjomand 2009: 22).

[4] The Iran–Iraq war (1980–8), supported by many Western powers simultaneously assisting both sides in their deadly conflict, allowed the regime to quell all opposition by accusing any dissenting voices of being aligned with external enemies who wish to derail the revolution (Ram 1992).

For decades the two main factions of reformists and conservatives have dominated electoral competition in Iran, but the playing field is far from level since the institutional structures privilege conservative-backed forces with the power to monitor and manage elections, including to vet candidates. Keshavarzian (2005) refers to the swings of control over elected institutions between hardliners and more moderate forces without disruption to the authoritarian status quo as 'fragmented authoritarianism', engendered by bodies established by the founders of the Islamic Republic to protect conservative clerical authority and prevent any radical transformation to the regime, despite the occasional victory for moderates or soft-liners. While the Council of Guardians, the office of the Supreme Leader, and the judiciary are on the 'forefront of blocking substantive and procedural policies aimed at moving Iran toward democracy', other state organisations, including state media and law enforcement, work to 'mollify protest through patronage' (Keshavarzian 2005: 80). Similarly, Mehran Kamrava (2010) argues that state leaders in authoritarian regimes create specific institutions to enhance their power and their political longevity. The limitations of Iran's electoral process are also clear from the frequent quarrels between the clerical-dominated and mostly unelected bodies from the office of Supreme Leader on down, and popularly elected bodies, such as the executive, on whether the Islamic Republic is legitimised by Islam as interpreted by the clerical oligarchy, or by the public's votes.[5]

Although previous research has examined the impact of Iranian factionalism on its regime type, institutional framework, and possibilities for democratisation (Azimi 1997, 2008; Arjomand 2009; Baktiari 1996; Kamrava 2010; Kazemian 2013; Moslem 2002), none has analysed its repercussions for women's rights, including women's access to political decision-making positions. In this chapter, I address this gap, arguing that Iran's factional politics and weak party structures have limited activists' opportunities to sustain pressure on male elites to address women's political

---

[5] A recent instance of this occurred in a speech by President Rouhani following his landslide re-election in 2017, where he quoted the first Shi'i Imam, Ali ibn Abi Talib: 'The source of legitimacy of a government should derive from people's votes.' The head of the Assembly of Experts, a body of high-ranking clerics responsible for appointing or removing the Supreme Leader, immediately responded that 'an Islamic government receives its legitimacy from *Imamate* (an Islamic leader), similar to leadership of the Prophet, and not from people's desires or votes' (Khayamdar 2017).

under-representation. The fragmented nature of the Iranian state, which undermines party competition, and its key features of pluralism, contestation, mass participation and representative bodies, also hampers women's access to political leadership in two main ways: by limiting women's organising and lobbying capacities; and by the regime's intentional marginalisation of reformist parties and figures sympathetic to women's expanded roles in formal politics.

Weak Party Structures and Limited Lobbying Capacities

Political parties, similar to electoral systems, play a key role in women's political representation, particularly women's presence in national parliaments. Research has identified a number of ways that political parties can enable women's access to political office. They include a strong organisational structure with the presence of female party members at the grass-roots levels, a leftist or liberal ideology, and the implementation of gender policy on candidate selection, such as quotas to guarantee women's nomination to key positions (Matland and Studlar 1996; Kittilson 2006; Wylie 2018). Additionally, well-developed parties, like those in Turkey, foster party competition by mobilising and politicising the public based on competing objectives and interests. As shown for Turkey in Chapter 4, competition among multiple parties provides an important structural opportunity for advocates of women's political representation, whereby activists can pressure party leaders to recruit or nominate more women as a means of competing for the votes of particular demographics and broadening their electoral appeal (Baldez 2004; Kenny and Mackay 2014; Krook 2009; Matland and Studlar 1996, 1998; Meier 2004). On the other hand, in two-party systems, or when parties are provisional or weak, activists have much less leverage for pressuring party leaders, and lack the structural support to train and back women for political leadership (Matland and Studlar 1996).

Iran's factional politics have severely curtailed the emergence of strong political parties with clear platforms, gender ideologies and widespread structures such as women's branches supporting female political empowerment.[6]

---

[6] Regardless of ideology, most political groups aspiring to elected office are not officially registered as 'parties' (Arjomand 2009; Zakizadah 2009). Conversely, entities which function primarily as interest groups in their quest to shape public policy and with no interest in electoral competition tend to register as parties. In fact, the first officially registered politi-

In Iran, parties are often provisional, forming in the context of elections as key political figures build coalitions for campaigning purposes, collaborating to create candidate lists. Acting more like elite blocs which coalesce to increase the chances of achieving some shared agenda, most parties in Iran have limited membership or plans to expand their reach to the public (Farhi 2015). Thus, while in Turkey as in most nations, parties aim to form and lead governments, in Iran the major parties usually arise from within government, as incumbents and their allies form coalitions to support candidates and increase their institutional impact.[7] Parties themselves generally consist of smaller groups which are inactive or dissolve from one election to the next. Factionalism and various legal limitations create the provisional and fluid nature of Iran's political parties, which makes them a moving target for any kind of lobby, and especially for a lobby focused on political 'membership' and rights, such as for women's political representation.

According to Hoodfar and Sadr (2009), of the hundreds of parties registered with the Iranian Interior Ministry, including eighteen women's parties, the majority resemble political or professional associations with particular political perspectives and agendas rather than conventional political parties. They are generally elite-based, in that key political figures form a party to further consolidate their political influence and represent their interests in Iran's power struggles. For instance, a handful of key governmental officials formed the right-wing Islamic Society of Engineers (*Jameh Islami Mohandesin*) in the late 1980s to consolidate and formalise the influence of engineers, professors and students of technical fields, and conservative technocrats in Iranian politics (Zandi 2014). For major elections, this party joins a coalition of larger conservative parties and provides them with the names of potential candidates to include on the main conservative candidate list. In a personal

cal party following the 1979 revolution was the Association of the Women of the Islamic Republic (*Jam'iat-e Zanan-e Jomhouri-e Islami*). The Association registered as a party to enhance its legitimacy among the many clerical associations of its time, and to highlight women's concerns.

[7] For instance, the Executives of Construction Party (*Hezb-e Kargozaran-e Saazandegi; or Kargozaran*) was founded in 1996 by the government of President Hashemi Rafsanjani, and has been inactive outside of major elections. Similarly, the reformist Islamic Iran Participation Front (*Jebheye Mosharekate Iran-e Islami*; 1998–2009) rose out of President Khatami's government, and its candidates later won the first city council and the sixth parliamentary elections.

interview with a political party official, as of 2021 there are more than thirty-five 'active political parties in Iran', though many are unknown to the general public and lack a formal platform (9 June 2021).

Given the absence of organised party structures and active membership, political groups and parties tend to enter coalitions with other like-minded groups, and together put forth one main factional candidate list. For instance, for the 2016 parliamentary elections, a coalition of more than twenty-six reformist and moderate groups formed to produce a single list of candidates, the List of Hope. Similarly, conservatives put forth one nationwide list under the Principlist Grand Coalition (see Figure 6.5 of previous chapter for these groups' lists for Tehran's district). Forming coalitions with moderates is particularly important for reformists trying to access the formal political arena, since the Council of Guardians overwhelmingly disqualifies candidates with alliances to the reformist camp, especially prominent ones. Elites play a key role in campaign outcomes: in 2016 former President Khatami's public announcement urging the electorate to support the List of Hope helped the list win 42 per cent of parliamentary seats (BBC Persian 2016). However, since candidate lists are products of political and strategic coalitions, once elected to parliament the individual members of parliament are not accountable to any specific party or group, and may vote on issues as they wish.[8]

The leadership of the majority of registered political parties is almost exclusively male, according to Elham (a pseudonym), a prominent female reformist party activist (personal interview, 13 June 2015). This includes reformist parties, despite their general support for women's political representation. According to her, 'Of (approximately) twenty-three reformist parties currently functioning in Iran, none are directed by women, and women are largely absent from their leadership cadre. This is the reason we have women's parties in Iran.'[9] During major elections women's parties lobby male elites to

---

[8] The absence of accountability among elected officials to a clear party platform also partly explains the low incumbency return rates in Iran's parliament, which has averaged approximately 30 per cent in nine parliamentary elections, as voters frequently punish individual candidates for their failures by voting them out of office (Borden 2016).

[9] Among reformist women's parties are the recently founded Society of Muslim Women's New Religious Thinking (*Jami'yyat-e Zanan-e Mosalman-e Nu Andish*), or the older Society of Women of the Islamic Revolution (*Jame'eh-ye Zanan-e Enqelab-e Islami*). There are conservative women's parties as well, including the long-established Zeinab Society (*Jameh Zeinab*).

include women from their ranks on the main factional candidate lists. Both reformist and conservative party women believe such parties are essential at this point in order to formally lobby male leaders for women's increased political access. Thus, in preparation for the 2016 parliamentary elections, Elham and her female colleagues attended the Coordination Council of the Reformist Front (*Shuray Hamahangy Jebhe Eslahat*) to pressure for the inclusion of at least 30 per cent women on the nationwide main reformist candidate lists. 'The greater number of organised women's groups present at these meetings, the more bargaining power we have (*qhodrat-e chaneh zani*),' Elham told me (personal interview, 13 June 2015).

Iranian women activists, particularly reformist women like Elham, continue to press for greater party infrastructure such as exists in Turkey, with women's wings and grass-roots women's party branches to help bring more women into political life.

> We need structures that lead to women's political empowerment. When I meet with our male colleagues, I remind them that they were not born political leaders, but became leaders from sufficient political exposure and experience. We need to open the gate of formal politics to women so that they can also gain such experience.

She continued, 'Parties can function as a bridge bringing women from their communities to formal political roles, similar to how they function in Turkey and most other countries' (personal interview, 13 June 2015).

Elham herself became politically active thanks to the unique structures of the reformist Islamic Iran Participation Front party (*Jebheye Mosharekate Iran-e Islami*; henceforth *Mosharekat*), which sought to facilitate women's inclusion. Recognising the potential of mobilising wider public support, key reformists founded *Mosharekat* following President Khatami's election in 1997, establishing structures that reached from the central level in Tehran to the municipal level in cities across Iran. *Mosharekat*'s gender-sensitive party rhetoric and its efforts to institutionalise women's inclusion distinguished it from all other parties. Under the leadership of key reformist women, including party executive board members Farideh Mashini – a graduate in women's studies, and Elahe Koolaee – a political science professor, *Mosharekat* institutionalised a women's commission at the central level, women's branches across the country, and a 30 per cent quota for women at all administrative levels of the party. Elham credits such organised structures in her home province as her gateway to party activism and political participation.

> I became active in politics by first joining my local *Mosharekat* branch office and gradually rose up from there. My early party experience introduced me to the nature of power and politics in Iran, and led me to recognise parties as great means to advance women's political participation. (Personal interview, 13 June 2015)

Based on her experiences, Elham has been writing and speaking about the ways parties can politically empower women, and believes the most significant of these are women's commissions and strong quota measures for women.

To integrate women and their concerns into the party, *Mosharekat's* female leaders created a Women's Commission at the party's Central Political Office (*Comissiun masa'eleh zanan dar daftar-e siasy*) to mainstream women's issues in all major party decisions and programmes, and ensure women's presence at various administrative levels. The Commission also played a role in publicising women's interests, which further strengthened the burgeoning Iranian women's rights movement at the time. For instance, it regularly organised public conferences and roundtables on women's rights as advocated by the new religious thinkers, and helped amplify reformist clerical voices in Iran, like Ayatollah Yousef Saanei and Mohammad Mojtahed Shabestari, on women's public roles, including access to political leadership (personal interview with Farideh Mashini, 4 July 2011).

The establishment of women's branches in every party office in the country aimed to mobilise and politicise women from the grass roots. Unlike most party women's branches at the time, which Mashini told me tended to 'create islands for party women' with few opportunities to ascend the party echelon, Mashini and her colleagues envisioned *Mosharekat's* women's branches as avenues for women's political empowerment.

> At first, I opposed women's branches since I feared they could end up separating women and their issues from men and the central party structure . . . creating more gender segregation. However, I was eventually convinced, when I kept hearing from our offices in smaller cities and towns that there are not enough women to fill the (internal) 30 per cent quota. As a way to politicise more women and help recruit them to the party, we established women's branches across the country, even in the most remote areas. I

realised that these branches can create a friendly atmosphere for women to encourage them to enter politics and help facilitate their rise to decision-making positions. (Personal interview, 4 July 2011).

To assist members of women's branches to translate their grass-roots political experiences into more formal political gains, *Mosharekat*'s Women's Commission designed training courses and workshops to encourage and support women's candidacy for political office. However, in 2009, the state banned the party before any training sessions could take place (personal interview with Farideh Mashini, 4 July 2011), making *Mosharekat*'s efforts to facilitate women's entry to political power both short-lived as well as limited by continuous resistance from male colleagues. In eleven years of existence, from 1998 to 2009, *Mosharekat* failed to fulfil its 30 per cent quota for women at most administrative levels, including in its central executive board, because male party leaders resisted giving up their seats to women. The party's final thirty-member executive board included only three women, with two more women among the five reserve board members. Mashini reflected on her uphill battle to convince her male colleagues of the importance of women's inclusion through quotas.

> We mentioned gender quotas at the party's first congress, which I did not expect would become so controversial ... We formulated it as 'affirmative action' and highlighted that it is difficult for women to enter male-dominated structures and become known to eventually get elected unless there are opportunities in place like quotas for women ... some very important reformist leaders criticised this proposition. (Personal interview with Farideh Mashini, 4 July 2011)

A male *Mosharekat* board member present at that congress told me that though he initially opposed Mashini's appeal for quotas, 'her devotion and hard work on this issue convinced us to support it at a later party congress' (personal interview, 27 May 2015). Despite its adoption, according to Mashini, the 30 per cent quota was never filled in part because of the male elites' unwillingness and claims that there were not enough qualified women to fill the quota at all administrative levels, particularly in provinces (personal interview, 4 July 2011). Furthermore, despite all efforts by the women members, *Mosharekat*'s quota never expanded to candidate party lists for national elections. To date, no party or group in Iran has adopted a gender quota for candidate party lists for major elections, partly because of the difficulty of applying a quota in Iran's many single-member districts.[10]

Before it had a chance to reach many of its objectives, following political unrest in 2009 the authorities dissolved *Mosharekat*, imprisoning many of its leaders, both male and female (BBC News 2010). Some former *Mosharekat* members went on to found the Union of Islamic Iran People Party (*Hezbe Etehad Mellat Iran Islami*; henceforth *Etehad*) in 2015, but it is uncertain whether this party will be able to establish a similar structure and outreach given the conservative hardliner position declaring many reformist leaders to be 'seditionists' (*fetneh-gar*). Currently five women sit on *Etehad*'s thirty-member central executive board, one of whom, Azar Mansouri, received significant support from the party congress to become secretary general.[11] Although the party platform outlines its commitment to women's equal rights, including access to decision-making positions, it has yet to adopt a gender quota, largely because factional competition and the majoritarian electoral system encouraging strategic alliances mean reformist coalitions often include moderates indifferent to the goal of women's political representation. Thus, reformist women like Elham believe women's parties are necessary to amass bargaining power with male elites.

Conservative party women have yet to see organisational structures aimed at integrating women into formal politics on par with those of *Mosharekat*. Given the dominant conservative gender ideology relegating women to the domestic sphere, most conservative party organisational structures for women focus on mobilising grass-roots campaigning for voter support rather than access to formal politics. Even the oldest and most established conservative parties in Iran, instrumental in the success of the revolution, rarely prioritised women's inclusion in the party structure. For instance, the Islamic Coalition Party (*Hezb-e motalefeh-e Islami*; henceforth *Motalefeh*), an influential conservative party with over fifty years of history, took measures to be inclusive of women in its structures only in 1996 when it established a women's division. In 2002, the party established at least one woman's branch in each of

---

[10] Of Iran's 207 electoral districts, 112 are single-member. Tehran is Iran's biggest electoral district with thirty seats, the next biggest district has only six (Asr Iran 2016; Borden 2016).

[11] At *Etehad*'s first party congress held in August 2015, Mansouri and the other candidate, Ali Shakouri-Rad, received the same number of votes from the over 200 party delegates to become the party's first general secretary. However, Mansouri reportedly withdrew in support of Shakouri-Rad (Radio Farda 2015a).

Iran's thirty-one states (*ostan*), placing 'pious, capable, and abiding women as their heads' (Resalat Newspaper 2010). According to the head of its women's branches, the party 'supports women's active participation in social and political fields, so long as the institution of family is protected and women's personal, religious and social status are respected' (Resalat Newspaper 2010). This partly explains why *Motalefeh* women's branches have never gained much recognition from party officials, nor been effective at mobilising women or as a conduit for aspiring female politicians. Instead, the Zeinab Society, with its history of organising and mobilising women on behalf of the conservatives, has acted as the de facto women's branch of *Motalefeh* (personal interviews with party women across the political spectrum, 2011 and 2015). The well-respected organisation has been at the forefront of advocacy for women's increased access to political office, which does not sit well with many conservative male elites.

In recent years, largely thanks to increasing pressure from women's rights groups on all political elites, *Motalefeh* has recruited token women to various leadership posts. As of 2017, three women sit on the thirty-member *Motalefeh* central board (13 per cent), two of whom (Fatemeh Rahbar and Laleh Eftekhary) served as MPs for three consecutive sessions from 2004 to 2016 (ILNA News Agency 2015). However, in part because of the Zeinab Society along with other conservative party women's increasing outspokenness against the discriminatory actions of conservative male leaders, *Motalefeh*'s elites have been mostly granting political office access to conformist women who serve as their mouthpieces and toe the party line. *Motalefeh*-backed women MPs' allegiance to conservative elites is apparent from their silence on bills or policies opposing women's public sphere activities including those limiting women's access to certain university-level fields of study and banning women from sports complexes, and on bills supporting polygamy and temporary marriage (Amirshahi 2016). Key leaders of the Zeinab Society, including Maryam Behrouzi, expressed disappointment in conservative women MPs for 'not representing women's interests' (personal interview, 21 July 2011). This means that when public pressure forces male conservative leaders to select female candidates or appoint women to positions, they handpick those who will support conservative gender ideology. In fact, the women MPs from *Motalefeh* did not come from the party structures but were recruited directly from state-dominated organisations such as the Islamic Republic of Iran Broadcasting (like Rahbar) or religious seminaries for women (like Eftekhary). Appointment of token women MPs who are mostly accountable to male party leaders has faced the public criticism of some outspoken conservative party women given their loss of patience at being intentionally sidelined, as I explain elsewhere (Tajali 2017).

Overall, the absence of organised party structures, including women's branches to help politicise women at the grass roots as seen for Turkey, greatly limits the capacity of Iranian women's rights activists to lobby political elites, while the formation of provisional parties for the duration of election periods leaves activists insufficient time or opportunity for lobbying party leaders to nominate women into leadership positions. The reformist *Mosharekat* has been the only party in post-revolutionary Iran which sought to institution-alise women's inclusion in formal politics largely thanks to the foresight of a few key party women; but as mentioned earlier, the state banned this party in 2009 before its Women's Commission and their training courses towards women's political representation took off the ground. Although reformist women's groups have sought to revive similar candidate training programmes in recent years, other institutional obstacles, in particular the regime's little tolerance for reformist party women, have limited their reach and scope, as explained below.

Institutionalising Elite Cleavages: Handpicking 'Acceptable' Women

In addition to facing weak, male-dominated party structures in Iran's majori-tarian electoral system, women aspiring to political office face another major hurdle: the candidate vetting process of the Council of Guardians. As outlined in the previous chapter, this institution severely impacts women's descriptive, substantive and symbolic representation by discouraging female candidacy, preventing the rise to power of prominent, outspoken women's rights advo-cates, and reinforcing the perception of the political arena as exclusively and appropriately male. To preserve Iran's male-dominated political institutions, the Council's vetting process enables ruling elites to marginalise women who threaten the status quo. The result has been 'unrepresentative' state institu-tions, since the Council grants access to only a few select women who meet ideological and religious 'credentials' determined by clerical and conservative elites.

The Council's handpicking of female parliamentary candidates intensified following the sixth parliament (2000–4), which included outspoken reformist female MPs Fatemeh Haghighatjoo, Elaheh Koolaee and Shahrbanoo Emani, among others. Despite numbering only thirteen of 290, the female MPs of the sixth parliament formed a vocal and active parliamentary women's caucus (*fraksion-e zanan*) – an informal cross-factional parliamentary women's group to address women's concerns. According to Haghighatjoo, this caucus successfully debated and passed many of the women's rights bills that had failed in the two previous parliaments, including a bill allowing unmarried women to access state scholarships for university study abroad (personal interview, 22 November 2015). And, when President Khatami failed to nominate any women ministers following his 2001 re-election, before giving their approval to Khatami's cabinet nominees during the parliamentary vote of confidence, the women's caucus required that they pledge to support women's interests within their ministries. On at least one occasion, the women's caucus helped prevent a reformist party member's appointment to a ministerial position, due to his lack of commitment to women's issues.

> Women's rights were so central, that I dared to oppose one nominee and berated him for having closed the advisory office to women's affairs in his ministry while he was serving as interim Minister, despite the fact that he was also a high-ranking member of *Mosharekat* party. And I received much backlash from my *Mosharekat* colleagues for this.

Haghighatjoo went on to credit many of the gains on women's rights during the sixth parliament to women's outspokenness and the occasional support they received from their male colleagues. 'On various occasions, our male reformist colleagues, including reformist clerics, would ask to speak on the parliament floor in defence of bills on women's rights, since this would be more effective in convincing the male-dominated parliament' (personal interview, 22 November 2015).

To prevent another parliament with similar composition, the conservatives, through the Council of Guardians, have since the sixth parliament increasingly refused the candidacy of many reformists, particularly those active on human rights, civil society development and democratic reform. For the 2004 seventh parliamentary elections the Council disqualified 3,600 out of 8,200 candidate applicants, mostly from the reformist faction, including eighty reformist incumbents, both male and female, who protested with a sit-in strike in parliament that had little impact (Arjomand 2009: 106). Haghighatjoo protested by officially resigning from parliament. In a farewell speech to the Iranian people, she stated

I am resigning from the 'house of the people', since I can no longer carry out my oath to defend and protect your rights and the Iranian constitution, and to protest the illegal and un-Islamic ways in which various state institutions handled the recent parliamentary elections. (Haghighatjoo 2004)

In that 2004 parliamentary election, token conservative women replaced all of the sixth parliament female MPs, some of whom continued to serve for the following three terms, until 2016.

The Council's sweeping disqualification of candidates to benefit the conservatives is now a reality of Iran's major elections. While such disqualifications are generally regardless of gender, a number of women's rights activists and scholars told me they believe the Council is less tolerant of outspoken and/or reformist female political aspirants than of their male counterparts (personal interviews, 2011, 2015 and 2016). In the previous chapter, Table 6.2 showed that while women constituted 11.8 per cent of total individuals who registered to stand as candidates in the 2004 parliamentary elections, they constituted only 9.3 per cent of those approved by the Council. For the 2016 parliamentary elections, when the number of women registered for candidacy was three times that of 2012 (1,234 versus 428), the Council disqualified 53 per cent of female and 48 per cent of all male registered candidates. Significantly, the tripling of aspiring female parliamentarians was in part due to a grass-roots campaign by women's rights activists to dramatically increase the number of female applicants for candidacy to increase the odds of women passing the Council's filtering process. While seemingly insignificant, the differing rates of male and female disqualification demonstrate the Council's intolerance for the candidacy of women's rights activists and prominent female reformists, many of whom were involved in this campaign. I will discuss this campaign towards the end of this chapter.

Though rejected candidates legally have a tiny window to appeal their disqualification, this is virtually impossible since the Council, which is required by law to issue a written explanation, generally cites Articles 28 or 30 of the Iranian Elections Act, which in very general terms justify disqualification based on either questionable allegiance to the Constitution and regime (Article 28), or support for anti-revolutionary or illegal groups (Article 30) (Dokouhaki and Tarighi 2000). For instance, in disqualifying incumbent reformist female MPs of the sixth parliament, including Haghighatjoo and

Koolaee, the Council claimed that their 'belief and commitment to Islam, the Islamic Republic, *Velayat-e Faqih* (office of the Supreme Leader), and the constitution' as outlined in Article 28 of the Elections Act, was in question (Ebrahimi 2004: 3). The Council has also repeatedly disqualified Azam Taleghani, a former parliamentarian and well-known religious woman activist with close links to the founders of the Islamic Republic, using Articles 28 and 30 of the Elections Act (Dokouhaki and Tarighi 2000). These articles are purposefully almost impossible to contest, thus allowing the Council to exclude with impunity women who might challenge the state structure or discriminatory legislation, or who simply do not support prevailing elite ideological and political positions (personal interview with a women's rights activist and registered parliamentary candidate, 14 February 2016).

Regardless, many women continue to push against the Council's relentless gender injustice and discrimination. Azam Taleghani at seventy-four continued to publicly register her candidacy for the presidency as discussed in the following chapter. Women's media has also played a major role in highlighting the Council's groundless disqualification of many qualified and respected women. For instance, when the Council disqualified Zhaleh Shaditalab, a renowned sociology professor and women's rights scholar, without any specific reasoning, despite her many attempts to obtain a viable explanation, she took her case to a women's magazine, which featured an interview where she challenged the Council's decision to disqualify her based on her 'questionable beliefs and commitment to the regime'. Noting her decades-long academic career and nine-year tenure consulting for the national Office of Planning and Budget, she states, 'Nothing in my areas of expertise nor professional history warrants my disqualification . . . I am an academic who has with upmost honesty worked for the scientific and cultural development of my country' (Dokouhaki and Tarighi 2000: 4). Still without any response, she sent her husband to the Council to request the specifics of her infractions, in case they necessitated him divorcing her. The Council's response was simply to tell him 'Go back to your life; there is no need to divorce her!' This scholar, who can now laugh as she recounts the story, told me, 'There is no competition (in Iran's elections), when someone like me, wishing to run as an independent, doesn't even stand a chance to be qualified to run for office' (personal interview, 16 July 2011).

While the Council of Guardians uses the public activities, speeches and publications of prominent party women, scholars and rights activists to determine their 'acceptability' for political office, it has other, often gendered ways of vetting ordinary women whose ideological and political positions are not public knowledge. In such cases it defers to determining women's eligibility based on factors such as dress, religious observance and memberships in female Islamic societies. Shahrzad (a pseudonym), a women's rights' advocate, explained the process as akin to a police investigation. 'The Council of Guardians employs around 200,000 individuals to investigate registered candidates' educational background, employment, and personal matters like candidates' family history, level of religiosity and political ideology.' I asked her how the Council determined a woman's level of religiosity or political ideology:

> They (the Council of Guardians' employees) have access to most records and resources during the filtration process. For instance, they determine a candidate's political ideology by checking to see if they were members of their universities' Islamic student associations, and look at the activities they were involved in as students. For religiosity, they may interview the neighbours to ask whether they attend the local mosque or the Friday prayer. (Personal interview, 16 July 2011)

Iranian women do tend to be active in various political and religious associations, including very high female membership in *Basij*, an auxiliary paramilitary volunteer militia tasked with supporting and protecting the regime's ideals through moral policing, social service and other political activities.[12] However, Iran's culture of gender segregation, particularly within conservative demographics, means women have less access than their male peers to many associations and organisations. For instance, a female student at a technical university who wanted to join her school's conservative-backed student association had to attend their all-male meetings for over a year before they even acknowledged her.

> I was a student just like them, but women were not welcome. I would enter the room, and they would not even look at me or greet me. After more than a year of attending all their meetings, they finally acknowledged me and I

---

[12] The exact number of female *Basij* members is not available, but research puts it at about 5 million as of 2010 (Golkar 2015: 113). Serving under the Islamic Revolutionary Guard Corps, the female arm of *Basij*, with branches in almost every town and city, is intended to cultivate future generations of female supporters of the regime and its ideology.

joined them. My persistence led a few other women to also join. (Personal interview, 8 June 2015)

Given these discriminatory challenges, women are therefore disadvantaged by a vetting process for political candidacy that values membership in important political and religious groups.

However, the most gendered aspect of the vetting process is the weighing of women's dress and appearance as a marker of political and religious affinity, a type of scrutiny rarely directed towards men.[13] Mandatory veiling places the onus for public religious expression exclusively on women, whose degree of *hijab* (Islamic covering) may vary. The most observant style (advocated by the ruling conservative elites) is hair completely covered and a full-length *chador*, an often black, tent-like covering, leaving only the face and hands exposed. A less conservative but very common style includes a long (at least knee-length) loose fitting coat (*manteau*), complemented with either a cape-like veil (*maghna'eh*) or headscarf (*roosari*) both of which cover the hair, neck and shoulders, leaving the face clear. Despite the regime's repeated efforts to make the *chador* mandatory for women in public, they have thus far failed.[14]

In 2000, this issue was highlighted when reformist women MPs of the sixth parliament advocating for less stringent dress codes entered parliament without a *chador*. Elaheh Koolaee, Tahereh Rezazadeh and Fatemeh Khatami faced protests from some male colleagues and extensive criticism in the conservative media. Koolaee explained her refusal to wear the *chador* as a way to emphasise individual freedom, stating: 'We cannot speak of freedom, when we do not grant freedom of dress' (Dokouhaki 2000: 2). She often stood out as the only non-*chador* wearing woman at political gatherings (see Figure 7.1). Her persistence on this issue likely played a role in her disqualification by the Council for candidacy in subsequent elections.

---

[13] Since the 1979 revolution, the Iranian regime has banned the sale of men's ties (though this is often ignored) and actively discourages men employed by the public sector, including all politicians, from wearing them with their suits when acting in any official capacity, since the tie is constructed by the regime as a symbol of Western decadence (Dehghan 2012). Despite this, there is little evidence that men's access to formal politics has been hampered because they choose to wear ties, unlike the situation for women with 'bad-*hijab*'.

[14] In fact, contrary to the regime's expectations women, particularly in larger cities, are increasingly appearing with 'bad-*hijab*', a term invented by the morality police to refer to *hijab* that exposes parts of the hair, or *manteaus* that are considered too tight, short or bright.

Figure 7.1 Elaheh Koolaee (centre, with light scarf and *manteau*) pushing the boundaries of state control over women's choice of *hijab*. (Credit: Tabnak News, https://cdn.tabnak.ir/files/fa/news/1392/5/16/278907_871.jpg.)

The regime's sensitivity on women's *hijab* reflects its ongoing evaluation of women's attire to determine their ideological tendencies. In early 2000, *Zanan* (Women) magazine published an article entitled 'Does this woman wear a chador or not?', highlighting the ways the Council uses women's dress to identify their allegiance to the regime (Dokouhaki and Tarighi 2000). While some conservative elites tolerated the presence of some evidently pious conservative women politicians, outspoken female MPs like Koolaee clearly tested their limits, and attire was used as a justification for excluding them. One Iranian women's rights activist I spoke with, who has extensively researched *hijab* in Iran, views mandatory veiling as a key feature of Iranian authoritarianism. 'Without the right to freedom of dress (*azadi-e pooshesh*) any demands for democracy, representation, and freedom within the Iranian context are meaningless, as half of the Iranian population is subject to a mandate which restricts their dress, behaviour, work, and even mobility.' He added that Iran's gender segregation policy in tandem with mandatory veiling has effectively created male-dominated fields, including politics, where genders rarely work side-by-side and men are unlikely to receive direct orders from a female superior (personal interview, 13 July 2011). The regulations and expectations surrounding women's dress contribute to what scholar Elin Bjarnegård (2015) refers to as homosocial capital,[15] which maintains male dominance in politics.

Most women aspiring to political office thus consciously decide to present themselves in ways that facilitate their acceptance by the candidate vetting institutions.[16] Sharareh Abdolhoseinzadeh, a doctoral student in Political Science who ran for local council elections, was among those women. Like many urban university women, Abdolhoseinzadeh normally dresses in a *manteau* with a shawl wrapped loosely around her head. When I met her at an ice-cream parlour at one of Tehran's high-end malls for our interview per her suggestion, with her style and impeccable colour coordination she looked as if she had just stepped off the page of a Persian fashion magazine. She wore a well-fitting mustard coloured coat over black pants, with a light brown leather purse and a colourful shawl in turquoise, orange and yellow. Her blond highlights were clearly visible from underneath her loose shawl. However, her campaign poster for the 2013 local council elections for Karaj – a Tehran suburb – told a different story. In it, she wears a *chador* and her hair is completely hidden under a colourful striped headscarf (see Figure 7.2). When I asked about her choice of dress for the poster, particularly the decision to wear a *chador*, she smiled and said, 'It was suggested by my male colleagues.' Sensing my interest in the contrast between her usual fashion choices and her self-presentation for the campaign, she continued, 'I agreed it was better if I wore the *chador* and appeared to be looking towards the future, but I also looked very beautiful' (personal interview, 8 June 2015). Her strategic choice was to comply with the state-endorsed dress code and appeal to conservatives, but wear a stylish scarf conveying a contemporary sensibility appealing to young voters.

[15] Homosocial capital, a political capital accessible only to men, is needed for electoral success. Homosocial capital has two main components: a perceived pragmatic necessity to build linkages to those with access to important resources in society and a more psychological desire to cooperate with individuals whose behaviour can be understood, predicted and trusted (Bjarnegård 2015).

[16] Unlike the vetting process for the presidency, parliament and the Assembly of Experts, the Council of Guardians does not vet candidates for local council elections, as local elections are under the jurisdiction of the Interior Ministry, which creates supervisory boards composed of parliamentary deputies acting on information from 'the Ministry of Intelligence and Security, local justice departments, registry offices, and the police' (Parsons 2010: 9).

Figure 7.2 Contrasting images of Sharareh Abdolhoseinzadeh: Local council election candidate. Abdolhoseinzadeh is pictured in a *chador* for her campaign poster for Karaj Local Council; her public academia.edu profile image shows her with a loose shawl and visible hair. (Credit: Courtesy of Sharareh Abdolhoseinzadeh; https://srbiau.academia.edu/shararehAbdo lhoseinzadeh.)

Although ultimately unsuccessful in her bid for a seat on the local council, Abdolhoseinzadeh's attention to her appearance on her campaign poster proved warranted. In that same election, based on her campaign poster photo, authorities unprecedentedly annulled the election of a local council member for 'failing to follow Islamic norms'. Fifty days after Nina Siahkali Moradi, a twenty-seven-year-old graduate student of architecture, was elected with roughly 10,000 votes as an alternate member of the Qazvin City Council, the local election supervisory board removed her under pressure from conservative religious groups. Officials had received written complaints condemning Moradi's 'vulgar and anti-religious' posters, and objecting to having 'a catwalk model on the council' (Gates 2013). Moradi's posters show her with her hair fully covered under large, stylish headscarves rather than a *chador* (see Figure 7.3). Although Moradi's case, covered by Iranian and international media, raised outcries from women's rights activists outraged by her removal following her legitimate and resounding win, she was not reinstated. According to a women's rights activist and academic, 'many (conservative) men can hardly tolerate women and girls out in public "defying *hijab*" in fashionable dress and makeup, let alone seeing them reach political office' (personal interview, 14 June 2015). The undemocratic and unconstitutional removal of elected female politicians for alleged dress code or other 'moral improprieties' has continued as officials try to keep reform-minded women out of political office.

Figure 7.3 Campaign posters of Nina Siahkali Moradi for the 2013 local council election. (Above campaign posters were disseminated via social media with no original source locatable.)

Emerging scholarship on violence against women in politics and elections sheds further light on the extreme reactions to the appearances of women who run for office. According to Mona Lena Krook (2017), such violence includes intimidation and harassment intended to quash women's political participation *as women*. Bjarnegård (2017) argues that actions intending to violate the personal integrity of female political candidates ultimately undermine the integrity of the election as a whole. I observed that conservative male elites' insistence on women's 'proper' Islamic dress, and defaming female candidates and politicians for more liberal forms of dress, is a form of violence against women, meant to discourage other women, particularly those with similar ideological positions, from participating in politics. Since the perpetrators are male state elites, this further complicates the possibilities for protesting and appealing such violations.

A notable instance of this occurred in 2016, when the Council of Guardians nullified the votes garnered by Minoo Khaleghi, a thirty-year-old PhD candidate who won the third highest number of votes for Isfahan's five-member district. Backed by the reformist faction for the parliament,

Khaleghi was a civil society actor, involved with NGOs on women's rights and the environment. However, just weeks after her election victory, the Council declared her votes 'null and void' without providing any specifics. After much public outcry and international coverage, the conservative-backed Iranian judiciary cited a number of photographs, which were 'leaked' on social media, 'showing her in public in Europe and in China without the obligatory Islamic headscarf', as reasons for her removal (Erdbrink 2016). Khaleghi's dismissal alarmed many reformists, given that the Iranian constitution empowers only parliament to review and reconsider the credentials of elected officials. Since the Council had already vetted and confirmed Khaleghi as a candidate, it was clear that her ousting was politically motivated.[17] Her removal underscored the power struggles between conservative and moderate or reformist forces in Iran. Although Khaleghi lost her seat for alleged 'un-Islamic' behaviour while abroad, during the same election re-elected conservative MP Nader Ghazipour faced no repercussions for his statement that 'Parliament is no place for donkeys and women' during a campaign rally. Although outgoing women MPs filed a lawsuit against Ghazipour for his 'obvious and blatant disrespect for women', he continued to hold his post (Esfandiari 2016).[18]

Clearly, despite regular elections, Iran's institutional factionalism, particularly the dominance of conservatives within many key state institutions, has greatly hindered women's access to politics and to positions of authority, while opportunities to pressure ruling elites to address the issue are few. Ongoing crackdowns on reformist parties by the authorities, coupled with hardliners' efforts to marginalise outspoken and active reformist women have not only negatively impacted reformists' attempts to focus on women's rights, they have also discouraged women across the ideological spectrum from running for office. And considering that men are mostly exempt from the measure used to evaluate aspiring female candidates' ideological stance,

---

[17] In a statement, Khaleghi dismissed the headscarf scandal as motivated by 'political greed' and reaffirmed her 'adherence to the principles of Islam'. Considering herself a victim of 'malicious attacks', Khaleghi called on the authorities to respect the 'people's votes, which the Supreme Leader recognizes as a basic human right', and punish those who sought to tarnish her reputation (Khaleghi 2016).

[18] The incident, which was covered by Iranian and international media, was condemned by Iranian women across the ideological spectrum, but efforts to have him removed from office were ultimately unsuccessful.

namely attire, women are particularly vulnerable to being forced from formal politics.

In what follows I elaborate further on the negative impacts of Iranian factionalism for the organising and campaigning efforts of women activists from both within and outside of party structures to increase women's access to political representation. Using the failed instance of a cross-party push for gender quotas, I demonstrate that Iran's factional divides and fierce power struggles have prevented key party women from the reformist and conservative factions from joining forces to demand increased political representation. I also show that limited party competition due to the absence of well-structured parties has forced Iranian women's rights activists to engage directly with the public on the issue of expanding women's access to political decision-making, with hopes that increased awareness will result in increased public pressure for change.

Failed Cross-factional Alliances for Gender Quota Adoption

Gender quotas to address women's political under-representation captured the attention of Iranian women activists following the 1995 World Conference on Women in Beijing. As more was published on the increasing implementation of quotas around the globe to address gender imbalance in politics, party women in Iran took up the call. While reformist party women, particularly those in *Mosharekat*, actively pursued gender quota adoption for internal party structures as well as party candidate lists, conservative party women lobbied conservative elites to increase the number of women on candidate lists for major elections. These efforts were largely unsuccessful: in the absence of widespread public pressure neither reformist nor conservative elites felt a need to respond to women's demands.

Gender quota debates in Iran reached a turning point in preparation for the eighth parliamentary elections in 2008, as influential women from reformist and conservative factions finally decided to unite to pressure party elites to demand a 30 per cent quota for women on candidate lists. Forming a coalition under the banner 'The House of Political Parties', a non-partisan institution created by reformists for politicians and activists from across the political spectrum to meet, the coalition issued a statement from Fatemeh Rake'i, a former reformist MP and at the time the head of the Women's Office of the House of Political Parties, detailing the significance of a 30 per cent quota and its support from both reformist and conservative women

(Asr Iran 2007). Male political elites on both sides were enraged that the women had reached across the political divide, and under intense pressure from both factions the alliance dissolved. According to Zahra (a pseudonym), a conservative women's rights activist, 'We are rarely able to get influential reformist and conservative women together around election times, because of resistance from male leaders. We have even been accused of treason when we try to reach across the aisle' (personal interview, 11 July 2011). Although the women's cross-party coalition was short-lived, the attempt signified that outrage over discrimination against women in politics had moved beyond factional and ideological boundaries.

The failure of this coalition again reveals the limitations to organising for female political representation under Iran's factional and majoritarian electoral system. In what for all practical purposes ends up as a two-party race between reformists and conservatives, neither faction sees any need to disrupt the status quo by promoting more female candidates. Unlike in Turkey, where smaller parties may prioritise women's nomination as a means of targeting a particular demographic, as some pro-Kurdish parties have done, in Iran the intense power struggles between male elites of both factions are not served by promoting influential women and they view any coalition between prominent party women across factions as a threat to electoral success and a betrayal of the party.

Though the shared demand for a gender quota remains, there have been no further attempts to ally on this issue to increase leverage. When I asked the Vice President for Women and Family Affairs under President Rouhani, Shahindokht Molaverdi, about the potential for another strategic alliance on gender quotas, she said that women's rights were no longer under attack as they had been when the coalition formed under President Ahmadinejad, and she emphasised the challenges involved, 'When it comes to parliamentary elections, it is about power, and each group tries to gain the most seats . . . I suspect that each group of women will pursue a (quota) measure separately' (personal interview, 6 June 2015).

Unable to pressure male political elites with a unified voice, women from each faction have been employing various pressure tactics. As described at the beginning of this chapter, conservative party women, initially under the leadership of Maryam Behrouzi, challenged women's exclusion by presenting a ten-member women-only list for Tehran during the 2008 parliamentary elections (Tabnak 2008). Given the significance of women's vote for both factions, this bold move intended to force male leaders to consider women's concerns. Conservative female MPS of the eighth and ninth parliament advocated for quota measures based on Behrouzi's proposal, demanding that a number of seats for each province be reserved for women, similar to Afghanistan's quotas.[19] Despite the support of conservative Speaker of the Parliament Ali Larijani, the proposal was not accepted. With their election in 2016, reformist-backed women of the tenth parliament unsuccessfully pursued their own legal quota measure that sought to ensure women compose at least 30 per cent of future electoral lists (Safari 2017).

The Campaign to Change the Face of Parliament

With party structures to directly pressure party elites absent, women's rights activists instead focus on mobilising the electorate to support improving women's access to political decision-making. This strategy seemed particularly crucial for the 2016 parliamentary elections, given the unfulfilled promises on this issue during the first term of moderate President Rouhani, elected in 2013. Rouhani's failure to appoint any women ministers was even more disappointing given the precedent set by his ultra-conservative predecessor, Mahmoud Ahmadinejad.[20]

Thus, a group of feminist activists launched a campaign shortly before the 2016 election with the slogan, 'Changing Parliament's Male Face'. To this end, the campaign organisers established three committees, each with a specific objective: the 'I will be a candidate' committee; the '50-seats for egalitarian women' committee, and the 'Red card for misogynous candidates' committee (Barlow and Nejati 2017). The first committee worked on increasing the number of registered female candidates, calculating that 'to see the election of at least 50 women, thousands of women who believe in gender equality should register for candidacy' as expressed in the campaign's social media posts. The strategy was to register so many female candidates that a sufficient number would pass the Council of Guardians' vetting process. This

[19] The proposal specified that Tehran's thirty-member district have at least ten seats reserved for women, provinces with five or more seats include at least two for women, with one seat for women in two-member districts (RadioZamaneh 2012).

[20] During both of his terms in office President Rouhani (2013–21) did appoint some women to his cabinet, mostly as vice presidents, in areas such as Women and Family Affairs, Environmental Protection, and Cultural Heritage, but none were ministers. Ahmadinejad appointed a woman as his Minister of Health during his second term in office (2009–13).

was successful – the number of registered women candidates tripled from 428 in the previous election of 2012 to 1,234. Directed at the Iranian electorate, the second committee sought to mobilise the public to vote for candidates who expressed gender egalitarian views, and to pressure candidates to address gender equality in their campaigns. The third committee publicised the voting records and views of incumbent and likely MPs on women's rights and gender equality, hoping that increased public awareness would help defeat misogynist candidates. Organisers publicised their messages (mostly in the form of short videos) and reports on social media and their website.

In the end, the campaign contributed to the election of a record number of women to the post-revolutionary parliament. Eighteen women, mostly backed by reformist and moderate forces, entered the parliament, though with the Council's annulment of Minoo Khaleghi's election the number dropped to seventeen. This amounts to 5.9 per cent female representation in parliament, roughly double that of the previous term. However, the most significant outcome of the campaign was that reformist-backed women replaced all of the female incumbents of the previous two terms, all of whom were linked to the conservative faction.

As I have argued elsewhere, the reformist-backed women of the tenth parliament acted critically on women's rights, which in turn led to greater hostility and harassment against them by the conservatives (Tajali 2022). Consequently, the 2020 elections for the eleventh parliament once again witnessed mass disqualifications of reformists, with efforts aimed at marginalising outspoken women. Such treatments, among other factors, led to a sense of hopelessness among Iranian women's rights groups, intensifying campaigns for boycott of the elections rather than expansion of women's access to the parliament. Absence of extensive women's organising and the willingness of elites to be inclusive of women led to the election of conservative women with poor records on women's rights in Iran's most politicised district, Tehran.

Conclusion

This chapter highlighted the negative implications of Iranian factionalism and weak party structures on efforts to address women's political underrepresentation. In addition to lacking direct channels through which to pressure party elites, and to the paucity of grass-roots mechanisms to mobilise and politicise women, party women activists across the political spectrum have been unable to form strategic alliances on common goals around the issue of women's access to formal politics. This is largely due to hostility between the two competing factions of conservatives and reformists, which obstructs any meaningful collaboration between conservative and reformist women. This is exemplified by the failed attempt at a coalition by women across party lines to pressure male elites for gender quota adoption. As well, in contrast to Turkey's organised party structures which foster multi-party competition, Iranian women's rights activists lack the opportunity structure to pressure male elites to expand women's political access and roles in what is essentially a two-party system. With the absence of well-organised and intentioned women's branches, Iranian women often become politicised through religious and military organisations such as the *Basij*, or women's religious seminaries. These organisations are the main conduit for most women (and men) to key positions in the Islamic Republic, thanks in large part to personal connections developed with prominent religious and political figures.

Iran's factionalism has also given rise to institutional fragmentation, which by design privileges the conservative faction and the hard-liner discourse on women's rights. This, I argued, has allowed the handpicking of conformist, conservative women for political decision-making positions, while quashing those with more independent and reformist positions. The heavy-handed process of disqualification has discouraged many Iranian women from pursuing political office, as has the sense that Iranian political institutions do not function to represent the public interest.

Despite the near exclusion of women from political decision-making, Iranian women continue to engage with the formal political arena to challenge the state's gender ideology by setting up their own political parties, pushing for candidacy in major elections, and raising public awareness about the importance of women's political leadership. Although Iran's conservative institutional dominance seeks to curtail women's activism in the formal political sphere, women are determined to gain their seats at the decision-making table. The following chapter will elaborate on how activists are strategically framing their efforts as they engage with elites to achieve their place in politics.

8

PIETY AND AGENCY: FRAMING WOMEN'S POLITICAL RIGHTS IN A THEOCRATIC STATE

Ultra-conservative President Mahmud Ahmadinejad (2005–13)[1] surprised everyone when he nominated three women to his cabinet in 2009 – everyone that is but the many women who had worked unceasingly for exactly that outcome. Zahra (pseudonym), at the time secretary of the Zeinab Society (*Jameh Zeinab*) and the Islamic Women's Coalition (*E'telaf Islami-e Zanan*), told me that from her perspective, the nominations were 'completely expected, since Ahmadinejad and his political allies were under great pressure from women's groups, and he is the type of person inclined to make bold moves' (personal interview, 11 July 2011). Ultimately only one of the three female nominees, Marzieh Vahid Dastjerdi, was approved by the conservative-dominated parliament. As Minister of Health, Vahid Dastjerdi became post-revolutionary Iran's first, and at time of writing only, female minister.

[1] Ahmadinejad represents a new conservative bloc in Iranian politics, referred to by some as ultra-conservative or 'revolutionary hardliner', whose populism, revolutionary idealism, militarism, and social justice orientation distinguishes them from old-guard conservatives and clerical elites (Arjomand 2009; Hoodfar and Sadr 2009; Sohrabi 2006). His proximity to Iran's paramilitary groups such as the *Basij*, led him to push for gender conservative policies, including expansion of the morality police that harassed and arrested those with 'bad-*hijab*', while he also restricted women's equal access to certain fields of study (personal interview with women's rights activists in Iran, 2009 and 2011). However, on a few occasions, when it was politically expedient, he did push for women's rights, such as his public advocacy for women's greater access to sports stadiums, resulting in some highlighting his pragmatism (Shahrokni 2020).

Despite her conservative affiliation, women across the ideological spectrum celebrated Vahid Dastjerdi's appointment as an important step towards the realisation of women's political rights, finally breaking the taboo on female authority in the theocratic state (Tajali 2011; Tohidi 2009). It was thus a great disappointment for women's rights activists when Ahmadinejad's successor, the moderate and reformist-backed President Hassan Rouhani (2013–21), failed to nominate any female ministers. Women's rights groups decried what they saw as 'a serious setback', and publicly accused the new president of ignoring the rights of half of Iran's population to be integrated into decision-making (Esfandiari 2013). Unfortunately, following his landslide re-election in 2017, Rouhani again nominated an all-male cabinet, though ongoing criticism from reformists led to the appointments of three women to less authoritative vice-presidential or presidential assistant posts (Dehghanpisheh 2017).[2]

Ahmadinejad's unexpected nomination of women for ministerial positions despite any record of a commitment to women's issues deserves our analysis. While conservative party recruitment of token numbers of women to political office has at times been associated with party shifts in ideology or leadership (Bayat 2007; Wickham 2015), this was not the case for Ahmadinejad and his allies, who maintained their conservative stance on gender. In light of this and the failure, despite campaign promises to the contrary, of the two more reformist-oriented presidents who served before *and* after Ahmadinejad (presidents Mohammad Khatami and Hassan Rouhani) to appoint any female ministers, it is important to evaluate what factors and actors resulted in Ahmadinejad's move.

As I demonstrate throughout this book, significant factors underlying noteworthy shifts in the rate of female political representation include women's organising and lobbying tactics, and political elites' willingness to respond to women's efforts. In Iran, numerous institutional features, including the absence of party competition, shape the opportunity structures and strategies used by Iranian women to expand female political representation. I argue that recent breakthroughs in female political representation, such as the appointment of the Islamic Republic's first female minister in 2009 and the

---

[2] In his two terms (2013–17; 2017–21), President Rouhani only appointed women to less authoritative positions that do not require Parliament's approval, such as vice-presidential positions or as ministry spokespersons.

near doubling of women's parliamentary presence in 2016 (from 3.1 to 5.9 per cent), are due to women's tactful usage of discursive opportunity structures. Specifically, demands for increased access to political decision-making, framed using the regime's own discourse, are more likely to resonate with ruling elites and to gain support from a wider spectrum of the population. Activists have thus strategically chosen to frame their demands using *religious* or *revolutionary* discursive opportunity structures that arise from within the context of the theocratic regime.

The regime's rhetoric of Islamic values has provided women's rights groups, particularly those with religious tendencies, with *religious discursive opportunities* for harnessing that rhetoric to reference the Quran and female religious figures such as Fatima and Zainab. This religious framing by women's rights advocates – which is particularly utilised by Islamic party women, but also by some secular activists – promotes women's political participation as inherent to Islam.

Women activists also frame demands for women's political representation through reference to revolutionary discourse, highlighting contradictions between the rhetorical gender ideology of the revolution and the actuality of women's political rights and roles in the decades since 1979. This discursive opportunity structure allows activists to demonstrate their allegiance to the Iranian regime while pressuring for reforms using the regime's own promises of Islamic justice and women's rights. The strategic use of regime founder Ayatollah Khomeini's revolutionary rhetoric, along with the discourse of 'gender justice', are presented by activists as indigenous approaches to redressing discrimination against the recruitment and nomination of women for political office. The gender justice – as opposed to gender equality – approach has enabled prominent Islamic women to tactfully demand affirmative action measures such as gender quotas to correct the systematic sidelining of qualified women from political office (Tajali forthcoming). My analysis exposes how women's rhetorical use of the regime's revolutionary ideals, in conjunction with their nuanced understanding of Islamic gender justice and its support of female political authority, led to effective campaigns by women activists to increase female access to parliament in the 2016 elections. The fluidity of Iranian women's framing tactics relative to the particular political and social contexts in which they operate at a given moment demonstrates their agency within a restrictive situation.

Given Iran's theocratic structure and the persistence of revolutionary ideals, pious women from reformist and conservative factions have formed more effective strategic coalitions addressing women's political under-representation than have activists who use secular discourses, including those referencing international human rights documents, since post-revolutionary elites have generally moved away from international human rights frameworks in favour of *Islamic* human rights. Thus, Iranian women's rights activists, as opposed to their Turkish counterparts, have been unable to successfully draw on international human rights documents such as CEDAW in their framing processes. The main factors underlying the framing of contemporary demands by rights activists for women's increased access to formal politics using regime discourse are the power of the clerical oligarchy within Iran's theocratic political structure, and the limited role of international pressure and influence in Iran, particularly regarding women's political rights.

Women's Framing Processes in Iran: Instances of Piety and Agency

According to political process theorists, the concept of discursive opportunity structures refers to institutionally anchored ideas that act as hegemonic discourses shaping the political meaning of given issues in a particular time and context. This conceptual tool helps illuminate which social movement frames are most apt to achieve the goals of a particular movement (Ferree 2003; Katzenstein 1998; McCammon 2013; McCammon *et al.* 2007). Movement actors utilise discursive opportunity structures in their framing processes and in the articulation of demands in order to facilitate their reception, particularly by elites, but also by the public. Discursive opportunity structures – understandings that resonate in the broader culture as sensible and legitimate – include a country's legal framework and its particular structuring of rights and duties, and institutional discourses such as party platforms and ideologies, all of which are harnessed by movement actors to express demands (Benford and Hunt 2003; McCammon *et al.* 2007).

In Chapter 5, I discussed and expanded on the distinctions between culturally resonant versus dissonant or radical frames[3] to illustrate how Turkish women's rights activists strategically select particular frames to engage political elites and garner public support in pursuit of their goal. I argued that pious women activists in Turkey, including AKP party members and supporters,

---

[3] Building on the work of Myra Marx Ferree (2003).

opted for a radical framing referencing secular human rights documents such as CEDAW to try and dislodge hegemonic ideas embedded in their political institutions. This discursive opportunity structure is not available to Iranian activists, who are thus limited to using politically and culturally resonant frames to try and convince elites and the public of the legitimacy of their demands. Thus, in Iran the analysis of framing processes must recognise religion as a discursive opportunity structure, since in a theocratic context most laws, as well as citizen's rights and duties, are mandated in religious terms.

Although an emerging body of literature considers women's activism in Muslim contexts, particularly that of pious and Islamic women[4] linked with religiously inspired and/or conservative parties and movements (Arat 2005; Ben Shitrit 2016a; Deeb 2006; Hafez 2011; Jad 2011; Mahmood 2005; Shehabuddin 2008; White 2002), not much is written on the strategic framing processes they engage in to enhance their rights. Given the significant role of religion in women's politicisation and mobilisation in Iran and other Muslim contexts, I argue that such an analysis of activists' framing strategies illuminates women's agency under specific micro and macro conditions.[5] This chapter contributes to the literature on women's political agency in religious contexts (whether Muslim or otherwise), challenging the assumption that women can only further their rights and tackle gender discrimination from a secular and feminist modelled framework (Ben Shitrit 2013; Hafez 2011; Katzenstein 1998; Mahmood 2005). By presenting pious women's efforts to increase female access to positions of political authority, my research emphasises the complexity of women's rights campaigning, including the use of religious framing and the flexibility to make strategic alliances across ideological tendencies.

Looking at how Islamic Iranian women activists frame their demands for access to political leadership also challenges the assumption that female political under-representation is due to Islam and its principles (Fish 2002; Inglehart and Norris 2003; Inglehart et al. 2003). My findings suggest that

---

[4] In Iran, women who wish to distinguish themselves from secular women (but also from the political label 'Islamist') refer to themselves as Islamic (*Islami*); in Turkey, practicing Muslim women refer to themselves as pious (*din-dar*), since they worry the label Islamic might be confused with pro-Shari'a/Islamist. One of the issues with comparative research is managing informants' use of context-embedded local terminologies.

[5] See Abrutyn (2013) and Gracey (2017) for further discussion of the complex macro/micro dynamics in the relation of religion to values and behaviour.

Islam, which, like any religion is subject to diverse interpretations, can serve as a source of inspiration and legitimacy for Islamic women's rights' activism and political aspirations.[6] Additionally, by highlighting compatibility between Islam and female authority, Iran's religious activists help shift the focus from religion per se to other factors contributing to women's political under-representation; among them, Iran's authoritarian political structure, its theocratic framework, factional politics, and undemocratic state–society relations play bigger roles in women's political under-representation than does Islam writ large.

Restoring 'Islamic Justice'

Zahra (pseudonym), a former secretary general of Iran's influential conservative women's organisation the Zeinab Society (introduced at the beginning of the chapter), met with me in a north-Tehran park on a warm summer day. She was welcoming and friendly and quickly made me feel at ease. Dressed in a brown, loose-fitting *manteau*, with a large, tightly wrapped headscarf fully concealing her hair, Zahra spoke at length about the patriarchal misinterpretations of Islam by clerics and the injustices these have created for women, including their marginalisation from political decision-making. She explained that religious reform, also referred to as new religious thinking, is a key strategy of many Islamic women activists as a corrective to centuries of male-dominated scriptural interpretation. Far from advocating secularisation of Iranian politics, she emphasised that the rights and status granted women *by* Islam need to be restored. Throughout our conversation she highlighted 'Islamic justice' (*a'dl*), emphasising its principle of anti-discrimination (*raf-e' tab'iez*) as foundational to running a government and passing legislation. 'If the Islamic state cannot guarantee justice and fair treatment of its citizens, it cannot be considered truly Islamic' (personal interview, 11 July 2011).[7]

Zahra lauded the Iranian Islamic women's movement (*Jonbesh-e zanan-e Islami*) for successfully highlighting instances of cultural, legislative and

---

[6] In recent decades, female religious activists have spearheaded the fight for many of the legal reforms the Islamic Republic has adopted to improve women's rights and status (Kar and Hoodfar 1996; Mir-Hosseini 1996; Paidar 1995).

[7] Despite her conservative party affiliation, Zahra echoes what many Iranian women's rights activists, particularly those from the reformist camp, have been arguing about Islam's compatibility with individual rights, freedoms and social justice (Alikarami 2014; Mir-Hosseini 2006b).

political discrimination and engaging with the clerical authorities to address them, noting that the consequent debates and discussions have been important to Iran's democratisation process. As a member myself of a transnational Muslim women's movement demanding 'democratisation of religious interpretation', I asked Zahra to elaborate on the movement's key strategy of including women-centred readings/interpretations of religious precepts.[8] She gave the example of the Zeinab Society's efforts to recast polygyny[9] as un-Islamic in contemporary Iran, since it creates injustice and hardship for women and their children, in contradiction with Islamic ideals.

> We argue that justice and fairness (*adl va edalat*) are at the core of Islam. Furthermore, protection of the family and its members, including children's rights are a major concern of Islam. If an Islamic society and its laws, culture, and economic order cannot guarantee fair treatment of *all* members of a polygynous family, then legislating polygyny is a *haram* act on the part of the state. (Personal interview, 11 July 2011)

Zahra said that while engaging in religious reinterpretation in contemporary Iran was challenging, she believed it to be the only viable approach: 'We are after all living under an Islamic state,' she told me. 'I am an Islamic (*Islami*) woman, and it is important to me that I challenge the clerics from within my faith and its writings.' Commenting on the Zeinab Society's perspective on women in politics, Zahra noted:

> Islam is a just religion, which holds women in great esteem. But throughout its history many of its gems (regarding women's rights) have been largely

---

[8] Here Iranian reformism's important distinctions between *fiqh* and Shari'a, that is between religion and interpretation of religion respectively, have been important to furthering women's demands for justice and equality while maintaining adherence to Islam. Within this framework, *fiqh* considers that historical interpretations of religious sources have been influenced by the interpreter's social and cultural realities, and are thus fallible. Reformists argue that *fiqh* has been mistakenly portrayed as Shari'a, the sacred totality of Islam free from clerical influence (Mir-Hosseini 2006b). This approach has supported women's position in two significant ways: (1) by allowing for argument against discriminatory rulings as juristic interpretations from a particular time and context which may no longer apply; and (2) by providing opportunities to challenge clerical interpretations as fallible, which in turn can decrease the influence and power of the clerical elite.

[9] Dominant interpretations of Islam allow for polygynous marriages, in that one man can marry up to four wives simultaneously, albeit with certain restrictions, such as equal treatment of the co-wives or permission of the first wife.

overlooked, while other rulings have been highlighted. For instance, while religious scholars emphasise *hijab*, they tend to ignore the story of *Bilquis* (Queen of Sheba), which justifies women in leadership roles.[10] As a religious women's organisation we seek to highlight such pearls of our faith that we feel have been ignored. (Personal interview, 11 July 2011)

When I asked about the religious expertise needed to challenge discriminatory religious rulings – since Iranian women have limited access to such training – Zahra explained, 'Many of us may not necessarily be able to interpret ourselves, but we can put the clerics on the spot by raising our questions directly from examples from religious texts.' The majority of these debates are carried out on the pages of women's journals or via state media – including TV shows on women's rights, which Zahra herself has produced and hosted – while the Islamic women's movement also recruits key male and female Muslim scholars, thus avoiding being labelled Western or 'un-Islamic'. 'Either way, there are some who label us as "feminist" (Western inspired), but we try to prevent this by formulating our demands in religious terms, with the help of influential and independent individuals with religious training.' Zahra herself had recruited one of the few Iranian *mujtahida* (feminine of *mujtahid* – a person recognised in the Shi'a tradition as an original authority in Islamic law), Ezat-ul-sadat Mirkhani, to serve as a permanent guest on her TV show (personal interview, 11 July 2011).

The focus on 'Islamic justice' is in fact a long-standing tactic of religious women's organising in Iran since the early years of the Islamic Republic, when the regime began to enact legal measures that relegated women to second-class citizenship. In response to discriminatory laws, especially regarding personal status, thousands of politicised Islamic women supporters of the revolution began to publicly criticise the regime for reneging on its promises to honour women and to uphold Islamic justice. Being publicly held to account became an embarrassment for the regime, and eventually the pressure resulted in revision of some aspects of family law. Islamic women, particularly the few who did manage to access state institutions such as parliament, played key roles in these legal reforms, using their positions to appeal directly to authorities

---

[10] Quran, chapter 27 *Al-Naml* (The Ant): 'I come to you from Sheba with sure news. I found a woman ruling over the people, she has been given many blessings and has a mighty throne!' (27: 22–4). The chapter (verses 22–44) goes on to praise Sheba for her wise choice to meet with King Solomon and accept to worship his creator (Mernissi 1991).

and to the public (Paidar 1995). Appropriating the regime's religious and revolutionary discourses, Islamic women activists have demanded expanded rights for women, including for child custody on behalf of the many mothers widowed during the Iran–Iraq war (1980–8), through reference to particular *ahadith* (sayings and actions of the Prophet Mohammad used as the basis for Islamic law) valuing motherhood as the highest and most desirable status for women (Kar and Hoodfar 1996).

Using similar framing processes, Islamic women activists have succeeded in bringing the issue of women's access to political office to the Iranian public sphere; the discussion has entered Iranian public discourse to the extent that many male leaders no longer feel comfortable ignoring demands for female access to leadership positions, forcing them to at least comment on it in their election campaigns.[11] Using the regime's own religious and revolutionary principles, Iranian women have tactfully highlighted the affinity between Islam and female authority, as well as the contradictions between revolutionary ideals and women's current political and social status in theocratic Iran.

Islamic women and religious discursive opportunities
Throughout the past decades, Iranian women's rights activists have learned to skilfully express their demands in ways that pressure the Islamic regime for reform while also highlighting their unquestionable allegiance to the Islamic Republic. Here, I explore their use of religious discursive opportunities to justify the call for increased female access to political office and to facilitate their participation in discursive politics. Following Mary Katzenstein's (1998) study of American feminist discursive politics in the US Catholic Church and military, I consider Iranian Islamic women's intentional reformulation of institutional gender discourse through writing, speeches and campaign slogans as strategic political actions. Rather than experiencing Islam as constraining their political rights, many Islamic women reference Islam as the source of gender egalitarianism, citing Quranic verses and the roles of influential female figures from early Islam. While many women shared with me

---

[11] Presidential candidates, especially from the reformist camp, have since the 1990s increasingly included support for women's rights, including women's access to political decision-making positions, in their campaigns. Coverage of this has been most prominent in women's journals, such as *Zanan* (Women) (Didban 2013; Kar 1996; Omidy 2001; Sherkat 1996; Tarighi 2001).

their faith-based personal conviction of women's qualification for political leadership, here I focus on the increasing promulgation of these religious understandings in the public sphere to engage the elites and the wider public. This framing occurs predominantly in print and on-line media, including women's journals and websites; and increasingly in mass media, through state-owned newspapers, radio and television.

The Quran, which Muslims believe is the revealed word of God, neither specifies nor denies gendered leadership. However, its verses have often yielded diverse and even opposing interpretations on particular matters, including women's access to positions of authority. For instance, while right's activists interpret the verses which praise the Queen of Sheba (*Bilquis*) in Chapter *Al-Naml* (The Ant) as justification for female authority, opponents support their perspective through their interpretation of verse 33 of Chapter *Al-Ahzab* (The Parties), which commands the wives of the Prophet to 'settle down in your homes, and do not mingle with the people excessively, like you used to do in the old days of ignorance . . .' as evidence that women's main duties lie in the domestic rather than public sphere. Reformists and feminist scholars lobbying for the expansion of women's rights in Islam are increasingly highlighting the Quranic verses that emphasise women's rights and gender egalitarianism, while advocating reinterpretation of verses that have been subject to patriarchal *mis*interpretations throughout the years (Mernissi 1991, 1993; Mir-Hosseini 1999, 2006b; Spellberg 1994).

Across the Iranian political spectrum, many religious women's rights activists, convinced of the 'Quran's inherently egalitarian message', highlight this in their campaigns to expand women's political rights (personal interviews with two women's rights activists, 10 July 2011 and 13 June 2015).[12] Referencing the Quran has been a particularly important strategy for pressuring male political elites and patriarchal institutions by accusing them of departing from the Quran's true message of justice and equality. Women's rights activist Azar Mansoury, a high-ranking reformist party member, prolific writer and advocate for women's access to political office, begins most of her articles and talks by referencing the Quran and other religious precepts. In a 2017 article in the major national newspaper *Hamshahri* (Fellow

[12] For example, verses 3: 195 and 33: 35, which emphasise the spiritual equality of men and women, stating that men and women will be equally rewarded or punished based on their actions.

Citizen), Mansoury likens those who argue against women in politics to the followers of the Taliban and Daesh (ISIS) who have a false understanding of Islam. 'In reality, in Islam there is no discrimination between women and men in political and social participation, and in fact, there are clear (Quranic) verses and models that encourage women's political participation.' She then outlines numerous Quranic verses that she argues treat women and men equally. The remainder of her article specifies ways women's political under-representation can be addressed through institutions, including the role of 'political parties in mainstreaming equal opportunities for women's political participation' (Mansoury 2017). Her calls for institutional reform based on Quranic references to socio-political gender egalitarianism are designed to resonate with elites, while her comparisons with Daesh and the Taliban are a tactful way to shame Iran's conservatives, who reject these groups' fundamentalist stands.

Through their writings, speeches and campaigning efforts, women activists have widely publicised the story of the Queen of Sheba to legitimise female leadership and political capacities. The Quranic passages recounting this story emphasise women's rationality, thoughtfulness and just leadership. The Queen of Sheba, presented in the Quran as the rightful ruler of her people, is faulted not for her gender, but because of her ignorance of monotheism, which she corrected using her own judgment and insights (Spellberg 1994). In her book *Zan* (Woman), Jamileh Kadivar, a former reformist parliamentarian and women's rights activist, references the Quran's description of the Queen of Sheba as 'a leader who is wise, not influenced by her emotions, and leads in a good manner', and concludes that 'women are qualified for politics ... and have qualities, which some male leaders lack!" (1996: 87). Other Quranic examples used by Islamic supporters of female political participation include stories highlighting women's allegiance (*ba'yah*) to the Prophet Mohammad independent of their husbands. Verse 12 of Chapter *Al-Mumtahanah* (She Who is to be Examined) praises the women who pledged allegiance to the Prophet, converting to Islam despite the hardships of this choice. One of my interviewees, a former reformist politician, cited women's *ba'yah* in early Islam as an example of women's independent political decision-making, noting some wives divorced their non-believer husbands to join the Prophet in his quest to spread Islam (personal interview, 13 July 2011). In 2021, high-ranking reformist women referenced the *ba'yah* to justify women's political leadership in their public statements and social media discussions as they campaigned in reformist Zahra Shojaee's attempt to become a presidential candidate.

Islamic women's rights activists have also used religious framing to challenge legal and institutional limits on women's access to certain political positions, such as the ambiguous constitutional requirement of *rijal* for presidential candidates as previously explained in Chapter 6. For decades prominent Islamic women have publicly demanded clarification of this term from the Council of Guardians, the body responsible for interpreting the Iranian constitution. In 1997, Azam Taleghani, a former parliamentarian and daughter of esteemed revolutionary leader Ayatollah Mahmood Taleghani, was the first Iranian woman to try and qualify as a presidential candidate. Taleghani also addressed the complex interpretations of *rijal* and their implications for women's political representation in her women's magazine, *Payam-e Hajar* (Hajar's Message). Researching the Quran's usage of the term, Taleghani argued, 'every time the term *"rijal"* appears in the Quran it is in reference to both genders and it simply means "humans" in plural form' (Taleghani 1997a). She cites Quranic verses in which it is impossible to interpret '*rijal* as only men,[13] arguing '*"rijal"* means men *and* women who are active in politics and society' (emphasis mine). To further legitimise her own interpretation, Taleghani (1997b) also presents interpretations of male religious scholars who argued the same position, including Allameh Seyed Mohammad Hussein Tabatabaei, a renowned Shi'a interpreter, and respected Islamic scholar Ali Tahmasebi.

As a high-profile Islamic woman and former parliamentarian with close ties to the regime's elites, Taleghani was well positioned to challenge the conservative elite's discriminatory interpretation of *rijal* using religious discourse, and framing her arguments in accordance with egalitarian Quranic precepts. Despite ongoing efforts by Taleghani and other women since 1997, the Council has yet to qualify a woman for presidential candidacy; however, women's persistent lobbying and attempts to register as presidential candidates have helped fuel ongoing public discussion around the issue and the meaning of *rijal*. Such discussions have forced the Council of Guardians to publicly downplay gender as a disqualifying factor for presidential candidacy,

---

[13] Such as chapter *Al-A'raf* (The Heights), which consists of conversation between occupants of hell and heaven (Quran 7: 46 and 48). Taleghani (1997b) states that, 'It is impossible that all those in hell and heaven are men.'

as it did in a statement during the 2009 elections (Alef 2009; Press TV 2009). This has not however pacified the Islamic women I interviewed, who are adamant 'only when the Council formally qualifies a woman for presidential candidacy, will this debate over *rijal* come to an end' (personal interview with Zahra, 30 May 2015). Indeed, in the run-up to the 2013 presidential election, Ayatollah Mohammad Yazdi, one of the twelve members of the Council of Guardians, declared that the law does not permit female candidates for president.[14] A number of high-ranking women publicly objected to his remarks, including long-term reformist politician Masoumeh Ebtekar, who published an article on the first page of the reformist daily *Bahar Newspaper* demanding 'How can the (Council of Guardians) disqualify all women for the presidency, when the Quran clearly gives the example of Sheba's leadership and her rational decision-making . . . which prevented war and bloodshed?' (Ebtekar 2013: 1). Islamic women's rights activists, extremely frustrated that qualified Iranian women are effectively barred from competing in presidential races, have kept up the pressure on this issue. In 2017 at the age of 73, exactly two decades after her initial campaign challenging the exclusionary interpretation of *rijal*, Taleghani once again defiantly registered her candidacy for president to demonstrate her persistence against hardliners (see Figure 8.1) (Esfandiari 2017; Ghazi 2017).

Islamic women also use religious framing to highlight the important roles of early female figures in Shi'a Islam, namely the Prophet Mohammad's daughter Fatima and granddaughter Zeinab. The revolution's founding ideologues Ali Shariati (1933–77), Ayatollah Khomeini (1902–89) and Ayatollah Motahhari (1919–79) effectively used them as examples of politically engaged women to mobilise the female populace against the monarchy;[15] today Iranian women use these same discourses as arguments to pressure male elites to expand women's access to political leadership. However, while in the late 1970s Shariati presented Fatima primarily as a loyal and stoic

---

[14] BBC Persian quoted Ayatollah Mohammad Yazdi: 'One of the women has declared that if she becomes president, half of her cabinet would consist of women . . . when the law doesn't even allow her to become president, how does she declare the composition of her cabinet?' (In Persian, available from: http://newsforums.bbc.co.uk/ws/fa/thread.jspa?forum ID=17015 (accessed 20 July 2013).)

[15] The ideal Muslim woman envisioned by the revolutionary ideologues, a devoted wife and mother in full *hijab* marching in the streets to defend Islamic values, quickly became an icon of the revolution.

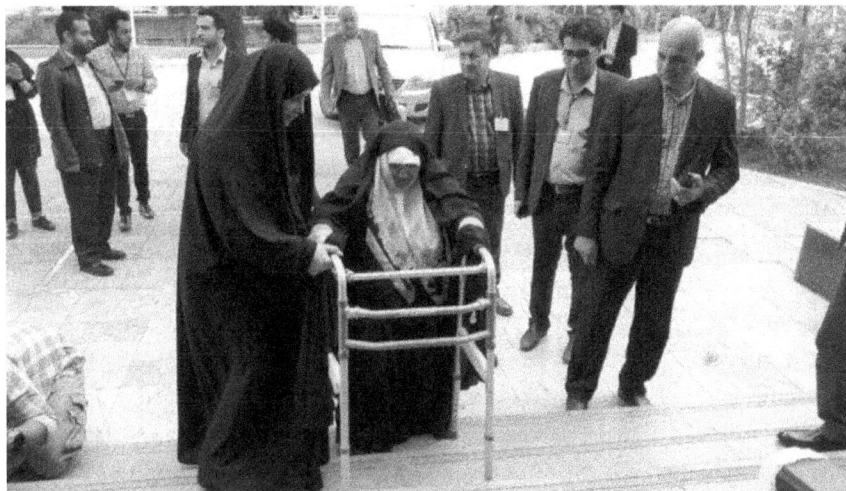

Figure 8.1 Azam Taleghani, using a walker, arrives at Iran's Interior Ministry to register as a candidate for the 2017 presidential election. (Credit: 'Azam Taleghani' by Tasmin News Agency is licensed under a Creative Commons Attribution 4.0 International Licence.)

daughter, wife and mother who silently suffered the injustices that followed her father's death (Mir-Hosseini 2002), in post-revolutionary Iran Islamic activist women, such as Monir Gorji and Massoumeh Ebtekar, have recast the Prophet's daughter to emphasise her 'role in the highest level of decision-making in the society of her time', which they argue 'powerfully challenges the way the Muslim feminine subject has been conceived, and . . . is being effectively utilized . . . to expand the public role of women' (as quoted in Pierce 2012: 345–6). For instance, former reformist politician and political scientist Jamileh Kadivar, in her 1996 book *Zan* (Woman), legitimises women's right to exercise political and religious authority by emphasising Fatima's role as an influential political leader. In her speeches and writing, Zahra Shojaee (2005), former Head of the Center for Women's Participation (CWP) under President Khatami (1997–2005), also highlights Fatima's outspokenness in support of her husband Ali's succession of the Prophet and leadership of the *ummah* (Islamic community). These interpretations contradict many of the earlier Fatima narratives born of the same classical Shi'i and Sunni sources.

Similarly, Iranian women's rights activists also reference Zeinab, the Prophet's granddaughter and Fatima's outspoken daughter, who confronted her brother Hussein's killer, Caliph Yazid – whose reign Shi'i Muslims did not recognise – and delivered an oft-quoted political speech supporting her brother's rebellion against the Caliph's abuse of power.[16] Revered with the honorific *hazrat Zeinab*, many Iranian women activists use Zeinab's defiance in the face of her brother's martyrdom as a model for women's political and public roles. Pioneering Iranian women's rights advocate and senior reformist party member Azar Mansoury, in an interview with *Shafaqna* (an online-based global Shi'a news agency), said, 'The character of Hazrat Zeinab should be introduced as an achievable model for our girls and women . . . as opposed to a holy figure whose status is unreachable' (Shafaqna and Mansoury 2018). In the interview, Mansoury urges readers to recognise the narratives of Zeinab as a powerful woman with leadership qualities and the strength of her convictions, and critiques the way 'our society sanctifies key Islamic figures by celebrating births or mourning deaths', none of which help 'solve any of our problems'. As in her many publications on women's political participation, here Mansoury warns of the repercussions of women's political marginalisation and advocates for measures such as parliamentary gender quotas, which have been adopted by other Muslim countries. Although a devout Muslim woman, Mansoury has been banned and disqualified by Iran's conservative-backed institutions from competing in popular elections due to her history of reformist activism.[17] She continues to publish and speak on women's political participation, tactfully wedding religious precepts with contemporary and internationally endorsed institutional mechanisms, such as gender quotas, to argue for women's increased political roles in Iran.

Islamic women and revolutionary discursive opportunities
In addition to the pragmatism of religious framing within Iran's theocratic structure, women's political rights activists also articulate their demands in

[16] Zeinab's speech after her brother Hussein's martyrdom has greatly influenced Shi'i political thought as the commemoration of *Ashura* – or the day of mourning of Hussein's martyrdom – entails references to Zeinab's words and deeds. Khomeini's (1982) own emphasis on Zeinab's heroic role in Shi'i Islam in his speeches during *Ashura*, has further encouraged Iranian women activists to highlight her role in their organising efforts (see Paidar 1995: 216–19).

[17] Following the contentious 2009 presidential elections, the opposition *Mosharekat* party was banned and among other party members Azar Mansoury, the party's Deputy Secretary General, was imprisoned for three years and banned from politics (BBC Persian 2010). In protest, she registers her candidacy for major elections, though the Council of Guardians repeatedly disqualifies her.

nuanced ways that draw directly from the regime's revolutionary discourse. The powerful gendered language used to mobilise masses of women in support of an Islamic republic during the 1978–9 popular revolution has come to serve as a discursive opportunity structure for addressing women's marginalisation from the political sphere by re-emphasising the promises of justice and equal participation. As outlined in Chapter 6, the Islamic regime's ideologues, including Ayatollah Khomeini, depended on mass participation for the revolution to succeed. However, women's political roles as envisioned (if not widely shared at the time) by the male founders of the revolution ranged from women's presence at street demonstrations and religious gatherings to their votes in support of an Islamic republic; the revolutionary leaders were not particularly concerned with women's own political and social ambitions, including leadership roles. In the decades since the revolution, Islamic women activists have however harnessed this revolutionary discourse to demand women's access to political office.

Esteemed as 'Imam' by many of the Islamic women I interviewed (both reformist and conservative), Khomeini's support for women's political participation during the early revolutionary era was their catalyst for engaging in formal politics. Former conservative-backed parliamentarian and two-time presidential candidate hopeful Rafat Bayat credited her entrance to formal politics to 'Imam Khomeini's teachings and his emphasis on women playing a visible role in the public and political spheres' (personal interview, 21 July 2011). Multiple women quoted Khomeini from a speech he gave soon after the fall of the Shah where he stated, 'Women should interfere in the destiny of their country.' For reformist party women this statement from the Imam legitimised women's active participation in all aspects of political and social life. However, as Elham (pseudonym), a prominent reformist party activist, noted, 'In close to four decades since the revolution, this remains an ideal' (personal interview, 13 June 2015). Since Khomeini's passing in 1989, and particularly since the conservative revival in the mid-2000s quashed the reformist era turn towards rights and democracy (1997–2005), influential party women across the political spectrum have increasingly drawn on Khomeini's words in their public statements and campaigns. By broadcasting women's contributions to the revolution and Khomeini's support for women's political participation, key Islamic women aim to pressure ruling elites and underscore the regime's departure from its revolutionary ideals and promises.

Since Khomeini's legacy concerning gender, including women's political roles, is somewhat ambiguous, this strategy is particularly important.[18] Iranian women continue to use Khomeini's women-friendly statements to challenge discrimination by male elites, keeping the issue in the public eye and on the political agenda. Responding to Ayatollah Mohammad Yazdi's 2013 declaration that Islamic law bars women from running for president, the Islamic Women's Coalition, consisting of high-ranking conservative and reformist women, published an open letter to Yazdi highlighting women's roles in recent Iranian history. The letter included a quote from Khomeini: 'Women of Iran have a bigger share of this movement and revolution than men, and this victory is thanks to fearless women', to challenge Yazdi's gender discrimination and underscore the anti-revolutionary character of his opinion. The letter went on: 'These women are still in the public sphere and continue to open paths' (Valimorad 2013). The Coalition's framing of its position using Khomeini's own words is particularly effective given the ideological divisions among Iran's ruling elites; it reminded conservative clerical authorities of Khomeini's support for female political engagement and underscored their departure from the revolutionary gender ideals he espoused, creating pressure on the clerics while highlighting Islamic women's commitment to the Islamic Republic and its founding ideals and values. In this instance, the Islamic Women's Coalition used available, deeply resonant political and religious discursive opportunity structures to directly respond to opponents of female leadership (Benford and Hunt 2003).

Notably, reference to revolutionary and religious ideals to advocate for women's greater political representation is not only limited to women, since key male political elites have also been expressing this support in similar terms. In his speeches, particularly to women activists and supporters, former President Rouhani has repeatedly justified the need to address discrimination against women in their equal access to politics through reference to the Quran, while also highlighted the double standards of the Islamic regime regarding women's political roles. In April 2021, as he was preparing to leave office, he expressed regret about his inability to appoint more women to his

---

[18] For instance, while Khomeini's policies of mandatory veiling and banning women from judgeship limit women's access to key formal political positions, his calls for women's votes and female access to higher education are deemed by many as designed to enhance women's access to the public sphere.

cabinet since his 'hands were tied', and noted that 'one of the greatest accomplishments of the revolution was its recognition of women's political rights'. After noting that some within the regime grant women a lower political status, he asked, 'If women are less qualified (in politics), then why do we ask them to come out and vote in our elections?' Emphasising women's qualities to be in political leadership, including those who served in his own cabinet, Rouhani stated, 'it is unjust that women compose half of our society, and yet we discriminate against their access to key posts' (Rouhani 2021).

A close analysis of such framing processes reveals that many influential figures within the Islamic Republic avoid feminism or arguments invoking 'gender equality'. This is because, as explained in Chapter 6, the regime's dominant gender ideology, as often emphasised by the Supreme Leader, preaches gender complementarity, while it dismisses gender equality and feminism, deemed to be Western weapons aimed at the destruction of Islamic society (Khamenei 2014). My interviews with key Iranian Islamic women leaders and women who have held official posts revealed that though many favour equal access to positions of authority, they avoid 'equal rights' language to prevent being labelled 'feminist' (personal interviews, 2009, 2011 and 2015). Instead, they justify their demands for increasing women's political representation using regime discourse, and drawing from religious and revolutionary values.

Appointment of the First Post-revolutionary Female Minister: Women's Strategic Framing in the Aftermath of Political Upheaval

As explained in the introduction of this chapter, the 2009 appointment of Marzieh Vahid-Dastjerdi as post-revolutionary Iran's first female minister was a long time in the making, influenced by many factors and actors. These include Iranian women's organising efforts, in particular the use of regime discourse by Islamic women to support the call for female ministers. Having already prepared the ground to demand increased female access to political decision-making, Islamic women's rights groups such as the Zeinab Society found important opportunity structures within the conservative elite hierarchy, which was eager to increase its electoral and political appeal after their contentious win in the 2009 presidential election. The mass protests that followed President Ahmadinejad's re-election, known as the Green Movement and including widespread support from Iranian women, severely undermined the legitimacy of the re-elected hardliner and his conservative backers. This provided an opening for Islamic women's rights activists, many of whom had strong linkages with Iran's ruling elites, to successfully lobby conservative male political elites to nominate a female minister (Shahrokni 2009; Tajali 2011).

The months prior to the 2009 presidential elections witnessed a flurry of organising by a great diversity of women's rights groups eager to address the discriminatory policies of the Ahmadinejad era and women's rights and status in Iranian politics (Tajali 2015b; Tohidi 2009). To strengthen their voices against the hardliners, women across the ideological spectrum formed strategic alliances to highlight that their demands superseded the factionalism and rivalries of Iranian politics. Taking advantage of pre-election political openings, two major coalitions were formed by women's groups to present their demands to the future president in a unified voice. The Convergence of Women (*Hamgarayee Zanan*; henceforth the Convergence), a coalition among mostly secular and reformist women, represented forty-two women's groups and 700 individual activists, including many who identified as feminists (Tohidi 2009). Rather than endorsing any particular presidential candidate, this coalition directed its campaigning efforts towards 'women's demands' (*motalebat-e zanan*).[19] Convergence worked tirelessly to inform Iran's electorate of the positions of all the presidential candidates on gender and women's rights, publicising the platforms of all four candidates on women's issues, which *except* for Ahmadinejad, included nominating female ministers.[20]

The second coalition, initiated by senior Zeinab Society members, brought together elite conservative and reformist women under the banner Islamic Women's Coalition (*Etelaf Islami-e Zanan*; henceforth the Coalition).

---

[19] The Convergence launched a Charter of Women's Rights in Iran (*Manshoor-e zanan-e Iran*) prior to the election, emphasising women's equal access to the public sphere, including formal politics. They also demanded that Iran join CEDAW to facilitate international accountability on women's rights. However, this coalition's activism came to an abrupt halt following the presidential election and the subsequent crackdown on women's rights activists.

[20] Prominent feminist film director Rakhshan Bani-Etemad documented the Convergence's efforts and made the film accessible for free on the internet prior to the elections. Particularly revealing in the film is that only Ahmadinejad refused to participate in an exchange with women's rights activists; the three other presidential candidates, including the military-backed conservative Mohsen Rezaee, commented on their plans for women's rights as their wives sat next to them (Bani-Etemad 2009; Tohidi 2009).

Like the Convergence, the Coalition did not endorse a particular presidential candidate; rather it publicly demanded that all four candidates put women's rights, especially women's political representation, at the centre of their policies. To distance itself from secular and feminist women's rights groups, the Coalition's public statements avoided any reference to the international human rights discourse, and highlighted its commitment to the Islamic Republic and founder Khomeini's ideals. In a strategic move, the Coalition announced itself by publicly launching its first manifesto on the thirtieth anniversary of the 1979 Islamic revolution. The first line of the manifesto, outlining the Coalition's objectives and demands, was a quotation from Khomeini: 'Women must participate in all affairs of the country' (Islamic Women's Coalition 2009). The text lauded the important anniversary, again using Khomeini's words to point out that the revolution was 'possible due to both women and men's efforts and sacrifices', and framed women's rights and the removal of gender discrimination as essential components of the Islamic regime's religious and revolutionary ideals. Women's lower status in contemporary Iran, the manifesto argued, is a result of a 'divergence from the ideals of the Islamic revolution . . . which was rooted in removal of injustice and discrimination'. Given that this coalition consisted of women who served in political positions in the Islamic state, their main emphasis was on women's increased access to leadership positions, including the adoption of gender quotas to ensure women's presence in the legislature.

The Coalition's discursive strategies situated the demand for women's increased access to positions of authority as an Islamic principal reiterated in Khomeini's teachings, rather than referring to any external, international codes. Given the conservative faction's fierce attacks against international human rights documents, particularly CEDAW, even the many reformist Coalition members who had campaigned for Iran to sign CEDAW during the reform era (1997–2005) refrained from any reference to international human rights documents.

Following the 2009 presidential elections, despite extreme opposition from a number of clerics, the Zeinab Society effectively seized the discursive and political opportunity structures available in the aftermath of the election turmoil to continue their lobbying for women's greater political presence. Given their ideological tendencies, Zeinab Society women had access to conservative elites dominating the political hierarchy who were anxious to win over alienated voter blocs including women, many of whom were angry and suspicious at the election results. The large-scale public demonstrations calling for transparent elections, which in turn challenged the regime's legitimacy on the heels of the 2009 election, provided Islamic women's rights groups with an important opportunity to convince their male leaders that women's appointment to political office could help ease tensions with some sections of the public in that political context. As learned Muslims with close links to the clerical establishment, senior Zeinab Society members were well positioned to use religious and regime discourse to publicly confront clerical opposition to female political authority. The Zeinab Society lobbied key conservative politicians, including President Ahmadinejad and the Supreme Leader Khamenei, effectively convincing them of the social and political expediency of appointing a female minister. Commenting on the process of Vahid-Dastjerdi's appointment, the Zeinab Society's former Director and Islamic Women's Coalition member Maryam Behrouzi told me:

> We met with Ahmadinejad and provided him with a list of qualified women who could serve as ministers . . . and then we met with the Supreme Leader to ensure that he didn't hold any reservations against women in leadership positions. Then we tirelessly lobbied the members of parliament to approve her nomination, which they did. (Personal interview, 18 July 2011)

The Zeinab Society's lobbying coincided with Ahmadinejad's need to establish his independence from various conservative factions and gain support from the broader Iranian public following the 2009 political crisis (Shahrokni 2009).[21] Zahra, the former high-ranking Zeinab Society member I interviewed in the north-Tehran park in July 2011, credited the significant victory of Ahmadinejad's appointment of a female cabinet minister largely to Behrouzi's tireless lobbying and meetings with key officials, including Khamenei and members of the United Front of the Followers of the Imam's and Leader's Line – a coalition of Iranian Principlist political groups (personal interview, 11 July 2011). Behrouzi herself shared with me the key

[21] According to Didban – a news source linked with government-based Fars News Agency – in the face of much clerical opposition, Ahmadinejad sought to justify his decision to include female ministers in his cabinet in 2009 in religious terms by stating that '50 of the 313 companions to Imam Zaman (Twelfth Shi'i Imam) were women', a claim that Iran's conservative clerics, among them city of Mashhad's Friday Prayer Imam, refuted (Didban 2013). Ahmadinejad failed to include any female ministers in his first cabinet, and resorted to a religious framing in 2009 largely following Islamic women's lobbying efforts.

role played by the Zeinab Society's face-to-face meetings with Khamenei, which eventually resulted in his approval of a female minister. The Society publicised Khamenei's endorsement to silence widespread clerical opposition (personal interview, 18 July 2011). Secular women's rights activists lauded the Islamic women's success in breaking the 'major taboo on female political leadership' (personal interviews, June and July 2011).

Similar to Turkey, the demand for increasing women's access to political decision-making positions had united diverse groups of Iranian women; despite their significant opposing political ideologies, key women from conservative and reformist factions joined forces to fight for women's political representation (Kadivar 2012). This coalition-building, and the strategic framing of demands in religious and revolutionary terms, also strengthened the Iranian women's rights movement in the face of extreme repression at the hands of ultra-conservatives. However, in 2013 with the election of moderate, reformist-backed President Rouhani, a resurgence in factionalism led to renewed divisions among elite women across ideological lines. The Islamic Women's Coalition, comprised of religious women from both factions, gradually became inactive as many of its high-ranking members chose factional over women's rights allegiance; several reformist women's rights activists who entered the new Rouhani government cut ties with their conservative counterparts to demonstrate their allegiance to the reformist camp. Likewise, many conservative women activists, who lost political clout and government posts in the 2013 election, objected to being used by the women's rights movement to woo conservatives in support of women's rights (personal interviews with Reformist and Conservative party women, May and June 2015). This seems to indicate that party politics once again superseded women's rights alliances. With more moderates in the executive branch, it was now up to reformist women to push their gender agenda and reverse some of the damage of the Ahmadinejad era. Reformist women's objectives to greatly improve women's access to politics during Rouhani's presidency however never materialised, given extensive conservative backlash against such efforts, including tying Rouhani's own hands to do more in this area (Rouhani 2021; Tajali 2020).

'Gender Justice': A Potential Route to Gender Quotas?

During President Rouhani's first term (2013–17), his Vice President for Women and Family Affairs, Shahindokht Molaverdi, used the term 'gender justice' in her speeches on women's status in Iran; the term was subsequently integrated into official government plans for gender and development, garnering national and international attention as various constituencies began debating Molaverdi's intentions and speculating as to her ideological tendencies. In the international press, a 2015 *BBC Persian* article titled, 'Rouhani's Vice President for Women: We Seek Gender Justice instead of (Gender) Equality', quotes Molaverdi as saying 'Gender justice, far from the extremes, aims to enhance women's status and to create a global model . . . that is acted on rather than merely talked about' (BBC Persian 2015). The article goes on to discuss women's lesser legal status relative to men in Iran and the declining rate of female employment. On the other hand, her emphasis on enhancement of women's status led some conservative forces inside Iran to attack her statements by arguing that 'Your suggestion of gender justice calls on United Nation's values and views on women and family . . . which are in conflict with Islamic views' (Student News Network 2015). Clearly, while some had interpreted Molaverdi's departure from 'gender equality' to signal diminished commitment to women's rights and acquiescence to Iran's entrenched patriarchy, others were concerned that her 'liberal thoughts' went too far and undermined the ideal of gender complementarity they considered essential to the 'institution of family in Iran's social structure' (Student News Network 2015).

Since I was in Iran during these debates, I asked women's rights activists and scholars, and Molaverdi herself, about the choice of the term 'gender justice'. A consultant and women's right's scholar at the office of the Vice President for Women and Family Affairs shared with me the reasoning behind the use of the term:

> During President Ahmadinejad's term (2005–13) to talk about gender equality meant that you are a feminist, which they (the government) equated to a crime. Also in 2014, the Supreme Leader declared that he does not believe in gender equality. Therefore, it has been important for us to try to arrive at another term to discuss women's rights. This is a tactic, although it all boils down to how you define gender justice. Justice for conservatives is when women stay home (*khane neshin*), while men are the breadwinners; whereas we say, women have been dealt the shorter end of the stick in Iran's male-dominated society for so long, so justice is to provide women with more opportunities. (Personal interview, 6 June 2015)

Later that day when I interviewed Molaverdi and asked her to elaborate on the decision to use the term 'gender justice', she laughed and said she was surprised by all the media attention. 'I keep being asked by journalists whether I believe in gender equality', she told me, adding that this gave her the impression that somehow gender justice and gender equality were being positioned by the media in opposition to each other. 'There is such a thing as gender equality . . . but what I am emphasising is that since women start from a lower status, they need extra opportunities to help them compensate. To me this is justice' (personal interview, 6 June 2015). I asked Molaverdi what she meant by 'extra opportunities' and about specific strategies the ministry had in mind concerning gender justice, especially regarding women's political representation. She immediately referred to gender quotas as 'a globally recognised tool' to help level the playing field for women in politics. Outlining the national plans for women's political empowerment and increasing women's descriptive *and* substantive political representation, Molaverdi stated:

> Our aim is to adopt national-level gender quotas, but there is opposition.
> The current women MPs (2012–16) oppose quotas in the form of reserving
> a specified number of parliamentary seats for women largely because both
> Iraq and Afghanistan adopted one after American intervention, so they feel
> that this is a Western method. (Personal interview, 6 June 2015)

During our interview, Molaverdi repeatedly affirmed her commitment to female access to political office and the importance of institutional support to achieve this, noting that with female political representation at 'only 3 per cent', gender quotas are an 'important affirmative action measure'. Molaverdi told me she supported broader quota measures than those favoured by current female MPs (all conservative allied),[22] who were calling for at least 30 per cent of candidate *lists* in Iran's few *multi-member districts* to be female.[23] Molaverdi felt this did not go far enough and wanted 30 per cent of *all seats* in parliament reserved for women, as is the case in Afghanistan and Iraq (Hoodfar and Tajali 2011). To date, all proposals for electoral gender quotas

[22] Prior to the end of their term, conservative women MPs in June 2015 proposed a bill requiring parties and coalitions to allocate at least 30 per cent of their election lists to women. However, the conservative-dominated parliament rejected this proposal (The Iran Project 2015).

[23] Of Iran's 207 electoral districts, ninety-five are multi-member with the majority having only two or three seats. Tehran is Iran's biggest electoral district with thirty seats, the next biggest district has only six (Asr Iran 2016; Borden 2016).

have been repeatedly rejected by parliament, largely due to conservative faction opposition (Deutsche Welle Persian 2015; The Iran Project 2015).

A year after I spoke with Molaverdi, Iran's Five-Year Development Plan for 2016–21[24] outlined her objectives on gender justice in a manner that seemed designed to avoid challenging the regime ideology of gender complementarity.[25] Rather than assessing her 'gender justice' approach as illustrative of antagonistic positions between religious 'gender justice' advocates and secular 'feminists' (Mir-Hosseini 2016), I see her emphasis on *justice* and Islamic values as a deliberate framing strategy to appeal to more conservative religious sectors of Iranian society, while her demands for changes to enhance women's social, political and economic status align with the position of secular women's rights activists who for decades have lobbied to eliminate social and legal discrimination against women. Many of the Iranian women's rights activists and scholars I spoke with said overall they approved of Molaverdi and her office's approach to women's rights issues, given the social and political constraints of the Iranian context. Her effectiveness was also apparent given that many hard-line conservatives sought to have her removed from her post as Vice President of Women and Family Affairs (Mir-Hosseini 2016). They eventually succeeded when in 2017 President Rouhani, presumably under pressure, removed her from her position and named her Special Assistant to the President for Citizenship Rights, a largely ceremonial

[24] The Law on the Sixth Five-Year Economic, Cultural, and Social Development Plan for 1396–1400 (2016–21), also referred to as the 'Sixth Development Plan', sets out the nation's development goals and objectives as articulated by the government and approved by parliament (Kordvani and Berenjforoush 2017). Article 101 states in part: 'to benefit the society with the human capital of women towards sustainable and balanced development (all bodies) are to apply the approach of gender justice based on Islamic principles in all of their policies, plans, and objectives . . .' (Tasnim 2017).

[25] Molaverdi is quoted in a 2016 Farsi language interview with Shahrdokht News Agency excerpted by the Tehran-based Organization for Defending Victims of Violence (ODVV) saying: 'Our main objective in the country's five-year development plan is the realisation of gender justice, . . . that will bring about justice in management, the job market and *various roles of men and women so that ultimately, we see a balance between women's activities and their jobs*. . . . In fact, we are pursuing fair access to resources and believe that justice supersedes equality' (my emphasis). It appears here that Molaverdi is suggesting women's labour market participation must be supported but this should not compromise their domestic roles. Thus, for example, she supports extended maternal leave and job protection. (http://www.odvv.org/news-844-The-Realisation-of-Gender-Justice-the-Main-Objective-of-Iran-in-the-Five-Year-Plan.)

appointment. Her continued outspokenness against gender discrimination in Iran eventually resulted in Molaverdi's forced resignation from government in November 2018 under an ambiguous interpretation of a law that banned the government from employing retirees (Shahrabi 2018).[26]

However, the nuanced framing and strategic approaches used by Molaverdi and her team have continued to significantly enhance the ability of women's rights activists to address the oft-used excuse of meritocracy (*shayesteh-salari*) to justify women's exclusion from political office. The acceptability of the gender justice framework provides women with more opportunities – such as a future quota as envisioned by Molaverdi – while it also challenges discrimination against qualified women, that is, discrimination based solely on gender. For decades politicians from both reformist and conservative camps have sidelined the issue of women's political representation by arguing that merit, rather than gender, should determine access to political office. Similar to other contexts, in Iran this has been used to justify the absence of women in government leadership posts, based on the argument that women lack sufficient political or leadership experience. Former reformist President Khatami used this meritocracy argument to support his failure to appoint women ministers during his two terms, 'given their limited executive experience', despite publication by the women's magazine *Zanan* of extensive profiles of various highly qualified women hoping to and eminently capable of leading a number of departments (Ebrahimi 2001; Omidy 2001; Tarighi 2001). Nevertheless, many conservative politicians continue to argue that affirmative action around gender is antithetical to merit-based appointment, especially regarding the office of presidency, which many continue to consider to be a male domain (Ghazi 2017; Khamenei 2014).

Through the frame of gender justice, I found women's rights activists across the ideological spectrum are challenging the fallacy of a lack of qualified women by highlighting the merits (*shayestegi*) of myriad highly competent female candidates. In an interview with the official parliament news agency (ICANA) where she vowed to 'decrease gender discrimination and

---

[26] Molaverdi's continued popularity among some reformists and women's rights advocates led to suggestions for her to be given governorship of one of Iran's provinces. Shortly after, she was forced to resign justified through a law that banned government employment of retirees. President Rouhani accepted her resignation. At age fifty-three, Molaverdi protested this forced resignation in a publicised letter to the President noting, 'Banning political participation is the violation of the most self-evident human right' (as quoted in Shahrabi 2018).

other forms of social injustice', reformist MP Fatemeh Zolghadr stated: 'Meritocracy is not in contradiction with appointing women to senior leadership posts', adding that *not* recruiting women for such positions undermines the merit argument:

> Although selection of leaders should be based on merit, without any regard to gender, unfortunately till now, in elections, meritocracy in its truest sense has not taken place since many qualified women who have for years worked alongside men are still absent from senior leadership posts.

She went on to criticise the absence of women ministers during both President Rouhani's terms (2013–21), asking 'How is it possible that from half of the society, not one single woman is qualified to become a minister?' (ICANA 2017). Another woman activist echoed this frustration:

> Some men, whom we had never heard of, became ministers overnight in President Ahmadinejad's cabinet, but meritocracy was never mentioned as a challenge to their appointment . . . however, when we have qualified women to fill only a few of the total seventeen or eighteen cabinet posts, suddenly their merit is questioned. (Personal interview, 10 June 2015)

Zolghadr and other women activists have strategically appropriated and transformed the rhetoric of *meritocracy* used by male elites to deny women's leadership capabilities, to shine light on eminently qualified women.

This skilful adoption of the meritocracy rhetoric by Iranian women activists aligns with an important recent shift in the literature on women and politics, which problematises male *over*-representation in political decision-making rather than female *under*-representation, highlighting the negative implications of male political dominance for representative democracy (Bjarnegård 2015; Murray 2014; Nugent and Krook 2016a). According to Rainbow Murray (2014: 520), 'Male overrepresentation itself compromises meritocracy and constrains the substantive representation of men as well as women'. As Murray explains, when men from a certain class and ethnicity dominate political institutions such as legislatures, the ability of elected governments to represent society in all its diversity is compromised. Furthermore, since men's dominance in political bodies renders them the de facto status quo, women, as political outsiders, have the burden of justifying their political presence. 'Men are required neither to prove their competence nor to justify their inclusion. This is not to say that individual men are immune to all scrutiny, but rather that the competence of men *as a category* is not questioned' (Murray 2014: 520–1).

Conceptualising different identities based on gender, ethnicity or class, as qualities (merit) that deserve representation in political institutions is fundamental to democratic and just governance, and increasingly demanded by women's rights groups everywhere, including in Iran.[27] However, Iranian Islamic women such as Molaverdi, the recent formulator of the gender justice discourse, have framed their demands for representation with reference to Iran's religious values and revolutionary ideals rather than democratic ones, in order to find resonance with the ruling elites. The emphasis on the indigenous origins of the demand for representation is a deliberate strategy to prevent backlash from conservatives critiquing the call for expansion of women's political roles as stemming from foreign influence.

Molaverdi's gender justice rhetoric and programming and its results have also served as an important campaigning tool to garner even more support among those who value women's increased public and political participation. Indeed, by April 2021, Rouhani boasted of increasing the percentage of women leaders and managers in the executive branch from five per cent to twenty-seven per cent, which was close to his initial goal of thirty per cent. Molaverdi and other post-holding women often shared statistics on their own social media accounts, crediting the Rouhani government's gender justice initiatives. 'Despite the heavy weight on their shoulders,' Molaverdi shared in a post, 'women in our society have proven their qualifications (*shayestegiha*) in balancing their social and family roles and satisfying their divine missions' (serving their communities). She ends the post stating: 'Democracy (*mardom-salari*) along with respect for religious and moral values, has the potential to protect the rights of all, including women.'

The impact of the gender justice frame on the 2016 parliamentary elections
A notable shift that correlated with the government's gender justice policy was the tripling of the number of female candidates for parliament and the near doubling of the percentage of female parliamentarians elected in 2016, to 5.9 per cent from 3.1 per cent the previous term. Given that a key goal

[27] According to a women's right's scholar consulting at the office of the Vice President for Women and Family Affairs, Iranian activists are very cognisant of the intersection of justice with class, ethnicity and other social markers (personal interview, 6 June 2015).

of 'gender justice' as articulated by the Office of Women and Family Affairs and in the Five-Year Development Plan was to increase women's numbers in senior leadership roles, reformist women activists felt legitimated in demanding women's parliamentary presence to further democratise the legislative branch; they extensively lobbied party elites to include female candidates, convincing the reformist coalition to adopt a 30 per cent female quota for their party lists. Reformist party leader Mohammad Reza Aref promoted this goal using gender justice rhetoric, but ultimately the reformist List of Hope (*Omid*) in Tehran's thirty-member district was slightly shy of its goal, managing to nominate eight women (26 per cent). While conservative party elites barely addressed women's political representation in the 2016 election, conservative party women did take the opportunity to press for women's increased parliamentary presence, albeit not explicitly using the language of gender justice (Alef 2015). As Figure 6.5 shows, the main candidate lists of conservatives included six women for Tehran (20 per cent).

In addition to lobbying party elites, women's rights activists also called on women to register as candidates to increase the likelihood that the Council of Guardians would qualify more female candidates. Both secular activists and reformist party women promoted and encouraged female candidacy in a loosely built alliance. While independent and secular women activists launched the 'Change the Male Dominated Face of Parliament Campaign'[28] prior to the elections, as explained in the previous chapter, renowned reformist women including Azar Mansoury initiated training courses and workshops around the country designed to identify, encourage and support qualified women to run for parliament.

Women's extensive organising around diversity and merit eventually led President Rouhani to publicly appeal to Iranian women to run for office, to show 'the world that in Iran nothing is based on gender, but rather that all affairs are based on meritocracy' (Radio Farda 2015b). A record number of women (1,234) registered as candidates, while the Council of Guardians disqualified a record number as well (648) as outlined in Table 6.2. Nonetheless, the number of women in parliament went from nine to seventeen, the highest rate of female representation ever in post-revolutionary Iran. This increase was largely thanks to the strategic framing processes chosen by activists to

---

[28] The reformist party women did not officially endorse the campaign, but the campaign certainly helped attract female reformist candidates.

resonate with religious and political elites, while still appealing to the central demands from the public for democracy and justice. In recent decades, international human rights discourses have been of limited use in the Iranian context, where they have been largely dismissed by high-ranking elites, authorities and clerics since the 1979 revolution.

CEDAW: A Battleground for Iran's Factional Politics

The 'international human rights discourse' rooted in Western liberal political theory and largely developed and legitimised by the UN, has not been welcomed by all governments, including that of the Islamic Republic of Iran, which associates it with Western dominance and imperialism. Instead, the Islamic regime claims 'Islamic human rights', based on Islamic justice, as equal to or surpassing secular rights ideals, enabling it to proclaim itself as a human rights abiding country in the world community, without yielding to Western influence (Osanloo 2009: 180–1). By using an Islamic human rights ideology, the regime emphasises its sovereignty both to its citizens and to the world, and can more easily denounce Western countries that criticise Iran's human rights record despite their own human rights violations.[29] However, notwithstanding its apparent rejection of international human rights discourse, Iran has nonetheless ratified several international documents, and attempted several times to gain a seat on the UN Human Rights Council, causing international criticism. Indeed, despite the outcry of human rights advocates both internationally and nationally, Iran has served twice as a member of the UN Commission on the Status of Women (CSW),[30] indicating that on some level the Islamic Republic wishes to be an

---

[29] For instance, Supreme Leader Khamenei criticised the US's maltreatment of prisoners at Guantanamo Bay (Isayev and Jafarov 2013), and denounced France's headscarf ban as infringing on the rights of its minority population to observe their religion. However, while such criticisms attempt to demonstrate Iran's acceptance of the liberal-based rationality associated with human rights and rule of law, Iranian women's rights activists have publicly pointed out that by the same token compulsory veiling also infringes on the rights of the minority non-Muslim population in the Islamic Republic.

[30] Iran agreed to withdraw from its 2010 bid for a seat on the Human Rights Council in exchange for securing uncontested membership in the CSW, a move criticised by much of the international community (Anderlini et al. 2010). In 2021, Iran was once again secretly elected to CSW, a move that was heavily criticised by many rights activists, though others welcomed it as they believed it might open Iran to greater international scrutiny on women's rights. Notably Iran was selected to serve on CSW in 2021 alongside Pakistan and

active player in the international human rights community. This willingness on the part of the government has led the Iranian women's rights movement to periodically consider international human rights documents as a possible route to enhancing women's rights. The reform era (1997–2005) created a window for women's rights activists to lobby for Iran to sign on to CEDAW, and ratification was debated several times by parliament. The reformist-dominated Sixth Parliament actually voted for CEDAW's ratification, but the Guardian Council, which is charged with vetting and approving all legislation, rejected the bill, declaring CEDAW incompatible with Islamic values (Koolaee 2012).

Over the years CEDAW has become a battleground for Iranian factionalism, where reformists and conservatives use women's rights as a flashpoint for their opposing ideologies, thus preventing ratification of this important document.[31] This has led many reformist women to abandon their decades-long fight for CEDAW's adoption, deeming it no longer viable as a strategy towards securing women's rights. For example, during the reform era (1997–2005), Shahindokht Molaverdi, as International Director of the now defunct Center for Women's Participation under President Khatami, was a major instigator pushing for CEDAW's ratification. However, in 2015, as the Vice President for Women and Family Affairs, CEDAW was entirely off her agenda:

> I believe that focus on CEDAW will distract us from addressing central women's rights issues by bringing up peripheral concerns and criticisms. We should not rely on an international convention to eliminate discrimination against women, and rather should work towards that goal with specific actions and plans. In addition, joining CEDAW has not meant elimination of all discrimination against women in the party countries, such as Saudi Arabia and many other countries. Because of these reasons, we will not

China, two states with similar poor records of human rights and women's rights.

[31] Nobel Peace Prize Laureate Shirin Ebadi lays the blame for Iran's failure to ratify CEDAW squarely on factionalism, suggesting that had conservatives held the power when parliament voted for CEDAW, the conservative-dominated Council of Guardians would have accepted ratification (Osanloo 2009: 189). Similarly, Iran's two terms on CSW (2010–4 and 2021–5) have both coincided with conservative-dominated parliaments, while reformist-oriented women such as Molaverdi have had limited roles and access to major international human rights bodies when they held formal posts.

pursue CEDAW. (Personal interview, 6 June 2015)

Molaverdi's more conservative women's rights peers, including Zahra, the former Secretary General of the Zeinab Society, have also been apprehensive of CEDAW. When I asked Zahra about CEDAW she explained:

> As soon as you go near CEDAW, you are attacked by (male elites) who label you as 'feminist' or Westernised (*gharb zadeh*). But I am saying that we do not even need CEDAW, when we have Islam, which in its true from is against all forms of discrimination. (Personal interview, 11 July 2011)

Unable to draw support from the international women's rights community or framework, particularly the UN and its declarations, Iranian women activists have increasingly turned to transnational activist networks operating from Muslim contexts. Significant support in the form of experience-sharing and strategy has come from the Muslim feminist research and advocacy network Women Living Under Muslim Laws (WLUML), which has provided Iranian women's rights activists with important tools and knowledge to lobby for increased female political representation. Towards this end, in 2009 the Women's Empowerment in Muslim Contexts (WEMC) project of WLUML organised a three-day workshop in Tehran on 'Discourses of Women's Electoral Politics and Quota Systems' for local women's rights activists. This workshop was tactfully organised ahead of the presidential election, at a time when political elites and candidates are most receptive to women's demands, and keen to appeal to the female electorate. Given my research interest on parliamentary gender quotas, the workshop's organiser, Homa Hoodfar, invited me to present on the global trend towards quota adoption and my findings concerning the relative effectiveness of various approaches from cases around the world.[32] The interest and insight generated by this workshop led to our co-authorship of a book on experiences with gender quotas around the globe: *Electoral Politics: Making Quotas Work for Women*, published by WLUML in 2011, with a Persian translation published in 2016, reprinted in 2020.[33]

---

[32] Other presenters included activists and quota advocates from Sri Lanka, India and the United States, who discussed their experiences with gender quotas, as well as related topics such as women's rights charters and constitutional reform.

[33] The idea for a guide for those advocating for women's political representation had been on WLUML's agenda since the 1995 World Conference for Women in Beijing; the book materialised after the 2009 WEMC workshop in Tehran, given the broad interest from

A number of women's rights activists who attended the WLUML workshop met with the reformist presidential candidate Mehdi Karroubi ahead of the 2009 elections to discuss the significance of women's political roles and gender quotas.

The lack of recourse to international human rights discourses in the Iranian context, for all the reasons stated above, has meant that in contrast with their Turkish counterparts, Iranian activists have had to appropriate regime discourse, in particular its religious and revolutionary elements, to articulate their demand for women's increased access to political office. We clearly see how the political and social context of a given period shapes the framing strategies of Iranian women's rights activists. Thus, during the reform era, there were efforts to engage with international human rights documents, but Iran's increasing marginalisation from the international community and hostility towards its rights discourses has led many activists to distance themselves from this framing. This flexibility in women's organising and lobbying and the fluidity of Iranian women's framing tactics relative to the socio-political specificities of a given moment, demonstrate their creativity and agency within a very restrictive environment. Using culturally and politically legitimate frames, women's rights advocates gain the widest possible public support and exert maximum pressure on elites to achieve increased female political representation and power. This agency is also evident in women's formation of issue-based strategic alliances across the ideological spectrum, depending on the political environment and the nature and extent of factional rivalry.

Conclusion

In recent decades, Iranian women's rights activists across the ideological spectrum have firmly established the issue of women's political rights and representation in the public discourse, and have made modest but notable gains in women's presence in political decision-making positions. Despite the numerous obstacles stemming from Iran's theocratic political structure and factionalism that hinder female access to leadership positions, Iranian women effectively take advantage of available opportunity structures to address female political under-representation. The current political climate of the theocracy

Muslim women activists in quota debates based on experiences with gender quota implementation around the globe to that point.

and subsequent discursive opportunity structures have led more and more women with strong religious convictions, both reformist and conservative, to become major players in the lobby to increase women's power in high-level politics. These women work on effectively framing their demand in a way that mobilises public support and pressures elites to address women's rights. The context of religiosity has in fact provided Islamic women, particularly those with ties to influential political and religious figures, with important opportunities to have their demands heard in formal politics.

In this chapter, I have shown how use of religious and revolutionary discourse to frame their demands has enabled Iranian women's rights activists to counter patriarchal interpretations concerning women's political roles. Secular and reformist women's political organising, coupled with the strategic lobbying power of Islamic women's rights activists, resulted in the eventual appointment of the first female minister in post-revolutionary Iran in 2009, as well as the notable increase in women's parliamentary presence in 2016. To legitimise female authority in Iran's theocratic context, Islamic women activists are particularly advantaged to appeal to and find resonance with the conservative elites. This chapter also argued that Islamic women activists are strategic in their framing, tactfully presenting their demands for affirmative action measures such as gender quotas using Islamically-inspired values such as 'gender justice' and avoiding exogenous frameworks and constructs which might open them to charges of 'Westernisation'. These framing strategies have resulted in the formation of important coalitions between ideologically diverse women's groups towards their common objectives, among them, increasing women's access to political decision-making. The effectiveness of women's organising has helped produce a female voting bloc, which male political leaders must consider when running for office. Significantly, when diverse women's rights groups collaborate, we also witness an improvement in women's substantive representation, as outspoken women enter key political posts largely thanks to women's organising and turning out to vote. However, with the absence of a meaningful affirmative action measure that is designed with direct input from women's rights advocates, women's political representation in Iran is likely to remain low.

9

CONCLUSION:
DEMANDING A SEAT AT THE TABLE

Women have played key roles in the political and social changes that continue to unfold in the Middle East and North African region and around the world. The pervasiveness of social media and the instantaneous spread of images across the globe mean that we are witness to women's significant presence at rallies in Iran, Turkey, and surrounding Muslim majority countries such as Sudan, Lebanon and Algeria, actively protesting undemocratic, corrupt, and unaccountable political systems alongside men. In their struggles for equal citizenship, women across the Muslim world have also been demanding greater access to political decision-making, an arena from which they have been largely marginalised. This book analysed the activities and strategies of women's rights groups around female political representation to explain women's gains in this area despite the significant constraints posed by gender discriminatory ideologies and undemocratic political parties and systems. Through a comparative study of two Muslim-majority countries in which conservative gender ideologies dominate, this research explored the underlying dynamics of these increases in Turkey and Iran, and by extension suggests an additional lens through which to analyse the status of women's political rights and roles in the Muslim world.

Recognising the many complex factors that impact women's access to political leadership, including institutional structures, contemporary and historical state ideologies, and political frameworks, many of which are not unique to the Muslim world, the book undertook a thorough analysis of how women's rights groups strategise to increase women's political representation.

Demonstrating the significant history of demands for greater access to political office and representational inclusion in both countries from women across the ideological spectrum, this book focused on the intersections of political and institutional structures, religious and cultural norms and values, and voter behaviour in terms of women's political representation. In this analysis, the book's findings elucidated the extent that Islam or Muslim culture hinders women's access to political office – as a number of previous scholarly works had suggested (Acar 1995; Afshar 1996; Fish 2002; Inglehart and Norris 2003; Joseph 2000; Moghissi 1999) – by comparing a secular Muslim society with an Islamic theocracy, both featuring the puzzling juxtaposition of highly politicised female demographics and relatively low female representation in high-level political posts.

My research here focused on deconstructing the assumption that it is Islam that keeps women out of political decision-making positions. An important empirical observation drove this inquiry into the relationship between Islam and female political representation: unexpected increases in female politicians representing *religious* political parties. In Turkey, a notable increase in the percentage of female parliamentarians coincided with the conservative, pro-religious AKP's rise to power; in Iran the first female minister of the Islamic Republic was nominated by ultra-conservative President Ahmadinejad and approved by a conservative-dominated parliament. In explaining these puzzling trends, witnessed in other Muslim majority countries as well including Yemen and Jordan (Clark and Schwedler 2003) and Tunisia (Marks 2013), I move away from an essentialist perspective of Islam as a barrier to women in politics, which fails to account for women's significant involvement in voter recruitment and political campaigning on behalf of religious and conservative parties, to consider that while some interpretations of Islam may work to hinder women's rise to political power, others support the presence of women in politics.[1] We also saw how both the 1979 Iranian revolution and the rise of Islamist parties in Turkey in the 1980s and 1990s provided pious women – previously largely absent from politics – with important opportunity structures that enabled their entry into the political arena, albeit primarily at informal levels. Women's decades of politicisation through involvement in

---

[1] While conservative patriarchal interpretations of Islamic texts are used to deny women political power, Muslim feminism sees Islam as promoting equal gender opportunity, including in politics.

religious political movements and activism at lower party echelons have legitimised their demands for increased access to high-level decision-making and
eventual rise, though in modest amounts, to such positions in the past decade.

My analysis of how Iranian and Turkish women's groups are demanding
a seat at the decision-making table highlights the nature of strategic interactions between women, political and religious elites, established institutions,
and the wider public, particularly the electorate. In this book, I argued that
the broader political and social contexts of Iran and Turkey provide local
women's groups with important opportunities to engage with political elites
and the electorate to address women's political under-representation, though
to different degrees. The findings of this research contribute to our understandings of women's rights in Muslim contexts, and also reveal the extent to
which Muslim women, as active agents, work to enhance their political rights
and status by strategically exploiting available opportunity structures.

Scholarship on the Muslim world has often portrayed Muslim women as
victims of patriarchal and traditional societies that grant women second-rate
citizen status (Acar 1995; Afshar 1996; Fish 2002; Inglehart and Norris 2003).
Such scholarly emphasis on gender discriminatory laws and practices regarding women's family, citizenship and civil rights, obscures the complex nature
of women's rights and status in many Muslim-majority countries, failing for
example to capture the dynamic that supported the appointment of a Muslim
woman Prime Minister in Turkey, or to account for the fact that women for
the past decades have been comprising the majority of university graduates
in Iran, at times even more than 60 per cent (Rezai-Rashti and Moghadam
2011). Although a growing body of literature emphasises Muslim women's
agency as they protest discriminatory treatments and employ diverse strategies to advance their social and political status (Abu-Lughod 1986; Fernea
1985; Kandiyoti 1989), very little research has analysed women's strategies
to expand their political rights and roles, particularly their access to formal
decision-making positions.

Through an in-depth study of women's organising efforts to reach high-
level political decision-making positions, this book presented both the agency
and the limitations of women to address their political under-representation
in Iran and Turkey. In the preceding chapters, I described a series of socio-
cultural and political/institutional obstacles that hinder the rise of Iranian
and Turkish women to political decision-making. I demonstrated that while
conservative interpretations of Islam, such as practices of gender segrega-

tion, can impede women's access to the male-dominated political sphere, a number of institutional obstacles such as undemocratic candidate selection procedures or institutional candidate vetting processes can also greatly limit women's rise to political decision-making. I highlighted women's agency and the multifaceted strategies they have tactically employed to build coalitions, garner support and amplify their voices. Through this research we have seen women's perseverance and preparedness to take advantage of available opportunity structures to enhance their political representation.

The findings have shown that demands for more female representation in Turkey and Iran have been strategically channelled through formal institutions as well as outside of them, and have been framed to both resonate with powerful elites or to challenge them while resonating with public opinion, whether national or international. Looking for immediate impact as well as deeper cultural change, Iranian and Turkish women's groups engaged directly with the state and its actors to address institutional obstacles, and sought to politicise the public regarding the significance of female representatives in decision-making bodies. I utilised two central elements of social movement theory: political opportunity structures and framing processes, to explain the nature of such interactions. Employing these two elements highlights both structures that impact women's political representation, as well as women's agency as they manipulate such structures to expand their roles in politics. In negotiating for increased access to political office, I also showed that women's groups were prepared to frame their demands in terms of the dominant discourse, even when that discourse ostensibly aims to disempower women; thus, for example, Islamic women's groups in Iran have taken advantage of the religious and revolutionary discursive opportunities offered by the theocratic regime, emphasising the Republic's ideological rhetoric supporting women's qualification for political office.

Imagining Women at the Decision-making Table

Leading up to the 2009 presidential elections in Iran, an episode of the British Broadcasting Corporation (BBC) Persian Television's interactive programme *Nobate Shoma* (Your Turn) asked viewers to share the names of individuals they wished would compete for the presidency.[2] Shirin Ebadi, the first female

---

[2] *Nobate Shoma* was an interactive BBC Persian TV show broadcast five days per week worldwide, during which viewers from around the world contribute via calls, emails and tweets in

Muslim Nobel laureate (2003),[3] was the person named most by both men *and* women. While respondents were exclusively viewers of BBC Persian TV who chose to participate, and thus certainly not representative of the larger Iranian population, it is nonetheless telling that a segment of Iranian society has no trouble imagining a woman in the highest executive position in the country, even though the state has thus far barred women from even being considered for this position.

In this book I showed that women's place at the decision-making table is just as much a demand of women's groups in Muslim-majority countries, such as Iran and Turkey, as it is in other parts of the world. Indeed, imagining women at the decision-making table drives much of women's activism in politics. Most Iranian and Turkish women are not satisfied with political roles limited to voting, voter recruitment and grass-roots organising; as this book demonstrated they are increasingly demanding their share of political power and influence. Regardless of their religious or ideological positioning, many women in Turkey and Iran have mobilised to increase their influence over formal politics. Their high rates of political participation in both countries is evidenced by the mobilisation of a female voting bloc in Iran that has impacted election results, and the significant involvement of Turkish women in grass-roots party organising, particularly in voter recruitment through women's branches since at least the 1990s. Male political leaders in both countries are aware of women's political might, and hence are increasingly taking measures to appeal to this section of the society, while elevating their own image domestically and internationally. Just months before the 2021 Iranian presidential election, outgoing President Hassan Rouhani publicly stated that

---

Persian to a discussion on a particular topic. While it is difficult to determine BBC Persian's reach among Iranians (and across various demographics), as it is accessed through satellite (which is illegal but widely used in Iran, particularly in urban settings) or Virtual-Private Network Internet access (which tech-savvy Iranians can easily acquire), a 2009 Council on Foreign Relations report estimated that in 2009 as many as eight million viewers regularly tuned into BBC Persian programming (Bruno 2009). The regime has attempted to counter this by confiscating satellite dishes and jamming signals, but without huge success as Iranians are determined to access non-state sanctioned media.

[3] Although Ebadi was not even a presidential hopeful, the callers' reasoning mostly ranged from because she is a believing Muslim, she has devoted herself to human rights, and that she would help bridge the current gap between Iran and the West.

women in our society have the main role, meaning that right now, if the women of our country choose to join forces and aim to bring a particular faction, party, or ideology to power, they have that capacity, as we have seen in many other previous elections. (Rouhani 2021)

The 2021 presidential elections also marked the first time in Iranian history that a woman sought to become a presidential candidate with a clear plan and having been endorsed by a number of reformist parties, though mostly women's parties. Zahra Shojaee, who had previously served in reformist President Khatami's cabinet, heading the Center for Women's Participation, distinguished herself from other previous women presidential hopefuls by launching a formal campaign from her party's headquarters, emphasising that Iran is ready to move beyond the debate on whether women can run for the presidency to truly evaluate a woman based on her qualifications and plans of action (Shojaee 2021). Although, as expected, the Council of Guardians did not approve her candidacy, Shojaee's mere attempt did energise a notable section of reformist women as they sought to publicise their presence at a time when large sections of the electorate advocated boycott of the elections, with hardliner Ebrahim Raisi expected to win unchallenged.

Women like Shojaee continue to rely of discursive opportunity structures of the theocratic regime to demand women's expanded access to politics. Islam, 'like all other major worldviews and religious traditions, has a full spectrum of potential symbols and concepts' (Esposito and Voll 1996: 7), which can be harnessed to support differing perspectives, including that of equality. Thus, while many factors, including patriarchal interpretations of Islam, may impact women's political rights and status in Muslim-majority countries, women's rights activists both secular and religious are continuously taking advantage of opportunity structures as they arise, strategically organising to expand their political rights and roles.

Opportunity Structures and Framing Processes

In this research I identified a number of opportunity structures that enable Turkish and Iranian women's groups to use strategic framing processes to challenge their marginalisation from formal political decision-making. One key political opportunity structure is the presence of organised party electoral competition, which enables effective lobbying of party leaders; such formal, multi-party system situations are enhanced when they operate in conjunction with woman-friendly electoral systems. These two factors played an important role for Turkish women when the small, liberal pro-Kurdish rights party BDP (*Baris ve Demokrasi Partisi*/Peace and Democracy Party) successfully implemented gender quotas during the 2007 elections, capturing the attention of the female electorate; key women's groups such as KADER (Association for the Support of Women Candidates) used this as an opportunity to pressure the leaders of the major parties to follow suit, suggesting they otherwise risked losing female supporters. The BDP's gender neutral approach to the framing of its 2007 quota inspired KADER to reframe its own original demand for a 30 per cent 'women's' quota in terms more palatable to patriarchal tastes, lobbying in the 2011 pre-election period for a 50 per cent 'gender' quota to be applied to closed party candidate lists. KADER also worked to focus voter attention on parties' commitments to social justice and gender equality as key criteria for winning votes. Such organising efforts have created mounting public pressure for gender balance in politics, resulting in a steady increase in the rate of female nominations by Turkey's two largest parties, the pro-religious AKP and secular CHP. In 2018, the AKP had a record 21 per cent female candidates (compared with 5 per cent in 2002); the CHP had 22.8 per cent (compared with 7.33 per cent in 2002). After the 2018 election, 18 per cent of AKP MPs were women, as were 12 per cent of CHP MPs. That election resulted in 104 parliamentary seats held by women (17.3 per cent), the highest level of female political representation since the founding of the Turkish republic in 1923 (see Tables 3.2–3.7).

While electoral party competition has provided an important opportunity structure for Turkish women's organising and lobbying, this is not the case for Iran, which lacks structured political parties with specific platforms and established recruitment processes. In Iran, political factions (*firaksiyun*), organised primarily around individual leaders (Amanat 2007; Arjomand 2009; Moslem 2002), masquerade as political parties which coalesce right before elections, putting out candidate lists for the elections. They campaign using the draw of prominent candidates rather than on specific party platforms (Azimi 1997; Moslem 2002). The provisional nature of Iranian political parties does not provide civil society groups, including women's groups, the same opportunity to extensively lobby or sustain pressure on party leaders and politicians that established multi-party political systems do; thus in Iran, advocates for increased female political representation at high levels must seek other opportunity structures. Additional institutional obstacles, including the Council of Guardians' undemocratic candidate vetting process and Iran's majoritarian electoral system in which voters cast ballots for individual candidates rather than party lists, also curtail the development of genuine party competition that might otherwise be used by women's groups to lobby political leaders. Consequently, Iranian women's rights activists often find themselves lobbying individual politicians or religious figures, and access to such individuals is highly dependent on women's own political, ideological and social positioning (personal interview with a prominent Islamic women's rights activist, 11 July 2011).

By looking at framing processes, this book also highlighted women's agency in strategically exploiting the opportunities that arise within the larger cultural and political contexts they inhabit. Using the concept of 'discursive opportunity structures' I showed that framing processes that tap into prevailing discourses to articulate demands are more likely to resonate with ruling political and religious elites and the electorate. I identified two discursive opportunity structures used in campaigns to increase women's political presence in Iran and Turkey; with broader socio-cultural and political currents favouring one or the other at a given moment, women's groups generally framed their demands according to either international human rights discourse or the local regime discourse.

Thus, we have seen how, in the early years of its rise to power, the AKP's pursuit of integration into the EU, coupled with its desire to distinguish itself from its Islamist predecessors, created a major opportunity structure for advocates of increased female representation. The AKP's moderate stance, in conjunction with various human rights-related commitments at the international level (such as Turkey's ratification of CEDAW; Erensü and Alemdaroğlu 2018; Marshall 2009), led to the framing of demands for female political inclusion in terms of international human rights discourse. This discursive opportunity structure was particularly salient for pious activists advocating for headscarved women's access to parliament. By framing this demand in secular terms without reference to religion, pious women's groups were able to demonstrate a commitment to secularism, resulting in a powerful convergence with secular feminist organisations; it also effectively pressured political elites seeking international acceptance. Thus, despite targeting their demands to the pro-religious AKP, pious activist groups strategically used rights-based framing; this drew the support of various international *and* local secular women's organisations, including the CEDAW Committee and KADER, for parliamentary access for headscarved women, further increasing their leverage over AKP party leaders. Although pious women's organising did not result in nomination of headscarved candidates by major parties for the 2011 elections, their efforts did eventually contribute to an official removal of the ban by AKP leaders in 2013. While Iran is one of the few countries (alongside the United States) that has not yet ratified CEDAW, I also showed that large sections of the Iranian women's movement are interested and have tried to get it ratified, highlighting the dynamic relation between political contexts and rights activism around international documents.

In Iran, the theocratic structure of the Republic, a lack of democracy, and marginalisation from the international community engendered a different approach to engaging with elites on the issue of women's political representation. Out of legal and tactical necessity, women's rights groups across the ideological spectrum frame and justify their demands by harnessing local regime discourse. In this regard I have demonstrated how state religion has provided an important discursive opportunity structure for women to frame their demand for political inclusion using religious texts and revolutionary discourse, including the words of the Islamic Republic's founder Ayatollah Khomeini. To resonate with both the wider public and ruling elites, many women's rights groups justify female access to positions of authority through reference to the Quranic story of the Queen of Sheba, as well as to the discourse of female equality used by religious leaders to mobilise the millions of women who were central to toppling the Pahlavi regime during the 1979 revolution. This woman-centred framing enables Iranian women's rights' activists to articulate their demands in terms of social justice and gender equality, as emanating directly from Islam and the Islamic Republic's founding revolutionary principles. By taking account of the broader political and cultural context in this way, this framing has been more effective in advancing Iranian women's rights than have attempts that reference international human rights standards.

Following Ferree and Merrill (2000), I also argued that these framing processes are deliberate and strategic, illustrating significant agency on the part women to further their objectives despite the perceived obstacles of the larger political and cultural contexts in which they operate. Given that cultural and political contexts are always in flux, women's framing processes may also shift over time. For instance, in Iran in the late 1990s, the rise of reformists eager to enhance relations with the international community provided

Iranian women's groups an opportunity to use a universal human rights discourse in their campaigns for women's rights. This approach was fruitful to some extent, but ended abruptly in the mid-2000s with the resurgence of ultra-conservative rule, which demonised all forms of Western influence, including liberal human rights discourse. This drastic shift in Iran's political context led women's rights groups to abandon rights-based framing in their advocacy for gender reform of political practices and to turn to the use of regime discourse to find resonance with conservative elites.

As demonstrated for both Iran and Turkey, women's strategic framing processes have resulted in important developments in both contexts. In Turkey, pious women chose to frame their demands using international human rights discourse, leading to important convergences between pious and secular women's groups that historically have rarely seen eye-to-eye on most issues. This development ahead of the 2011 parliamentary elections strengthened the Turkish women's movement and increased its political lobbying potential. Similarly, Iranian women's strategic framing using religious and revolutionary discourses has achieved significant improvements in Iranian women's rights since the founding of the Islamic Republic, as both secular and pious women's groups recognise religious reinterpretation as the most effective route for addressing gender discriminatory rulings and practices. This realisation led to important convergences among women's groups across the ideological spectrum, which has helped create a strong and unified Iranian women's movement. In both Turkey and Iran, strategic alliances and campaigns among diverse women's groups have helped politicise the female electorate; in Iran this has at times resulted in successful mobilisation of a female voting bloc that cast ballots according to its own collective interests rather than along political lines.[4] Iranian women's political might at the

---

[4] An important instance of this occurred with the landslide victory of reformist President Khatami in 1997, largely due to the women's and youth vote, mobilised by campaigning efforts by activists highlighting his gender inclusive public statements and promises. More recently (presented in Chapter 7), women's grass-roots campaigning during the 2016 parliamentary elections using the slogan 'to change the male-dominated face of parliament' helped ensure that every incumbent conservative woman MP not supportive of women's rights was replaced by female MPs who actively campaigned to enhance women's rights and status. One the other hand, women are key actors in boycotting elections in which women's rights are not emphasised or have marginalised moderate and reformist groups, as occurred during the 2020 parliamentary elections (Tajali 2020).

polls has forced political elites across the political spectrum to take women's demands into account during election periods. In Turkey, however, a female voting bloc has not emerged, largely due to deep-rooted ideological divergences, particularly between secular and pious women's groups, which often fall victim to Turkey's polarising party politics.

Structure and Agency amid Rapid Political and Social Change

What I have presented in the previous chapters has significant implications for our understanding of political and social change and of democratisation in Muslim contexts. Despite important differences between women, as a broad social category they share a common interest in demanding political representation to address their historical exclusion from politics, which in turn helps democratise politics. Literature on democratisation argues that a synthesis of *human agency* and *structure* is required for the successful consolidation of democracy (Mahdavi 2008; Mahoney and Snyder 1999). Because 'structures both enable and limit human agency' (Mahoney and Snyder 1999: 13), a nation's transition to democracy depends not only on civil society actors (instigators of democracy), but also on historical and structural factors that provide a series of opportunities or constraints for social and political actors (Mahdavi 2008; Huntington 1991).

These factors significantly shape not only civil society strategies, but also at times their outcomes and the extent to which their objectives are achieved. The degree to which activism for women's inclusion in the political arena is part of a broader civil society call for democratisation is highly predicated on a nation's political context and institutional structures – including political party hierarchies, constitution, electoral system, the priorities of elites, and state ideology, among others. In many Muslim societies, woman's rights movements have in the past been relegated to the back burner by leftist and liberal democracy movements that argued democratisation was a *prerequisite* to gender equality. Nevertheless, women's rights movements, by definition representing half the population in the fight for representation, often constitute a major force *of* democratisation, a claim that is also made for the cases of Iran and Turkey (Hoodfar and Sadr 2009; Tajali 2011, 2016b).

By placing women's efforts to secure equal representation in politics at its centre of analysis, this book has shown the conditions that enable local women's groups in Iran and Turkey to expand women's political roles, emphasising the dynamic interaction between women as agents on the one hand, and state and institutional structures on the other. This frame of analysis is highly relevant given the continuous political shifts unfolding throughout the Middle East and North Africa (MENA), many of which are opening up avenues for women's activism. Indeed, political uprisings, constitutional redrafting, electoral reform and domestic crises occurring in many MENA countries can provide local women's rights groups with important political and discursive opportunities to demand women's increased presence in political decision-making, as Tripp and others have shown for many post-conflict countries in Africa experiencing civil upheaval (Tripp 2015; Tripp *et al.* 2009). While these authors cite autonomous local women's movements as one of the most important determinants for the expansion of women's rights under these conditions, they also recognise other factors such as the spread of international norms, foreign aid, the influence of global and regional women's movements, and new government resources to implement reforms related to women's rights (Tripp *et al.* 2009). However, to achieve meaningful change, local women's groups have to be prepared to take advantage of the opportunity structures that arise.

Iran and Turkey, two of the most populous countries in the Middle East,[5] have not been immune to large-scale public calls for democracy and rule of law such as have happened in other countries in the region during the 'Arab Spring' protests. These mass demonstrations, in which women have been highly implicated, triggered widespread debate around gender dynamics and women's political roles. For example, in Iran, the prominent role of women's organising in the Green Movement uprisings that protested the contentious 2009 re-election of President Ahmadinejad solidified the unquestionable significance of women as key civil society actors in the Iranian political arena. The Iranian state's crackdown on Green Movement sympathisers included arresting and banning from politics a number of high-ranking reformist women activists and politicians.

Similarly, in Turkey, AKP leaders in recent years have come down hard on civil society groups, including women's organisations and activists peacefully protesting increasingly repressive government policies and measures; notably, harsh measures against protestors followed the 2013 Gezi Park protests. That same year, Reporters Without Borders (RSF) called Turkey 'the

---

[5] After Egypt with roughly 99.5 million population, Iran and Turkey are the two most populous MENA countries with 85 and 81 million population respectively (CIA 2019).

world's biggest prison for journalists',[6] after the state detained scores of media personnel, among them many female journalists and activists; detentions of journalists continue in alarming numbers (Eski 2019; Kestler-D'Amours 2013; McCarthy 2018). However, at the same time that they are cracking down on civil society activism in the wake of mass protests, Iranian and Turkish authorities have taken conciliatory actions that appear designed to appease women's groups. Just months after the 2009 uprisings, Iran's conservatives appointed a female minister in a move to distinguish themselves from more fundamentalist forces. And shortly after the Gezi Park protests in Turkey, Recep Tayyip Erdogan, at the time Turkey's Prime Minister, now President, announced the lifting of the headscarf ban, a key demand of women's campaigning and of the female members of his support base. Even more telling of the government's strategic attempts to placate female AKP supporters was the record number of women nominated and elected by AKP in the 2018 parliamentary elections following the transition to a presidential system that further concentrated the power held by Erdogan since 2002.

The AKP's ideological record has arguably been quite inconsistent throughout its two decades in power, evident by its drastic shifts in most of its initial policy plans in the post-Gezi era. For example, the party fully reversed its stance on Kurdish rights, becoming increasingly nationalistic and hostile to the Kurdish minority. As well, in direct contrast to its earlier efforts to democratise the state by limiting the role of the military and the judiciary, the party currently monopolises power over these institutions, undermining checks and balances. However, the AKP has remained consistent in ensuring a certain level of women's descriptive representation in formal politics, and its recruitment and nomination of women have risen steadily over its years in power, with the single exception of the November 2015 snap elections. Nevertheless, it is important to highlight that despite leaderships' apparent support for women's political presence, and AKP's modest measures to increase nomination of women during parliamentary elections (which is higher than secular CHP though not the pro-minority HDP), the party's gender ideology

---

[6] RSF (*Reporters Sans Frontières*/Reporters Without Borders) is a Paris-based international NGO working to support freedom of information and of the press. It monitors incarceration of journalists worldwide. Its 2013 World Press Freedom Index which ranked Turkey 154th out of 179 countries can be found here: https://rsf.org/en/world-press-freedom-index-2013.

has always remained conservative, with frequent attacks on women's rights and liberties particularly in recent years. Indeed, despite women's extensive protests, including by many pious women, Erdogan's AKP unilaterally withdrew from the Istanbul Convention 2021, an important international tool that aimed to protect women against domestic violence and other violations.

Thus, in my analysis I especially credit party women's own roles in demanding greater access to political leadership, emphasising that they are not passive bystanders despite their allegiance to conservative religious parties, but are rather prepared agents who take advantage of new openings that come with changed parameters to demand their rights. Women's rise *and* fall from political power are complicated phenomena that do not neatly align with the rise and fall of reformist or repressive agendas. States may concurrently enact both repressive and reformist measures in attempts to keep or gain as much popular support as possible, maintaining a delicate balance as they take with one hand and give with the other (Erensü and Alemdaroğlu 2018; Tripp 2019).

The Relationship between Women's Representation and Democracy

A key trend observed in both case studies is that women's descriptive representation did at times grow in times of increased authoritarianism and democratic backsliding. Though seemingly counterintuitive, this trend is not unique to Iran and Turkey; it has been documented in a number of previous studies, including by Aili Mari Tripp (2019) who exposes the conditions under which Arab autocracies adopt women's rights, including expanding their access to political office. Significantly, while Tripp finds that political expediency was a primary motivation for the support of women's rights policies by autocratic leaders in the Maghreb (Algeria, Morocco and Tunisia), these policies have nonetheless had positive impacts on women's rights in various domains, including in family law and political representation, compared with their counterparts in other Middle Eastern countries. While in this book I have focused primarily on women's descriptive representation, and the strategies and efforts that increase women's presence as political office holders for conservative and religious parties, I recognise that women's substantive representation requires its own analysis. This is an important direction for future research, and deserves a momentary digression here.

Regardless of the different political, social and historical contexts in Iran and Turkey, and of the diverse female constituencies within each nation, women in both countries have been demanding greater levels of political representation in order to facilitate better representation of their rights and interests in male-dominated bodies. Despite the absence of a critical mass (i.e. female parliamentary representation that has reached the recommended 20–30 per cent) of women in politics, we have nonetheless witnessed the passage of some women-friendly laws. In Iran, despite women's extensive marginalisation from politics, a number of outspoken female 'critical actors' opposed to the regime's gender discriminatory policies have won political seats and have been lauded by feminists for their roles in the passage of several legislation supportive of women's rights (Tajali 2022). For example Shahindokht Molaverdi, former Vice President for Women and Family Affairs, has actively pushed for women's greater access to the public sphere, while Faezeh Hashemi Rafsanjani, both as an elected MP and a key member of the women's movement, has been increasingly critical of discrimination against women in the Islamic Republic, including of their limited access to sports or physical activity that she argues jeopardises women's health, an approach that can more easily find resonance in Islamic circles. However, Iran's theocratic regime has demonstrated little tolerance for outspoken women, silencing and removing them from office, and sometimes even succeeding in reversing policy and legislative gains they have won for women (Tajali 2020).

In Turkey, much of the progress on women's rights has been championed by female activists and politicians, some of whom worked on gender policy reforms for decades before they materialised. Despite their low numbers, women critical actors pose a threat to patriarchal attitudes and practices, resulting in their harassment and occasionally their removal at the hands of male elites. Given that no ideological group is homogenous, such critical actors also emerge from among conservative party women, as I have demonstrated in the previous chapters. What seems to matter more for women's substantive representation is the election or appointment of outspoken women, as opposed to a large number of women, thus challenging the conventional understanding of the link between women's descriptive and substantive representation (Childs and Krook 2008, 2009). The expansion of women's political representation in undemocratic and closed contexts is thus complex and driven by multiple factors, resulting in varying degrees of women's descriptive, substantive and symbolic representation (Pitkin 1972), and by extension the quality of democracy in those contexts.

As noted in the first chapter, I problematise the assumption that the mere presence of women in political decision-making bodies equates a democratic turn. Indeed, women's access to politics when facilitated by autocratic leaders can at times lead to the selection of women who help maintain the patriarchal status quo and continue to limit rights for marginalised social groups (e.g. LGBT communities). However, I have also demonstrated the need for a more nuanced analysis of religious political groups and the potential some of their discourses hold for women's political empowerment. Although most patriarchal party elites aim to increase women's political representation in token numbers, sustained grass-roots pressure and the need to remain competitive has led these same party leaders to be more responsive to public and female constituency demands, thus increasing the odds that outspoken women will gain seats and render parliamentary bodies more representative. Although in undemocratic contexts, such gains can be reversed as leaders further concentrate their own powers or manipulate procedures and structures in order to ban parties and activists from participating in politics, such reversals are not without cost to their reputation and legitimacy, since the expansion of women's political rights for a given period has normative implications for a public that demands democracy, human rights and rule of law. In this sense, as long as regular elections are held – even when they are not free or fair – discourses and dialogue around such concerns will continue to have momentum.

Future research would do well to explore the complex relation between women's political roles and democracy, with attention to the multiple and ever shifting factors that impact both. In this book, I highlighted the opportunities that can arise out of religious discourses, which previous scholarship has often overlooked as a source for women's empowerment. Thus, in examining the agency of pious women in Iran and Turkey I looked to the possible role of religious discourses in expanding women's access to positions of authority. This contrasts with previous work suggesting the agency of pious women stems *from* their adherence to subjugation as interpreted by male leaders, for example as described for Egyptian women actors in that county's religious political movement by Saba Mahmood (2005). My analysis of women's organising in Iran and Turkey shows that many pious Muslim women, while deriving their subjectivity from religion, in their specific cultural and political contexts view Islam and religious teachings as more effective and important tools for contesting patriarchy and gender discrimination than, for example, international human rights discourses. Expectedly, many other factors deserve close analysis, including the extent and conditions under which pious women politicians aim to represent women and address their rights despite their party or ideological affiliation.

Future research might also expand investigation on the nature of strategic interactions between women's groups and state authorities as political and social changes continue to unfold across the MENA region. Keeping in mind that feminist scholarship is continuously re-conceptualising women's political activism and influence, further research can identify other factors shaping activism for the expansion of women's political roles. Understanding the roles and positions of local women's movements and feminist forces in fostering female access to positions of authority in these contexts, and deconstructing the significance of women's activism in democratisation processes, will also help answer questions regarding the direction women might look towards to increase their role and influence in policy making. Lastly, given the transnational spread of norms and ideals across borders, particularly on gender roles across the MENA region, scholars should analyse the impact and potential of such connections to deliver meaningful change for women, especially for contexts in which support from international bodies is limited.

APPENDIX

List of Iranian and Turkish Women's Groups Interviewed for this Research

Political Parties and Coalitions in Iran

Party or coalition	Ideological tendency	Years active	Founder/key figure(s)
WOMEN'S PARTIES OR GROUPS			
Zeinab Society (*Jameh Zeinab*)	Conservative	1986–present	Maryam Behrouzi
Fatemiyoun Society (*Jami'yat-e Fatemiyoun*)	Conservative	2006–present	Tahereh Rahimi
Islamic Women's Coalition (*E'telaf Islami-e Zanan*)	Coalition of elite conservative & reformist women	2009–present	Masoumeh Ebtekar, Maryam Behrouzi & Touran Valimorad
Society of Women of the Islamic Revolution (*Jame'eh-ye Zanan-e Enqelab-e Islami*)	Reformist	1987–present	Azam Taleghani
Iranian Women Journalists Association (*Anjoman-e Ruznamehnegaran-e Zan-e Iran*)	Reformist	1999–present	Zhaleh Faramarzian, Shahindokht Molaverdi & Ashraf Geramizadegan

Political Parties and Coalitions in Iran (*cont.*)

Party or coalition	Ideological tendency	Years active	Founder/key figure(s)
Society of Muslim Women's New Religious Thinking (*Jami'yyat-e Zanan-e Mosalman-e Nu Andish*)	Reformist	2007–present	Fatemeh Rake'i
Convergence of Women (*Hamgarayee Zanan*)	Coalition of key secular & reformist women	2009	Noushin Ahmadi-Khorasani, Shahla Lahiji & Elaheh Koolaee
GENERAL PARTIES IN WHICH WOMEN HELD/HOLD LEADERSHIP ROLES OR THAT HAD/HAVE GENDER QUOTAS			
Islamic Iran Participation Front (*Jebheye Mosharekate Iran-e Islami* or *Mosharekat*)	Reformist	1998–2010	Ali Shakurirad
Union of Islamic Iran People Party (*Hezbe Etehad Mellat Iran Islami*)	Reformist	2015–present	Ali Shakurirad & Azar Mansouri

Notes: Above are instances of registered Iranian political parties and groups that have been key actors on women's political participation and representation. Membership of these parties and groups are often fluid, with some individuals joining and founding a few simultaneously. As many of these parties are formed by and around influential political figures, their popularity and clout can decline with the passing of that figure, as has occurred with the Zeinab Society since Maryam Behrouzi's passing in 2012.

Women's Organisations and Political Parties in Turkey

Party or organisation	Tendency	Years active	Founder/(some) key figures
WOMEN'S ORGANISATIONS			
Association for the Support of Women Candidates (KADER)	Secular feminist	1997–present	Şirin Tekeli Current chairwoman since 2017: Nuray Karaoglu
Women and Democracy Association (KADEM)	Pious (pro-AKP government)	2013–present	Sezen Gongur Current chairwoman: Saliha Okur Gumrukcuoglu
Women's Rights Organization against Discrimination (AKDER)	Pious	1999–present	Fatma Benli, Neslihan Akbulut
Capital City Women's Platform (CCWP)	Pious	1995–2019	Fatma Benli, Hidayat Tuksal
Women Entrepreneurs Association of Turkey (KAGIDER)	Largely non-ideological but with secular leanings	2002–present	Meltem Kurtsan, Gulseren Onanc
POLITICAL PARTIES (WHOSE ACTIVISTS AND MEMBERS WERE INCLUDED IN THIS RESEARCH)			
Justice & Development Party (*Adalet ve Kalkinma Partisi* – AKP)	Conservative (centre right)	2001–present	Recep Tayyip Erdogan & other former Welfare (*Refah*) and Virtue (*Fazilet*) party members
Republican People's Party (*Cumhuriyet Halk Partisi* – CHP)	Social Democratic (centre left)	1919–present	Mustafa Kemal Ataturk Current leader since 2010: Kemal Kilicdaroglu
People's Democratic Party (*Halkların Demokratik Partisi* – HDP)	Liberal and pro-minority (leftist)	2012–present	Fatma Gök, Selahattin Demirtas, Figen Yuksedag
Nationalist Movement Party (*Milliyetçi Hareket Partisi* – MHP)	Ultraconservative nationalist (Far right)	1969–present	Alparslan Türkeş Current leader since 1997: Devlet Bahceli
Felicity Party (*Saadet*)	Conservative Islamist (Far right)	2001–present	Necmettin Erbakan, Recai Kutan
Peace and Democracy Party (*Baris ve Demokrasi Partisi* — BDP)	Social Democratic and pro-Kurdish (leftist)	2008–14	Selahattin Demirtaş, Gültan Kışanak

Notes: Above are instances of registered Turkish women's organisations and general political parties whose leaders and members were included in this research on the topic of women's political participation and representation. Membership of these parties and groups are often fluid, with some individuals active on behalf of a few simultaneously. Organisations and parties dissolve as they either fold into new organisations and groups, or as a result of disagreements among the leadership.

REFERENCES

Abou-Zeid, Gihan (2006), 'The Arab Region: Women's Access to the Decision-Making Process across the Arab Nations', in Drude Dahlerup (ed.), *Women, Quotas and Politics*, New York, NY: Routledge, pp. 168–93.

Abrutyn, Seth (2013), 'Reconceptualizing the Dynamics of Religion as a Macro-Institutional Domain', *Structure and Dynamics* 6 (3): 1–21.

Abu-Lughod, Lila (1986), *Veiled Sentiments: Honor and Poetry in a Bedouin Society*, Berkeley, CA: University of California Press.

Acar, Feride (1995), 'Women and Islam in Turkey', in Sirin Tekeli (ed.), *Women in Modern Turkish Society: A Reader*, London: Zed Books, pp. 46–65.

Adams, James (2012), 'Causes and Electoral Consequences of Party Policy Shifts in Multiparty Elections: Theoretical Results and Empirical Evidence', *Annual Review of Political Science* 15 (1): 401–19.

Afary, Janet (1996), *The Iranian Constitutional Revolution, 1906–1911: Grassroots Democracy, Social Democracy, and the Origins of Feminism*, New York, NY: Columbia University Press.

—— (2005), 'Civil Liberties and the Making of Iran's First Constitution', *Comparative Studies of South Asia, Africa and the Middle East* 25 (2): 341–59.

Afshar, Haleh (1982), 'Khomeini's Teachings and Their Implications for Women', *Feminist Review* 12: 59–72.

—— (1996), 'Women and the Politics of Fundamentalism in Iran', in Haleh Afshar (ed.), *Women and Politics in the Third World*, London: Routledge, pp. 121–41.

—— (2002), 'Competing Interests: Democracy, Islamification and Women Politicians in Iran', *Parliamentary Affairs* 55 (1): 109–18.

Ahmadi-Khorasani, Noushin (2013), 'Video and Image Report of the Women's Collaborative Meeting on Women's Demands (In Persian)', *Feminist School*, http://feministschool.com/spip.php?article7316.

Ajiri, Denise Hassanzade (2016), '"Reality is Even Worse": Reformist Hopefuls Banned from Iran's Parliamentary Poll', *The Guardian*, 19 January 2016, https://www.theguardian.com/world/iran-blog/2016/jan/19/iran-guardian-council-blocks-reformists-february-parliamentary-poll.

AK-DER (2019), 'Women's Rights Organization against Discrimination: About Us', *AK-DER,* http://ak-der.org/en/who-we-are.

AK Parti (2011), *Ak Party Women's Branch Headquarters*, Ankara: Ak Parti, http://www.akparti.org.tr/media/275538/ak-party-womens-branch-headquarters.pdf.

—— (2018), *Constitutional Reform: What is Changing?*, Ankara: Ak Parti, https://www.akparti.org.tr/media/277012/constitutional-reform-what-is-changing.pdf.

Aksoy, Hürcan Aslı (2015), 'Invigorating Democracy in Turkey: The Agency of Organized Islamist Women', *Politics & Gender* 11 (1): 146–70, https://doi.org/10.1017/S1743923X1500001X.

Al Jazeera (2013), 'Iran Rejects Women Presidential Hopefuls', *Aljazeera (English)*, 17 May 2013, http://www.aljazeera.com/news/middleeast/2013/05/201351754634102939.html.

Alamdari, Kazem (2005), 'The Power Structure of the Islamic Republic of Iran: Transition from Populism to Clientelism, and Militarization of the Government', *Third World Quarterly* 26 (8): 1285–301, https://doi.org/10.2307/4017715.

Alef (2009), 'Council of Guardians: Woman can Become Candidates for the Presidency (In Persian)', *Alef News*, 11 April 2009, http://old.alef.ir/vdcir5a5.t1apq2bcct.html?43462.

—— (2015), 'Women's Quota in Election Lists: A Feminist or Reformist Mindset? (In Persian)', *Alef News*, 3 December 2015, http://akharinkhabar.ir/analysis/2308319.Alef.

Alikarami, Leila (2014), 'CEDAW and the Quest of Iranian Women for Gender Equality', *OpenDemocracy*, 18 December 2014, https://www.opendemocracy.net/en/5050/cedaw-and-quest-of-iranian-women-for-gender-equality/.

Alvarez, Sonia E. (1990), *Engendering Democracy in Brazil: Women's Movements in Transition Politics*, Princeton, NJ: Princeton University Press.

Amanat, Abbas (2007), 'From Ijtihad to Wilayat-I Faqih: The Evolution of the Shiite Legal Authority to Political Power', in Abbas Amanat and Frank Griffel (eds), *Shari'a: Islamic Law in the Contemporary Context*, Stanford, CA: Stanford University Press, pp. 120–36.

Amenta, Edwin, and Neal Caren (2004), 'The Legislative, Organizational, and Beneficiary Consequences of State-oriented Challengers', in David Snow, Sarah Soule and Hanspeter Kriesi (eds), *The Blackwell Companion to Social Movements*, Oxford: Blackwell, pp. 461–88.

Amenta, Edwin, and Drew Halfmann (2012), 'Opportunity Knocks: The Trouble with Political Opportunity and what you can do about it', in Jeff Goodwin and James M. Jasper (eds), *Contention in Context: Political Opportunities and the Emergence of Protest*, Stanford, CA: Stanford University Press, pp. 227–39.

Amin, Camron Michael (2002), *The Making of Modern Iranian Woman: Gender, State Policy, and Popular Culture, 1865–1946*, Gainesville, FL: University Press of Florida.

—— (2008), 'Globalizing Iranian Feminism, 1910–1950', *Journal of Middle East Women's Studies* 4 (1): 6–30.

Amirshahi, Farnoosh (2016), 'More than an Ornament: Iran's "Female Statesmen" and Elections', *The Guardian*, 19 February 2016, https://www.theguardian.com /world/iran-blog/2016/feb/19/iran-women-candidates-rights-elections.

Amnesty International (2011), 'Iranian Women Fight Controversial "Polygamy" Bill', *Amnesty International*, 30 November 2011, https://www.amnesty.org/en /latest/news/2011/11/iranian-women-fight-controversial-polygamy-bill/.

Anderlini, S. B., Hadi Ghaemi and Dokhi Fassihian (2010), 'Iran, Gender Discrimination, and the UN Women's Commission', *Foreign Policy*, 27 April 2010, http://mideast.foreignpolicy.com/posts/2010/04/27/iran_gender_discri mination_and_the_uns_womens_commission.

Anil, Ela, Canan Arin, Ayse Berktay Hacimirzaoglu, Mehves Bingollu and Pinar Ilkkaracan (2002), *The New Legal Status of Women in Turkey*, Istanbul: Women for Women's Human Rights (WWHR)–New Ways.

Annesley, Claire, Karen Beckwith and Susan Franceschet (2015), 'What is 'Merit' Anyway? On Using Gender Quotas in Cabinet Appointments', *UK PSA Women & Politics Specialist Group*, 5 November 2015, https://psawomenpolitics.com /2015/11/05/what-is-merit-anyway-on-using-gender-quotas-in-cabinet-appoin tments/.

Arat, Yeşim (1989), *The Patriarchal Paradox: Women Politicians in Turkey*, Cranbury, NJ: Fairleigh Dickinson University Press.

—— (1998), 'A Woman Prime Minister in Turkey', *Women & Politics* 19 (4): 1–22, https://doi.org/10.1300/J014v19n04_01.

—— (1999), 'Democracy and Women in Turkey: In Defense of Liberalism', *Social Politics: International Studies in Gender, State & Society* 6 (3): 370–87.

—— (2000), 'From Emancipation to Liberation', *Journal of International Affairs* 54 (1): 107.

—— (2004), 'Rethinking the Political: A Feminist Journal in Turkey, *Pazartesi*, *Women's Studies International Forum* 27 (3): 281–92, https://doi.org/10.1016 /j.wsif.2004.06.007.

—— (2005), *Rethinking Islam and Liberal Democracy: Islamist Women in Turkish Politics*, Albany, NY: State University of New York Press.

Araujo, Clara, and Ana Isabel Garcia (2006), 'Latin America: The Experience and the Impact of Quotas in Latin America', in Drude Dahlerup (ed.), *Women, Quotas and Politics*, New York, NY: Routledge, pp. 83–111.

Arjomand, Said Amir (2009), *After Khomeini: Iran under his Successors*, New York, NY: Oxford University Press.

Asr Iran (2007), 'Rake'i Proposed the Formation of a Large Coalition among Women (In Persian)', *Asr Iran News*, 26 September 2007, http://www.asriran.com/fa /news/26051/%D8%B1%D8%A7%DA%A9%D8%B9%DB%8C-%D8%AE %D9%88%D8%A7%D8%B3%D8%AA%D8%A7%D8%B1-%D8%AA %D8%B4%DA%A9%DB%8C%D9%84-%D8%A7%D8%A6%D8%AA %D9%84%D8%A7%D9%81-%D8%A8%D8%B2%D8%B1%DA%AF -%D8%B2%D9%86%D8%A7%D9%86-%D8%B4%D8%AF.

—— (2016), 'Complete List of Reformist Candidates across the Country', *Asr Iran News*, 24 February 2016, http://www.asriran.com/fa/news/453349/%D8 %A7%D8%B3%D8%A7%D9%85%DB%8C-%D9%86%D9%87%D8 %A7%D9%8A%D9%8A-%DA%A9%D8%A7%D9%86%D8%AF%DB %8C%D8%AF%D8%A7%D9%87%D8%A7%DB%8C-%D8%A7%D8 %B5%D9%84%D8%A7%D8%AD-%D8%B7%D9%84%D8%A8%D8 %A7%D9%86-%D8%AF%D8%B1-%D8%B3%D8%B1%D8%A7%D8 %B3%D8%B1-%D8%A7%DB%8C%D8%B1%D8%A7%D9%86-%D8 %A8%D8%B1%D8%A7%DB%8C-%D8%A7%D9%86%D8%AA%D8 %AE%D8%A7%D8%A8%D8%A7%D8%AA-%D9%85%D8%AC%D9 %84%D8%B3-%D8%AF%D9%87%D9%85.

Atasoy, Yildiz (2005), *Turkey, Islamists and Democracy: Transition and Globalization in a Muslim State*, Library of Modern Middle East Studies, New York, NY: I. B. Tauris.

Avramopoulou, Eirini (2013), 'Signing Dissent in the Name of "Woman": Reflections on Female Activist Coalitions in Istanbul, Turkey', *The Greek Review of Social Research (Επιθεώρηση Κοινωνικών Ερευνών)* 140 (December), https://doi.org /10.12681/grsr.67.

Azimi, Fakhreddin (1997), 'On Shaky Ground: Concerning the Absence or Weakness of Political Parties in Iran', *Iranian Studies* 30 (1/2): 53–75.

—— (2008), *The Quest for Democracy in Iran: A Century of Struggle against Authoritarian Rule*, Cambridge, MA: Harvard University Press.

Badran, Margot (1995), *Feminists, Islam, and Nation: Gender and the Making of Modern Egypt*, Princeton, NJ: Princeton University Press.

—— (2002), 'Islamic Feminism: What's in a Name?', *The Feminist eZine*, http://www.feministezine.com/feminist/international/Islamic-Feminism-01.html.

Baktiari, Bahman (1996), *Parliamentary Politics in Revolutionary Iran: The Institutionalization of Factional Politics*, Gainesville, FL: University Press of Florida.

Baldez, Lisa (2002), *Why Women Protest: Women's Movements in Chile*, Cambridge: Cambridge University Press.

—— (2004), 'Elected Bodies: The Gender Quota Law for Legislative Candidates in Mexico', *Legislative Studies Quarterly* 29 (2): 231–58.

—— (2014), *Defying Convention: U.S. Resistance to the UN Treaty on Women's Rights*, New York, NY: Cambridge University Press.

Baldez, Lisa, and Celeste Montoya Kirk (2005), 'Gendered Opportunities: The Formation of Women's Movements in the United States and Chile', in Lee Ann Banaszak (ed.), *The U.S. Women's Movement in Global Perspective*, Lanham, MD: Rowman & Littlefield Publishers, pp. 170–93.

Banaszak, Lee Ann, Karen Beckwith and Dieter Rucht (2003). 'When Power Relocates: Interactive Changes in Women's Movements and States', in Lee Ann Banaszak, Karen Beckwith and Dieter Rucht (eds), *Women's Movements Facing the Reconfigured State*, New York, NY: Cambridge University Press, pp. 1–29.

Bani-Etemad, Rakhshan (2009), *We are Half of Iran's Population* [film], http://www.youtube.com/playlist?list=PL324C7549DCFD1551.

Barlow, Rebecca, and Fatemeh Nejati (2017), 'Impact and Significance of the 2016 "Campaign to Change the Male Face of Parliament" in Iran', *Social Movement Studies* 16 (3): 361–8, https://doi.org/10.1080/14742837.2016.1271741.

Baron, Beth (2005), *Egypt as a Woman: Nationalism, Gender, and Politics*, Berkeley, CA: University of California Press.

Batchelor, Tom (2018), 'Turkey Still Wants "Full Membership" of EU, Erdogan Says', *The Independent*, 26 March 2018, https://www.independent.co.uk/news/world/europe/erdogan-turkey-eu-full-membership-european-union-commitment-president-a8274166.html.

Bayat, Asef (2007), *Making Islam Democratic: Social Movements and the Post-Islamist Turn*, Stanford, CA: Stanford University Press.

BBC News (2010), 'Iranian Court Bans Two Leading Opposition Parties', *BBC News*, 27 September 2010, http://www.bbc.com/news/world-middle-east-11421538.

—— (2017), 'Turkey Reverses Female Army Officers' Headscarf Ban', *BBC News*, 22 February 2017, https://www.bbc.com/news/world-europe-39053064.

BBC Persian (2010), 'Azar Mansoury is Sentenced to Three Years in Prison (In Persian)', *BBC Persian*, 14 March 2010, http://www.bbc.com/persian/iran/20 10/03/100313_u03-mansouri-mosharekat-sentenced.

—— (2015), 'Rouhani's Vice President for Women: We Seek Gender Justice instead of (Gender) Equality (In Persian)', *BBC Persian*, 21 May 2015, http://www.bbc.com/persian/iran/2015/05/150521_l45_molaverdi_gender_justice _women.

—— (2016), 'Rouhani Government Supporters' Victory in the Second Round of Elections Secure them with Relative Majority of the Parliament (In Persian)', *BBC Persian*, 30 April 2016, http://www.bbc.com/persian/iran/2016/04/1604 28_l45_ir94_election_runoff_results.

Beck, Linda J. (2003), 'Democratization and the Hidden Public: The Impact of Patronage Networks on Senegalese Women', *Comparative Politics* 35 (2): 147–69, https://doi.org/10.2307/4150149.

Beckwith, Karen (2000), 'Beyond Compare? Women's Movements in Comparative Perspective', *European Journal of Political Research* 37 (4): 431–68.

Ben Shitrit, Lihi (2013), 'Women, Freedom, and Agency in Religious Political Movements: Reflections from Women Activists in Shas and the Islamic Movement in Israel', *Journal of Middle East Women's Studies* 9 (3): 81–107.

—— (2016a), *Righteous Transgressions: Women's Activism on the Israeli and Palestinian Religious Right*, Princeton, NJ: Princeton University Press.

—— (2016b), 'Authenticating Representation: Women's Quotas and Islamist Parties', *Politics & Gender* 12 (4): 781–806, https://doi.org/10.1017/S174392 3X16000027.

Bend, Jill (1988), 'Turkey "the Fight Is against Power"', *Women Living Under Muslim Laws – Dossier 4*: 30–2.

Benford, Robert, and Scott Hunt (2003), 'Interactional Dynamics in Public Problems Marketplaces: Movements and the Counterframing and Reframing of Public Problems', in James Holstein and Gale Miller (eds), *Challenges and Choices: Constructionist Perspectives on Social Problems*, New York, NY: Aldine de Gruyter, pp. 153–86.

Benford, Robert, and David Snow (2000), 'Framing Processes and Social Movements: An Overview and Assessment', *Annual Review of Sociology* 26: 611–39.

Benli, Fatma (2010a), *European Court of Human Rights: Under the Light of Leyla Sahin Decision*, Istanbul: AKDER Publications.

—— (2010b), 'Turkey's Sixth Report on its Compliance with the Convention on the Elimination of All Forms of Discrimination against Women', Istanbul: The Coalition for the Partial Preliminary Evaluation Report by 71 NGOs,

http://www2.ohchr.org/english/bodies/cedaw/docs/ngos/CPRER_Tur
key46.pdf.

Benstead, Lindsay J. (2016), 'Why Quotas are Needed to Improve Women's Access
to Services in Clientelistic Regimes', *Governance* 29 (2): 185–205, https://doi
.org/10.1111/gove.12162.

Berktay, Fatmagul (2004), *The Position of Women in Turkey and in the European
Union: Achievements, Problems, Prospects*, Istanbul: Ka-der Press.

Biagini, Erika (2016), 'The Egyptian Muslim Sisterhood between Violence, Activism
and Leadership', *Mediterranean Politics* 22 (1): 35–53, https://doi.org/10.1080
/13629395.2016.1230943.

—— (2020a), 'Islamist Women's Feminist Subjectivities in (R)evolution:
The Egyptian Muslim Sisterhood in the Aftermath of the Arab Uprisings',
International Feminist Journal of Politics 22 (3): 382–402, http://doi.org/10.10
80/14616742.2019.1680304.

—— (2020b), 'Islamist Women's Activism under Morsi's Government (2011–
2013): Political Inclusion, Gender and Discourse', *Egypte/Monde Arabe* 21:
37–55, https://doi.org/10.4000/ema.11592.

Bilgili, Nazli Cagin (2011), 'Bridging the Gender Gap in Turkish Politics: The
Actors Promoting Female Representation', *European Perspectives* 3 (2): 105–29.

Birch, Nicholas (2011), 'Turkey: Religious Conservatives Confront Headscarf
Dilemma as Election Looms', *Eurasianet*, 11 April 2011, https://eurasianet.org
/turkey-religious-conservatives-confront-headscarf-dilemma-as-election-looms.

Bjarnegård, Elin (2015), *Gender, Informal Institutions and Political Recruitment:
Explaining Male Dominance in Parliamentary Representation*, London: Palgrave
Macmillan.

—— (2017), 'Gender and Election Violence: Advancing the Comparative Agenda',
Comparative Politics Newsletter 27 (1): 11–15.

Borden, Emma (2016), 'Demystifying Iran's Parliamentary Election Process',
Brookings, 9 February 2016, https://www.brookings.edu/blog/markaz/2016/02
/09/demystifying-irans-parliamentary-election-process/.

Bruno, Greg (2009), 'The Media Landscape in Iran', *Council on Foreign Relations*,
22 July 2009, https://www.cfr.org/backgrounder/media-landscape-iran.

Buyuk, Hamdi Firat (2020), 'Istanbul Convention's Fate Splits Turkish President's
Supporters', *Reporting Democracy*, 10 August 2020, https://balkaninsight.com
/2020/08/10/istanbul-conventions-fate-splits-turkish-presidents-supporters/.

Cavdar, Gamze (2006), 'To Branch or Not to Branch? Women and Political Parties
in Turkey', *Kadin/Woman 2000* 7 (1): 91–126.

CEDAW Committee (2010), 'Concluding Observations of the Committee on the
Elimination of Discrimination against Women', *Convention on the Elimination*

of all Forms of Discrimination against Women, CEDAW/C/TUR/6/United Nations, https://www2.ohchr.org/english/bodies/cedaw/docs/co/CEDAW-C-TUR-CO-6.pdf.

Chappell, Louise A. (2002), *Gendering Government: Feminist Engagement with the State in Australia and Canada*, Vancouver, BC: UBC Press.

Charrad, Mounira (2001), *States and Women's Rights: The Making of Postcolonial Tunisia, Algeria, and Morocco*, Berkeley, CA: University of California Press.

Childs, Sarah, and Mona Lena Krook (2006), 'Gender and Politics: The State of the Art', *Politics* 26 (1): 18–28, https://doi.org/10.1111/j.1467-9256.2006.00247.x.

—— (2008), 'Critical Mass Theory and Women's Political Representation', *Political Studies* 56 (3): 725–36, https://doi.org/10.1111/j.1467-9248.2007.00712.x.

—— (2009), 'Analyzing Women's Substantive Representation: From Critical Mass to Critical Actors', *Government and Opposition* 44 (2): 125–45, https://doi:10.1111/j.1477-7053.2009.01279.x.

CIA (2019), 'The World Factbook', *CIA*, https://www.cia.gov/library/publications/the-world-factbook/.

Ciftci, Sabri, F. Michael Wuthrich and Ammar Shamaileh (2019), 'Islam, Religious Outlooks, and Support for Democracy', *Political Research Quarterly* 72 (2): 435–49, https://doi.org/10.1177/1065912918793233.

Cinar, Alev (2008), 'Subversion and Subjugation in the Public Sphere: Secularism and the Islamic Headscarf', *Signs: Journal of Women in Culture and Society* 33 (4): 891–913.

Cindoglu, Dilek (2011), *Headscarf Ban and Discrimination: Professional Headscarved Women in the Labor Market*, Istanbul: TESEV Publications, http://www.tesev.org.tr/Upload/Publication/2011b868-60a8-492a-a170-0e2dca71b84b/headscarf-book.pdf.

Cindoglu, Dilek, and Gizem Zencirci (2008), 'The Headscarf in Turkey in the Public and State Spheres', *Middle Eastern Studies* 44 (5): 791–806, https://doi.org/10.1080/00263200802285187.

Çitak, Zana, and Özlem Tür (2008), 'Women between Tradition and Change: The Justice and Development Party Experience in Turkey', *Middle Eastern Studies* 44 (3): 455–69, https://doi.org/10.1080/00263200802021616.

Clark, Janine Astrid, and Jillian Schwedler (2003), 'Who Opened the Window? Women's Activism in Islamist Parties', *Comparative Politics* 35 (3): 293–312.

Cleveland, William L. (2004), *A History of the Modern Middle East*, 3rd edn, Cambridge, MA: Westview Press.

Collins, Aengus (2010), 'The Trouble with Turkey's Closed-List Elections', *Istanbul*

Notes, 17 October 2010, https://istanbulnotes.wordpress.com/2010/10/17/the
-trouble-with-turkeys-closed-list-elections/.

Commission on the Status of Women (1995), *Monitoring the Implementation of the
Nairobi Forward-Looking Strategies for the Advancement of Women*, New York,
NY: United Nations, https://digitallibrary.un.org/record/208684.

Connell, R. W. (1990), 'The State, Gender, and Sexual Politics: Theory and
Appraisal', *Theory and Society* 19 (5): 507–44.

Cook, Steven A. (2016), 'How Erdogan Made Turkey Authoritarian Again', *The
Atlantic*, 21 July 2016, https://www.theatlantic.com/international/archive/2016
/07/how-erdogan-made-turkey-authoritarian-again/492374/.

Dahlerup, Drude (1988), 'From a Small to a Large Minority: Women in Scandinavian
Politics', *Scandinavian Political Studies* 11 (4): 275–98, https://doi.org/10.1111
/j.1467-9477.1988.tb00372.x.

—— (2006), 'Introduction', in Drude Dahlerup (ed.), *Women, Quotas and Politics*,
New York, NY: Routledge, pp. 3–31.

—— (2008), 'Gender Quotas: Controversial but Trendy', *International Feminist
Journal of Politics* 10 (3): 322–8.

Dahlerup, Drude, and Lenita Freidenvall (2005), 'Quotas as a "Fast Track" to Equal
Representation for Women', *International Feminist Journal of Politics* 7 (1):
26–48, https://doi.org/10.1080/1461674042000324673.

Daragahi, Borzou (2017), 'Iranian Women and Young Give Moderate President a
Second Term', *BuzzFeed*, 20 May 2017, https://www.buzzfeed.com/borzoudar
agahi/iran-election.

Davachi, Azadeh (2016), 'Disqualifying Women: Strategic Omission or Resistance
to Change (In Persian)', *The Feminist School*, https://www.tribunezamaneh.com
/archives/90553.

De Groot, Joanna (2010), 'Feminism in Another Language: Learning from
"Feminist" Histories of Iran and/or from Histories of Iranian "Feminism" since
1830', *Women: A Cultural Review* 21 (3): 251–65, https://doi.org/10.1080/09
574042.2010.513489.

Deeb, Lara (2006), *An Enchanted Modern: Gender and Public Piety in Shi'i Lebanon*,
Princeton, NJ: Princeton University Press.

Dehghan, Saeed Kamali (2012), 'Cutting Ties: Iran Moves to Enforce Ban on
Symbol of Western Decadence', *The Guardian*, 31 May 2012, https://www.the
guardian.com/world/2012/may/31/ties-iran-ban.

Dehghanpisheh, Babak (2017), 'Iranian President Names Three Women to
Government Posts after Criticism', *Reuters*, 9 August 2017, https://www.reut
ers.com/article/us-iran-politics/iranian-president-names-three-women-to-gover
nment-posts-after-criticism-idUSKBN1AP1PB.

Deutsche Welle Persian (2015), 'New Support for 30% Quotas for Women in the Parliament (In Persian)', *Deutsche Welle Persian*, 14 December 2015, http://www.dw.com/fa-ir/%D8%AD%D9%85%D8%A7%DB%8C%D8%AA%D9%87%D8%A7%DB%8C-%D8%AA%D8%A7%D8%B2%D9%87-%D8%A7%D8%B2-%D8%B7%D8%B1%D8%AD-%D8%B3%D9%87%D9%85%DB%8C%D9%87-%DB%B3%DB%B0-%D8%AF%D8%B1%D8%B5%D8%AF%DB%8C-%D8%B2%D9%86%D8%A7%D9%86-%D8%AF%D8%B1-%D9%85%D8%AC%D9%84%D8%B3/a-18916732.

Diamond, Larry Jay (2002), 'Thinking About Hybrid Regimes', *Journal of Democracy* 13 (2): 21–35, https://doi.org/10.1353/jod.2002.0025.

Didban (2013), 'Women in the Eleventh Cabinet: Presidential Candidates' Thoughts on Women's Presence in the Cabinet (In Persian)', *Didban News*, http://didban.ir/fa/news/4403/%D8%B2%D9%86%D8%A7%D9%86-%D8%AF%D8%B1-%DA%A9%D8%A7%D8%A8%DB%8C%D9%86%D9%87-%DB%8C%D8%A7%D8%B2%D8%AF%D9%87%D9%85.

Dogan, Yonca Poyraz, Pinar Ilkkaracan and Hidayat Tuksal (2013), 'Two Views: Pinar Ilkkaracan and Hidayet Seftakli Tuksal', *Turkish Review* 21 (3): 182–8.

Dokouhaki, Parastoo (2000), 'Political Groups are to Blame for the Decrease in the Number of Women Parliamentarians! (In Persian)', *Zanan Magazine* 64.

Dokouhaki, Parastoo, and Noushin Tarighi (2000), 'Does she Wear a Chador or not? (In Persian)', *Zanan Magazine* 59.

Ebrahimi, Zahra (2001), 'Efforts for Women's Ministership in the Parliament's Alleys (In Persian)', *Zanan Magazine* 77.

—— (2004), 'Women, Strike, Resignation (In Persian)', *Zanan Magazine*, January.

Ebtekar, Massoumeh (2013), 'Capabilities of "Rijal" Women (In Persian)', *Bahar Newspaper* 129, 22 May.

Ehsani, Kaveh, Arang Keshavarzian and Norma Claire Moruzzi (2009), 'Tehran, June 2009', *MERIP: Middle East Research and Information Project*, http://www.merip.org/mero/mero062809.

Eisenstein, Hester (1983), *Contemporary Feminist Thought*, Woodbridge, CT: Twayne Publishers.

Eisinger, Peter K. (1973), 'The Conditions of Protest Behavior in American Cities', *The American Political Science Review* 67 (1): 11–28.

Ekim, Sinan, and Kemal Kirisci (2017), 'The Turkish Constitutional Referendum, Explained', *Brookings Institute*, 13 April, https://www.brookings.edu/blog/order-from-chaos/2017/04/13/the-turkish-constitutional-referendum-explained/.

Eligur, Banu (2010), *The Mobilization of Political Islam in Turkey*. New York, NY: Cambridge University Press.

Erdbrink, Thomas (2016), 'She Won a Seat in Iran's Parliament, but Hard-Liners Had Other Plans', *The New York Times*, 11 May, https://www.nytimes.com/20 16/05/12/world/middleeast/iran-parliament-minoo-khaleghi.html.

Erensü, Sinan, and Ayça Alemdaroğlu (2018), 'Dialectics of Reform and Repression: Unpacking Turkey's Authoritarian "Turn"', *Review of Middle East Studies* 52 (1): 16–28, https://doi.org/10.1017/rms.2018.8.

Esfandiari, Golnaz (2013), 'Perhaps Bowing to Pressure, Rouhani Appoints Women to Iranian Parliament', *RadioFreeEurope*, 13 August, https://www.rferl.org/a/ro hani-woman-cabinet-iran/25074111.html.

—— (2016), 'Iranian Lawmaker Says Parliament Is no Place for Women, Donkeys', *RadioFreeEurope*, 3 March, https://www.rferl.org/a/iran-lawmaker-parliament-no-place-for-women-donkeys/27587883.html.

—— (2017), 'No Woman has ever run for Iranian President. Will Azam Taleghani be the First?', *RadioFreeEurope*, 19 April, https://www.rferl.org/a/iran-taleghani-woman-president-election/28439661.html.

Eski, Beril (2019), 'Turkey: The World's Largest Prison for Journalists', *Amnesty International*, https://www.amnesty.org/en/latest/news/2019/05/turkey-the-wo rlds-largest-prison-for-journalists/.

Esposito, John L., and John Obert Voll (1996), *Islam and Democracy*, New York, NY: Oxford University Press.

Evans, Tyler, and Esin Efe (2012), *Who's Who in Turkey's Justice and Development Party*, Washington, DC: The Washington Institute for Near East Policy, https:// www.washingtoninstitute.org/uploads/Documents/pubs/AKP_Bios6.pdf.

Fabbrini, Sergio (2010), 'Faction', in Mark Bevir (ed.), *Encyclopedia of Political Theory*, Thousand Oaks, CA: Sage Publications, pp. 491–2.

Farhi, Farideh (2015), 'The Parliament | The Iran Primer', *United States Institute of Peace*, http://iranprimer.usip.org/resource/parliament.

Fazli, Sahan (2020), 'Ak Party Women Branch Headquarters are on the Move against Coronavirus: Taking Public's Pulse (In Turkish)', *Yeni Safak*, 3 April, https://www.yenisafak.com/koronavirus/ak-parti-kadin-kollari-koronaviruse-ka rsi-harekete-gecti-halkin-psikolojisi-olculuyor-3532736.

Fernandes, Sujatha (2005), 'Transnationalism and Feminist Activism in Cuba: The Case of Magín', *Politics & Gender* 1 (3): 431–52, https://doi.org/10.1017/S17 43923X05050117.

Fernea, Elizabeth Warnock (1985), *Women and the Family in the Middle East: New Voices of Change*, Austin, TX: University of Texas Press.

Ferree, Myra Marx (2003), 'Resonance and Radicalism: Feminist Framing in the Abortion Debates of the United States and Germany', *American Journal of Sociology* 109 (2): 304–44, https://doi.org/10.1086/378343.

Ferree, Myra Marx, and David A. Merrill (2000), 'Hot Movements, Cold Cognition: Thinking about Social Movements in Gendered Frames', *Contemporary Sociology* 29 (3): 454–62.

Ferree, Myra Marx, and Carol McClurg Mueller (2004), 'Feminism and the Women's Movement: A Global Perspective', in David A. Snow, Sarah A. Soule and Hanspeter Kriesi (eds), *The Blackwell Companion to Social Movements*, New York: Wiley, pp. 576–609.

Fish, M. Steven (2002), 'Islam and Authoritarianism', *World Politics* 55 (1): 4–37.

Franceschet, Susan, and Jennifer M. Piscopo (2008), 'Gender Quotas and Women's Substantive Representation: Lessons from Argentina', *Politics & Gender* 4 (3): 393–425, https://doi.org/10.1017/S1743923X08000342.

Gamson, William, and David Meyer (1996), 'Framing Political Opportunity', in Doug McAdam, John D. McCarthy and Mayer N. Zald (eds), *Comparative Perspectives on Social Movements: Political Opportunities, Mobilizing Structures, and Cultural Framings*, New York, NY: Cambridge University Press, pp. 275–90.

Gardels, Nathan, and Elif Shafak (2018), 'Opinion | Authoritarianism is Changing the Very Fabric of Society', *Washington Post*, 26 June, https://www.washington post.com/news/theworldpost/wp/2018/06/26/turkey-election/.

Gates, Sara (2013), 'Nina Siakhali Moradi, Iranian Councilwoman-Elect, Disqualified for Being "Too Attractive"', *HuffPost*, http://www.huffingtonpo st.com/2013/08/15/nina-siakhali-moradi-disqualified-iran-too-attractive_n_37 62532.html.

Ghazi, Fereshteh (2017), 'Presidential Elections: Sidelining Women for the Twelfth Time', *BBC Persian*, 22 April, http://www.bbc.com/persian/iran-39668510.

Gheytanchi, Elham (2008), 'Women's Rights Activists are not a Threat to Iran's National Security', *HuffPost*, 19 February, https://www.huffpost.com/entry/wo mens-rights-activists-a_b_87391

Gillespie, Andra, and Melissa R. Michelson (2011), 'Participant Observation and the Political Scientist: Possibilities, Priorities, and Practicalities', *PS: Political Science and Politics* 44 (2): 261–5.

Gol, Nuray (2009), 'Women's Participation Issue and Analysis of Woman Organization Structure in Turkey: A Comparison of KA.DER (Association for Supporting and Training Women Candidates) and Türk Kadinlar Birligi (Turkish Women Union)', *Thinking Gender Papers, UCLA Center for the Study of Women*, http://escholarship.org/uc/item/2jc4v0hs.

Gole, Nilufer (1996), *The Forbidden Modern: Civilization and Veiling*, Ann Arbor, MI: University of Michigan Press.

Golkar, Saeid (2015), *Captive Society: The Basij Militia and Social Control in Iran*, New York, NY: Columbia University Press.

Gracey, Kellen J. (2017), 'The Macro Polity and Public Opinion in Religious Context', PhD Dissertation, Iowa City, IA: University of Iowa, https://ir.uio wa.edu/etd/5762.

Granqvist, Hilma (1947), *Birth and Childhood among the Arabs: Studies in a Muhammad Village in Palestine*, Helsingfors: Soderstroms.

Gulalp, Haldun (2005), 'Enlightenment by Fiat: Secularization and Democracy in Turke', *Middle Eastern Studies* 41 (3): 351–72, https://doi.org/10.1080/00263 200500105984.

Gunduz, Zuhal Yesilyurt (2004), 'The Women's Movement in Turkey: From Tanzimat towards European Union Membership', *Perceptions* IX (Autumn): 115–34.

Gurbey, Sinem (2009), 'Islam, Nation-State, and the Military: A Discussion of Secularism in Turkey', *Comparative Studies of South Asia, Africa and the Middle East* 29 (3): 371–80.

Gurbuz, Seyma Nazli (2018), 'Turkey Enters Electoral Process with Highest Ratio of Female Parliamentary Candidates Ever', *DailySabah*, 22 May, https://www.dai lysabah.com/elections/2018/05/23/turkey-enters-electoral-process-with-highest -ratio-of-female-parliamentary-candidates-ever-1527015974.

Hafez, Sherine (2011), *An Islam of Her Own: Reconsidering Religion and Secularism in Women's Islamic Movements*, New York, NY: New York University Press.

Haghighatjoo, Fatemeh (2004), 'Full Text of Fatemeh Haghighatjoo's Resignation Letter, Reformist Member of the Sixth Parliament (In Persian)', *Gahar*, https:// gahar.ir/%D8%A8%DB%8C%D9%88%DA%AF%D8%B1%D8%A7%D9 %81%DB%8C-%D9%81%D8%A7%D8%B7%D9%85%D9%87-%D8 %AD%D9%82%DB%8C%D9%82%D8%AA-%D8%AC%D9%88/.

Hamandishi Zanan (2013), 'Statement about Selection Criteria of Women Ministers in the New Government (In Persian)', *Iran-Emrooz*, 23 July, http://www.iran -emrooz.net/index.php/news1/46707/.

Hansen, Henny Harald (1961), *The Kurdish Woman's Life*, Copenhagen: Abe Books.

Hasan, Ahmad (1971), 'Social Justice in Islam', *Islamic Studies* 10 (3): 209–19.

Hern, Erin (2017), 'The Trouble with Institutions: How Women's Policy Machineries Can Undermine Women's Mass Participation', *Politics & Gender* 13 (3): 405–31, https://doi.org/10.1017/S1743923X16000519.

Holland, Lisa (2013), 'Iran Presidential Election: Women Banned', *Sky News*, 17 May, https://news.sky.com/story/iran-presidential-election-women-banned-10 445501.

Hoodfar, Homa (1992), 'The Veil in Their Minds and on Our Heads: The Persistence of Colonial Images of Muslim Women', *Resources for Feminist Research* 22 (3/4): 5–18.

—— (1997), *Between Marriage and the Market: Intimate Politics and Survival in Cairo*, Berkeley, CA: University of California Press.

—— (1999), *The Women's Movement in Iran: Women at the Crossroads of Secularization and Islamization*, Grabels Cedex, France: Women Living Under Muslim Laws (WLUML).

Hoodfar, Homa, and Shadi Sadr (2009), 'Can Women Act as Agents for the Democratization of Theocracy in Iran?', Geneva, Switzerland: United Nations Research Institute for Social Development.

Hoodfar, Homa, and Mona Tajali (2011), *Electoral Politics: Making Quotas Work for Women*, London: Women Living Under Muslim Laws (WLUML).

Howe, Marvine (2000), *Turkey Today: A Nation Divided over Islam's Revival*, Boulder, CO: Westview Press.

Htun, Mala, Marina Lacalle and Juan Pablo Micozzi (2013), 'Does Women's Presence Change Legislative Behavior? Evidence from Argentina, 1983–2007', *Journal of Politics in Latin America* 5 (1): 95–125, https://doi.org/10.1177/186 6802X1300500105.

Hughes, Melanie M. (2009), 'Armed Conflict, International Linkages, and Women's Parliamentary Representation in Developing Nations', *Social Problems* 56 (1): 174–204.

Huntington, Samuel P. (1991), *The Third Wave: Democratization in the Late 20th Century*, Norman, OK: University of Oklahoma Press.

—— (1996), *The Clash of Civilizations and the Remaking of World Order*, New York, NY: Simon and Schuster.

Hurriyet Daily News (2012), 'CHP Women's Branch Head Resigns for Praising Family Minister', *Hurriyet Daily News*, 7 November, http://www.hurriyetdai lynews.com/chp-womens-branch-head-resigns-for-praising-family-minister--3 4148.

ICANA (2017), 'Zolghard: Meritocracy is not in Contradiction with Using Women for Senior Leadership Posts (In Persian)', *Islamic Consultative Assembly News Agency (ICANA)*, 11 September, http://www.icana.ir/Fa/News/347771/%D8 %B4%D8%A7%DB%8C%D8%B3%D8%AA%D9%87-%D8%B3%D8 %A7%D9%84%D8%A7%D8%B1%DB%8C-%D8%AA%D9%86%D8 %A7%D9%82%D8%B6%DB%8C-%D8%A8%D8%A7-%D8%A7%D8 %B3%D8%AA%D9%81%D8%A7%D8%AF%D9%87-%D8%A7%D8 %B2-%D8%B2%D9%86%D8%A7%D9%86-%D8%AF%D8%B1-%D9 %BE%D8%B3%D8%AA%E2%80%8C%D9%87%D8%A7%DB%8C

-%D8%A7%D8%B1%D8%B4%D8%AF-%D9%85%D8%AF%DB%8C
%D8%B1%DB%8C%D8%AA%DB%8C-%D9%86%D8%AF%D8%A7
%D8%B1%D8%AF.

Ilkkaracan, Pinar (1997), *A Brief Overview of Women's Movement(s) in Turkey*, Women for Women's Human Rights Report No. 2, Istanbul: USAID, https://www.popline.org/node/309367.

ILNA News Agency (2015), 'Motalefeh's Central Executive Board have been Elected (In Persian)', *Iranian Labour News Agency*, 18 October, http://www.ilna.ir/بخش-%D8%B3%DB%8C%D8%A7%D8%B3%DB%8C-3/314534-%D8%A7%D8%B9%D8%B6%D8%A7%DB%8C-%D8%B4%D9%88%D8%B1%D8%A7%DB%8C-%D9%85%D8%B1%DA%A9%D8%B2%DB%8C-%D8%AD%D8%B2%D8%A8-%D9%85%D8%A4%D8%AA%D9%84%D9%81%D9%87-%D8%A7%D9%86%D8%AA%D8%AE%D8%A7%D8%A8-%D8%B4%D8%AF%D9%86%D8%AF-%D8%A7%D8%B3%D8%A7%D9%85%DB%8C.

Inglehart, Ronald, and Pippa Norris (2003), *Rising Tide: Gender Equality and Cultural Change around the World*, New York, NY: Cambridge University Press.

Inglehart, Ronald, Pippa Norris and Christian Welzel (2003), 'Gender Equality and Democracy', *Comparative Sociology* 1 (3–4): 321–46.

'International Alliance of Women Records' (n.d.), *Five College Archives & Manuscript Collection*, https://asteria.fivecolleges.edu/findaids/sophiasmith/mnsss330.html (accessed 9 April 2019).

International IDEA, and Stockholm University (2018), 'Gender Quotas Database'," *Gender Quotas Around the World Database*, https://www.idea.int/data-tools/data/gender-quotas.

Inter-Parliamentary Union (2019), 'Women in National Parliaments', *IPU: Statistical Archive*, http://archive.ipu.org/wmn-e/classif-arc.htm.

—— (2021), 'Monthly Ranking of Women in National Parliaments', *IPU Parline: Global Data on National Parliaments*, https://data.ipu.org/women-ranking?month=10&year=2021.

Iqtidar, Humeira (2011), *Secularizing Islamists? Jama'at-e-Islami and Jama'at-Ud – Da'wa in Urban Pakistan*, London: University of Chicago Press.

Iran Newspaper (2015), 'Tripling of Women's Candidacy for the Tenth Parliament (In Persian)', *Iran*, 27 December, 6110 edn.

IRNA (2017), '1,636 Candidates File for Iran's Presidential Elections: Official (In Persian)', *Islamic Republic News Agency*, 15 April, http://www.irna.ir/en/News/82494032/.

Isayev, Saeed, and Temkin Jafarov (2013), 'Ayatollah Khamenei: U.S Policy Doesn't

Care about Human Lives', *Trend*, http://en.trend.az/regions/iran/2186569
.html.

Islamic Women's Coalition (2009), 'The First Manifesto of the Islamic Women's
Coalition (In Persian)', *Iranzanan* (blog), http://www.iranzanan.com/point_of
_view/cat_7/000046.php.

Jad, Islah (2011), 'Islamist Women of Hamas: Between Feminism and Nationalism',
Inter-Asia Cultural Studies 12 (2): 176–201, https://doi.org/10.1080/14649373
.2011.554647.

—— (2018), *Palestinian Women's Activism: Nationalism, Secularism, Islamism*,
Syracuse, NY: Syracuse University Press.

Janaati, Mohammad Ebrahim, and Heidar Zaifi (2005), 'Not Women-ocracy, nor
Men-ocracy, but Meritocracy (In Persian)', *ISNA*, 28 June.

Jasper, James M. (2012), 'Introduction: From Political Opportunity Structures to
Strategic Interaction', in Jeff Goodwin and James M. Jasper (eds), *Contention
in Context: Political Opportunities and the Emergence of Protest*, Stanford, CA:
Stanford University Press, pp. 1–36.

Jayawardena, Kumari (1986), *Feminism and Nationalism in the Third World*, New
York, NY: Zed Books.

Joseph, Suad (2000), 'Gendering Citizenship in the Middle East', in Suad Joseph
(ed.), *Gender and Citizenship in the Middle East*, Syracuse, NY: Syracuse
University Press, pp. 3–30.

KADEM (2019), 'KADEM Campaigns', *KADEM Organization*, https://kadem.org
.tr/tag/kadin-ve-demokrasi-bulusmasi/.

KADER (2017), 'Election Campaigns and Activities', KA.DER Organization
Campaign for Turkish 2017 Constitutional Change Referendum: 'Go to Polls
and Show Your Power', *KA-DER*, http://ka-der.org.tr/en/gallery/.

Kadivar, Jamileh (1996), *Zan [Woman]* (In Persian), Tehran: Etela'at Press.

—— (2012), 'Women and Executive Power', in Tara Povey and Elaheh Rostami-
Povey (eds), *Women, Power and Politics in 21st Century Iran*, Burlington, VT:
Ashgate, pp. 121–36.

Kamali, Fatemeh (2017), 'Gender Quotas are in Conflict with Meritocracy (In
Persian)', *Setareh Sobh Newspaper*, 19 April.

Kamrava, Mehran (2010), 'Preserving Non-Democracies: Leaders and State
Institutions in the Middle East', *Middle Eastern Studies* 46 (2): 251–70, https://
doi.org/10.1080/00263200902811353.

Kandiyoti, Deniz (1987), 'Emancipated but Unliberated? Reflections on the Turkish
Case', *Feminist Studies* 13 (2): 317–38.

—— (1988), 'Bargaining with Patriarchy', *Gender and Society* 2 (3): 274–90.

—— (1989), 'Women and the Turkish State: Political Actors or Symbolic Pawns?', in Nira Yuval-Davis, Floya Anthias and Jo Campling (eds), *Woman, Nation, State*, London: Macmillan, pp. 126–49.

—— (1991), 'End of Empire: Islam, Nationalism and Women in Turkey', in Deniz Kandiyoti (ed.), *Women, Islam, and the State*, Philadelphia, PA: Temple University Press, pp. 22–47.

Kang, Alice (2009), 'Studying Oil, Islam, and Women as if Political Institutions Mattered', *Politics & Gender* 5 (4): 560–68, https://doi.org/10.1017/S174392 3X09990377.

—— (2015), *Bargaining for Women's Rights: Activism in an Aspiring Muslim Democracy*, Minneapolis, MN: University of Minnesota Press.

Kantola, Johanna (2006), *Feminists Theorize the State*, New York, NY: Palgrave Macmillan.

Kaplan, Hilal (2018), 'Women's r-Evolution in Turkey under Erdogan's AKP', *Alaraby*, 22 June, https://www.alaraby.co.uk/english/comment/2018/6/22/wo mens-r-evolution-in-turkey-under-erdogans-akp.

Kar, Mehranguiz (1996), 'Women on the Way: A Report on Women's Presence in Elections (In Persian)', *Zanan Magazine* 28.

—— (2000), *Women's Political Participation: Obstacles and Opportunities* (In Persian), Tehran: Entesharat Roshangaran va Motale'at Zanan.

—— (2005), 'Women's Political Rights after the Islamic Revolution', in Lloyd Ridgeon (ed.), *Religion and Politics in Modern Iran: A Reader*, New York, NY: I. B. Tauris, pp. 253–85.

Kar, Mehranguiz, and Homa Hoodfar (1996), 'Women and Personal Status Law in Iran: An Interview with Mehranguiz Kar', *Middle East Report* 198: 36–8.

Kardam, Nuket (2004), 'The Emerging Global Gender Equality Regime from Neoliberal and Constructivist Perspectives in International Relations', *International Feminist Journal of Politics* 6 (1): 85–109.

Katzenstein, Mary Fainsod (1998), *Faithful and Fearless: Moving Feminist Protest inside the Church and Military*, Princeton, NJ: Princeton University Press.

Kausar, Zinat (1997), *Political Participation of Women: Contemporary Perspectives of Gender Feminists and Islamic Revivalists*, Kuala Lumpur, Malaysia: A. S. Noordeen.

Kavakci, Merve (2010), *Headscarf Politics in Turkey: A Postcolonial Reading*, New York, NY: Palgrave Macmillan.

Kazemian, Morteza (2013), 'Blinds of Political Parties and Rouhani's Government (In Persian)', *BBC Persian*, 20 August, http://www.bbc.co.uk/persian/blogs/20 13/08/130820_blog_l44_nazeran_rohani_parties.shtml (accessed 23 November 2021).

Keck, Margaret E., and Kathryn Sikkink (1998), *Activists Beyond Borders: Advocacy Networks in International Politics*, Ithaca, NY: Cornell University Press.

Keddie, Nikki R. (2007), 'Iranian Women's Status and Struggles since 1979', *Journal of International Affairs* 60 (2): 17–33.

Kemal, Mustafa (1935), *Ataturk's Address to the International Women's Congress*, presented at the International Women's Congress, Istanbul, Turkey, 22 April, http://www.ataturksociety.org/about-ataturk/political-and-cultural-reforms/.

Kenny, Meryl, and Fiona Mackay (2014), 'When is Contagion not very Contagious? Dynamics of Women's Political Representation in Scotland', *Parliamentary Affairs* 67 (4): 866–86, https://doi.org/10.1093/pa/gss109.

Keshavarz, Fataneh (2009), 'Windows on Iran'. *Windows on Iran 98* (blog), 3 December, https://windowsoniran.wordpress.com/2009/12/03/windows-on-iran-98/.

Keshavarzian, Arang (2005), 'Contestation without Democracy: Elite Fragmentation in Iran', in Marsha Pripstein Posusney and Michele Penner Angrist (eds), *Authoritarianism in the Middle East: Regimes and Resistance*, Boulder, CO: Lynne Rienner Publishers, pp. 63–90.

—— (2007), *Bazaar and State in Iran: The Politics of the Tehran Marketplace*, Cambridge: Cambridge University Press.

—— (2009a), 'How Islamic was the Revolution?', *Middle East Research and Information Project* 39 (250): 12.

—— (2009b), 'Regime Loyalty and Bāzārī Representation under the Islamic Republic of Iran: Dilemmas of the Society of Islamic Coalition', *International Journal of Middle East Studies* 41 (2): 225–46.

Keshavarzian, Arang, and Naghmeh Sohrabi (2017), 'Lessons Learned (and Ignored): Iran's 2017 Elections in Context', *MERIP: Middle East Research and Information Project*, 26 May, http://www.merip.org/mero/mero052617-0.

Kestler-D'Amours, Jillian (2013), 'Turkey: "World's Biggest Prison" for Media', *Al Jazeera*, 17 February, https://www.aljazeera.com/indepth/features/2013/02/201 3217124044793870.html.

Keysan, Asuman Ozgur (2012), 'EU Civil Society and Voices of Women's Organizations in Turkey', paper presented at the *European Consortium for Political Research (ECPR)*, Bremen, Germany, https://ecpr.eu/Filestore/Paper Proposal/f0e43353-6325-4a42-b45b-16f97460caaf.pdf.

Khaleghi, Minoo (2016), 'Statement of Minoo Khalegi (In Persian)', *Tabnak News*, 23 March, http://www.tabnakesfahan.ir/fa/news/201446/%D9%85%D9%86 %D8%AA%D8%AE%D8%A8-%D8%B3%D9%88%D9%85-%D8%B1 %D8%AF-%D8%B5%D9%84%D8%A7%D8%AD%DB%8C%D8%AA -%D8%B4%D8%AF%D9%86%D8%B4-%D8%B1%D8%A7-%D9%82 %D8%A8%D9%88%D9%84-%D9%86%D8%AF%D8%A7%D8%B1 %D8%AF-%D8%AE%D8%A7%D9%84%D9%82%DB%8C-%D8%AE

%D9%88%D8%A7%D8%B3%D8%AA%D8%A7%D8%B1-%D8%A8
%D8%B1%D8%AE%D9%88%D8%B1%D8%AF-%D8%A8%D8%A7
-%D9%85%D8%AA%D8%AE%D9%84%D9%81%DB%8C%D9%86
-%D8%B4%D8%AF.

Khamenei, Ali Hosseini (2014), 'Discussion on Women and Employment', *Khamenei.ir*, 19 April, http://farsi.khamenei.ir/video-content?id=26153.

Khayamdar, Majid (2017), 'Does the Islamic Republic of Iran Receive its Legitimacy from God or the People? (In Persian)', *BBC Persian*, 20 June, http://www.bbc .com/persian/40349525.

Khorasani, Noushin Ahmadi, and Parvin Ardalan (2003), *The Senator: Mehranguiz Manoutchehrian's Efforts on the Context of Women's Activities Concerning Equal Rights in Contemporary Iran* (In Persian)', Tehran: Towse'e Publication.

Kian-Thiebaut, Azadeh (2002), 'Women and the Making of Civil Society in Post-Islamist Iran', in Eric Hooglund (ed.), *Twenty Years of Islamic Revolution: Political and Social Transition in Iran since 1979*, New York, NY: Syracuse University Press, pp. 56–73.

Kittilson, Miki Caul (2006), *Challenging Parties, Changing Parliaments: Women and Elected Office in Contemporary Western Europe*, Columbus, OH: Ohio State University Press.

Koolaee, Elaheh (2012), 'Women in the Parliament', in Tara Povey and Elaheh Rostami-Povey (eds), *Women, Power and Politics in 21st Century Iran*, Burlington, VT: Ashgate, pp. 137–52.

—— (2015), 'Justice and Development Party Women's Success (In Persian)', *Arman Daily*, 13 June.

Kordvani, Amir, and Poulad Berenjforoush (2017), 'Iran Approves the Sixth Development Plan to Boost Investment', *Lexology*, 21 April, https://www.lexolo gy.com/library/detail.aspx?g=9a25e9cc-44d0-45fa-9a54-905de434fc66.

Kriesi, Hanspeter (1995), 'The Political Opportunity Structure of New Social Movements: Its Impact on Their Mobilization', in J. Craig Jenkins and Bert Klandermans (eds), *The Politics of Social Protest: Comparative Perspectives on States and Social Movements*, Minneapolis, MN: University of Minnesota Press, pp. 83–98.

Krook, Mona Lena (2006), 'Reforming Representation: The Diffusion of Candidate Gender Quotas Worldwide', *Politics & Gender* 2 (3): 303–27.

—— (2009), *Quotas for Women in Politics: Gender and Candidate Selection Reform Worldwide*, Oxford: Oxford University Press.

—— (2017), 'Violence Against Women in Politics', *Journal of Democracy* 28 (1): 74–88, https://doi.org/10.1353/jod.2017.0007.

Krook, Mona Lena, and Sarah Childs. 2010. "Women, Gender, and Politics: An

Introduction." In *Women, Gender, and Politics: A Reader*, 3–18. New York: Oxford University Press.

Krook, Mona Lena, and Fiona Mackay (eds) (2011), *Gender, Politics and Institutions: Towards a Feminist Institutionalism*, New York, NY: Palgrave Macmillan.

Kuru, Ahmet (2006), 'Reinterpretation of Secularism in Turkey: The Case of the Justice and Development Party', in M. Hakan Yavuz (ed.), *The Emergence of a New Turkey: Democracy and the AK Parti*, Salt Lake City, UT: University of Utah Press, pp. 136–59.

—— (2009), *Secularism and State Policies toward Religion: The United States, France, and Turkey*, New York, NY: Cambridge University Press.

Kuru, Ahmet and Alfred Stepan (2012), *Democracy, Islam, and Secularism in Turkey*, New York, NY: Perseus Books Group.

Kurzman, Charles (1996), 'Structural Opportunity and Perceived Opportunity in Social-Movement Theory: The Iranian Revolution of 1979', *American Sociological Review* 61 (1): 153–70, https://doi.org/10.2307/2096411.

Larserud, Stina, and Rita Taphorn (2007), *Designing for Equality: Best Fit, Medium Fit and Non-Favorable Combinations of Electoral Systems and Gender Quotas*, Stockholm, Sweden: International IDEA, http://www.idea.int/publications/de signing_for_equality/upload/Idea_Design_low.pdf.

Liu, Dongxiao (2006), 'When Do National Movements Adopt or Reject International Agendas? A Comparative Analysis of the Chinese and Indian Women's Movements', *American Sociological Review* 71 (6): 921.

Lovenduski, Joni, and Pippa Norris (eds) (1993), *Gender and Party Politics*, London: Sage Publications.

Lutfi, Manal, and Yousef Saanei (2007), 'The Women's Mufti: Interview with Grand Ayatollah Yousef Saanei', *Asharq Al*-Awsat, https://eng-archive.aawsat.com /theaawsat/features/the-womens-mufti-interview-with-grand-ayatollah-yousef -saanei.

Macdonald, Alastair (2018), 'Turkey Taking "Huge Strides" Away from European Union: Top EU Official', *Reuters*, 17 April, https://www.reuters.com/article/us -eu-turkey-idUSKBN1HO22G.

MacKinnon, Catharine A. (1983), 'Feminism, Marxism, Method, and the State: Toward Feminist Jurisprudence', *Signs* 8 (4): 635–58.

Mahdavi, Mojtaba (2008), 'Rethinking Structure and Agency in Democratization: Iranian Lessons', *International Journal of Criminology and Sociological Theory* 1 (2): 142–60.

Mahmood, Saba (2005), *Politics of Piety: The Islamic Revival and the Feminist Subject*, Princeton, NJ: Princeton University Press.

Mahoney, James, and Richard Snyder (1999), 'Rethinking Agency and Structure in the Study of Regime Change', *Studies in Comparative International Development* 34 (2): 3–32.

Maksoud, Hala (1991), 'Yesim Arat, The Patriarchal Paradox: Women Politicians in Turkey (Book Review)', *International Journal of Middle East Studies* 23 (4): 678–80.

Manning, Kimberley (forthcoming), *Revolutionary Attachments: Party Families and the Gendered Origins of Chinese State Power*, New York, NY: Cornell University Press.

Mansoury, Azar (2017), 'Azar Mansoury: Deputy of Society of New Religious Thinking Muslim Women (In Persian)', *Hamshahri*, 2 March, http://shoaresal .ir/fa/news/102476/%D8%A2%D8%B0%D8%B1-%D9%85%D9%86%D8 %B5%D9%88%D8%B1%DB%8C-%D9%82%D8%A7%D8%A6%D9 %85%E2%80%8C%D9%85%D9%82%D8%A7%D9%85-%D8%AC%D9 %85%D8%B9%DB%8C%D8%AA-%D8%B2%D9%86%D8%A7%D9 %86-%D9%85%D8%B3%D9%84%D9%85%D8%A7%D9%86-%D9%86 %D9%88%D8%A7%D9%86%D8%AF%DB%8C%D8%B4.

Marks, Monica (2013), 'Women's Rights before and after the Revolution', in Nouri Gana (ed.), *The Making of the Tunisian Revolution: Contexts, Architects, Prospects*, Edinburgh: Edinburgh University Press, pp. 224–51.

Marshall, Gul Aldikacti (2009), 'Authenticating Gender Policies through Sustained-Pressure: The Strategy Behind the Success of Turkish Feminists', *Social Politics: International Studies in Gender, State & Society* 16 (3): 358–78, https://doi.org /10.1093/sp/jxp014.

Martin, Patricia Yancey (1990), 'Rethinking Feminist Organizations', *Gender & Society* 4 (2): 182–206, https://doi.org/10.1177/089124390004002004.

Matland, Richard E. (2005), 'Enhancing Women's Political Participation: Legislative Recruitment and Electoral Systems', in Julie Ballington and Azza Karam (eds), *Women in Parliament: Beyond Numbers*, Stockholm, Sweden: International IDEA, pp. 93–110, http://www.idea.int/publications/wip2/upload/WiP_inlay .pdf.

Matland, Richard E., and Donley T. Studlar (1996), 'The Contagion of Women Candidates in Single-Member District and Proportional Representation Electoral Systems: Canada and Norway', *Journal of Politics* 58 (3): 707–33.

—— (1998), 'Gender and the Electoral Opportunity Structure in the Canadian Provinces', *Political Research Quarterly* 51 (1): 117–40, https://doi.org/10.1177 /106591299805100105.

McAdam, Doug (1997), *Social Movements: Readings on their Emergence, Mobilization, and Dynamics*, ed. David A. Snow, Los Angeles, CA: Roxbury Publications.

McAdam, Doug, Sidney G. Tarrow and Charles Tilly (2001), *Dynamics of Contention*, New York, NY: Cambridge University Press.

McCammon, Holly (2013), 'Discursive Opportunity Structures', in D. A. Snow, D. Della Porta, P. G. Klandermans, D. McAdam (eds), *Blackwell Encyclopedia of Social and Political Movements*, Malden, MA: Blackwell Publishing.

McCammon, Holly, Courtney Sanders Muse, Harmony D. Newman and Teresa M. Terrell (2007), 'Movement Framing and Discursive Opportunity Structures: The Political Successes of the U.S. Women's Jury Movements', *American Sociological Review* 72 (5): 725–49.

McCarthy, Niall (2018), 'Where the Most Journalists are Imprisoned Worldwide [Infographic]', *Forbes*, https://www.forbes.com/sites/niallmccarthy/2018/12/13/where-the-most-journalists-are-imprisoned-worldwide-infographic/.

Meier, Petra (2004), 'The Mutual Contagion Effect of Legal and Party Quotas: a Belgian Perspective', *Party Politics* 10 (5): 583–600, https://doi.org/10.1177/1354068804045389.

Meliha, Benli Altun, and Ozlem Tur (2005), *Turkey: Challenges of Continuity and Change*, New York, NY: Routledge.

Mernissi, Fatima (1991), *The Veil and the Male Elite: A Feminist Interpretation of Women's Rights in Islam*, New York, NY: Perseus Books.

—— (1993), *The Forgotten Queens of Islam*, Minneapolis, MN: University of Minnesota Press.

Merry, Sally Engle (2006), *Human Rights and Gender Violence: Translating International Law into Local Justice*, Chicago, IL: University of Chicago Press.

Meyer, David S. (2004), 'Protest and Political Opportunities', *Annual Review of Sociology* 30: 125–45, https://doi.org/10.1146/annurev.soc.30.012703.110545.

Meyer, David S., and Debra C. Minkoff (2004), 'Conceptualizing Political Opportunity', *Social Forces* 82 (4): 1457–92.

Mies, Maria (1986), *Patriarchy and Accumulation on a World Scale: Women in the International Division of Labour*, New York, NY: Zed Books.

Migdal, Joel S. (2001). *State in Society: Studying How States and Societies Transform and Constitute One Another*, New York, NY: Cambridge University Press.

Milani, Mohsen (2013), 'Why the Islamic Republic Disqualified One of its Founding Fathers from Running for President', *The Atlantic*, 7 June, https://www.theatlantic.com/international/archive/2013/06/why-the-islamic-republic-disqualified-one-of-its-founding-fathers-from-running-for-president/276671/.

Milliyet Haber (2018), 'AKP Parliamentary Candidate List (in Turkish)', MİLLİYET HABER – TÜRKİYE'NİN HABER SİTESİ, 2018, http://www.milliyet.com.tr/ak-parti-milletvekili-listesi-siyaset-2119578/.

Mir-Hosseini, Ziba (1996), 'Stretching the Limits: A Feminist Reading of the Shari'a in Post-Khomeini Iran', in Mai Yamani and Andrew Allen (eds), *Feminism and Islam: Legal and Literary Perspectives*, New York, NY: New York University Press, pp. 285–320.

—— (1999), *Islam and Gender: The Religious Debate in Contemporary Iran*, Princeton, NJ: Princeton University Press.

—— (2002), 'Religious Modernists and the "Woman Question": Challenges and Complicities', in Eric Hooglund (ed.), *Twenty Years of Islamic Revolution: Political and Social Transition in Iran since 1979*, Syracuse, NY: Syracuse University Press, pp. 74–95.

—— (2006a), 'Is Time on Iranian Women Protester's Side?', *MERIP (Middle East Research and Information Project)*, 16 June, https://merip.org/2006/06/is-time -on-iranian-women-protesters-side/.

—— (2006b), 'Muslim Women's Quest for Equality: Between Islamic Law and Feminism', *Critical Inquiry* 32 (4): 629–45, https://doi.org/10.1086/508085.

—— (2007), 'The Politics and Hermeneutics of Hijab in Iran: From Confinement to Choice', *Muslim World Journal of Human Rights* 4 (1).

—— (2016), 'The Islamic Republic's War on Women', *Foreign Policy*, 29 August, https://foreignpolicy.com/2016/08/29/the-islamic-republics-war-on-women-ir an-feminism/.

Mir-Hosseini, Ziba, Mulki Al-Sharmani and Jana Rumminger (eds) (2015), *Men in Charge? Rethinking Authority in Muslim Legal Tradition*, London: Oneworld Publications.

Moghadam, Valentine (2013), *Modernizing Women: Gender and Social Change in the Middle East*, 3rd edn, Boulder, CO: Lynne Rienner Publishers.

Moghissi, Hiadeh (1999), *Feminism and Islamic Fundamentalism: The Limits of Postmodern Analysis*, New York, NY: Zed Books.

Mohanty, Chandra Talpade (1984), 'Under Western Eyes: Feminist Scholarship and Colonial Discourses', *Boundary* 2 (12/13): 333–58. https://doi.org/10.23 07/302821.

Molaverdi, Shahindokht (2003), 'The Law's Role in Preventing or Reserving Violence against Women (In Persian)', *Hoghooghe Zanan Magazine*.

—— (2006), 'Women in Politics: Still the Second Sex (In Persian)', *Hoghooghe Zanan Magazine*.

—— (2007), *Women: Towards Gaining Power* (In Persian)', Tehran: Society for Protection of Women's Human Rights.

—— (2008), 'Men's Role in the Realization of Gender Equality (In Persian)', *Hoghooghe Zanan Magazine*.

—— (2014), *International Standards of Women's Rights* (In Persian)', Tehran: University of Tehran Press.

Moslem, Mehdi (2002), *Factional Politics in Post-Khomeini Iran*, Syracuse, NY: Syracuse University Press.

Murray, Rainbow (2014), 'Quotas for Men: Reframing Gender Quotas as a Means of Improving Representation for All', *American Political Science Review* 108 (3): 520–32.

—— (2015), 'What Makes a Good Politician? Reassessing the Criteria Used for Political Recruitment', *Politics & Gender* 11 (4): 770–6.

Najmabadi, Afsaneh (2000), '(Un)Veiling Feminism', *Social Text* 18 (3) [64]: 29–45.

Nashat, Guity (1980), 'Women in the Islamic Republic of Iran', *Iranian Studies* 13 (1/4): 165–94.

Norris, Pippa, and Ronald Inglehart (2002), 'Islamic Culture and Democracy: Testing the "Clash of Civilizations" Thesis', *Comparative Sociology* 1 (3–4): 235–63.

Nugent, Mary, and Mona Lena Krook (2016a), 'All-Women Shortlists: Myths and Realities', *Parliamentary Affairs* 69 (1): 115–35, https://doi.org/10.1093/pa/gsv015.

—— (2016b), 'Gender Quotas Do Not Pose a Threat to "Merit" at Any Stage of the Political Process', *Democratic Audit UK*, 19 February, http://www.democraticaudit.com/2016/02/19/gender-quotas-do-not-pose-a-threat-to-merit-at-any-stage-of-the-political-process/.

Oladi Ghadikolaei, Samaneh (2009), 'The Involvement of Iranian Women in Civil Society: Religious and Secular Activism in Perspective', *Zaytoon* 1: 17–30.

Omidy, Samar (2001), 'Khatami: "Selection of a Female Minister Is Not Necessary" (In Persian)', *Zanan Magazine* 79.

Ortbals, Candice, Meg Rincker and Celeste Montoya (2012), 'Politics Close to Home: The Impact of Meso-level Institutions on Women in Politics', *Publius: The Journal of Federalism* 42(1): 78–107, https://doi.org/10.1093/publius/pjr029.

Osanloo, Arzoo (2006), 'The Measure of Mercy: Islamic Justice, Sovereign Power, and Human Rights in Iran', *Cultural Anthropology* 21 (4): 570–602, https://doi.org/10.1525/can.2006.21.4.570.

—— (2009), *The Politics of Women's Rights in Iran*, Princeton, NJ: Princeton University Press.

OSCE/ODIHR (2007), *Republic of Turkey Early Parliamentary Elections 22 July 2007: Election Assessment Mission Report*, Warsaw, Poland: OSCE Office for Democratic Institutions and Human Rights (OSCE/ODIHR), https://www.osce.org/odihr/elections/turkey/29181?download=true.

Paidar, Parvin (1995), *Women and the Political Process in Twentieth-Century Iran*, New York, NY: Cambridge University Press.

—— (2001), *Gender of Democracy: The Encounter between Feminism and Reformism in Contemporary Iran*, Geneva, Switzerland: UNRISD.

Parsons, Nigel (2010), 'Electoral Politics in Iran: Rules of the Arena, Popular Participation, and the Limits of Elastic in the Islamic Republic', *The Middle East Institute Policy Brief* 30 (November), http://www.mei.edu/sites/default/files/pu blications/Parsons_0.pdf.

Pateman, Carole (1988), *The Sexual Contract*, Stanford, CA: Stanford University Press.

Paxton, Pamela, and Melanie M. Hughes (2007), *Women, Politics, and Power: A Global Perspective*, Los Angeles, CA: Pine Forge Press.

—— (2013), *Women, Politics, and Power: A Global Perspective*, 2nd edn, Thousand Oaks, CA: SAGE Publications.

Paxton, Pamela, Melanie M. Hughes and Jennifer L. Green (2006), 'The International Women's Movement and Women's Political Representation, 1893–2003', *American Sociological Review* 71 (6): 898–920.

Paxton, Pamela, Sheri Kunovich and Melanie M. Hughes (2007), 'Gender in Politics', *Annual Review of Sociology* 11 (1): 263–84.

Phillips, Anne (1991), *Engendering Democracy*, University Park, PA: Penn State Press.

—— (1995), *The Politics of Presence*, New York, NY: Clarendon Press.

—— (1998a), 'Democracy and Representation: Or, Why Should it Matter Who Our Representatives Are?', in Anne Phillips (ed.), *Feminism and Politics*, New York, NY: Oxford University Press, pp. 224–40.

—— (ed.) (1998b), *Feminism and Politics*, New York, NY: Oxford University Press.

Pierce, Matthew (2012), 'Remembering Fatimah: New Mean of Legitimizing Female Authority in Contemporary Shi'i Discourse', in Masooda Bano and Hilary Kalmbach (eds), *Women, Leadership and Mosques: Changes in Contemporary Islamic Authority*, Boston, MA: Brill, pp. 345–64.

Pitkin, Hanna F. 1972. *The Concept of Representation*. Berkeley, CA: University of California Press.

Press TV (2009), 'Iran "Does Not Rule out Female Presidency"', *Press TV*, 11 April, http://edition.presstv.ir/detail/91141.html.

Radio Farda (2013), 'Member of Parliament: The Bill Limiting Passports for Women Under 40-Years Has Been Dismissed (In Persian)', *Radio Farda*, 21 February, https://www.radiofarda.com/a/f11-passport-restrictions-for-women-dismissed /24908064.html.

—— (2015a), 'Ali Shakouri-Rad first General Secretary of Union of Islamic Iran People Party (In Persian)', *Radio Farda*, 21 August, https://www.radiofarda.com /a/f4_iran_islamic_alliance_party_shakoorirad/27200031.html.

—— (2015b), 'Rouhani Insists on the Importance of Women's Candidacy in the Elections (In Persian)', *Radio Farda*, 22 November, https://www.radiofarda.com/a/f35_iran_plmnt_elections_dec21/27439824.html.

RadioZamaneh (2012), 'Demands to Increase Women's Numbers in the Iranian Parliament (In Persian)', *RadioZamaneh News*, 15 January, https://www.radiozamaneh.com/39324 (accessed 23 November 2021).

Ram, Haggay (1992), 'Crushing the Opposition: Adversaries of the Islamic Republic of Iran', *Middle East Journal* 46 (3): 426–39.

Ramirez, Francisco O., Yasemin Soysal and Suzanne Shanahan (1997), 'The Changing Logic of Political Citizenship: Cross-National Acquisition of Women's Suffrage Rights, 1890 to 1990', *American Sociological Review* 62 (5): 735.

Randall, Vicky (1982), *Women and Politics*, London: Macmillan.

Rao, Shakuntala (1999), 'Woman-as-Symbol: The Intersections of Identity Politics, Gender, and Indian Nationalism', *Women's Studies International Forum* 22 (3): 317–28, https://doi.org/10.1016/S0277-5395(99)00033-3.

Resalat Newspaper (2010), 'Seyedeh Fatemeh Fakhr: "Better Laws Support Women's Participation in the Society" (In Persian)', *Resalat Newspaper* 7068, 26 August, http://www.magiran.com/npview.asp?ID=2142565.

Reynolds, Andrew (1999), 'Women in the Legislatures and Executives of the World: Knocking at the Highest Glass Ceiling', *World Politics* 51 (4): 547–72.

Rezai-Rashti, Goli, and Valentine Moghadam (2011), 'Women and Higher Education in Iran: What are the Implications for Employment and the "Marriage Market"?', *International Review of Education* 57 (3–4): 419–41. https://doi.org/10.1007/s11159-011-9217-9.

Ross, Michael L. (2008), 'Oil, Islam, and Women', *The American Political Science Review* 102 (1): 107–23.

Rouhani, Hassan (2021), 'President's Speech in Meeting with Women and Family Activists (In Persian)', *Islamic Republic News Agency*, 17 April, https://www.irna.ir/news/84298688/%D8%B3%D8%AE%D9%86%D8%A7%D9%86-%D8%B1%D8%A6%DB%8C%D8%B3-%D8%AC%D9%85%D9%87%D9%88%D8%B1-%D8%AF%D8%B1-%D8%AF%DB%8C%D8%AF%D8%A7%D8%B1-%D9%81%D8%B9%D8%A7%D9%84%D8%A7%D9%86-%D8%AD%D9%88%D8%B2%D9%87-%D8%B2%D9%86%D8%A7%D9%86-%D9%88-%D8%AE%D8%A7%D9%86%D9%88%D8%A7%D8%AF%D9%87.

Rule, Wilma (1994), 'Parliaments of, by, and for the People: Except for Women?', in Wilma Rule and Joseph Francis Zimmerman (eds), *Electoral Systems in Comparative Perspective: Their Impact on Women and Minorities*, Westport, CT: Greenwood Press, pp. 15–30.

Rule, Wilma, and Joseph Francis Zimmerman (eds) (1994), *Electoral Systems in Comparative Perspective: Their Impact on Women and Minorities*, Westport, CT: Greenwood Press.

Sabbagh, Amal (2005), 'The Arab States: Enhancing Women's Political Participation', in Julie Ballington and Azza Karam (eds), *Women in Parliament: Beyond Numbers*, Stockholm, Sweden: International IDEA, pp. 52–71, http://www.idea.int/publications/wip2/upload/WiP_inlay.pdf.

Sadiqi, Fatima (2006), 'The Impact of Islamization on Moroccan Feminisms', *Signs: Journal of Women in Culture and Society* 32 (1): 32–40, https://doi.org/10.1086/505277.

Safari, Zeinab (2017), 'We Seek Positive Discrimination for Women in the Parliament (In Persian)', *Etemad*, 16 July.

Safshekan, Roozbeh, and Farzan Sabet (2010), 'The Ayatollah's Praetorians: The Islamic Revolutionary Guard Corps and the 2009 Election Crisis', *The Middle East Journal* 64 (4): 543–58, https://doi.org/10.3751/64.4.12.

Saidzadeh, Mohsen (1998), *What is Women's Role in the Civil Society?* (In Persian)', Tehran: Nashr Ghatreh.

Sanasarian, Eliz (1982), *The Women's Rights Movement in Iran: Mutiny, Appeasement, and Repression from 1900 to Khomeini*, New York, NY: Praeger Publishers.

Sanij, Neda (2017), 'Why are Women not Becoming Tehran's Mayor (In Persian)?', *BBC Persian*, 12 June, http://www.bbc.com/persian/40232898.

Sapiro, Virginia (1998), 'When are Interests Interesting? Problem of Political Representation of Women', in Anne Phillips (ed.), *Feminism and Politics*, New York, NY: Oxford University Press, pp. 161–92.

Schwindt-Bayer, Leslie A., and William Mishler (2005), 'An Integrated Model of Women's Representation', *The Journal of Politics* 67 (2): 407–28, https://doi.org/10.1111/j.1468-2508.2005.00323.x.

Schwindt-Bayer, Leslie A., and Michelle M. Taylor-Robinson (2011), 'Introduction: The Meaning and Measurement of Women's Interests', *Politics & Gender* 7 (3): 417–18, https://doi.org/10.1017/S1743923X11000213.

Sedghi, Hamideh (2007), *Women and Politics in Iran: Veiling, Unveiling, and Reveiling*, Cambridge: Cambridge University Press.

Sehlikoglu, Sertaç (2013), 'Vaginal Obsessions in Turkey: An Islamic Perspective', *OpenDemocracy*, 18 February, https://www.opendemocracy.net/en/5050/vaginal-obsessions-in-turkey-islamic-perspective/.

—— (2018), 'Revisited: Muslim Women's Agency and Feminist Anthropology of the Middle East', *Contemporary Islam* 12 (1): 73–92, https://doi.org/10.1007/s11562-017-0404-8.

Sevinc, Ozgenur (2018), 'New Parliament Welcomes More Women in Politics to

Improve Turkey's Governance', *DailySabah*, 28 June, https://www.dailysabah .com/elections/2018/06/29/new-parliament-welcomes-more-women-in-politi cs-to-improve-turkeys-governance-1530210978.

Shaditalab, Jaleh (2006), 'Islamization and Gender in Iran: Is the Glass Half Full or Half Empty?', *Signs: Journal of Women in Culture and Society* 32 (1): 14–21.

Shafaqna, and Azar Mansoury (2018), '"Introduction of Hazrat Zeinab as an achievable model for women": An Interview with Azar Mansoury (In Persian)', *Shafaqna*, 2 April, https://fa.shafaqna.com/news/547289/.

Shaheen, Kareem (2018), 'Turkish Opposition Parties Unite against Erdoğan in Elections', *The Guardian*, 2 May, https://www.theguardian.com/world/2018 /may/02/turkish-opposition-parties-unite-against-erdogan-elections.

Shahrabi, Shima (2018), 'A Government Feminist Bids a Sad Goodbye (In Persian)', *IranWire*, 26 November, https://iranwire.com/en/features/5663.

Shahrokni, Nazanin (2009), 'All the President's Women', *MERIP (Middle East Research and Information Project)* 253, https://merip.org/2009/12/all-the-presi dents-women/.

—— (2020), *Women in Place: The Politics of Gender Segregation in Iran*, Oakland, CA: University of California Press.

Shalaby, Marwa (2016), 'Women's Political Representation and Authoritarianism in the Arab World', *Project on Middle East Political Science (POMEPS) Studies* 19: 45–51.

Shariati, Ali (1981), *Fatima Is Fatima* (In Persian), Tehran: Shariati Foundation.

Shehabuddin, Elora (2008), *Reshaping the Holy: Democracy, Development, and Muslim Women in Bangladesh*, New York, NY: Columbia University Press.

Shekarloo, Mahsa (2005), 'Iranian Women Take on the Constitution', *MERIP (Middle East Research and Information Project)*, 21 July, https://merip.org/2005 /07/iranian-women-take-on-the-constitution/.

Sherkat, Shahla (1996), 'What Does Faezeh Hashemi Say? (In Persian)', *Zanan Magazine* 28.

Shively, Kim (2005), 'Religious Bodies and the Secular State: The Merve Kavakci Affair', *Journal of Middle East Women's Studies* 1 (3): 46–72, https://doi.org/10 .2307/40326871.

Shojaee, Zahra (2005), *For Tomorrow's Women: Selection of Zahra Shojaee's Speeches and Articles* (In Persian)', Tehran: Soor-e Mehr Publishings.

—— (2021), 'Zahra Shojaee: My Presence in the Elections is not Ceremonial', *Ensaf News*, 21 May, http://www.ensafnews.com/295280/زهرا-شجاعی-حجاب-اجباری-ی یک-خطابود/.

Simmons, Beth (2009), *Mobilizing for Human Rights: International Law in Domestic Politics*, New York, NY: Cambridge University Press.

Sirman, Nuket (1989), 'Turkish Feminism: A Short History', *Women Living Under Muslim Laws*, Dossier 5–6: 1–10.

Snow, David A., and Robert D. Benford (1988), 'Ideology, Frame Resonance, and Participant Mobilization', *International Social Movement Research* 1 (1): 197–217.

Sohrabi, Nader (2011), *Revolution and Constitutionalism in the Ottoman Empire and Iran*, New York, NY: Cambridge University Press.

Sohrabi, Naghmeh (2006), 'Conservatives, Neoconservatives and Reformists: Iran after the Election of Mahmud Ahmadinejad', *Middle East Brief: Crown Center for Middle East Studies*, 1–5.

Spellberg, D. A. (1994), *Politics, Gender, and the Islamic Past: The Legacy of Aisha Bint Abi Bakr*, New York, NY: Columbia University Press.

Stephan, Rita (2010), 'Couple's Activism in Lebanon: The Legacy of Laure Moghaizel', *Women's Studies International Forum* 33 (6): 533–41.

Student News Network (2015), 'Why Have You Pursued Liberal Thought in Your Plans?: Women and Family Affairs Should Be Run in Accordance to Iranian Islamic Values (In Persian)', *Student News Network*, 25 April, http://snn.ir/fa /news/404805.

Tabnak (2008), 'At Last Conservative Women Give a Separate List (In Persian)', *Tabnak News*, 19 March, www.tabnak.ir/fa/print/7667.

—— (2010), 'Polygamy and Remarriage: Main Challenges of the Family Protection Bill (In Persian)', *Tabnak News*, 26 August, http://www.tabnak.ir/fa/news/1165 60/%D8%A7%D8%B2%D8%AF%D9%88%D8%A7%D8%AC-%D9%85 %D8%AC%D8%AF%D8%AF-%D9%88-%DA%86%D9%86%D8%AF-% D9%87%D9%85%D8%B3%D8%B1%D9%8A-%DA%86%D8%A7%D 9%84%D8%B4-%D9%87%D8%A7%D9%8A-%D8%A7%D8%B5%D9% 84%D9%8A-%D9%84%D8%A7%D9%8A%D8%AD%D9%87-%D8%A E%D8%A7%D9%86%D9%88%D8%A7%D8%AF%D9%87.

Tajali, Mona (2011), 'Notions of Female Authority in Modern Shi'i Thought', *Religions* 2 (3): 449–68, https://doi:10.3390/rel2030449.

—— (2013), 'Gender Quota Adoption in Post-Conflict Contexts: An Analysis of Actors and Factors Involved', *Journal of Women, Politics, and Policy* 34 (3): 261–85, https://doi.org/10.1080/1554477X.2013.820115.

—— (2014), 'Women's Dress and the Politics of Access to Political Representation in Contemporary Turkey', *Anthropology of the Middle East* 9 (2): 72–90, https:// doi.org/10.3167/ame.2014.090206.

—— (2015a), 'The Promise of Gender Parity: Turkey's People's Democratic Party (HDP)', *OpenDemocracy*, 28 October, https://www.opendemocracy.net/5050/ mona-tajali/promise-of-gender-parity-turkey-s-people-s-democratic-party-hdp.

—— (2015b), 'Islamic Women's Groups and the Quest for Political Representation in Turkey and Iran', *The Middle East Journal* 69 (4): 563–81, http://dx.doi.org /10.3751/69.4.14.

—— (2016a), 'Women's Rise to Political Office on Behalf of Religious Political Movements', *Project on Middle East Political Science (POMEPS) Studies* 19: 17–21.

—— (2016b), 'Women Are Not "Foot-Soldiers": A Comparative Analysis of Women's Political Participation in Iran and Turkey (In Persian)', *Zanan Emrooz Magazine*, January.

—— (2017), 'Protesting Gender Discrimination from Within: Women's Political Representation on Behalf of Islamic Parties', *British Journal of Middle Eastern Studies* 44 (2): 176–93, https://doi.org/10.1080/13530194.2017.1281570.

—— (2020), 'Women Politicians of Iran on Women's Rights: Critical Actors or Futile Figureheads', *Jadaliyya*, 5 March, https://www.jadaliyya.com/Details/40 788/Women-Politicians-of-Iran-on-Women%E2%80%99s-Rights-Critical-Actors-or-Futile-Figureheads-40788.

—— (2022), 'Women's Substantive Representation in the Islamic Republic of Iran: The Potential of Women Critical Actors', *Politics & Gender*, doi 10.1017/ S1743923X21000416.

—— (forthcoming), '"Gender Justice" versus "Gender Equality": Elite Women's Framing for Political Representation in Iran and Turkey', *Journal of Middle East Women's Studies*.

Taleghani, Azam (1997a), 'Adoption without Clarification: A Review of the Adoption of the Constitutional Requirements for Presidency (In Persian)', *Payam-e Hajar*, 1997.

—— (1997b), 'Why Did I Become a Presidential Candidate? (In Persian)', *Payam-e Hajar*, 1997.

Tarighi, Noushin (2001), 'Will Women Ministers Finally Happen? (In Persian)', *Zanan Magazine* 77 (June).

Tarrow, Sidney G. (1998), *Power in Movement: Social Movements and Contentious Politics*, 2nd edn, Cambridge: Cambridge University Press.

Taş, Hakkı (2015), 'Turkey – from Tutelary to Delegative Democracy', *Third World Quarterly* 36 (4): 776–91, https://doi.org/10.1080/01436597.2015.1024450.

Tasnim (2017), 'Full Text of the Law on the Sixth Development Plan', *Tasnim News*, 18 March, /fa/news/1395/12/28/1360457/%D9%85%D8%AA%D9% 86-%DA%A9%D8%A7%D9%85%D9%84-%D9%82%D8%A7% D9%86%D9%88%D9%86-%D8%A8%D8%B1%D9%86%D8%A7% D9%85%D9%87-%D8%B4%D8%B4%D9%85-%D8%AA%D9%88% D8%B3%D8%B9%D9%87.

Tavernise, Sabrina (2008), 'Under a Scarf, a Turkish Lawyer Fighting to Wear It',

New York Times, 9 February, https://www.nytimes.com/2008/02/09/world/eu rope/09benli.html.

Tekeli, Sirin (1981), 'Women in Turkish Politics', in Nermin Abadan-Unat, Deniz Kandiyoti and Mubeccel Belik Kiray (eds), *Women in Turkish Society*, Leiden: Brill, pp. 293–315.

—— (1995), 'Introduction: Women in Turkey in the 1980s', in Sirin Tekeli (ed.), *Women in Modern Turkish Society: A Reader*, London: Zed Books, pp. 1–21.

—— (2010), 'The Turkish Women's Movement: A Brief History of Success', *Quaderns de La Mediterrània* 14: 119–23.

Terman, Rochelle (2010), 'The Piety of Public Participation: The Revolutionary Muslim Woman in the Islamic Republic of Iran', *Totalitarian Movements and Political Religions* 11 (3–4): 289–310, https://doi.org/10.1080/14690764.2010 .546086.

The Associated Press (2011), 'Turkey: Ruling Party Criticized over Headscarves', *CTV News*, 12 April, https://www.ctvnews.ca/turkey-ruling-party-criticized-ov er-headscarves-1.630419.

The Iran Project (2015), 'Iran Disapproves Allocating 30% of Majlis Electoral Lists to Women', *The Iran Project*, 20 June, https://theiranproject.com/blog/2015/06 /20/iran-disapproves-allocating-30-of-majlis-electoral-lists-to-women/.

Tohidi, Nayereh (2009), 'Women and the Presidential Elections: Iran's New Political Culture', *Informed Comment*, http://www.juancole.com/2009/09/tohidi-wom en-and-presidential-elections.html.

Torfeh, Massoumeh (2008), 'Iranian Women Crucial in Majlis Election', *BBC News*, 30 January, http://news.bbc.co.uk/2/hi/middle_east/7215272.stm.

Towns, Ann E. (2010), *Women and States: Norms and Hierarchies in International Society*, New York, NY: Cambridge University Press.

Tran, Mark (2009), 'Ahmadinejad Nominates Women to Cabinet', *The Guardian*, 16 August, https://www.theguardian.com/world/2009/aug/16/ahmadinejad-no minates-women-cabinet.

Tremblay, Pinar (2015), 'Women Were Big Losers in Turkey's Elections', *Al-Monitor*, https://www.al-monitor.com/pulse/originals/2015/11/turkey-women-are-losers -turkish-elections-akp.html.

Tripp, Aili Mari (2004), 'The Changing Face of Africa's Legislatures: Women and Quotas', in Julie Ballington (ed.), *The Implementation of Quotas: African Experiences*, Stockholm, Sweden: IDEA, International Institute for Democracy and Electoral Assistance, pp. 72–7, http://www.idea.int/publications/quotas_af rica/upload/IDEA_no3.qxd.pdf.

—— (2006), 'Why So Slow? The Challenges of Gendering Comparative Politics',

Politics & Gender 2 (2): 249–63, https://doi.org/10.1017/S1743923X0624 1047.

—— (2013), 'Political Systems and Gender', in Georgina Waylen, Karen Celis, Johanna Kantola and Laurel Weldon (eds), *The Oxford Handbook of Gender and Politics*, New York, NY: Oxford University Press, p. 872.

—— (2015), *Women and Power in Post-Conflict Africa*, New York, NY: Cambridge University Press.

—— (2019), *Seeking Legitimacy: Why Arab Autocracies Adopt Women's Rights*, New York, NY: Cambridge University Press.

Tripp, Aili Mari, and Alice Kang (2008), 'The Global Impact of Quotas: On the Fast Track to Increased Female Legislative Representation', *Comparative Political Studies* 41 (3): 338–61, https://doi.org/10.1177/0010414006297342.

Tripp, Aili Mari, Dior Konate and Colleen Lowe-Morna (2006), 'Sub-Saharan Africa: On the Fast Track to Women's Political Representation', in Drude Dahlerup (ed.), *Women, Quotas and Politics*, New York, NY: Routledge, pp. 112–37.

Tripp, Aili Mari, Isabel Casimiro, Joy Kwesiga and Alice Mungwa (2009), *African Women's Movements: Changing Political Landscapes*, New York, NY: Cambridge University Press.

Tugal, Cihan (2009), *Passive Revolution: Absorbing the Islamic Challenge to Capitalism*, Stanford, CA: Stanford University Press.

Tunkrova, Lucie (2010), 'The EU Accession Process and Gender Issues: Central Europe and Turkey', presented at the *Fifth Pan-European Conference on EU Politics, Porto, Portugal, 23–6 June 2010*, http://www.jhubc.it/ecpr-porto/virtu alpaperroom/011.pdf.

Turam, Berna (2007), *Between Islam and the State: The Politics of Engagement*, Stanford, CA: Stanford University Press.

Turan, Ilter (2007), 'Unstable Stability: Turkish Politics at the Crossroads?', *International Affairs* 83 (2): 319–38.

Turkish Interior Ministry (2013), *Graphs of NGOs*, http://www.dernekler.gov.tr/in dex.php?option=com_content&view=category&layout=blog&id=52&Itemid= 12&lang=tr.

Unal, Ali (2017), 'AK Party Women's Branch Head Selva Çam: We Want to Increase Women's Participation in Politics and Business', *DailySabah*, 2 October, https:// www.dailysabah.com/politics/2017/10/02/ak-party-womens-branch-head-selva -cam-we-want-to-increase-womens-participation-in-politics-and-business.

Vakil, Sanam (2011), *Women and Politics in the Islamic Republic of Iran: Action and Reaction*, New York, NY: Bloomsbury.

Valdini, Melody E. (2019), *The Inclusion Calculation: Why Men Appropriate Women's Representation*, New York, NY: Oxford University Press.

Valimorad, Touran (2013), 'A Letter to Ayatollah Yazdi from the Islamic Women's Coalition (In Persian)', *Khabaronline*, 17 May, https://www.khabaronline.ir /news/293508/%D9%86%D8%A7%D9%85%D9%87-%D8%A7%DB%8C -%D8%A8%D9%87-%D8%A2%DB%8C%D8%AA-%D8%A7%D9%84 %D9%84%D9%87-%DB%8C%D8%B2%D8%AF%DB%8C-%D8%A7 %D8%B2-%D8%B7%D8%B1%D9%81-%D8%A7%D8%A6%D8%AA %D9%84%D8%A7%D9%81-%D8%A7%D8%B3%D9%84%D8%A7 %D9%85%DB%8C-%D8%B2%D9%86%D8%A7%D9%86-%D8%B1 %D9%88%D8%B3%D8%AA%D8%A7-%D9%88-%DA%A9%D8%AF %D8%9%AE%D8%AF%D8%A7.

Virgint, Erin (2016), 'Electoral Systems and Women's Representation', Research Publications, *Library of Parliament*, https://lop.parl.ca/sites/PublicWebsite/defa ult/en_CA/ResearchPublications/201630E.

Waylen, Georgina (2007), *Engendering Transitions: Women's Mobilization, Institutions, and Gender Outcomes*, New York, NY: Oxford University Press.

Weeks, Ana Catalano, and Lisa Baldez (2015), 'Quotas and Qualifications: The Impact of Gender Quota Laws on the Qualifications of Legislators in the Italian Parliament', *European Political Science Review* 7 (1): 119–44, https://doi.org/10 .1017/S1755773914000095.

White, Jenny (2002), *Islamist Mobilization in Turkey: A Study in Vernacular Politics*, Seattle, WA: University of Washington Press.

—— (2012), *Muslim Nationalism and the New Turks*, Princeton, NJ: Princeton University Press.

—— (2013), 'Breaking news: Women in Trousers', *Kamilpasha.com*, http://kami lpasha.com/?p=7553 (accessed 23 November 2021).

—— (2014), 'Turkey at a Tipping Point', *Current History: A Journal of Contemporary World Affairs* 113 (767): 356–61.

Wickham, Carrie Rosefsky (2015), *The Muslim Brotherhood: Evolution of an Islamist Movement*, Princeton, NJ: Princeton University Press.

Wuthrich, F. Michael (2015), *National Elections in Turkey: People, Politics, and the Party System*, Syracuse, NY: Syracuse University Press.

Wylie, Kristin N. (2018), *Party Institutionalization and Women's Representation in Democratic Brazil*, New York, NY: Cambridge University Press.

Yavuz, Hakan (2009), *Secularism and Muslim Democracy in Turkey*, New York, NY: Cambridge University Press.

Yavuz, Hakan, and John L. Esposito (2003), 'Introduction: Islam in Turkey: Retreat from the Secular Path?', in Hakan Yavuz and John L. Esposito (eds), *Turkish Islam and the Secular State: The Gulen Movement*, Syracuse, NY: Syracuse University Press, pp. xiii–xxxiii.

Young, Lisa (2006), 'Women's Representation in the Canadian House of Commons', in Linda J. Trimble, Marian Sawer and Manon Tremblay (eds), *Representing Women in Parliament: A Comparative Study*, New York, NY: Routledge, pp. 47–66.

Zakizadah, Ismat (2009), *The Workings of Parties and Elections: With a Structural View in the Islamic Republic of Iran* (In Persian), Tehran: Arad Kitab: Kahkashan-i Danish.

Zald, Mayer (1996), 'Culture, Ideology, and Strategic Framing', in Doug McAdam, John D. McCarthy and Mayer N. Zald (eds), *Comparative Perspectives on Social Movements: Political Opportunities, Mobilizing Structures, and Cultural Framings*, New York, NY: Cambridge University Press, pp. 261–74.

Zandi, Mohammad Ali (2014), 'Islamic Society of Engineers', *Baqir Al-Ulum Research Center*, 14 November, http://pajoohe.ir/%D9%85%D9%82%D8%A7%D9%84%D8%A7%D8%AA%D9%81%D8%B1%D9%87%D9%86%DA%AF-%D8%B9%D9%84%D9%88%D9%85-%D8%A7%D9%86%D8%B3%D8%A7%D9%86%DB%8C-%D9%88-%D8%A7%D8%B3%D9%84%D8%A7%D9%85%DB%8C-%D9%85%D9%88%D8%B6%D9%88%D8%B9%DB%8C%D8%B9%D9%84%D9%88%D9%85-%D8%B3%DB%8C%D8%A7%D8%B3%DB%8C%D9%85%D8%B3%D8%A7%D8%A6%D9%84-%D8%A7%DB%8C%D8%B1%D8%A7%D9%86%D8%AC%D8%A7%D9%85%D8%B9%D9%87-%DB%8C-%D8%A7%D8%B3%D9%84%D8%A7%D9%85%DB%8C-%D9%85%D9%87%D9%86%D8%AF%D8%B3%DB%8C%D9%86__a-1331-46346-9478-9487-46568.aspx.

Zheng, Wang (2005), '"State Feminism"? Gender and Socialist State Formation in Maoist China', *Feminist Studies* 31 (3): 519–51, https://doi.org/10.2307/2045 9044.

Zibak, Fatma (2011), 'Is Turkey Ready for a Headscarved Deputy?', *Today's Zaman*, 27 March, http://www.todayszaman.com/newsDetail_getNewsById.action?loa d=detay&newsId=239331&link=239331.

INDEX

EU representative:
Easy Access System Europe
Mustamäe tee 50, 10621 Tallinn, Estonia
Gpsr.requests@easproject.com

www.ingramcontent.com/pod-product-compliance
Lightning Source LLC
Chambersburg PA
CBHW050332270326
41926CB00016B/3427